EROTIQUE DIGITALE

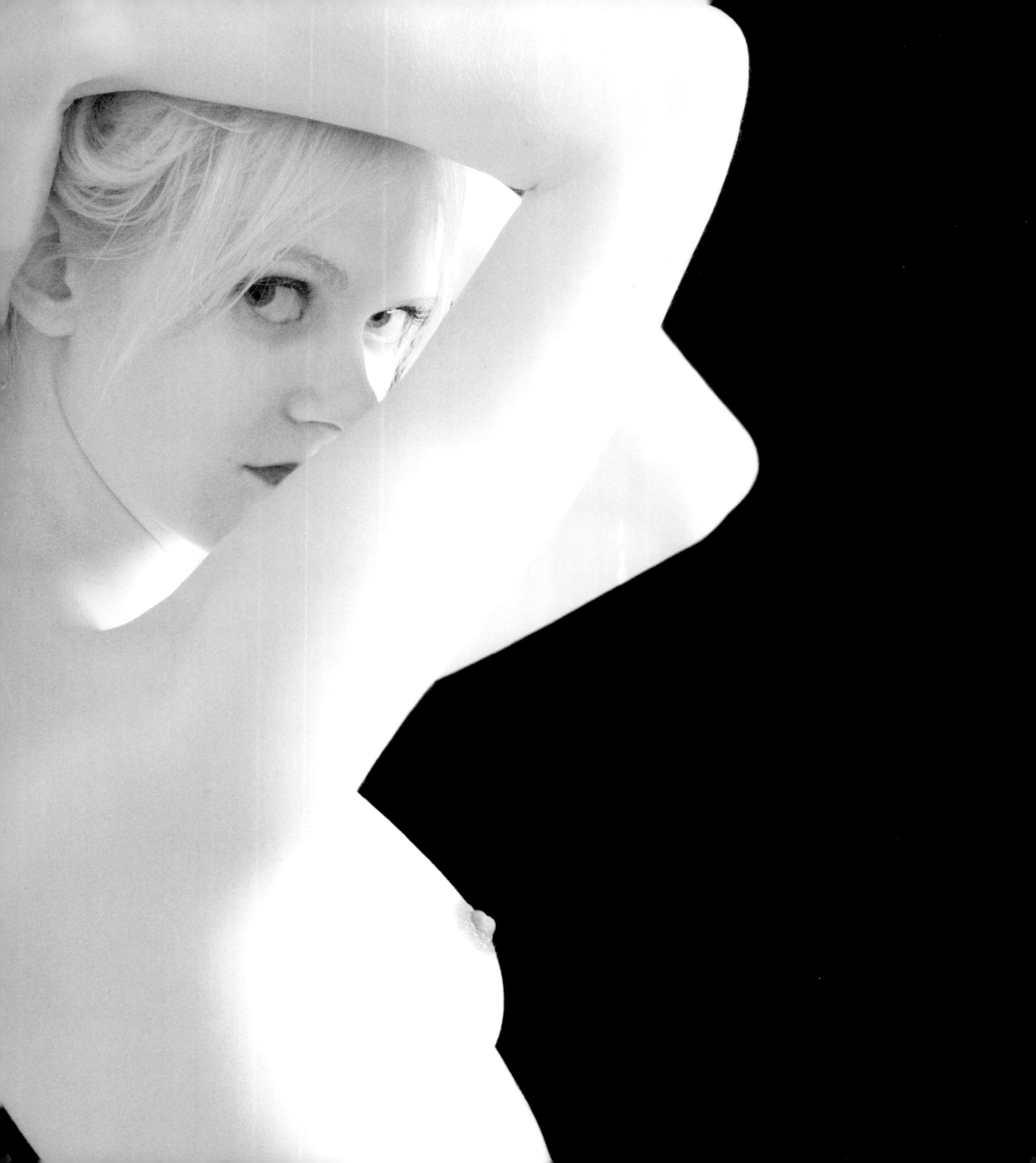

EROTIQUE DIGITALE

The Art of Erotic Digital Photography

Roderick Macdonald & Minnie Cook

THOMSON
COURSE TECHNOLOGY
Professional ■ Trade ■ Reference

First published in the United States in 2005 by
Course PTR, a division of Thomson Course Technology.

For Course PTR
Publisher: Stacy L. Hiquet
Senior Marketing Manager: Sarah O'Donnell
Marketing Manager: Heather Hurley
Associate Marketing Manager: Kristin Eisenzopf
Associate Acquisitions Editor: Megan Belanger
Manager of Editorial Services: Heather Talbot
Market Coordinator: Elizabeth Furbish

ISBN: 1-59200-526-8

5 4 3 2 1

Library of Congress Catalog Card Number: 2004109493

Educational facilities, companies, and organizations interested in multiple copies of this book should contact the publisher for quantity discount information. Training manuals, CD-ROMs, and portions of this book are also available individually or can be tailored for specific needs.

COURSE PTR,
A Division of Thomson Course Technology
(www.courseptr.com)
25 Thomson Place
Boston, MA 02210

This book was conceived, designed, and produced by
The Ilex Press Limited
Cambridge
England

Publisher: Alastair Campbell
Executive Publisher: Sophie Collins
Creative Director: Peter Bridgewater
Design Manager: Tony Seddon
Managing Editor: Tom Mugridge
Editor: Kylie Johnston
Designer: Jonathan Raimes
Junior Designer: Jane Waterhouse
Development Art Director: Graham Davis
Technical Art Editor: Nicholas Rowland

Printed in China

For more information on this title please visit:
www.web-linked.com/erotus

contents

The erotic in the 21st century

Erotic photography occupies the ground that lies between the highly formal, almost abstract "fine art" nude, and the omnipresent, pervasive world of pornographic and "glamor" images. In terms of themes and subjects, it's concerned with desire, sexuality, and sexual activity and our responses to them, and also with the anxiety that goes with these aspects of human experience. In terms of style and expression, it spans a range so wide that it defies definition or categorization. In terms of technique, as we'll see throughout *Erotique Digitale*, photographers who work in this field employ digital methods at every level, from making simple corrections to exposure and contrast, to reshaping, fragmenting, or multiplying the body and locating it in a fantasy world.

If you're a digital photographer who's interested in developing your skills in erotic photography, then this book will give you an idea of the fundamental techniques, as well as showing you some of the best of current work, as a spur and inspiration for your own image-making. If you're a non-photographer with an interest in this subject, then you'll enjoy the diversity of approaches and ideas to be found in the Showcase section of the book; and you'll also gain some insight into what the main digital methods are, and how they're used. (For more technical and detailed instruction in digital photographic techniques, consult Roderick Macdonald's *Digital Nude Photography*, published by Muska & Lipman, an imprint of Thomson Course Technology PTR.)

Erotic images often avoid the brightly lit nude: as painters and sculptors have known for centuries, the erotic often works best by implication, provoking the viewer's imagination, rather than overt statements. (They don't even have to be images of human subjects: Robert Mapplethorpe's flower photographs, like Georgia O'Keefe's flower paintings, are unmistakably sexually charged.)

What makes an image erotic? Inevitably, this depends on the viewer's response, and reflects how strongly the image connects with their fantasies and imagination, as much as it depends on the photographer's intention. My erotic image may be for you no more than a nude; on the other hand it may strike you as unquestionably pornographic. One of the challenges in assembling this book has been to find images which would strike most viewers as erotic, but which would at the same time represent the most advanced, challenging, and inspirational creative ideas and digital techniques.

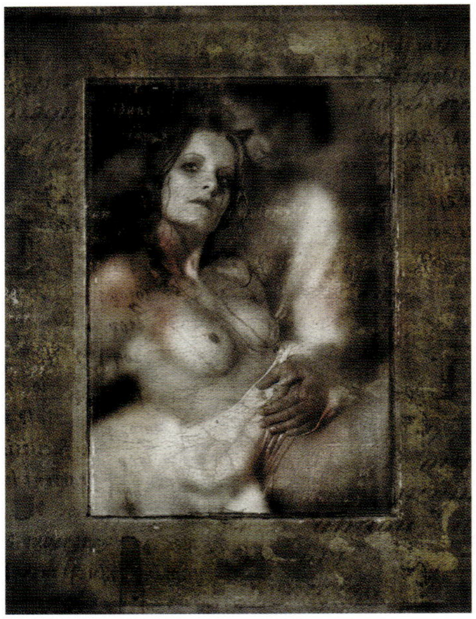

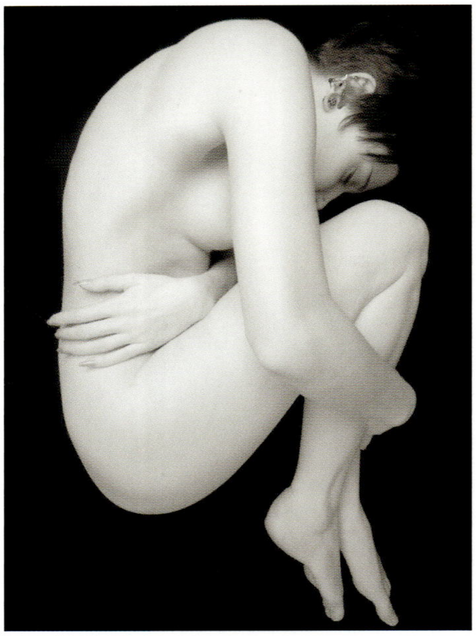

ABOVE AND TOP: The traditional "fine art" nude often uses the simplest of means; eroticism may call for a more complex, layered image. In each case the photographer seeks to create a completed work within which every element seems to fit naturally.

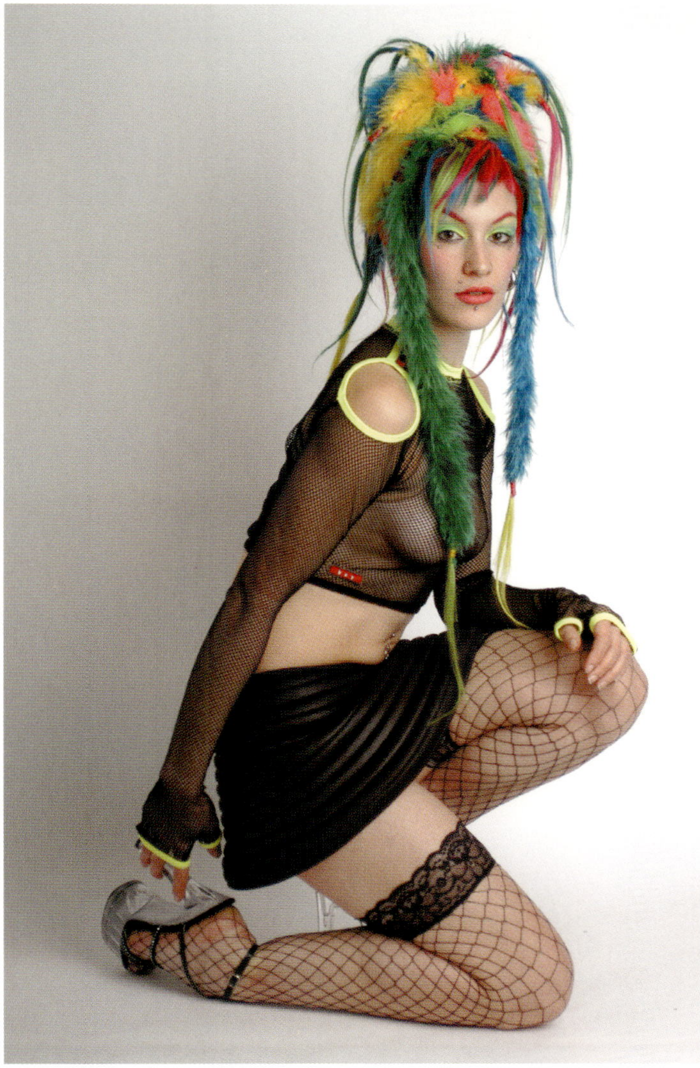

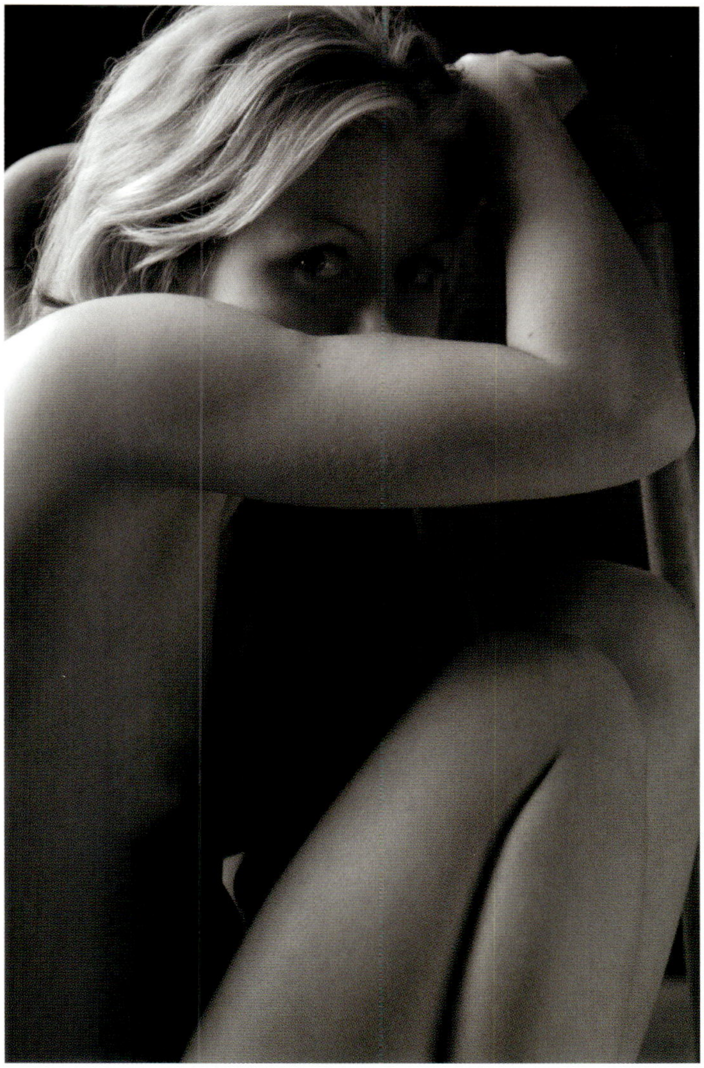

ABOVE LEFT AND RIGHT: Brightly lit but not nude; nude but concealed in shadow: two ways of challenging the viewer's imagination.

RIGHT AND FAR RIGHT: Some erotic images work through very simple, classic elements; others generate their impact through a carefully ordered complexity.

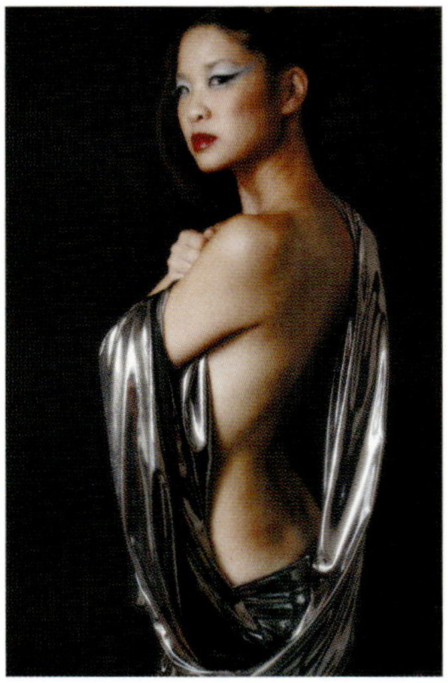

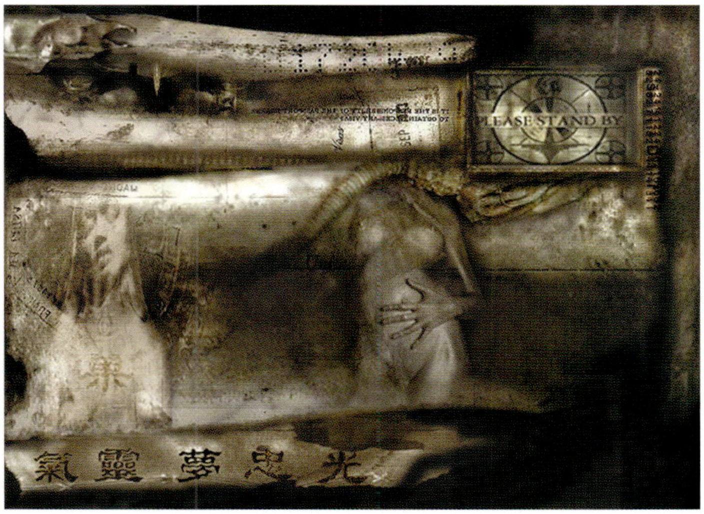

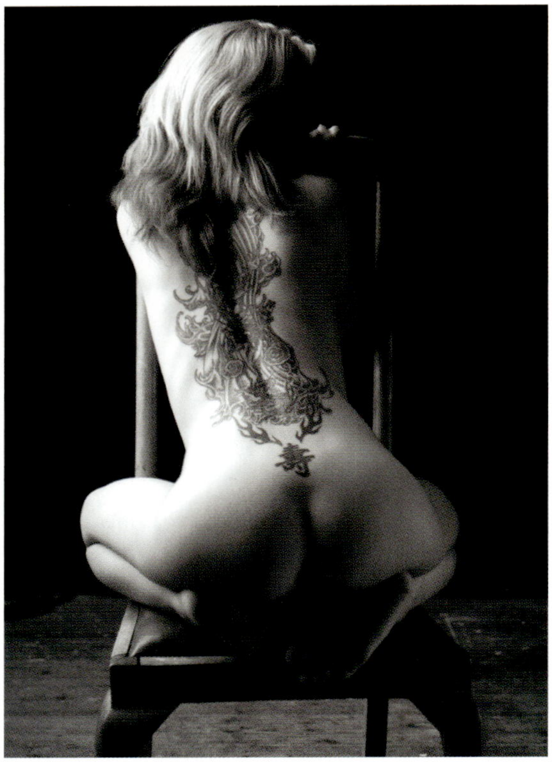

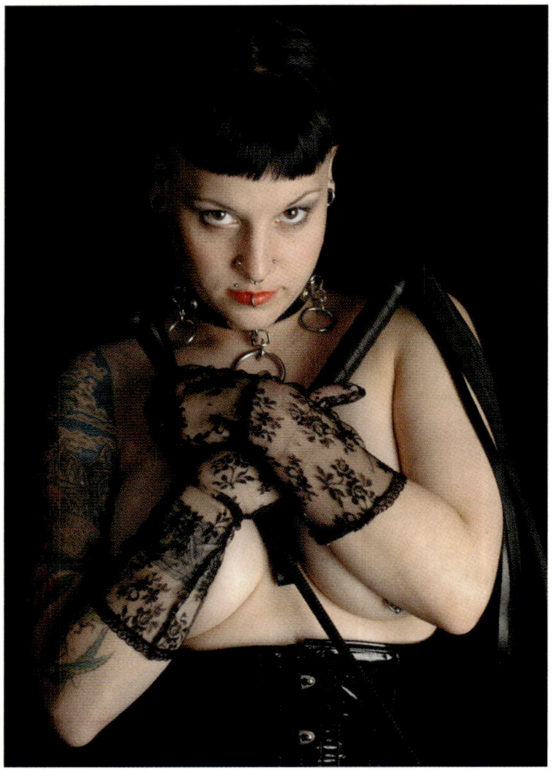

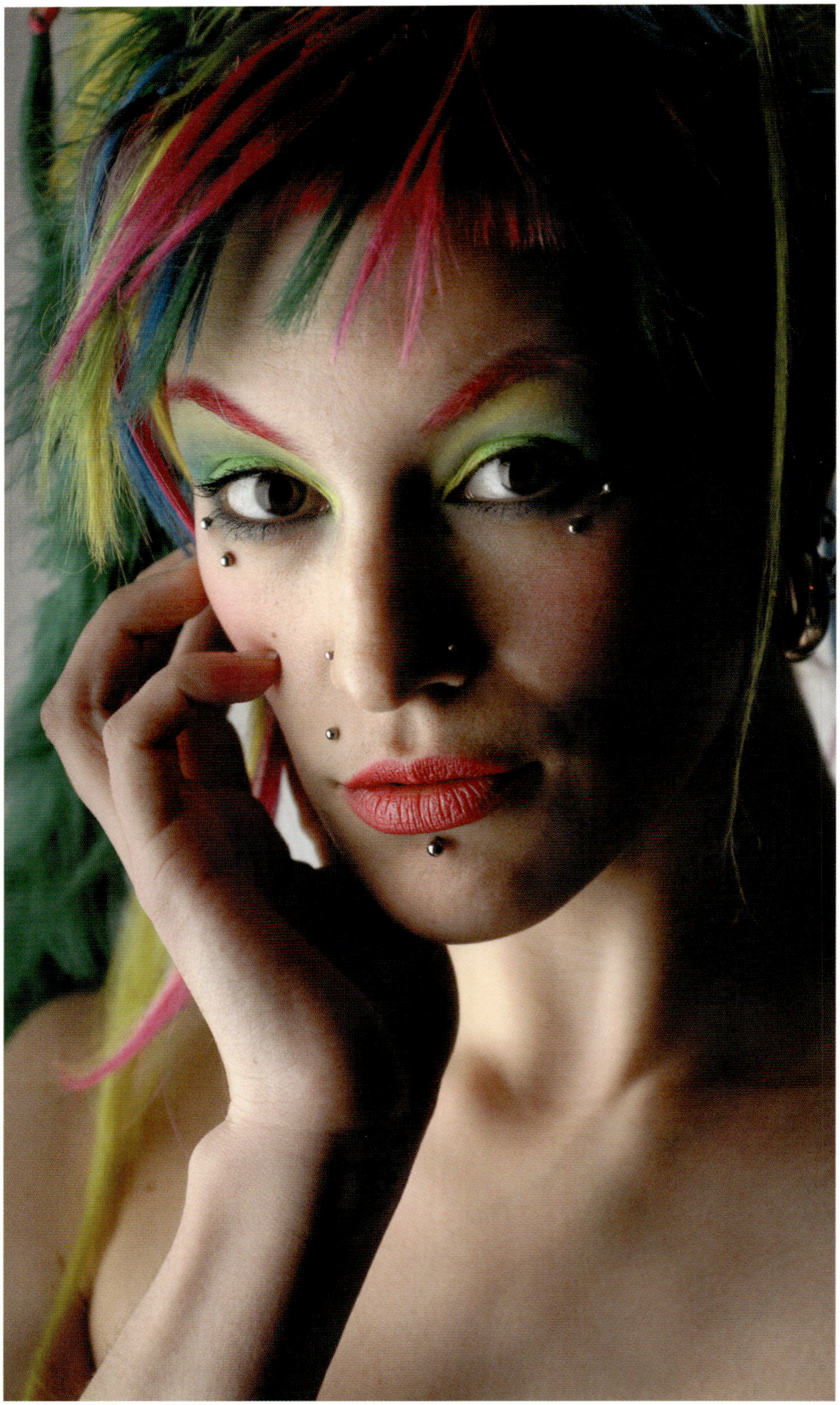

It's clear, looking at this work, how much the creation of erotic images has benefited from the advent of the digital era, with its powerful tools, which enable spectacular manipulation of the original image. This approach to photography doesn't necessarily require a digital camera, but it does rely on computers and image-editing software to achieve its effects. For example, good image-editing programs provide extraordinarily subtle ways of rendering black-and-white images, at least comparable to those of traditional photographic printing. But the computer also offers reproducibility: you can print as many copies of the image as you want, and know that they will all be identical, without having to strive to dodge and burn each print just like the previous one.

So, on the one hand, the erotic image in the twenty-first century experiments with the exciting and challenging new possibilities of digital media. On the other, it also reflects changing sexual values and lifestyles. For example, small digital cameras capable of producing clear, sharp images have had an impact in documenting the sexual "underground"—often just referred to as the Scene—which is a feature of the erotic life of many countries. While this kind of photography doesn't play a prominent part in *Erotique Digitale*, it has contributed to a higher profile for, and greater acceptance of, a range of different sexual lifestyles. And this in turn has led to serious photographers incorporating elements of these lifestyles into their imagery.

Linked to this involvement of the Scene in serious erotic photography is the growing use of "alternative" models. These are models who by their use of unconventional fashion, hair-styles, and body modifications, such as tattoos and piercings, create in themselves new, challenging, and often controversial forms of physical beauty, which stand in opposition to the mainstream.

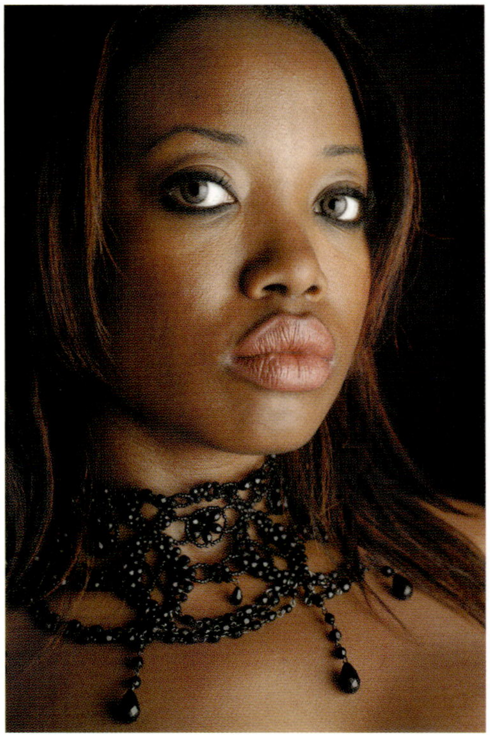

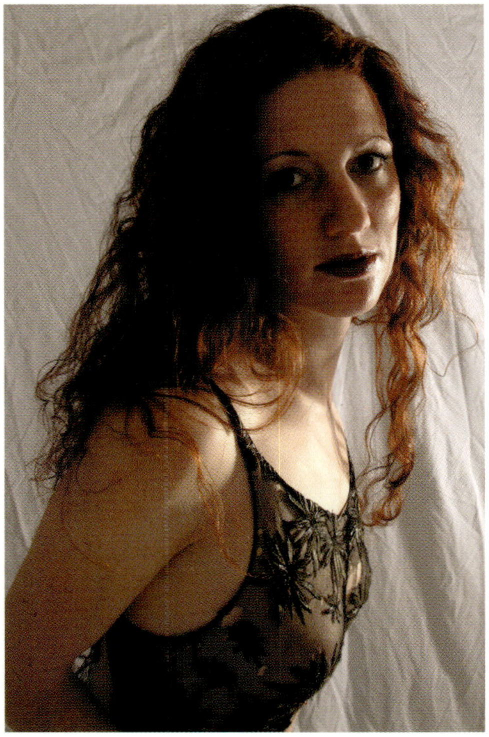

ALL IMAGES: The erotic photographer chooses between the many "looks" that different models offer, but expressive facial features, whether "natural" or the product of elaborate makeup or body modification, are among the most important considerations.

The photographers: six of the best

Here we survey the work of six of the outstanding photographers whose work appears in the Showcase section of *Erotique Digitale*. Their work stands as a summation of what is being achieved in this rich, sophisticated, and diverse field of creativity today.

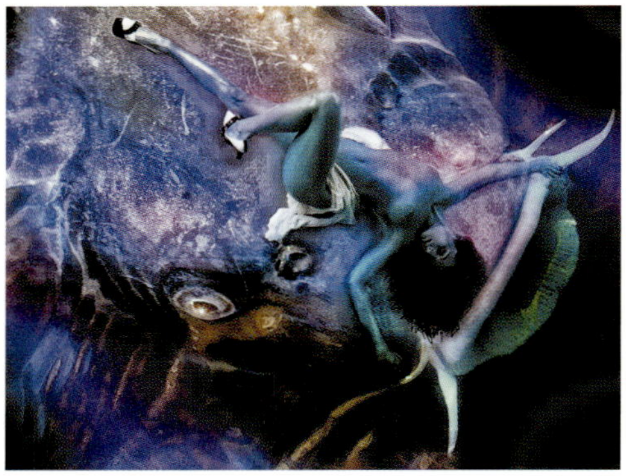

G. W. Burns

If the computer provides the tools for digital manipulation, it's still the artist whose imagination, vision, and skill are essential to the finished work. G. W. Burns shows this process at work. Here a fantasy scene is created, bringing a vivid sensuality to bear on an image inspired by Moby Dick, but perhaps even more suggestive of one of the Greek legends of the abduction of a beautiful woman by some supernatural creature. The blending of the top layer (the model) with the underlying image of the fish is perfectly achieved; but what gives the picture its impact is the imaginative use of digitally created color in it, which shifts it utterly out of the "real" world into the realm of the mythical.

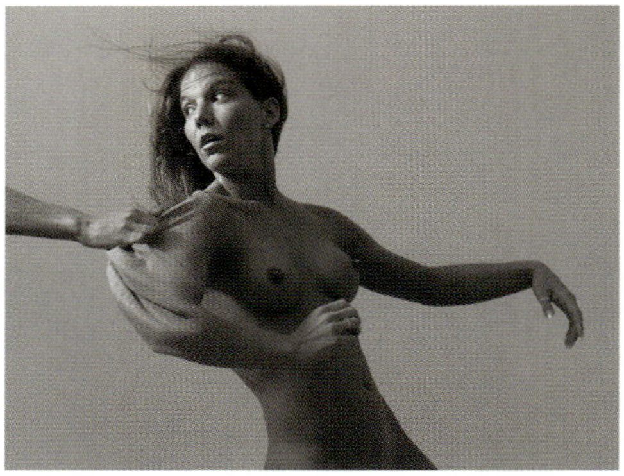

Christopher Donovan

Christopher Donovan's stunning portfolio in this book almost defies categorization, ranging from joyous pastoral to dark reflections on mortality and human fragility. Here pre-planning and pre-visualization of the image is essential, in order to ensure that the physical elements of the image are correctly shot to enable them to be digitally combined. The result is deceptively simple, but note, for example, the precisely controlled lighting which clearly shows us the fear in the model's expression, while leaving the light in the rest of the image restrained and sombre. The image recalls the Greek myth of Eurydice, dragged back into the underworld just at the moment she seems to have achieved her freedom. However, in this image, with its horror-film-like vision of the body as soft and almost plastic, the myth is seen through very modern eyes. This is a dark eroticism indeed.

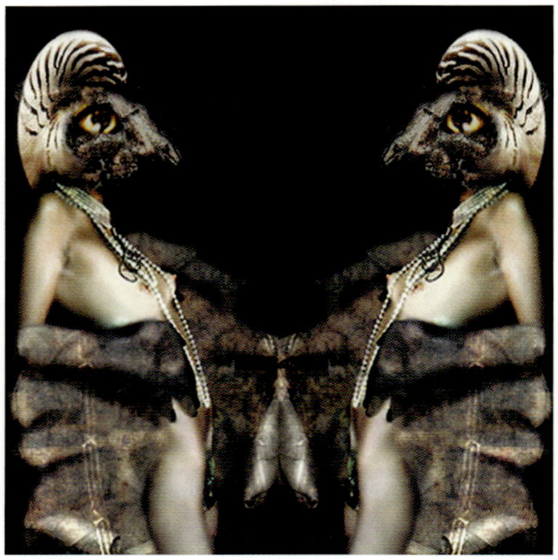

Derek Caballero

In Derek Caballero's work we remain in mythical regions, where extraordinary beings are created out of the seamless fitting together of what might seem like very disparate elements. In this image his meditation on female power is not without its element of anxiety, conveyed by the use of tiger skulls as helmets and reinforced by the symmetry of the two figures, which suggests two superhuman guardians of some dark and mysterious space, whose sideways gaze is fixed penetratingly on the viewer. It's fascinating to read the list of "ingredients" in this image: as well as the tiger-skull and the model with her pearls and collar, Caballero used leaves, a nautilus shell, an image of someone else's eye, a length of fabric, and a metal sunglasses case! Some of these elements were planned, some were found by chance; and the photographer's eye and skill meld them all triumphantly together.

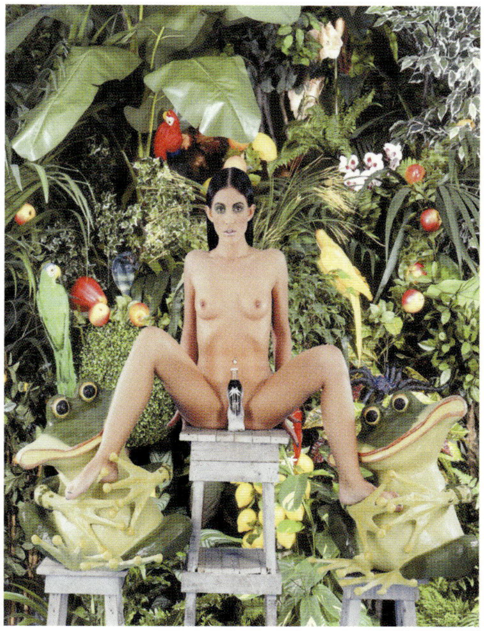

Holger Maass

His finished pictures will always have been run through some digital manipulation and adjustment, but for Holger Maass the process of making an image often literally requires construction, of the physical sets and props that frame the model(s). Whereas most of the other photographers in *Erotique Digitale* would see themselves as individual creative artists, Maass' work is thus a team effort, bringing in experts in a number of visually related fields. His stylish approach to photography, and the purposes for which his images are conceived, gives them a glitzy, super-real feeling, full of vivid colors and allusions to other arts, such as painting and film. This is a very knowing aesthetic, which plunders the common visual language of advertising, marketing, and the global village for elements that it cheerfully and wittily exploits.

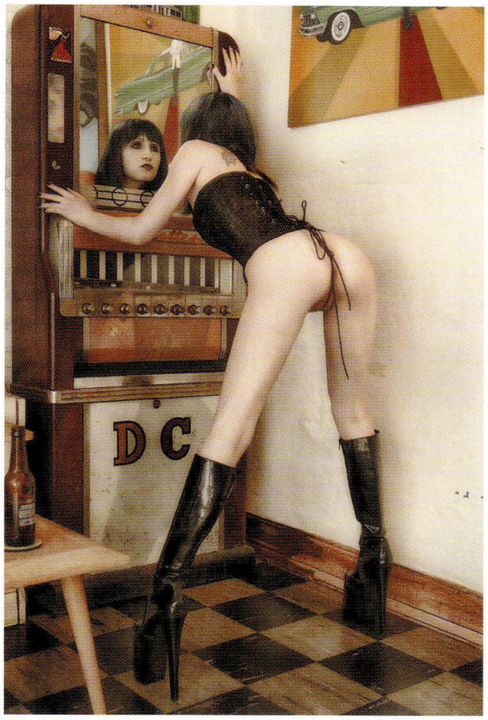

Chris Gustafson

Many photographers fall into the trap of slavishly applying the "painterly" effects and filters which image-editing programs provide. The results usually look like bad paintings, or bad photographs, or both. In Chris Gustafson's work we enter a world of desire and sexual provocativeness where the conventional look of the photographic image has been superseded by a new and different vision of the body, with textures and colors which may be reminiscent of the work of great airbrush artists like Vargas, but which are at the same time entirely original. You can sum it up by saying that it's all done with layers and filters, but that hardly does justice to the smooth, almost glowing skin tones and glittering highlights that are characteristic of Gustafson's work, combined with well-chosen locations and props.

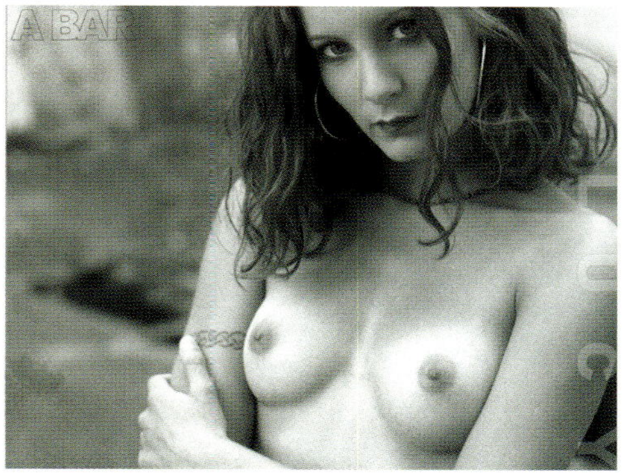

Roberto Segate

Roberto Segate's work spans two distinct styles, which still have in common the use of text—language, words—as an element that is both within and outside the image. Segate works with film and scans his photographs, before building them up into multi-layered exchanges of words and emotions that reflect on sexual anxiety. The sequence from which this image is taken works by creating a tension or contradiction between the model's pose and expression, and the text. If you look at the images of the model without reading the words, the model looks sexy, erotic, challenging, but available. Once you've read the words, however, the model's gaze becomes ambiguous, and even aggressive.

Tools

Digital technology has opened up the world of erotic photography to a new audience. Many of you will be familiar with the tools and techniques involved, but some of you will not. This section discusses some of the factors you might want to consider in choosing the "hardware"—a camera and computer, and the picture-editing software.

This book is an inspirational guide to the world of erotic digital photography, not another "how-to" manual, but this early part will familiarize you with some of the methods used by the artists we'll be looking at later on.

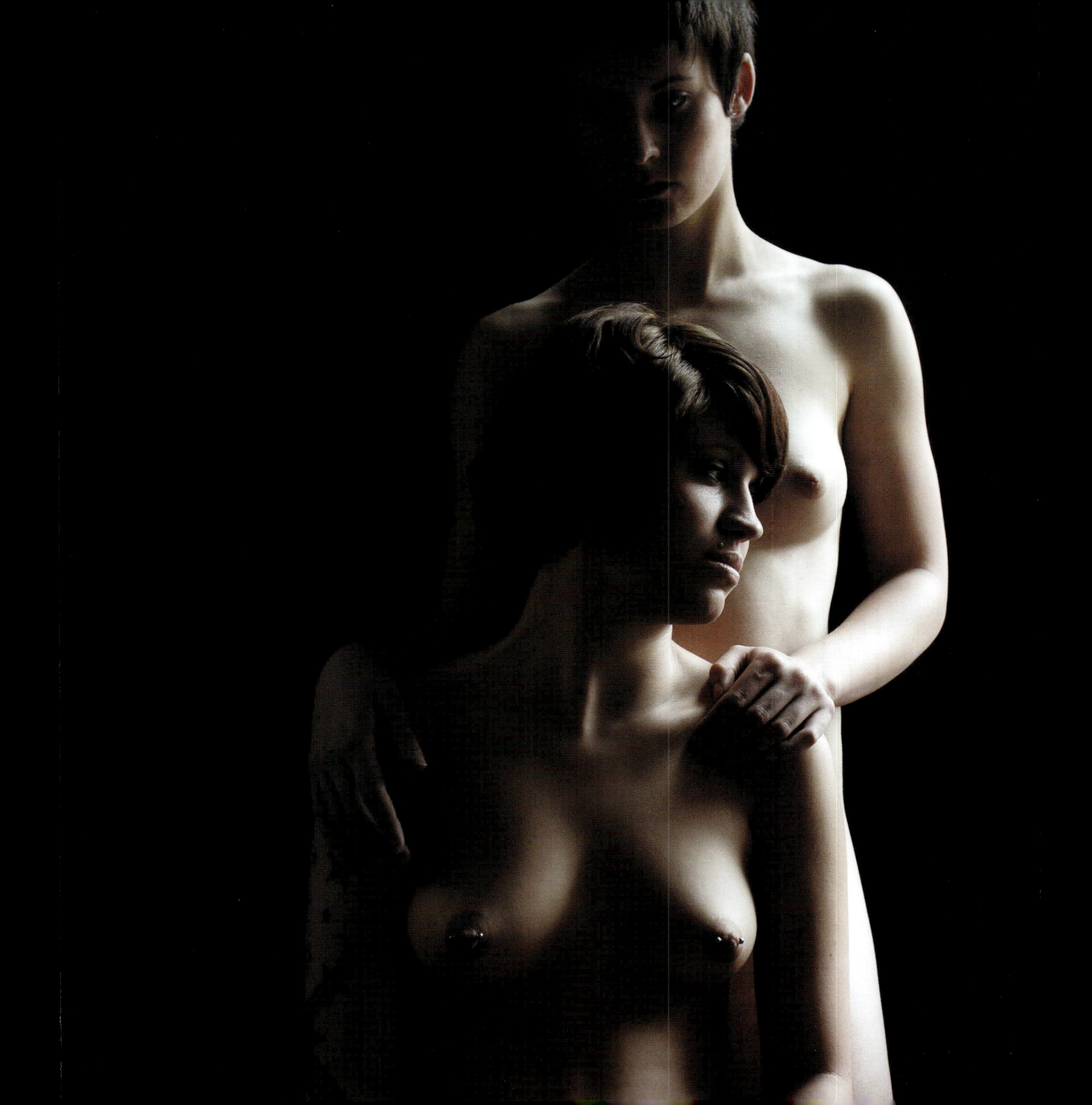

Hardware

In terms of set-up costs, digital photography with a good-quality camera is actually quite expensive, compared to getting started in film photography. But for the enthusiastic photographer the many freedoms and possibilities that digital offers, and the longer-term savings it brings, are still very attractive. You have probably already made the switch, but in case you haven't, there are some very good reasons for "going digital."

First—and this is particularly important in the field of erotic photography—digital photography is discreet. You don't have to entrust your films to a lab: the whole production process is under your own control.

Secondly, digital cameras give you immediate feedback. You can see the image on the camera's monitor immediately after you take it, enabling you to adjust the lighting, focus, exposure, or pose, and then reshoot. This works particularly well on cameras that offer supporting features such as histograms, overexposure indicators, and zoomable monitors. As a corollary of this, digital photography is more open to experimentation. You can try out ideas extensively—angles, poses, locations, lighting—where it would have been inconvenient and expensive to do the same thing on film.

Digital running costs are relatively low. You need only print the images you want, and once you've gained some experience with editing you can be confident that even the first print of an image will be correct—no more printing test strips! And of course you don't need a darkroom to work in. What's more, once you've edited an image to perfection, you can print as many copies as you want, confident that they will all be identical. Put this all together and, depending on how enthusiastic a photographer you are, you should find that a digital camera pays for itself in a year or two.

Finally, there's the question of exhibition. Since photography began, there's never been a photo gallery to compare to the Web. If you want to share your images with the widest imaginable audience, there are many websites devoted to photography and to erotic photography in particular. Or you could create your own website....

Inevitably, digital has its drawbacks. Up front, you have a fairly large set-up cost if you really want serious results. You need not only a good camera, but a good computer, monitor, and software. You'll need a lot of storage capacity on the computer, and a reliable method of backing up/archiving your work. And if you want to show your work extensively on the Web, a fast Internet connection will be important too.

In some regards, all but the very best digital cameras deliver less than they promise. Most offer a range of ISO settings, typically from 100 to 1600, but even on a high-end camera like the Nikon D100, the level of digital noise at ISO settings much above 400 is unacceptable.

Similarly, dynamic range can be an issue, particularly when working outdoors. Compared to a slow, fine-grain monochrome film, your digital camera may have more difficulty handling strong highlights and deep shadows in the same shot. This can also be a problem with film, and it's always possible to bracket exposures, of course, but you may find that you have to work around this aspect of digital cameras more frequently than you would with film. In addition many digital cameras produce very noticeable artifacts, often in the form of spurious color fringes, around overexposed areas.

Should these drawbacks put you off? Not at all. The further we go into this book, the more the advantages of shooting digital will become clear.

The Alternative

Of course, you don't have to take a completely digital route to gain the benefits of digital image-editing and exhibition on the Web. A few photographers still prefer to shoot on 35mm or medium-format film and transfer their images onto the computer through a scanner. The most common type is an A4 flatbed scanner, which can be used to scan prints or slides at resolutions of up to 9,600 dpi (although some models may need an optional adapter to scan slides and transparencies). These also have the advantage that they can scan other physical objects, including textiles, paintings, books, or magazines.

Alternatively, you could invest in a film scanner. These are designed specifically to scan 35mm negatives or slides (and larger transparencies on some models) at resolutions of 2,800 dpi and upward while maintaining the highest levels of tonal and color accuracy. If you want to continue working on film, the best way to move images into the digital domain is to have them burnt onto a Photo CD by the processing lab when you have the film processed. This will give you high-resolution images in a durable form, which also forms an archive of all your originals.

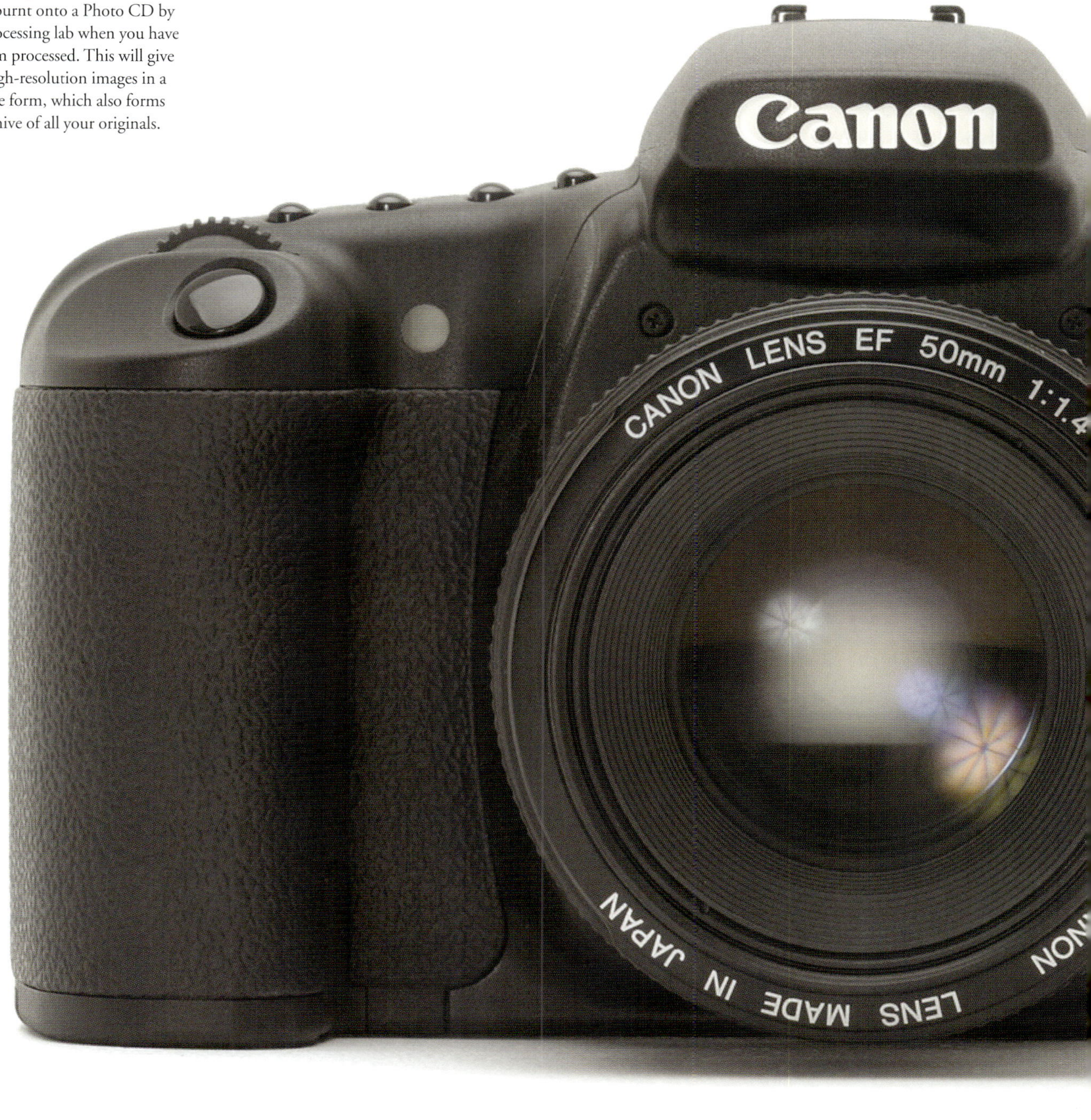

RIGHT: There are different routes into digital photography. Either buy your own digital camera or use your 35mm camera, and scan the results on a scanner or have them burnt onto a Photo CD.

Selecting a digital camera

There's now a bewildering range of digital cameras on the market. At the top of the range are digital backs which attach to 4x5 and medium-format camera bodies. Next come the so-called Digital SLR cameras, such as the Nikon D2, Nikon D70, the Canon EOS-1Ds, and the Fujifilm FinePix S3 Pro. These look and work like a 35mm film camera, accepting interchangeable lenses and using an optical viewfinder (as well as a monitor on which to view images after they've been taken). Below these comes a huge range of digital cameras with non-interchangeable lenses and, depending on price, more or fewer features. In terms of quality and features, you pretty much get what you pay for.

If you already own a 35mm camera with a range of interchangeable lenses, your choice when you "go digital" may be to buy a body by the same maker, so that you can continue to use your lenses. If not, read on....

Manufacturers release new and updated versions of their cameras frequently, but there's a minimum set of features to look for on whichever camera you choose:

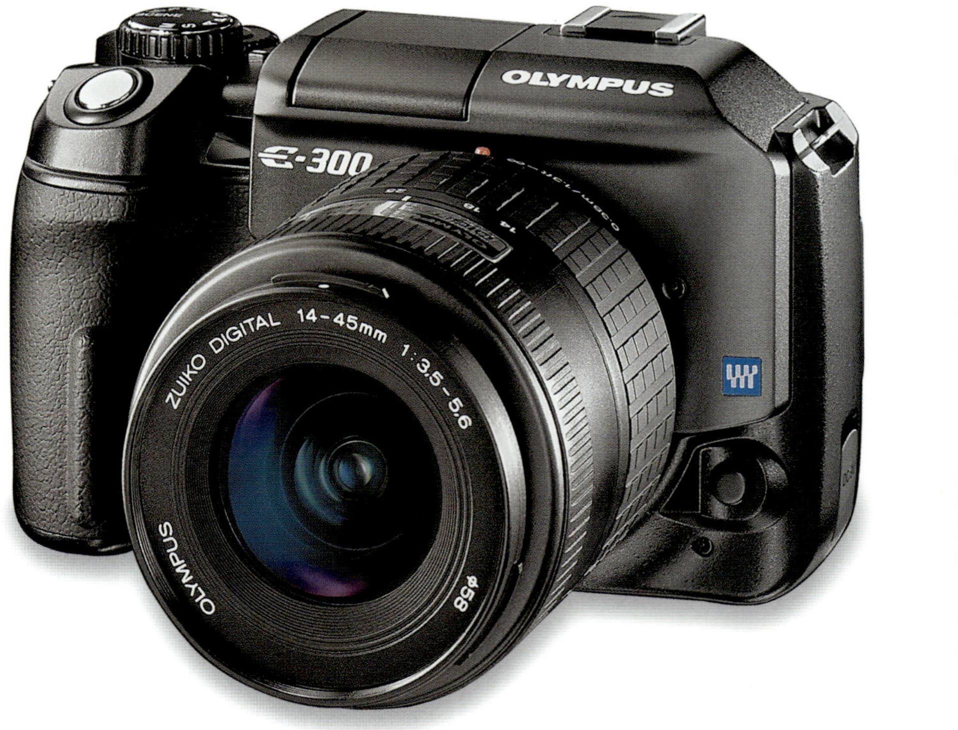

∗ The larger the image the camera produces, the better. It's sensible to go for a camera with an image size of at least 4 megapixels, and the majority of "serious" digital cameras now feature resolutions of 6 megapixels and above.

∗ The camera should have a hot shoe or a sync cable socket so that you can connect flash heads to it, and a threaded socket so you can mount it on a tripod.

∗ You should be able to override the camera's automatic settings, so that you can manually select shutter speed or aperture (or preferably both) in order to control depth of field, switch off the built-in flash, and adjust the color balance to handle different light sources.

∗ Three features are useful on the monitor: a histogram display to assess the exposure of each shot; a highlight indicator to see which areas of the image are overexposed; and a zoom facility so that you can zoom in on details to check focus, lighting, the model's expression, etc.

∗ On some cheaper cameras you may encounter a noticeable delay between pressing the button and the shutter opening. Not a problem perhaps with carefully set up studio shots, but a killer for spontaneity!

∗ It's probably desirable that the camera you select has the capacity to save images in RAW format. RAW images are saved without any compression, which makes them much cleaner (no compression artifacts) and more flexible when you come to edit. RAW images are much larger than JPEGs and so take much longer to save when you shoot them (about 40 secs per image on a Nikon D100). They're also slower to edit, but they do let you use the full capacity of your camera. You may not shoot RAW very often, but for occasions when you want the best possible results, RAW is the way to work.

ABOVE: The E-300 is the second "Four Thirds" system digital SLR from Olympus and is targeted at the more affordable end of the market. The E-300 has an 8-megapixel Kodak CCD sensor and a 4/3 system lens mount.

OPPOSITE PAGE, TOP: Website www.dpreview.com is an extremely useful resource for making informed comparisons between digital cameras on the market.

OPPOSITE PAGE, BOTTOM: One of the most important prosumer digital camera of 2004, the Cybershot DSC-F828 combines a high-quality mechanically linked zoom lens combined with the resolution of an 8-megapixel CCD.

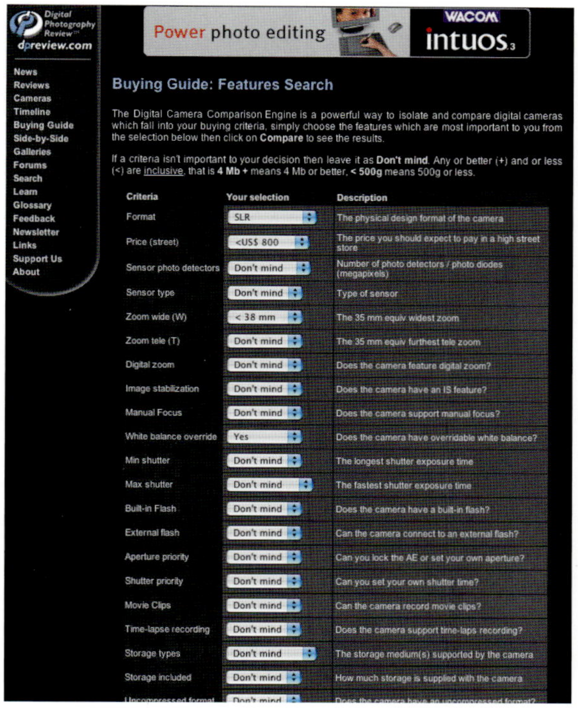

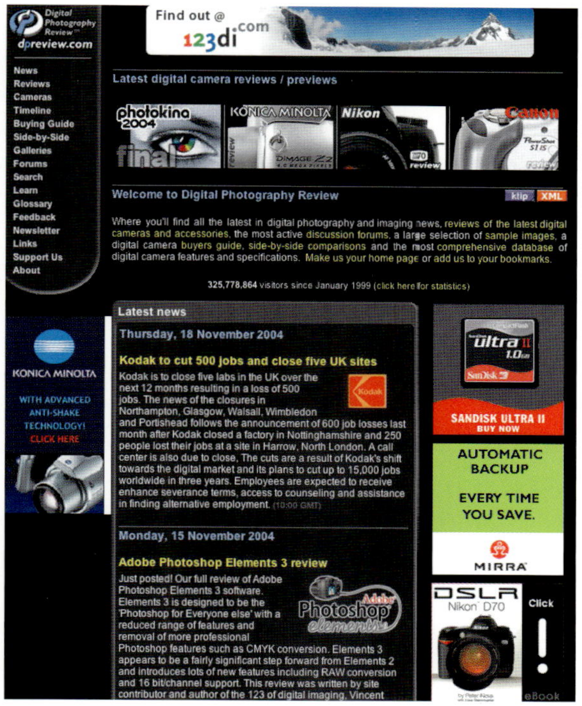

Decision time

When it comes to making your mind up what to buy, there's a range of sources of advice. Photography magazines carry reviews of current cameras, and usually have websites on which reviews of older cameras are archived. Good photography shops may also offer advice which is unbiased as well as knowledgeable. Friends will usually be happy to talk about what they like and don't like about their cameras—biased advice, certainly, but based on real experience.

Pretty well every camera manufacturer has a website, and these are useful for finding out what's available, for getting access to technical specifications, and checking what additional lenses are available for the camera you're considering.

Finally, the website www.dpreview.com carries detailed, thorough, and well-written reviews of digital cameras; it's the best source of information I know, but is appropriately cautious in making recommendations.

The Lens

If you're going for a camera with a non-interchangeable lens, a big optical zoom (6x or better) is very useful. Ignore the camera's digital zoom if it has one—the quality of the images this produces is likely to be very disappointing.

Despite the manufacturer's hype, a big zoom isn't everything, so on cameras with non-interchangeable lenses, you should always check the aperture range as well. This is the widest aperture you can use at different positions of the zoom lens. For example on a Nikon Coolpix 5700, the lens has a maximum aperture of f2.8 when zoomed out, but stops down to f4.2 as you zoom in. This makes it more difficult to work with shallow depth of field when you're zoomed in.

Again, on cameras with non-interchangeable lenses, check which lens attachments are available, such as wide-angle and telephoto converters, and fish-eye adapters. These are often designed to fit only one or two specific models in the manufacturer's range.

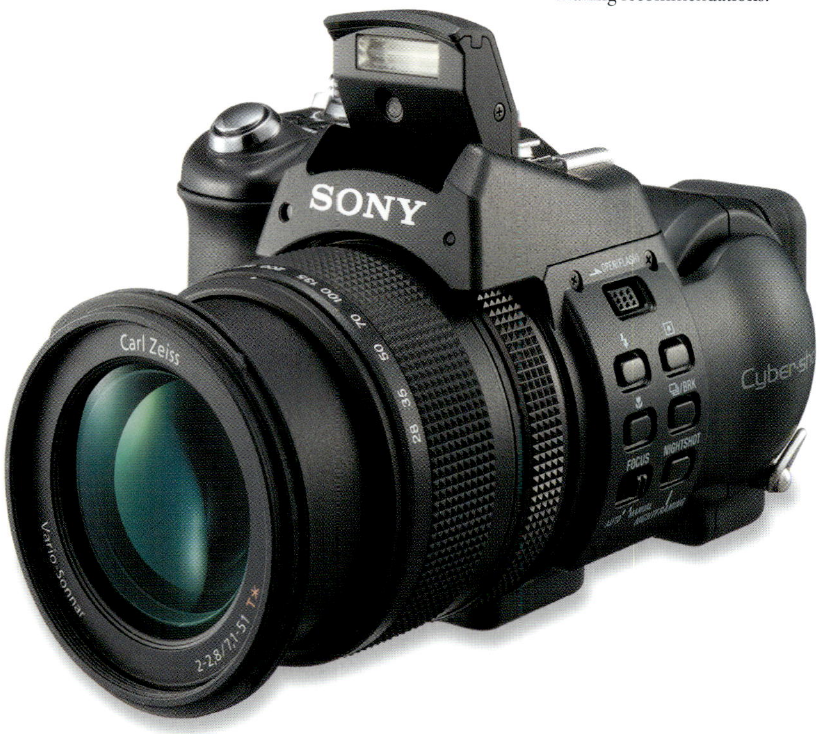

Choosing a computer

If you're buying a computer primarily for photo-editing, then Apple's range of Macintosh computers deserves serious consideration. While less popular than Windows PCs, Macs are designed with image-processing as a core function (both still images and video). They also work very effectively as general-purpose domestic computers, using Apple's Unix-based OS X operating system, which has proved extremely rugged and reliable.

If your interests extend to video production as well as photography, then Macs are even more attractive, because you can run Apple's brilliant video-editing applications, Final Cut Express and Final Cut Pro on them. I'd better declare my prejudices: I use Macintosh computers, and like many Mac users I'm passionate about the virtues of Apple's machines. So my heartfelt advice would be, "buy a Mac!" But most of the world uses Windows PCs, and a reliable PC is a perfectly satisfactory machine for image-editing and manipulation. I've taught Photoshop for many years in a lab equipped with PCs, without any difficulties.

If you've decided that you're going for a PC, then your choice will probably be determined by a whole range of considerations to do with price, bundled software, support, etc.

Whatever your choice, it's worth considering whether a laptop computer would be better for you than a conventional desktop machine. Many laptops are more than powerful enough to handle picture-editing, and their portability can be very useful. You can download images during location shoots, in order to see them at a reasonable size, and burn CDs immediately. Some cameras come with software that lets you connect them to a laptop via a Firewire cable, and "take" pictures directly onto the laptop's hard drive.

Whatever computer you choose, these are important considerations:

✱ Install as much memory as you can afford. Although Photoshop will run with less, a gigabyte of memory no longer seems excessive, for either PC or Mac, and half a gigabyte (512MB) is a sensible minimum for normal use. In any case, more memory will make complex editing applications run much more smoothly and rapidly. It's usually cheaper to buy a computer with lots of memory than to buy it with less and have it upgraded later, but this isn't always the case. Some major manufacturers charge a premium for additional RAM.

✱ Choose a big hard drive. A high-quality (6-megapixel) image downloaded from my Nikon D100 is about 1.5 megabytes, because it's been compressed as a medium-quality JPEG file. If I edit it and want to save the edited version in an uncompressed format, such as .tif or .psd, that file will be over 17MB. In other words, 60 uncompressed images will take up more than a gigabyte of storage. We said earlier that one of the advantages of working in the digital domain is the freedom it gives you to experiment. The downside of that freedom is that you will fill up your hard drive surprisingly quickly with experimental shots and edits! As with memory, it's usually cheaper to buy a computer with the biggest hard drive available already fitted, rather than buy a smaller drive and have it upgraded later. Having said that, however large the hard drive you buy, you will eventually fill it up if you keep all or most of your images immediately accessible on the hard drive, rather than archiving them, so additional hard drives may also become necessary.

✱ You'll need at least two USB and one Firewire port, although more than one is helpful. It's also useful to have ports on the front of the computer so you can plug devices into them easily. You will need them to connect your camera, plus your printer, scanner, digital video camera, and any external hard disk, CD, or DVD drives should you need them.

RIGHT: A PC, such as this Sony Vaio, will be a perfectly adequate set-up for image-editing and manipulation.

BELOW RIGHT: Apple Macs are designed with image-processing as a core function and are brilliant for running video-editing applications, too.

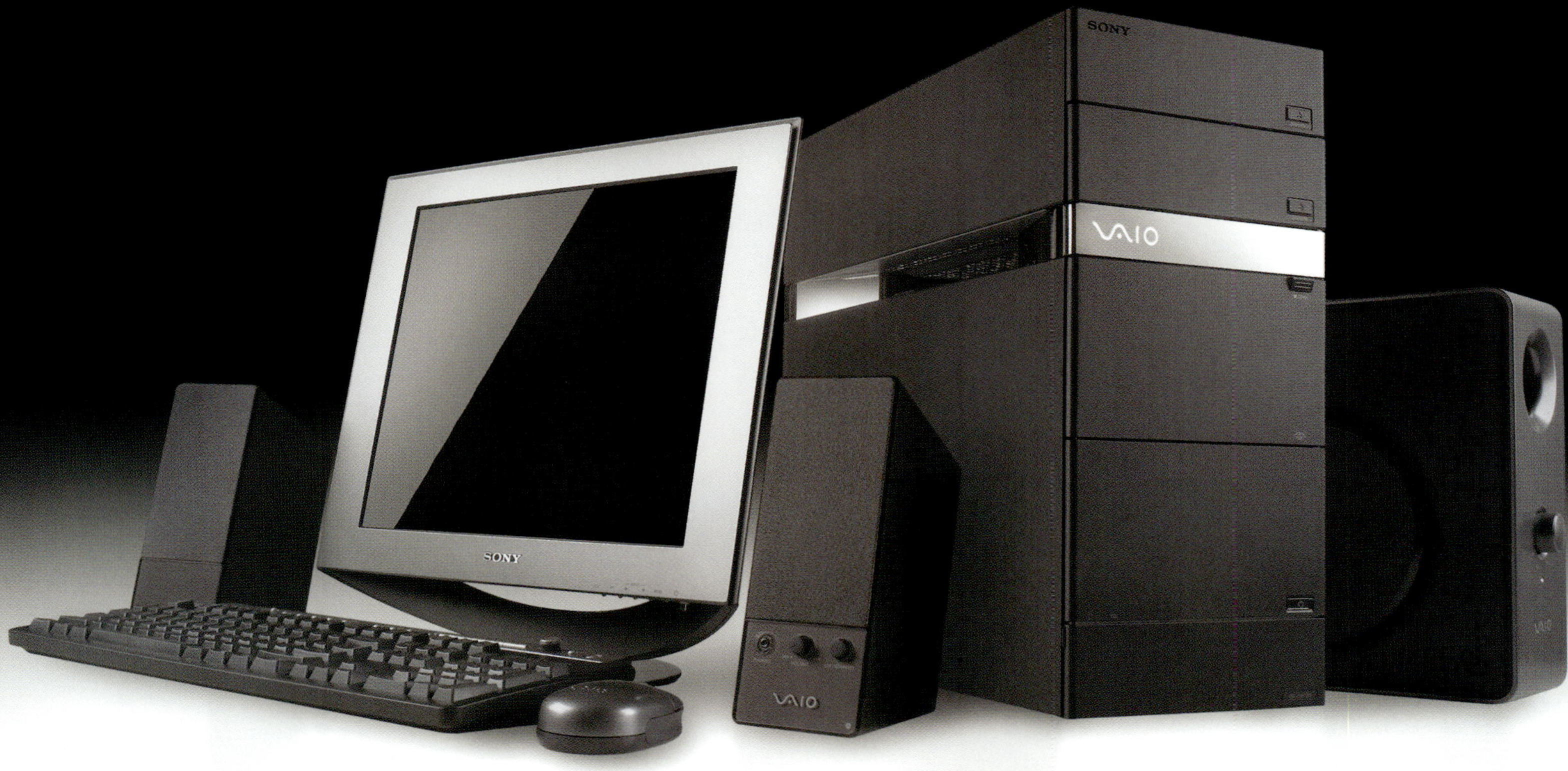

* Your computer must have a CD or preferably DVD writer. The simplest way to archive images, and to send them to photo labs, is on a CD or DVD. CDs hold at least 650MB, and the blank media are very cheap; DVD media are more expensive, but will currently hold up to 4.7 GB, with higher capacity on the way. DVD writers will also write CDs, as well as playing CDs and DVDs.

* If you're buying a desktop system, splash out on a large screen. The bigger the screen (at least 21-inch), the less time you'll spend scrolling your image around to get to the area you want to edit, or moving other windows out of the way. Again, at the time of writing, only the most expensive flat panel (LCD) screens are regarded as suitable for serious image-editing, in terms of stability and color accuracy (see the section on Color Management, p24). High-quality, traditional cathode ray tube (CRT) screens from manufacturers such as Sony, LaCie, and Mitsubishi are more modestly priced. The ideal solution is in fact to have two screens side by side: one for the image, the other for all the other windows, menus, and tools.... If you opt for this solution, two 17-inch monitors will work effectively.

To sum up: any modern computer should be able to process photographic images without difficulty. But the more you can incorporate the features described above, the easier and faster the work will be.

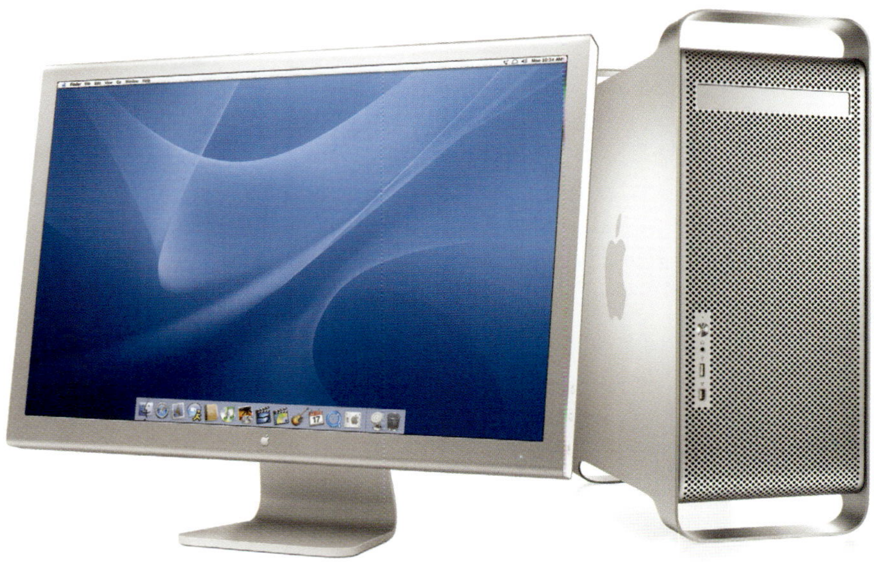

Additional peripherals

I work with a graphics tablet and stylus, rather than a mouse. This gives more control over the delicate use of brushes and other picture-editing tools, and is much less stressful on the wrist and fingers than a mouse. It's fine for all other applications, such as word-processing or spreadsheets, as well. Speaking of health and safety, don't neglect your working environment! Picture-editing is a lot more intensive than word-processing or web-browsing, so if you don't already have them, treat yourself to a well-designed chair and a work surface that places your keyboard and screen at the right height for you. Make sure you have good lighting, too.

If, like me, you prefer to have easy access to your collection of images, rather than storing them offline on CDs or DVDs, you may want to consider adding a couple of external hard drives to your system. External USB and Firewire Drives from manufacturers such as LaCie are cheap and reliable, and fast enough for picture-editing.

We've discussed archiving images onto CD or DVD. It's also important to back up current work. You can do this using rewritable CD or DVD (CD-RW, DVD-RW) or DVD-ROM, or by using a second hard drive to copy the contents of your working hard drive onto. Whichever method you choose, you should back up regularly, preferably every day.

Rather than hooking your camera directly up to your computer to download images, you may want to consider buying a media reader, such as those made by Belkin (www.belkin.com). This is a small device, with a slot to accept whatever type of storage card your camera uses, which plugs into a USB or Firewire port. As you fill each storage card up, you take it out of the camera, slot it into the media reader and leave it to download, while you load a fresh card into the camera and continue shooting. It does save time.

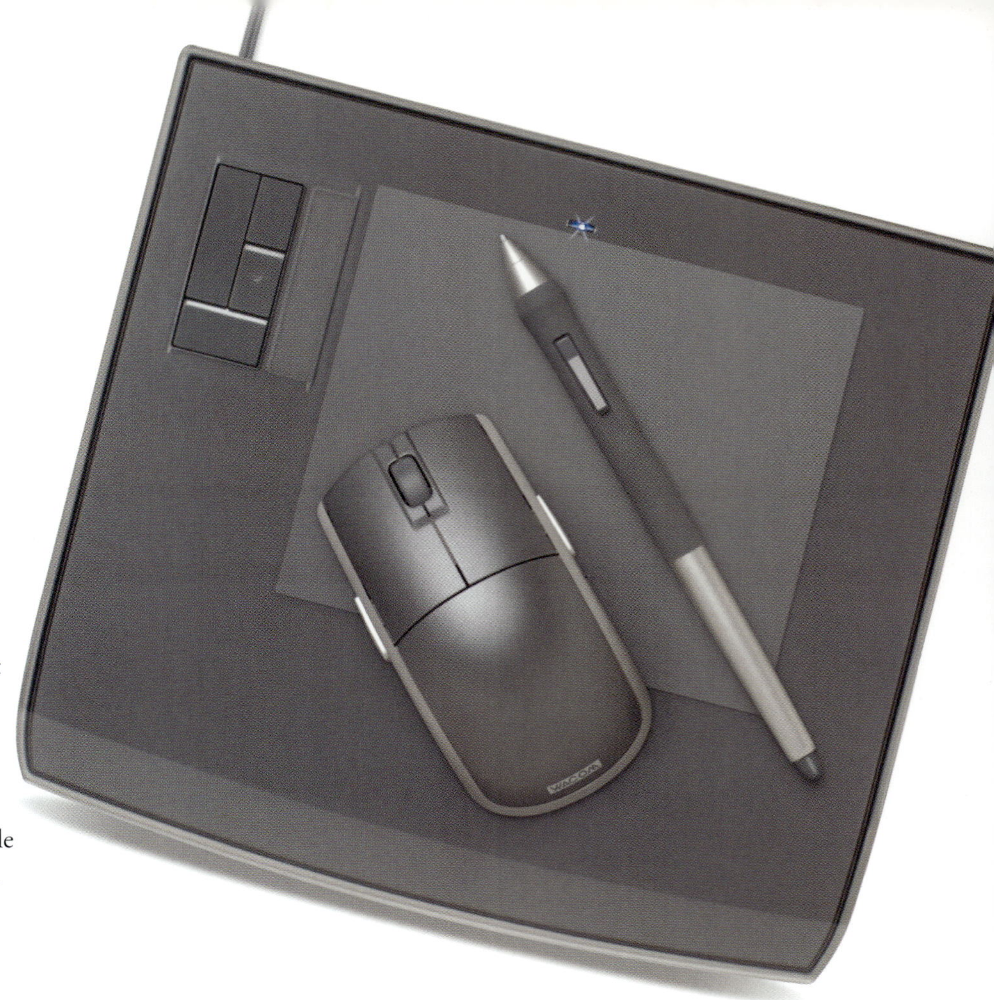

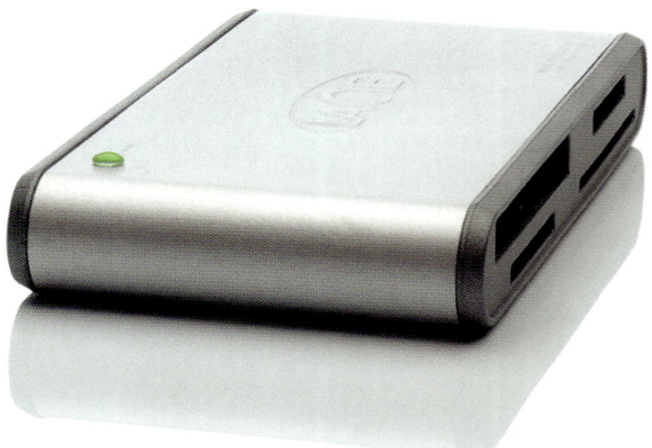

ABOVE: The highly recommended Wacom tablet and stylus.

LEFT: The LaCie card reader is cheap and reliable and makes for speedy picture-editing.

Printers

Color inkjet printers designed for photographic work are produced by, among others, Epson, Canon, Lexmark, and Hewlett-Packard. A4 printers are very cheap (their ink cartridges may be less so!) and A3 printers are also becoming more affordable. Basic printers will print in four colors (cyan, magenta, yellow, and black) whereas more advanced ones will add, for example, light cyan and light yellow inks to achieve more vivid and realistic colors. The printer you choose should be capable of printing at least 720 dpi (dots per inch). A range of papers is available also, of different weights and with different finishes, of the kinds familiar from traditional photo printing, such as glossy and matte.

The problems I've encountered using non-proprietary ink cartridges have led me to stick to buying Epson inks for my Epson printer. But there are two specialist companies that are worth looking into. Lyson (www.lyson.com) make a range of wide-gamut and archival inks, mainly for Epson printers. Wide-gamut inks enable the printer to capture a wider range of tones and colors than conventional inks, and archival inks are designed to last longer. Piezography (www.piezography.com) produces high-quality inks for black-and-white printing on Epson printers. Instead of the six different colors described above, Piezography uses six different shades of gray and black to provide very rich and finely graduated monochrome tones.

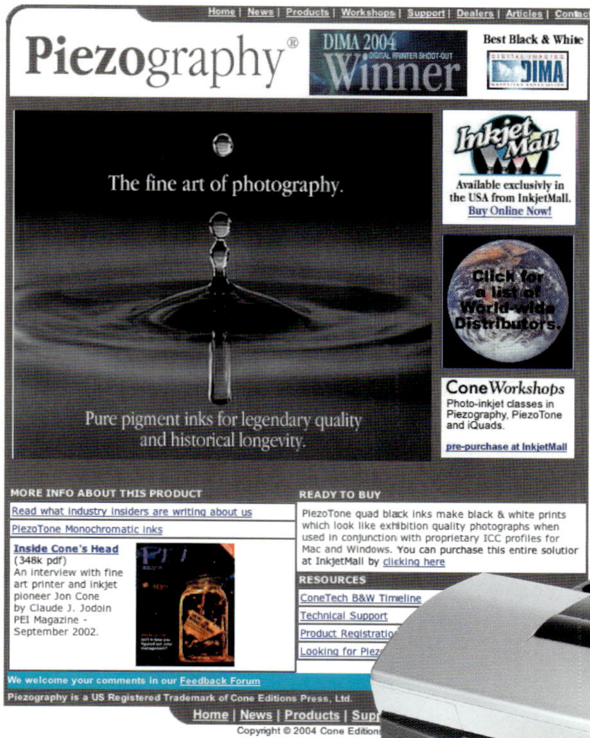

LEFT: Piezography supplies high-quality inks for black-and-white printing.

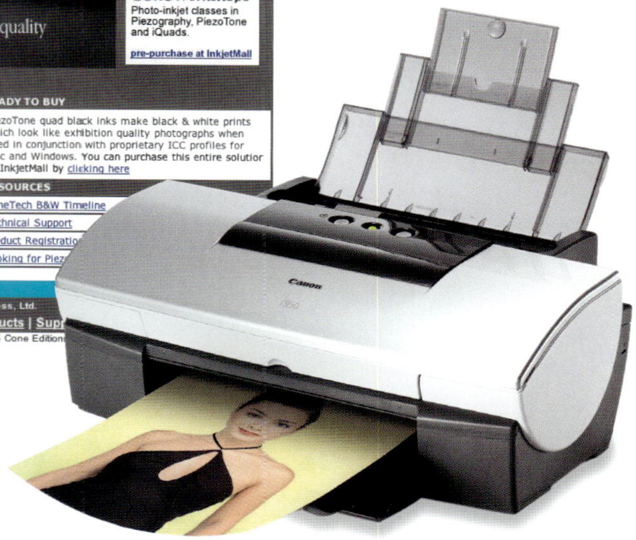

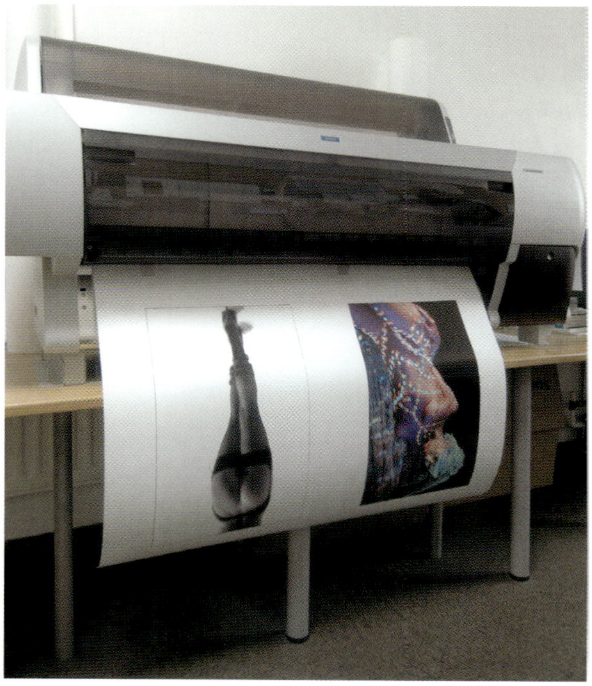

ABOVE AND LEFT: A4 printers are very cheap and larger printers are becoming more affordable all the time.

Image-editing software

Adobe Photoshop has become more or less the industry standard for image-manipulation; I don't know a digital photographer who doesn't use it in one version or another, whatever else they may use. It's a very powerful, very robust program that runs on both Mac and Windows computers. It's also pretty expensive, but Adobe have produced Photoshop Elements (also run on both Mac and Windows) which is about one-tenth of the price of "full" Photoshop, and has most of its features. No one who can afford Photoshop would choose to make do with Elements, but Elements is none the less a very useful package. Even on the most ambitious montages, it might slow down your creativity but it certainly won't frustrate it.

What does Photoshop do for the photographer? Everything! You use it to carry out basic tasks such cropping an image, scaling it, maximizing its dynamic range, and retouching flaws and blemishes on the subject. You can manipulate the colors in the image, either to make them look "correct" or to creatively distort them. You can do this for the image as a whole, or by using Photoshop's selection tools, for any part of it. You can use Photoshop's filters to change the textures and surfaces of the image or any part of it; and you can use Photoshop's layers and blends to combine images in limitless different combinations. And when you've finished creating your image you can use Photoshop to save it in formats suitable for anything from displaying it on your website, through printing it on your inkjet printer, to having it printed onto photographic paper at a lab.

There are other applications that either compete with Photoshop or complement its advanced feature set. These include JASC's Paint Shop Pro and Corel's Photo-Paint and Painter (from www.corel.com). The latter is particularly interesting. Often referred to as a "natural medium" program—one that lets you create digitally the different qualities of traditional artists' media such as paint, ink, chalk, even etching acid, on different surfaces such as (digital) paper and canvas—it's aimed principally at artists and illustrators. However, its appeal to photographers is that it lets you apply these same media to your photographs.

Paint Shop Pro is a relatively inexpensive, Windows-only program that provides many of the facilities of Photoshop, alongside some "painterly" features similar to those of Painter. The factor that makes it worthy of attention is that it provides some of the high-end color control and photographic adjustment tools that Photoshop Elements omits at a far lower price than Photoshop itself. This combination of powerful features and a low price point has won Paint Shop Pro a sizable following among Windows image-editors, though Photoshop remains the professional choice.

We'll hear about these packages from the photographers who use them throughout the book. As well as editing your pictures, you need to be able to keep track of them. Photoshop includes a Browse option that lets you look at all the images in a folder at once, but other applications are available. These range from consumer-level programs (the bundled iPhoto application on the Mac and Adobe Photoshop Album and JASC Paint Shop Pro Studio on Windows) to professional-level packages such as Extensis Portfolio or iView MediaPro. They let you organize your images and browse through via thumbnails and text tags, enabling you to sift thousands of shots without having to work through every picture on your hard drive. This can be a genuine timesaver.

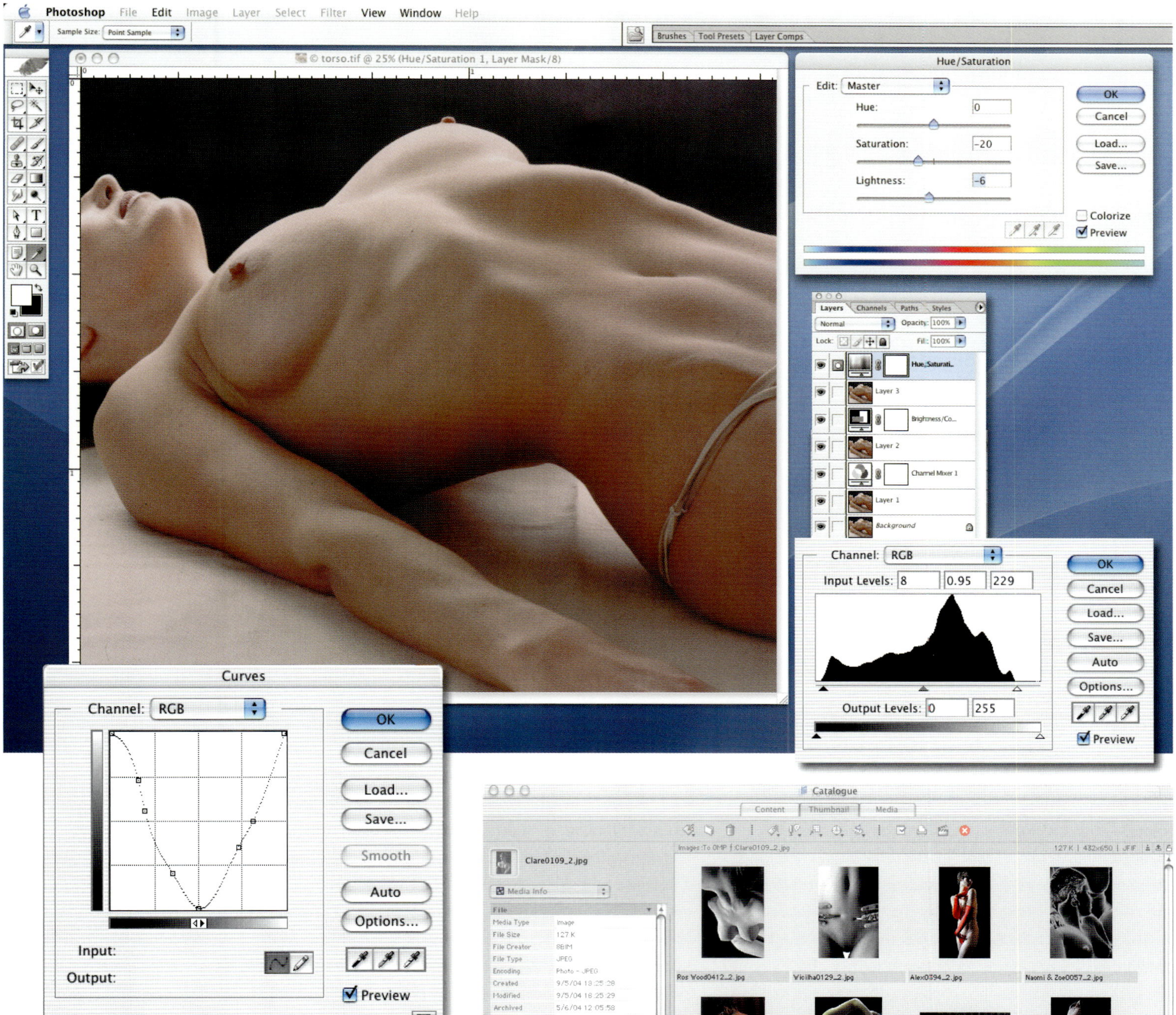

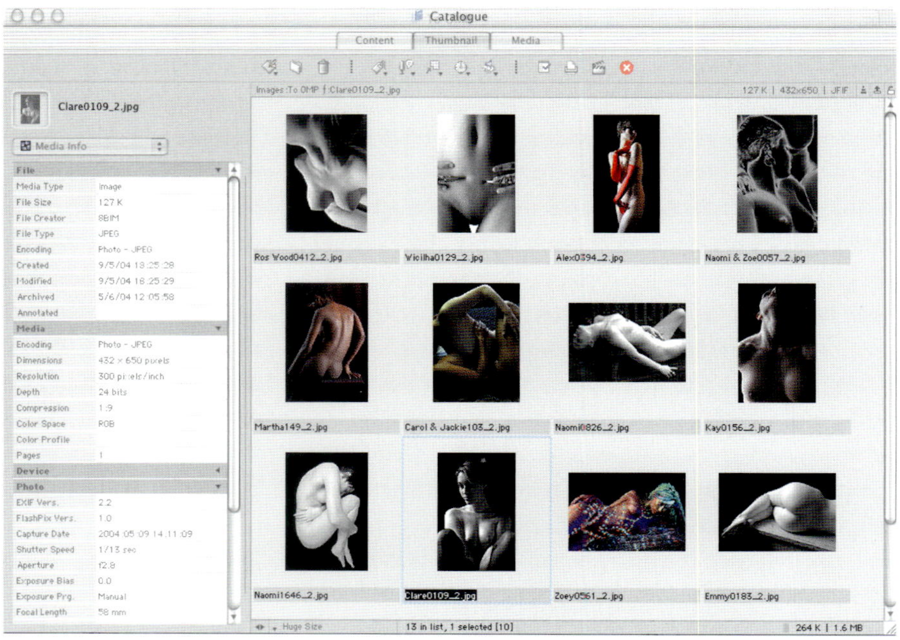

ABOVE: Using Photoshop enables you to both correct and enhance your photos to creative effect.

RIGHT: Photoshop includes a Browse option which lets you look at your images at handy thumbnail size.

Color management

Before we get further in, we also need to talk about color management. Too many digital photographers ignore this issue, and will spend hours working on the colors and tones in an image and then wonder why their image doesn't look like it should on another screen or—even worse—in print.

To understand why, we need to understand how color works in the digital realm. Each pixel in an image is described by a set of numbers that specify the pixel's position in a particular color space, which contains a certain range (or "gamut") of colors: for example in RGB mode there are three numbers that give the values for red, green, and blue for that pixel. However, the appearance of the pixel may vary when displayed or output on different devices, such as monitors or printers, because each device has a particular way of translating the raw numbers into visual color. If you ever see the same image displayed on two computer monitors from different manufacturers, side by side, you'll see what I mean.

Now consider the digital photography production chain. You shoot a picture on your digital camera. You view that picture on a computer screen, then print it on a printer or send it off to be processed in a lab. Your hope, in all of this, is that the colors in the final print will come out identical to those you saw on the monitor when you were editing the picture (which generally means you want them to look "lifelike"). But there's scope for error or inaccuracy at every stage: the camera may not "see" the colors in the scene perfectly; the colors, brightness, or contrast of your screen may be off, thus distorting your judgment of what you see when you edit the picture; and the printer or processing lab may produce a further shift away from what you originally saw.

To sort out these problems matching colors, and getting consistency thoughout this process, we need a system that interprets and translates color accurately between devices. A color-management system (CMS) compares the color space in which a color was created to the color space in which the same color will be output, and makes the necessary adjustments to represent the color as consistently as possible among different devices.

At its simplest, using color management involves applying a profile or "tag" to each image file, which tells the computer, the monitor, and the printer how to interpret the raw numbers of the file. A profile systematically describes how color numbers map to each particular color space. By tagging an image with a color profile, you provide a definition of actual color appearances in the image. You also need to set your monitor up correctly, so that the colors you see on screen are as accurate as possible. Some image-editing programs, including Photoshop, allow you to select the best profile for your purposes, depending on how your images are going to be printed or displayed.

It's worth also saying a little more about two of the other color spaces available in Photoshop. As well as RGB (which matches digital cameras), you also have a choice of CMYK and Lab. CMYK (Cyan, Yellow, Magenta, and blacK) corresponds to the four inks commonly used for color printing on offset printing presses, as well as on inkjet printers. The Lab color space consists of a luminance or lightness component (L) and two chromatic components: the "a" component (from green to red) and the "b" component (from blue to yellow). This comes closest to covering the whole gamut of colors visible to the human eye.

Most photographers work in RGB, even if the work is intended to be printed on a four-color printer, converting the file to CMYK only after it's been edited. The reason for this is that the CMYK color space is smaller than the RGB color space (i.e. it contains fewer colors), and is likely to limit your flexibility in editing. But many professionals edit in Lab mode, because of its broad gamut, switching back into RGB mode to get access to the features not available in Lab (not all Photoshop filters are available in Lab for example). If you're working from PhotoCDs, Lab is closest to the color mode used by the lab to scan your image onto the PhotoCD.

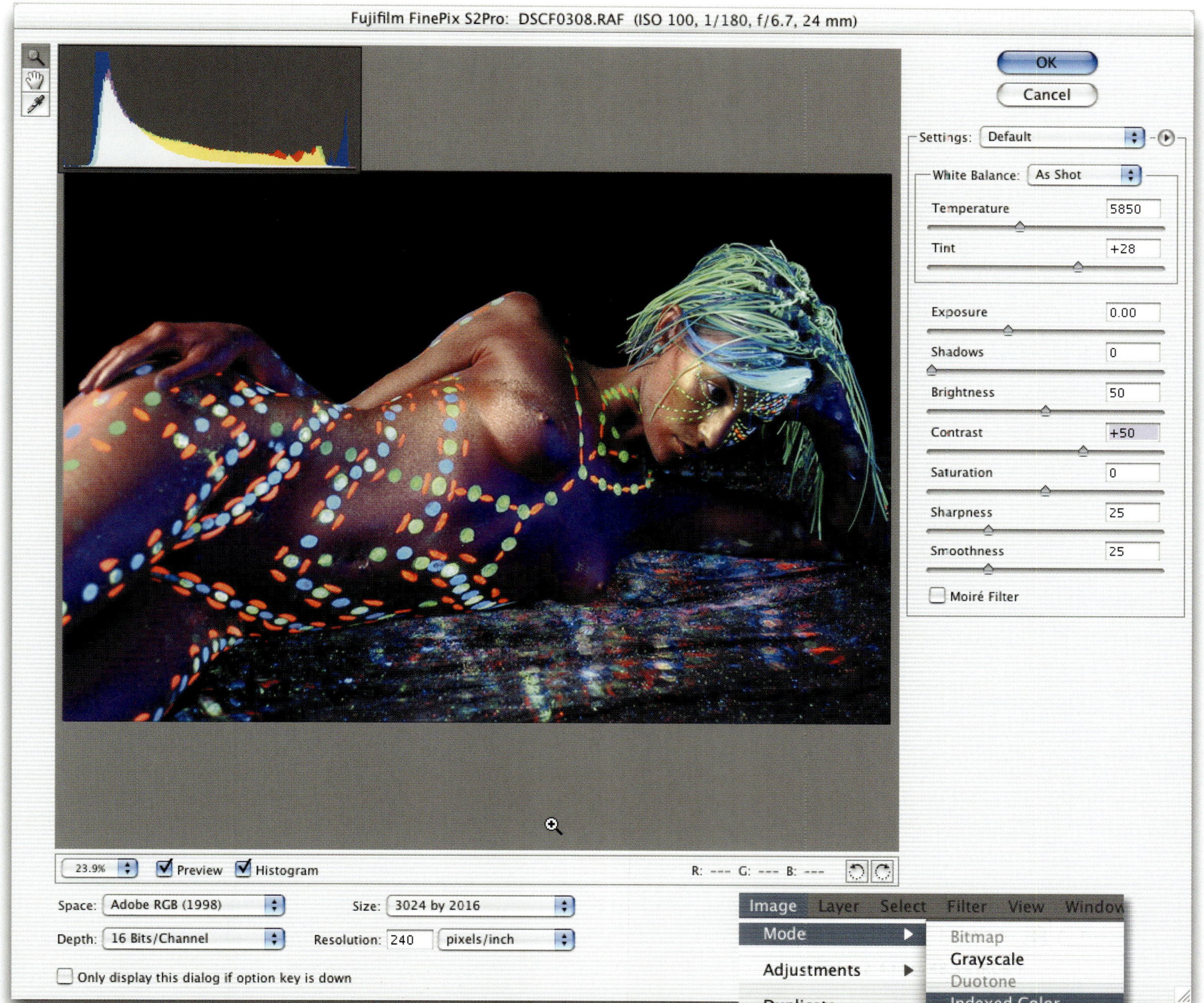

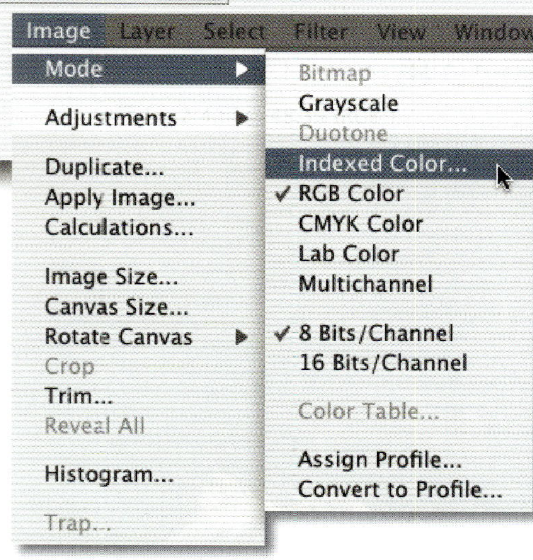

ABOVE: Editing a RAW file. Note the wide range of controls available in this mode (to the right of the image), which makes it an ideal tool for doing very precise picture-editing on an image such as this one, with its rich and subtle range of color, light, and shade.

The histogram, top left, reflects dynamically any adjustments made to the image as you edit it. Note also the Space setting, bottom left, which shows the color management tag currently applied to the image.

Techniques

Photo-retouching, which used to be the preserve of highly skilled professionals, is now within the scope of any capable photographer. Throughout this section, we'll cover how to use Adobe Photoshop—the industry standard image-editing application—to "clean up" and correct images, subtly altering or enhancing them without the viewer being aware that anything has been done. Typical processes here include removing skin blemishes, making eyes brighter, enhancing skin tones, and filling in overexposed areas.

We also deal with some of the basic tools for manipulating the image beyond merely making it look "right": different methods for creating monochrome and negative images, for example, as well as a first look at the remarkable power and creative possibilities offered by layers and blending.

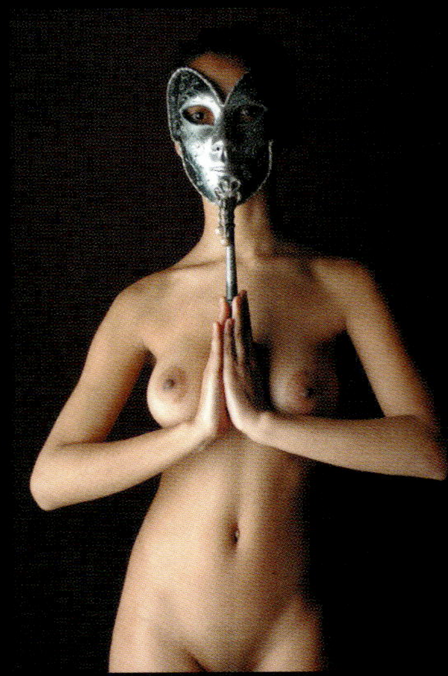

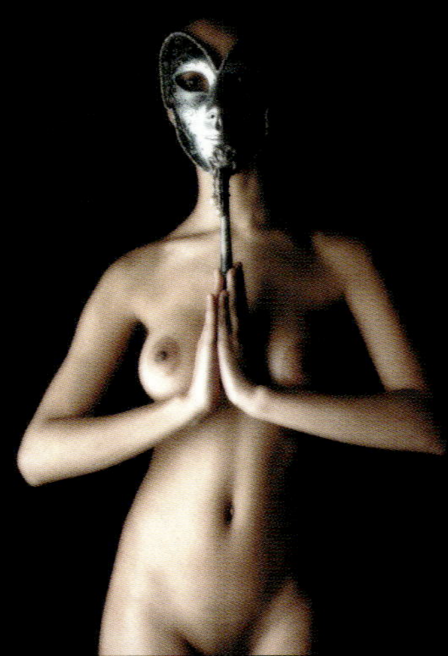

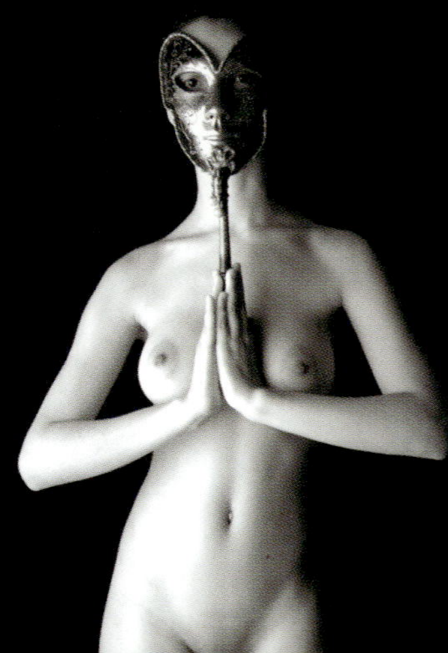

Starting with an original image, we can provide a different background, add grain and mute its tonal range, convert it to black and white, or give it a strikingly painterly look.

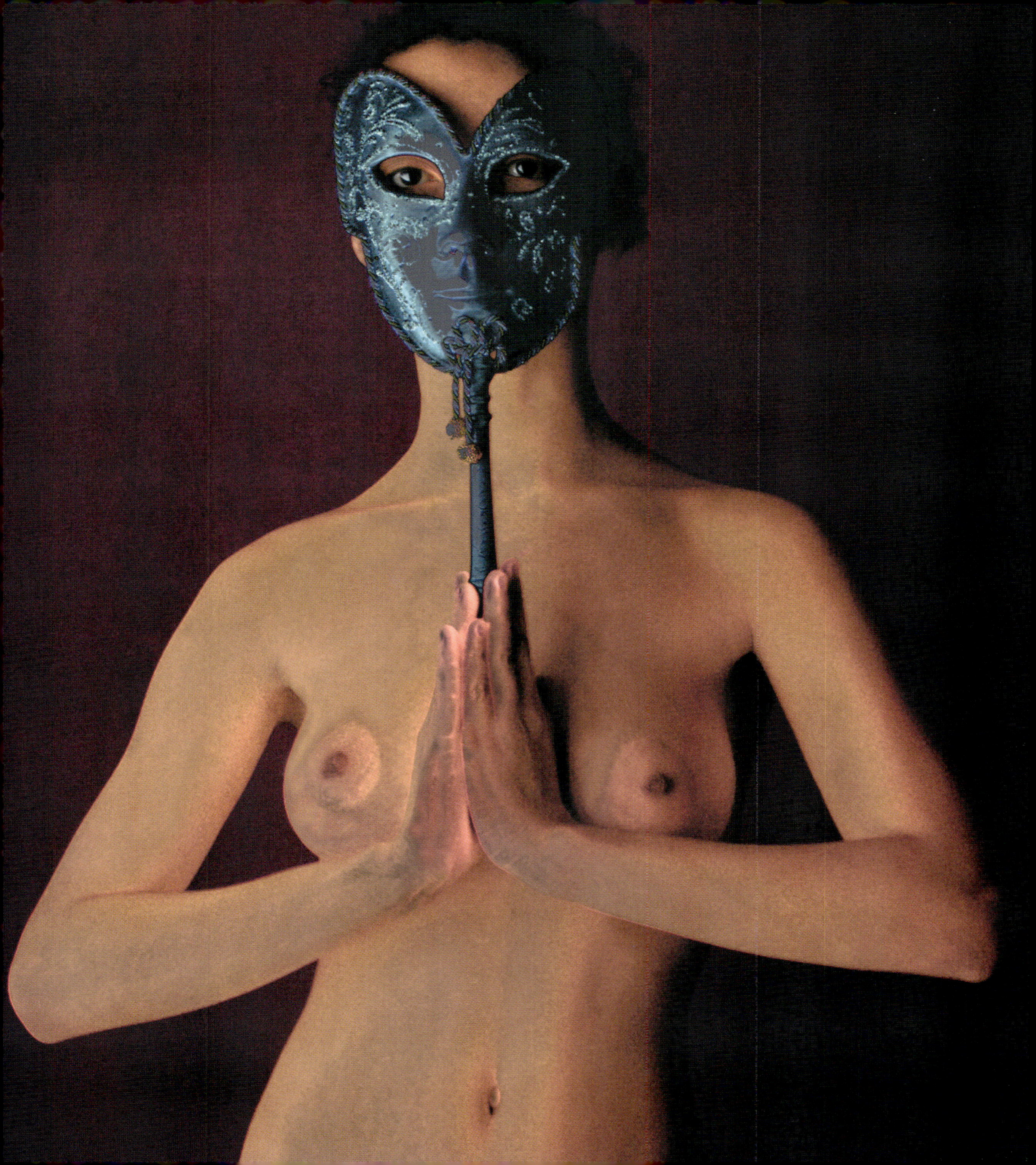

BELOW: In this pair of images, the overall brightness and contrast have been improved, the overexposed areas on the model's left breast and shoulder have been subtly filled in, the sunlight on the arm and seat of the bench has been reduced, and a little sharpening has been applied.

RIGHT: Not all digital cameras allow you to shoot in monochrome. This is a straightforward conversion of a color image to black and white, but notice that the shadow on the model's face has been lightened.

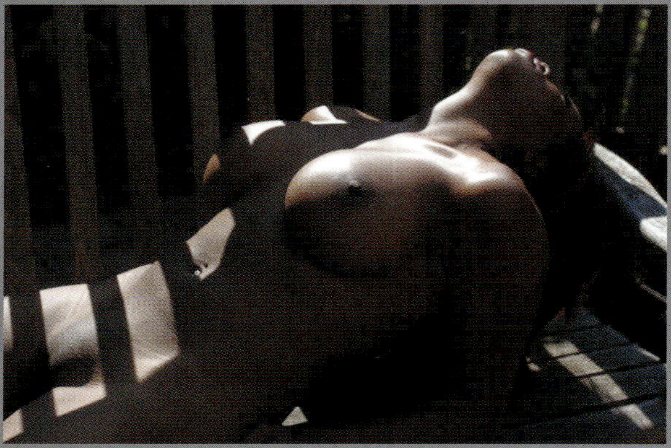

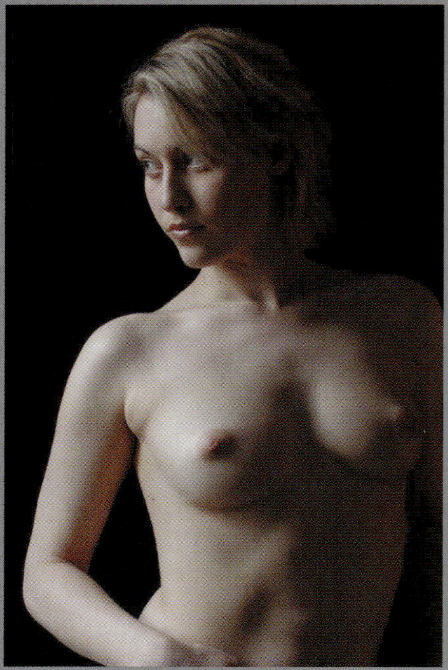

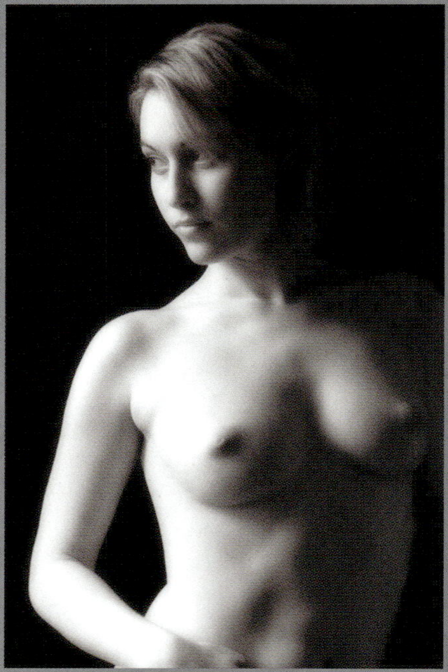

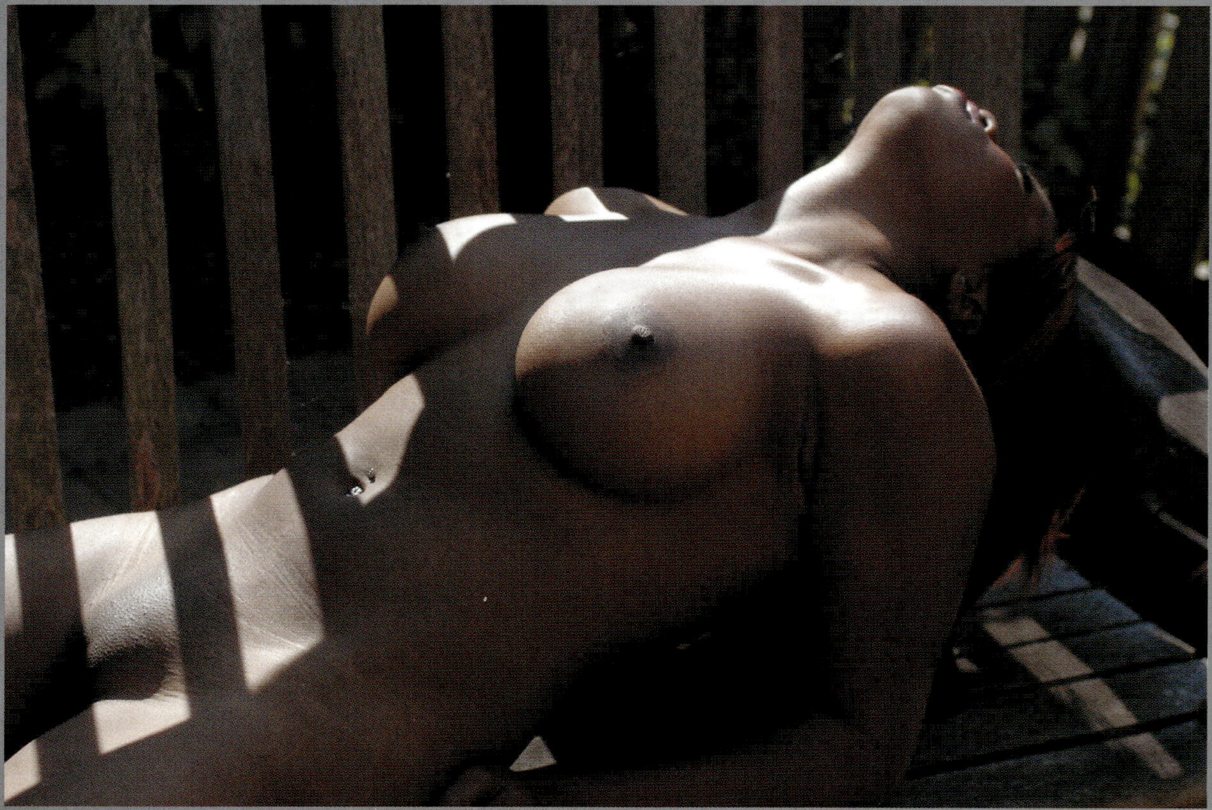

RIGHT AND BELOW: The overexposed sky has been cropped, and the wall and greenery "extended" to fill in the top left corner; the background has been blurred further, emphasizing the model by making the depth of field shallower; some skin blemishes have been removed, the brightness and contrast of the picture have been improved, enriching the tone of the model's skin, and the picture has also been sharpened.

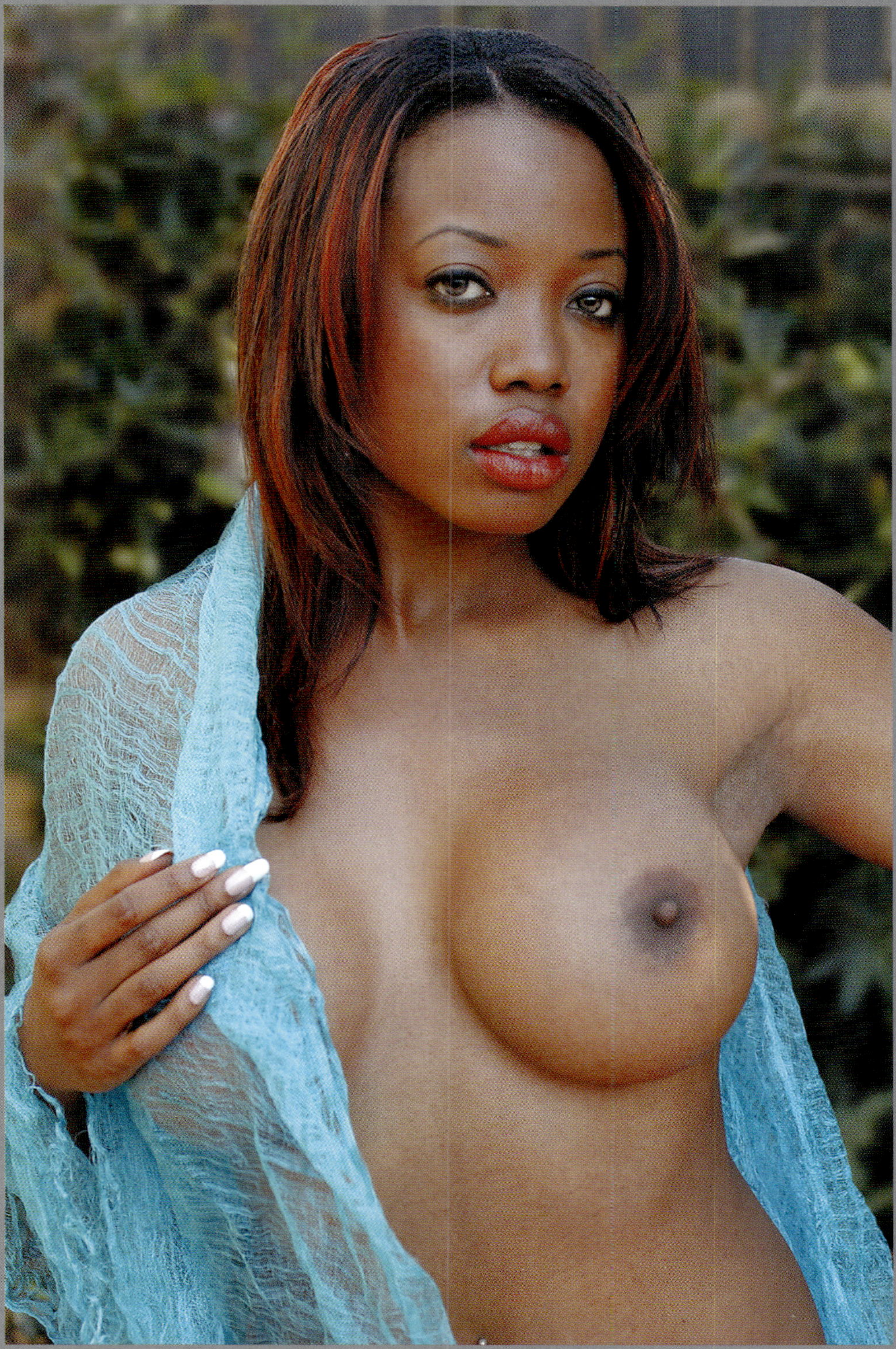

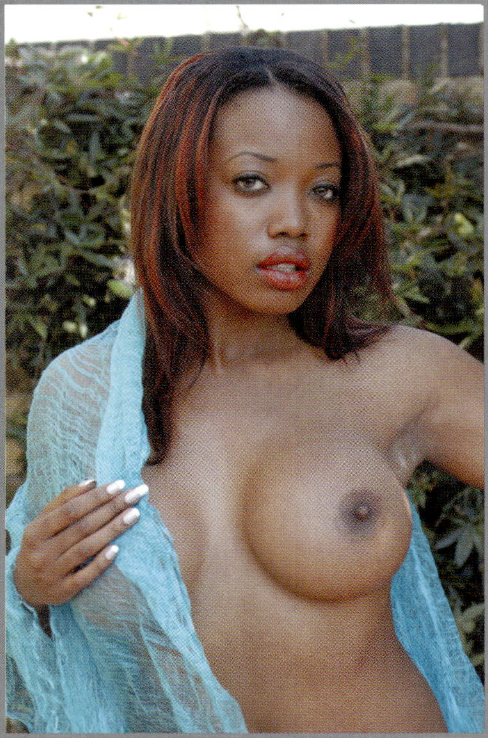

Fixing pictures in Photoshop

Before we get started, a word about keeping your images secure. If there's one hard-and-fast rule in editing pictures on a computer, it has to be "never edit the original file!" Always make a copy of the original file, whether it's from your digital camera or from a scanner, and edit that copy. If you're working on film, and you have your images scanned and/or transferred to PhotoCD, the problem won't arise, because PhotoCDs are "read-only." The only way to save any changes you make will be by saving the file as a copy of the original, onto your hard drive. Follow this basic rule, and you can edit without inhibition, knowing that if you have to start again from the beginning, you still have the original file, safe and unchanged.

Specular highlights

One of the most common faults that needs fixing in a photograph is overexposure: a shiny line down the nose, or a bright white patch on the breast or shoulder. These burnt-out areas (known as specular highlights) contain no detail at all, so they have to be filled by copying parts from elsewhere in the image.

To do this we use the Clone tool, which was designed for just this job. We'll create an empty layer above the image and carry out our changes on that, to avoid altering the image itself. This is a technique that lets you edit your pictures non-destructively; that is, every change you make can be reversed, to bring you back to the original unchanged image, even after you've saved, closed, and reopened the file. This is one of Photoshop's most valuable features.

By default the layer the image sits on is called the Background layer; the new empty layer is Layer 1.

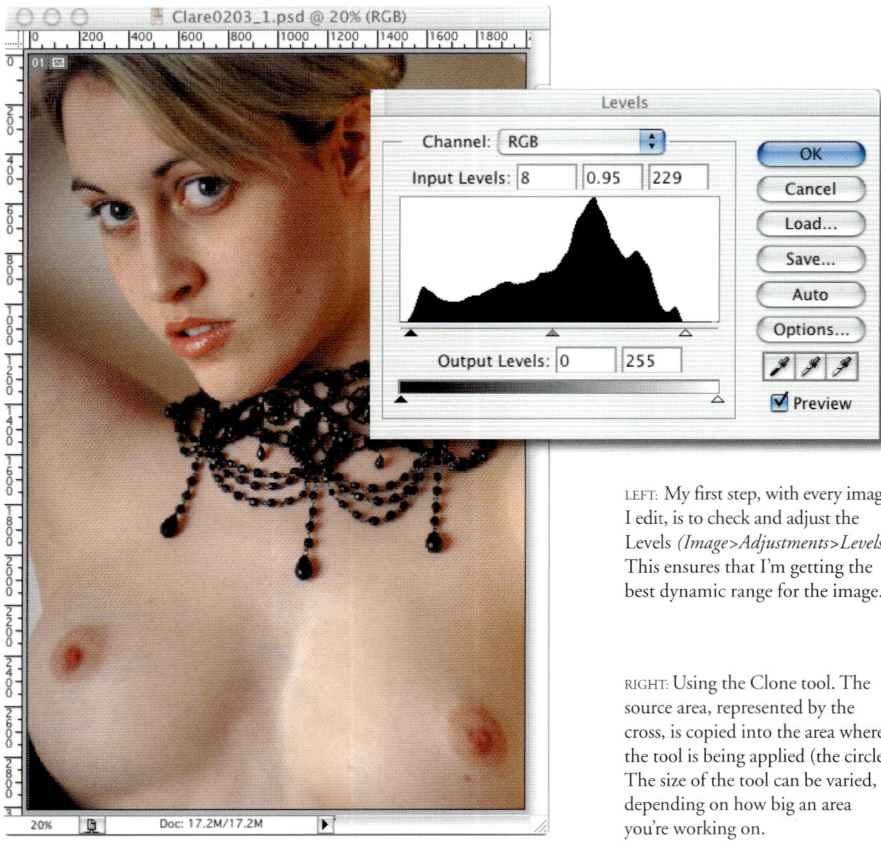

LEFT: My first step, with every image I edit, is to check and adjust the Levels *(Image>Adjustments>Levels)*. This ensures that I'm getting the best dynamic range for the image.

RIGHT: Using the Clone tool. The source area, represented by the cross, is copied into the area where the tool is being applied (the circle). The size of the tool can be varied, depending on how big an area you're working on.

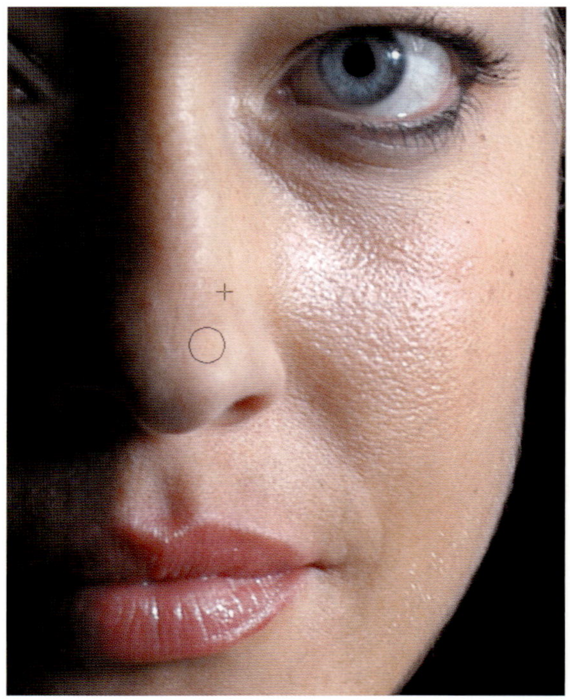

RIGHT: There's a noticeable specular highlight on the tip and ridge of the model's nose, as well as on her left cheek.

BELOW: We use the Clone tool in Layer 1 to copy an area of skin from the Background layer which will match the skin surrounding the highlights. Usually you'll find a suitable area close to the highlight, but sometimes you may need to look further afield (you can even copy skin from a different picture). It's usually most effective to leave the highlight area a little brighter than its surroundings, so that it remains consistent with the nearby shadows. As well as the highlight on the nose, you may want to reduce the highlight on the model's cheek.

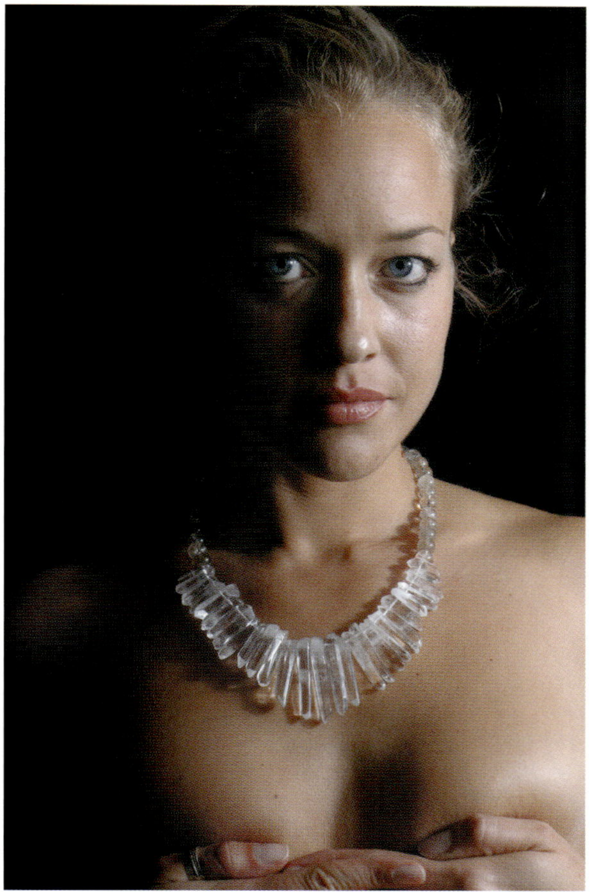

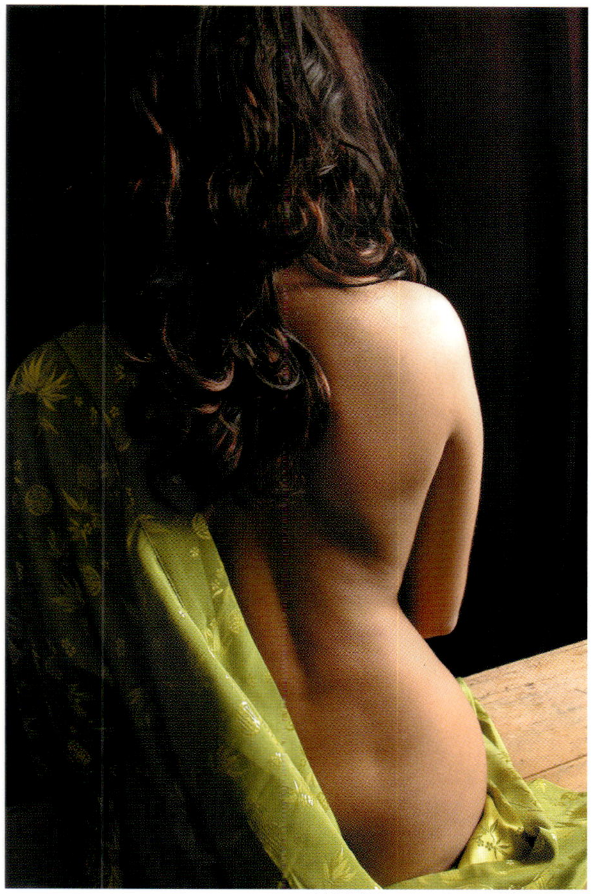

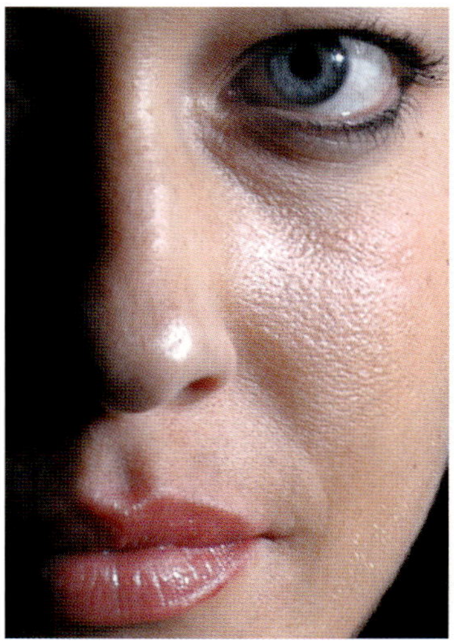

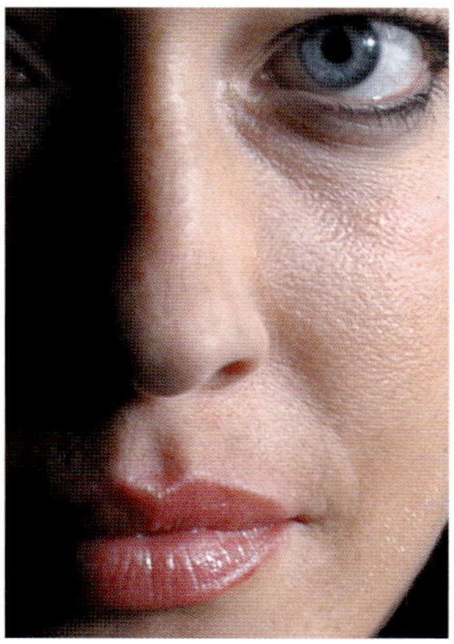

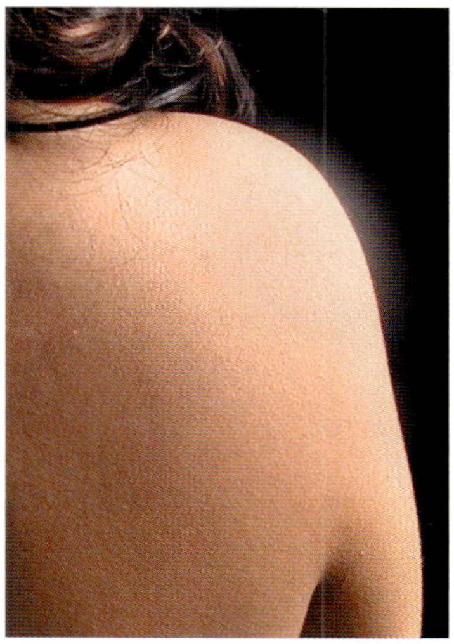

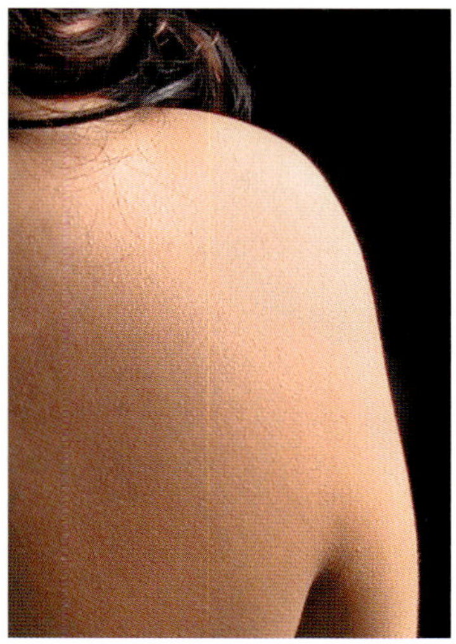

ABOVE: In this example there's a large specular highlight on the model's shoulder. Again we use the Clone tool, this time with a larger diameter, to fill it in. If we spill over the edge of the shoulder onto the background, that won't matter. We can use the Eraser tool to clean up the background, which is quicker and easier than trying to stay within the outline of the shoulder.

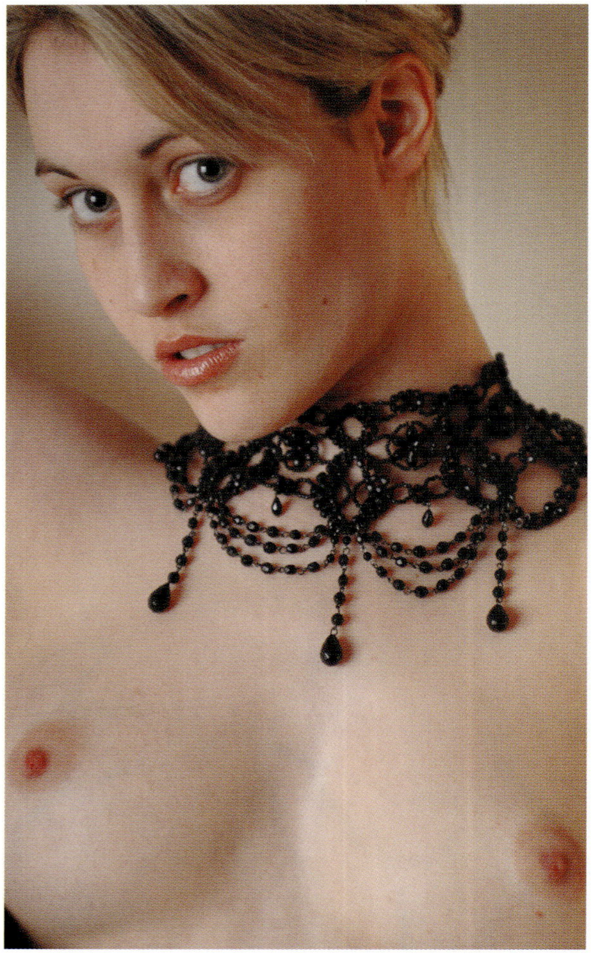

RIGHT AND BELOW: The small blemishes on Clare's skin are dealt with by using Photoshop's Patch tool. Just make a lasso around a blemished area, then drag the lasso to an area of smooth skin. The smooth skin is copied over the blemish and takes on the texture, lighting, and shading of the underlying area where you've positioned it. It's also possible to set the Patch tool so that you carry out this process in reverse: select the area of smooth skin first, then drag it over the blemish. This seems to me to work less well, as it's often hard to judge the size of the area of smooth skin you'll need.

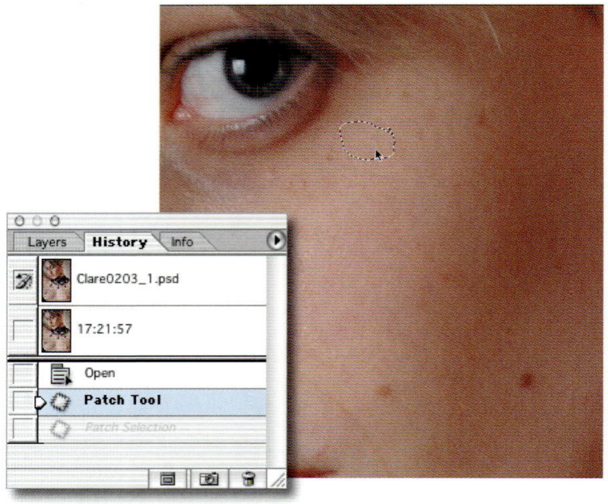

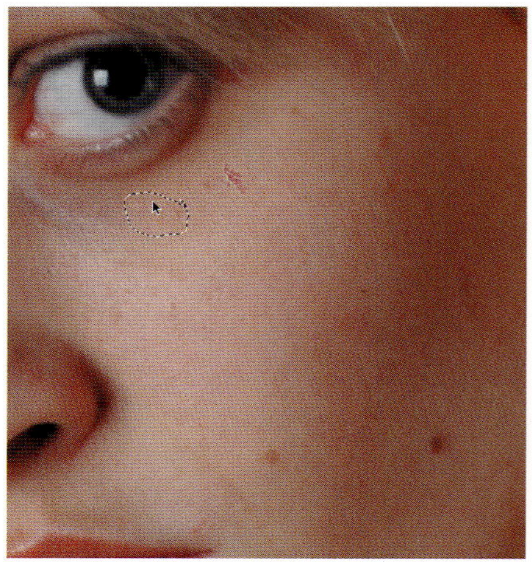

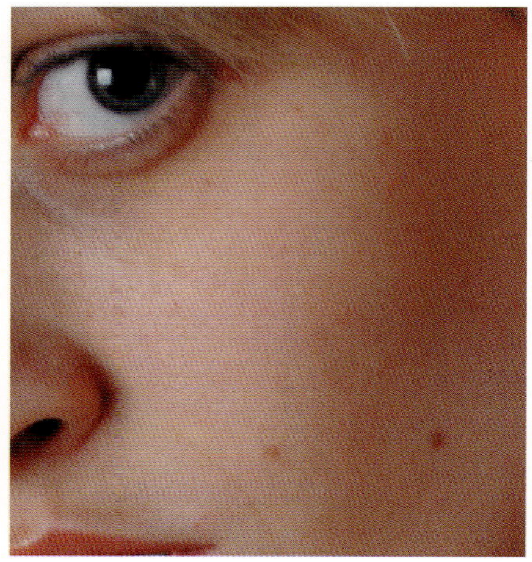

Blemishes

Even the most gorgeous model will have a few blemishes. So we'll take this image of Clare, remove the blemishes, and enhance her eyes and mouth.

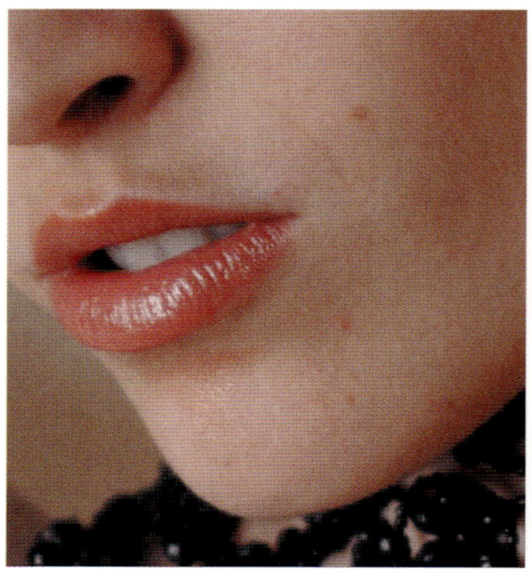

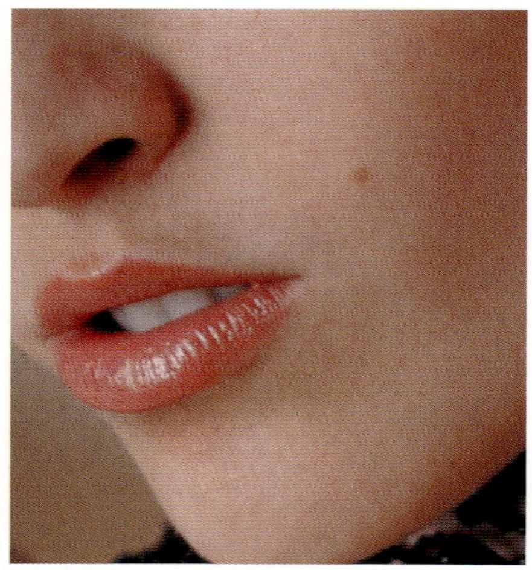

RIGHT: Before and after using the Patch tool.

Enhancements

Now for some enhancements. For many of these Photoshop gives you a choice of methods. Here I'm going to carry them all out by using adjustment layers. Adjustment layers are a powerful feature of Photoshop that again enable you to edit non-destructively. (We'll go into more detail about layers, and the related use of blend modes, on pages 46-49.)

Adjustment layers are a surprisingly fast way of making changes. Be careful when you paint out the mask not to drift outside the area the color of which you want to change. Photoshop helps by providing you with both a white and a black paintbrush when you work on masks. Changes to masks are non-destructive, so you can paint and repaint white and black over each other until you get the perfect result.

Another useful feature of adjustment layers is that they retain all the settings you've chosen. So if you need to remind yourself how you achieved a certain effect, all you have to do is find an image that used that effect, open the file and double-click in turn on each of the adjustment layers.

We'll start with the eyes and teeth. I've cheated a little here—as it happened, the same amount of whitening seemed to work for eyes and teeth, so I did them together, rather than treating them separately.

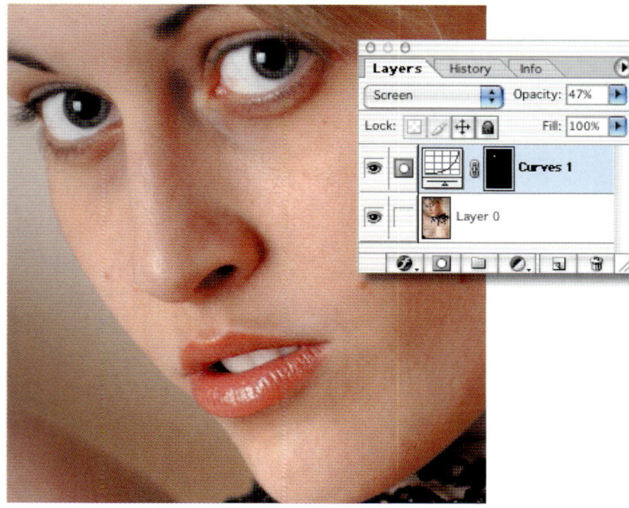

RIGHT: I've chosen the Curves adjustment layer, then set its blend mode to Screen, which has the effect of lightening and brightening the whole image. Next I apply a mask (the black box in the layers window on the right) which has the effect of cancelling out the Screen effect, except where I paint three white openings in the mask, over the eyes and teeth, thus revealing the brighter version created by the Screen blend. By itself, the effect of this would be to make the eyes and teeth look far too white, so I've reduced the opacity of the mask (to 47% in this case) which looks just right.

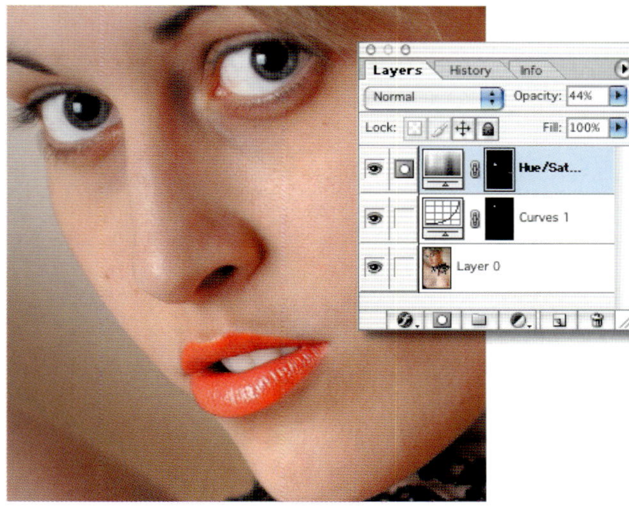

RIGHT: Next, the mouth needs a Hue/Saturation layer, which I can use to slightly adjust and intensify the color of the model's lips. As with the eyes, the changes I make effect the whole of the image, so once more I use a mask, and this time paint out just the area of the mask over the mouth. An Opacity of 44% seems about right here.

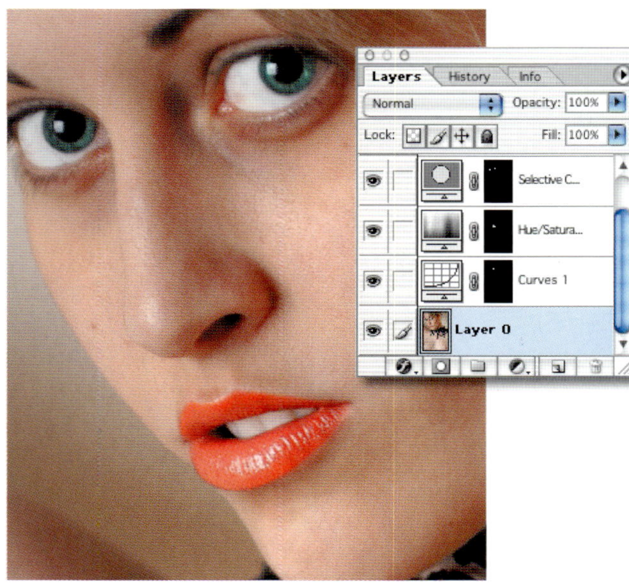

RIGHT: Back to Clare's eyes. This time we'll enhance their irises. Changing their color requires a Selective Color adjustment layer. By playing with the extensive controls available in this layer, and once more masking out the whole of the image apart from the area whose color I want to change. I can give her green eyes (or almost any other color). Opacity here works well at 60%.

We have two more alterations to make. I'm going to slightly darken the nipples, to make a stronger contrast with Clare's pale skin, and I'm going to redden her hair (to go with the green eyes). We'll do this with two more adjustment layers.

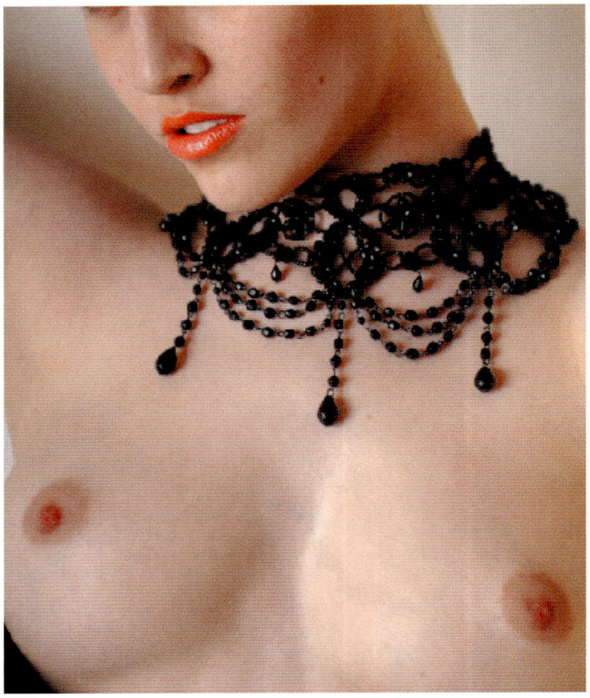

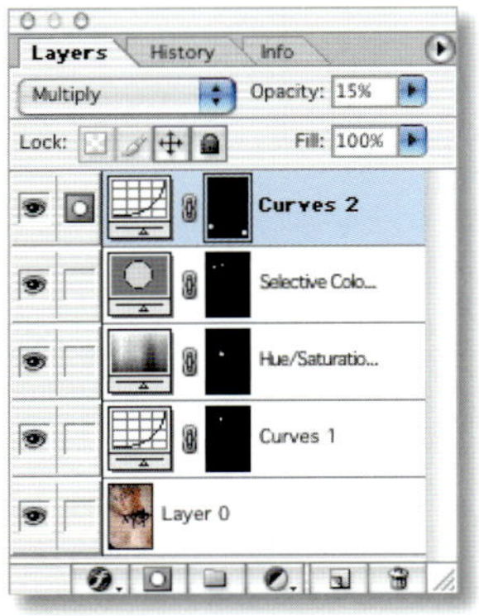

LEFT: The nipples are done using the Curves layer, but this time the blend mode is set to Multiply, which selectively darkens the layer. Only a small amount of Opacity (15%) is needed. Hair, because of its complex textures and irregular shapes, is usually the most time-consuming part of an image to alter.

BELOW: Finally for this image, we'll give Clare's skin a soft, glamorous finish. To do this we create a duplicate layer of the image, then apply Gaussian Blur to it repeatedly with a low setting to build up the level of blur we want. We can also adjust the Opacity of the top layer to get the right combination of "real" skin texture and smoothed texture: about 75% here. To finish the skin, we make a mask for the top layer and use it to paint out all the areas which aren't skin: background, eyes, teeth, hair, eyelashes and eyebrows. And we'll paint out the lips as well, to get the best effect from their highlights.

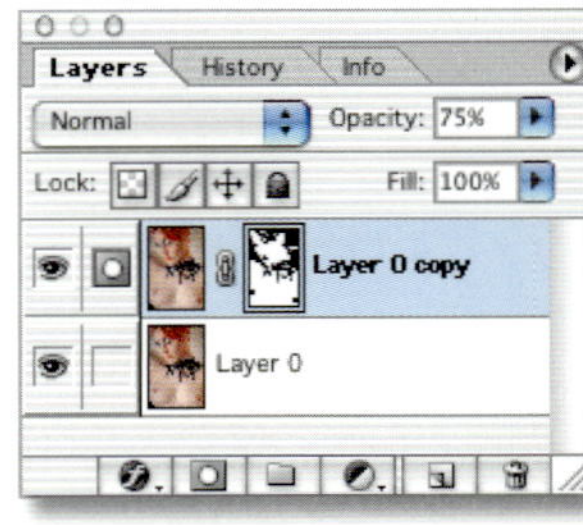

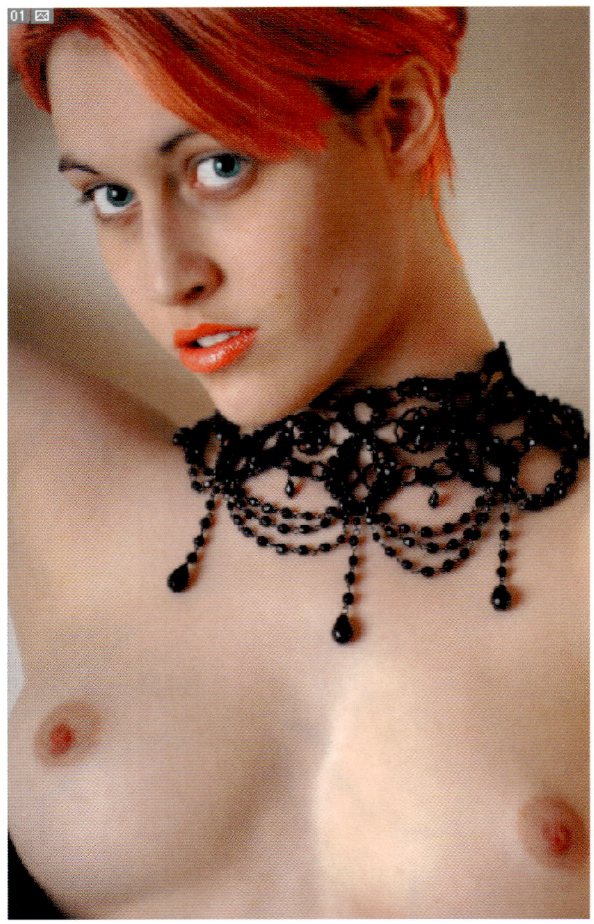

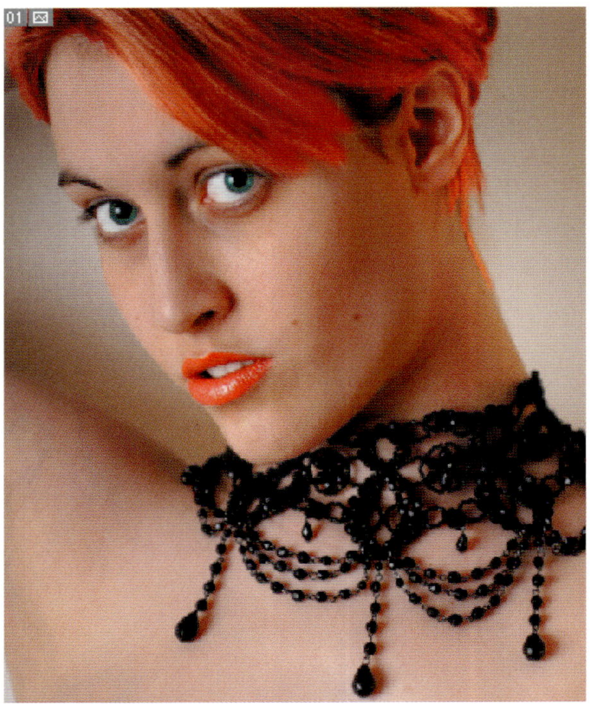

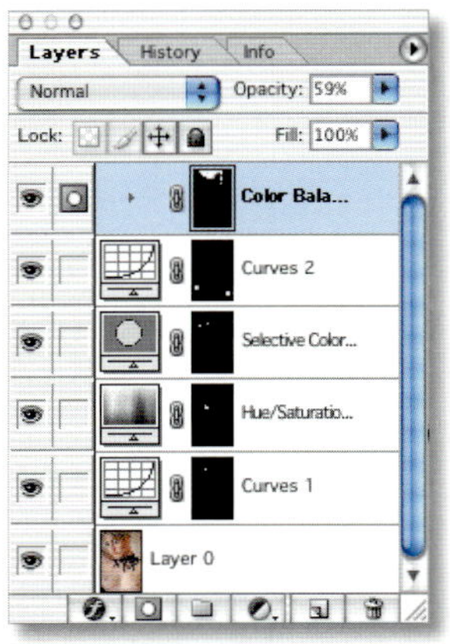

LEFT: To change the hair color we use the Color Balance layer, which again has a powerful and flexible set of controls.

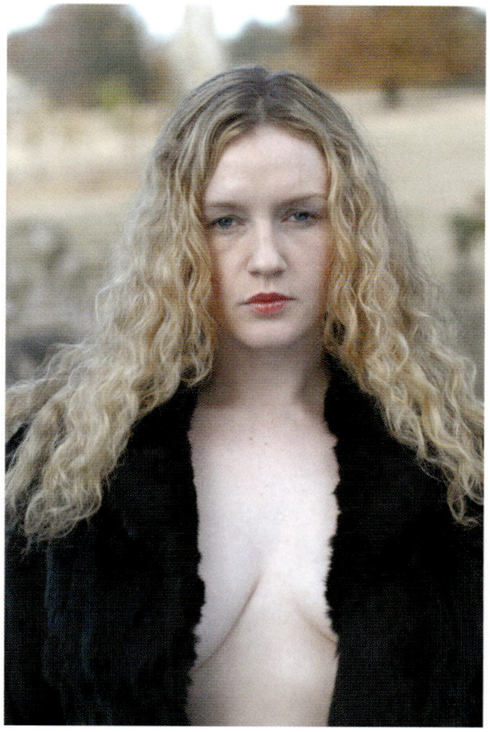

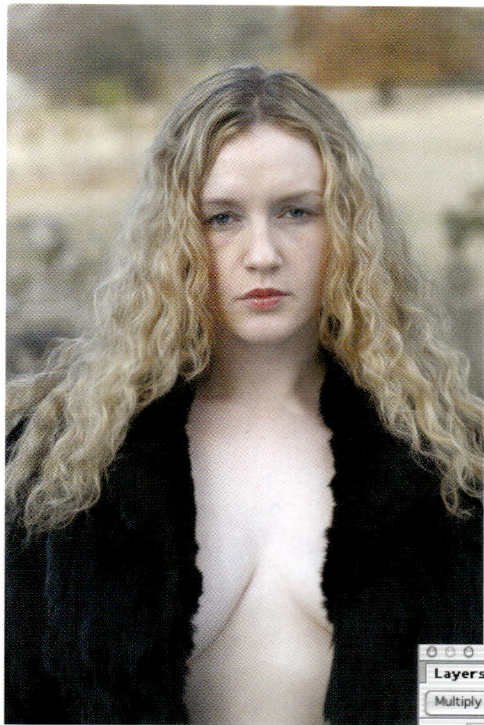

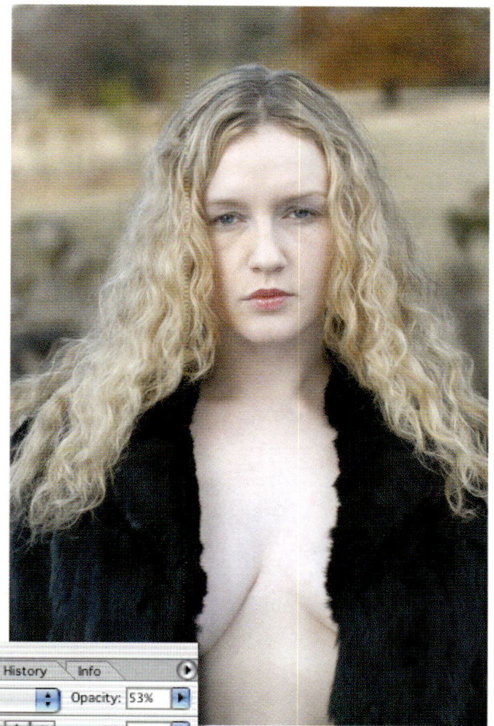

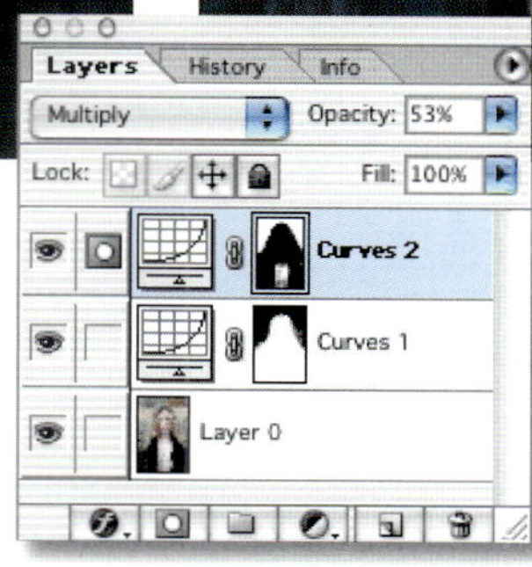

Fixing backgrounds

So far we've concentrated on the model. We may also need to make similar alterations to the background of an image.

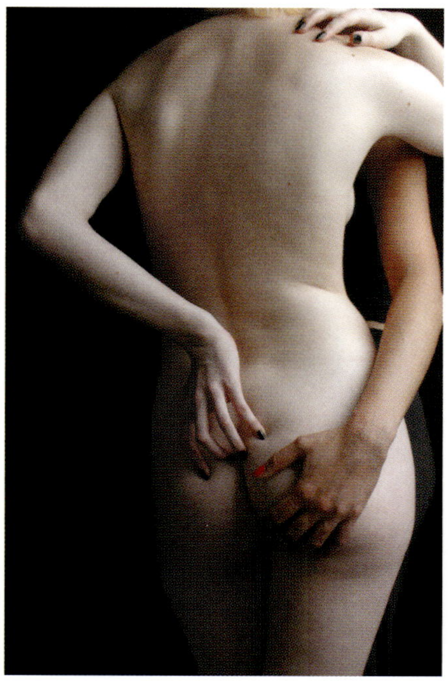

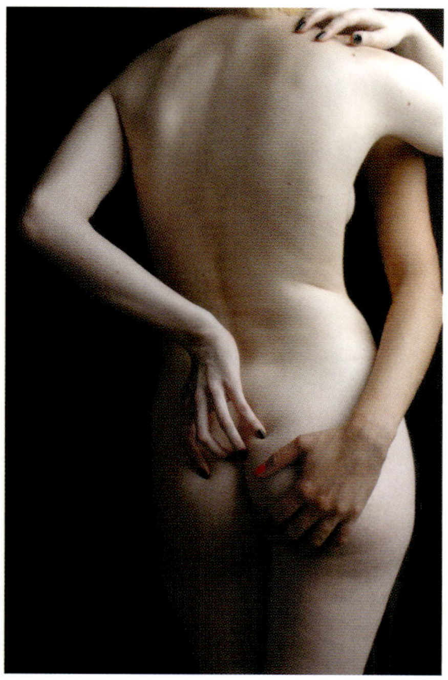

LEFT: In this example, a shot taken on the spur of the moment at the end of a shoot, the problem is slightly different. I want to make the rest of the model with the tanned arm disappear from the shot. I can clone her out easily, as before cleaning up any overspill with the Erase tool.

ABOVE: In the example, above, you can see at the top of the picture a characteristic feature of most digital cameras—the "fringing" effect which often occurs on boundaries where specular highlights meet dark areas. Rather than crop the top of the image, I'll use the Clone tool to fill in the highlights. Fortunately the picture was taken with fairly shallow depth of field and the background is blurred, which makes the task easier!
Finally I'll use a couple of adjustment layers and masks to make the model a little brighter, and the background a little darker.

Hi- and Lo-key effects

"Hi-key" and "Lo-key" have become rather broad and vague terms in digital photography. Here I use them to mean images that are predominantly made up of very bright or very dark tones, respectively. In both cases, however, good images will still use the whole range of tonality: this distinguishes them from images that are simply over- or underexposed.

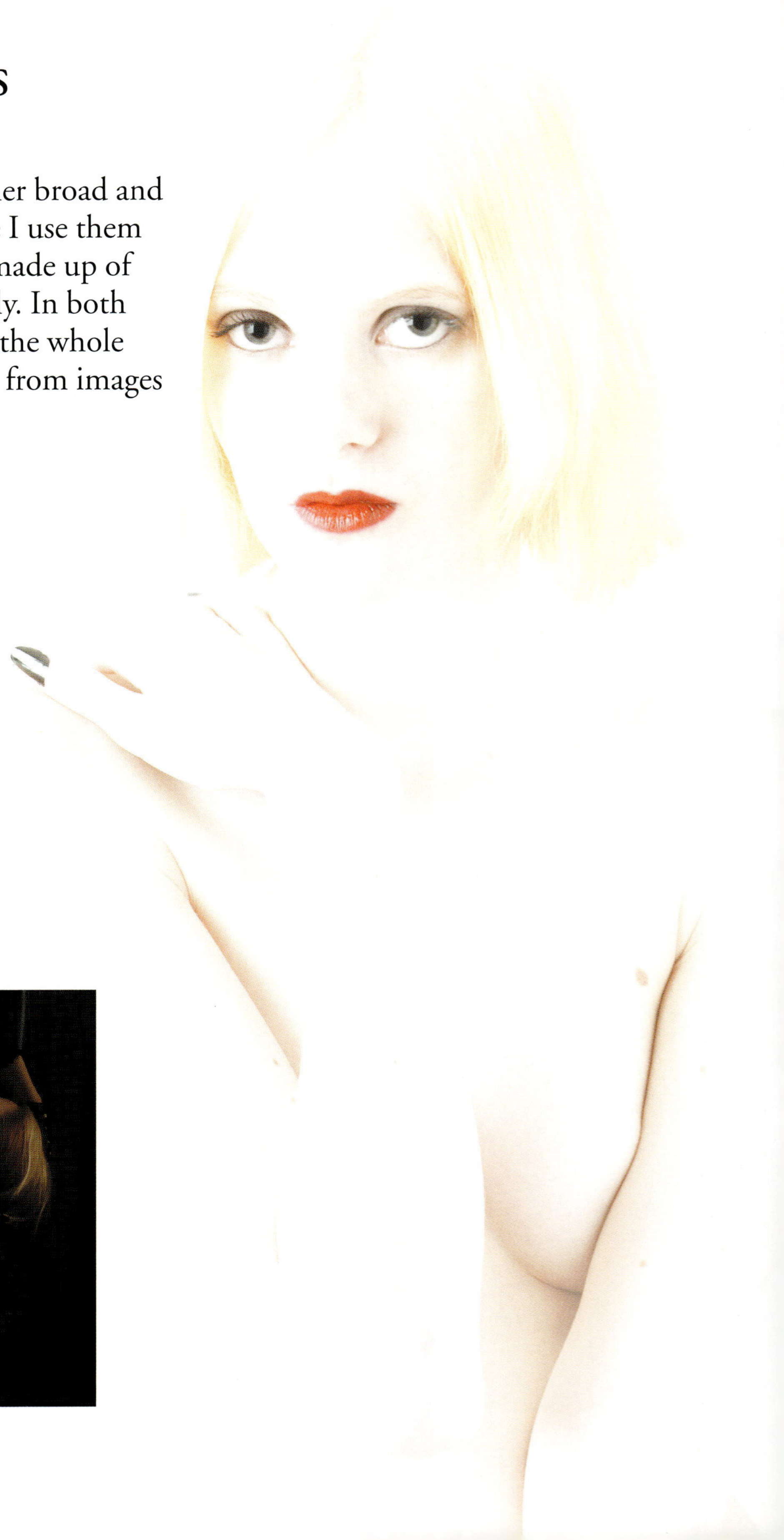

BELOW: The easiest way to create a low-key image is, again, to shoot it that way. But we can also use layers and blends to lower the key of a "normal" image.

RIGHT: For all the power of computers and picture-editing applications, the easiest way to create a hi-key image is to shoot it that way.

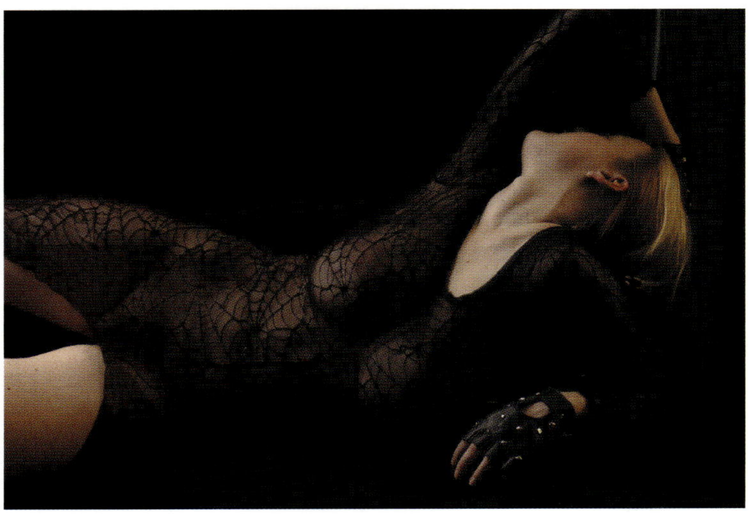

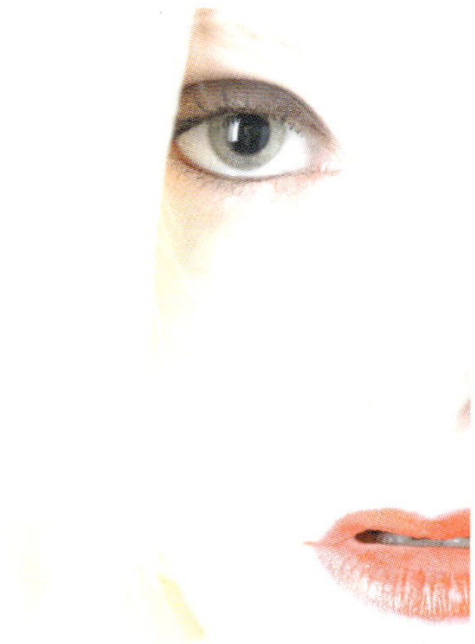

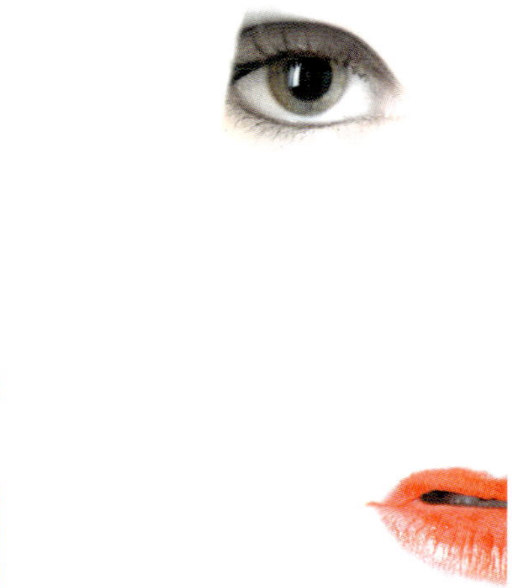

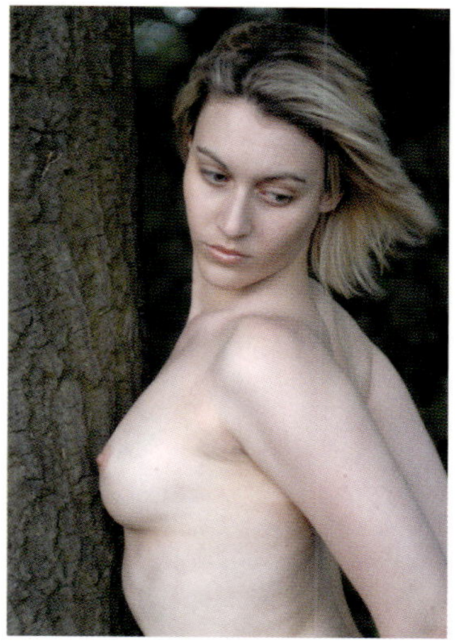

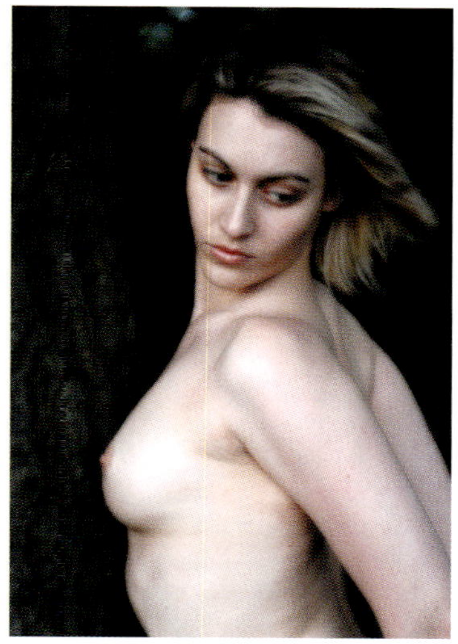

ABOVE LEFT AND RIGHT: Starting from a deliberately overexposed image like this, it's easy to make a hi-key version by adjusting levels, brightness, and contrast, and doing a little retouching. Checking the levels of the hi-key version confirms that it runs the full gamut of tonality. As with most hi-key images, this one requires the viewer to see the implied edges and shapes without which it isn't complete.

BELOW LEFT: Let's take a more "middle of the road" example. The simplest way to increase the overall brightness of the image is to repeatedly duplicate the original layer and apply the Screen blend mode to each copied layer.

BELOW CENTER: I've increased the brightness three times. This lifts the skintones and preserves quite a lot of the shadow, but perhaps not quite enough. The nipple has also nearly vanished. It may be that the image needs to be a little clearer and less implied. We can achieve this by burning in the top edge of the model's arm (the lower edge is less visible, but I think the image will work without adding emphasis to it), and then by darkening the nipple.

BELOW RIGHT: As we've increased the brightness of the picture by adding layers in Screen mode, the easiest way to achieve this is by creating a layer mask for each of the upper layers and painting out the nipple in each layer mask, thus making it visible as it appears in the bottom layer.

ABOVE LEFT: In this example, we can darken the image selectively by duplicating the layer, then changing the blend mode of the top to Multiply. Multiply will make the whole image darker, but will darken the dark tones most. Skintones will look oversaturated as a result of this, so we can use *Image >Adjustments>Hue/Saturation* on the top layer to reduce the Saturation and give the skintones a more natural look. At the same time the light/dark balance can also be adjusted by varying the Opacity of the upper layer.

ABOVE RIGHT: Finally I've added some blur to the top layer. One of the side effects of Multiply is that it tends to accentuate any unevenness of skintones. Applying *Filter>Blur>Gaussian Blur* to the top layer will compensate for this, without in fact having much of a blurring effect on the lighter areas of the image.

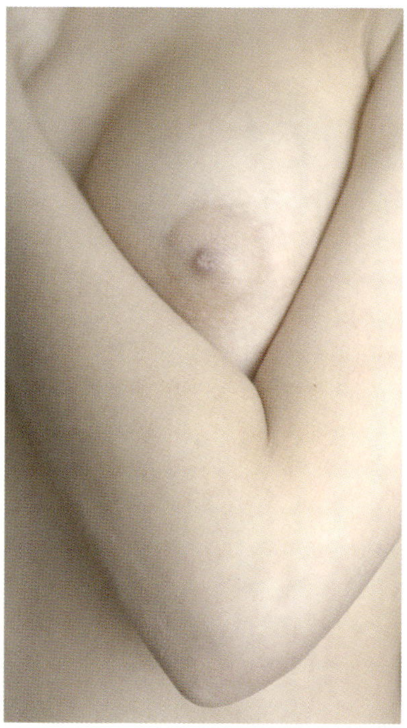

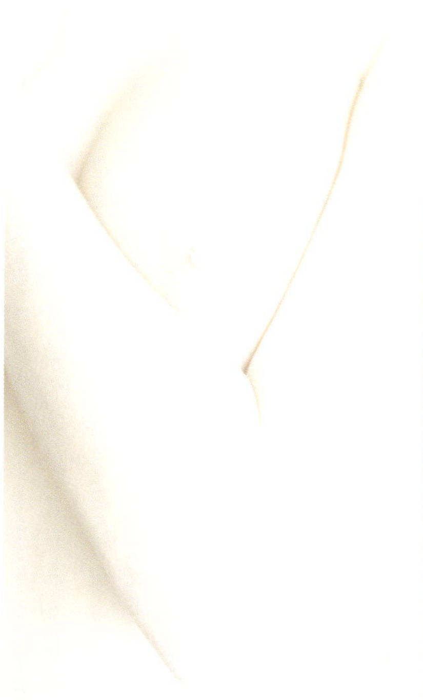

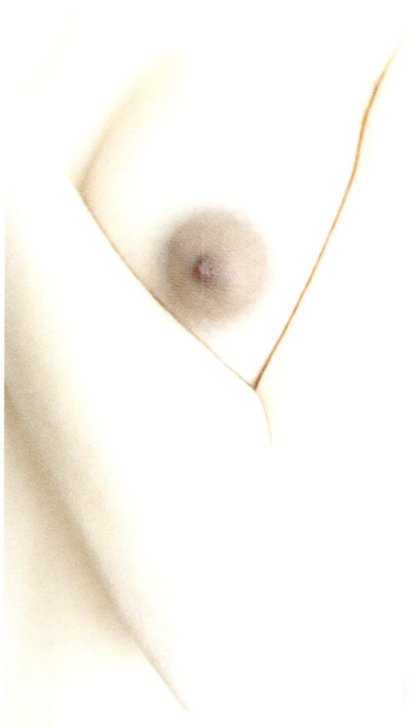

Color shifts and negatives

Photoshop makes it easy to shift the color either of the whole of an image or a selected area. Negative images can be created in several ways, using *Image>Calculations*, for example. Just remember that flat images don't always have the same impact.

In this example I'll change the color of Zenith's boots and gloves. The task will be made more challenging by the many fractured reflections in the background.

There are several ways to make selective color shifts. For example, you could use the Magic Wand, which is designed to let you select elements of an image that have a similar color and tone, and a range of Lasso tools with which you can draw around an area. However, many professional Photoshop users prefer to use layer masks to isolate areas of an image, and that's the method we'll use here.

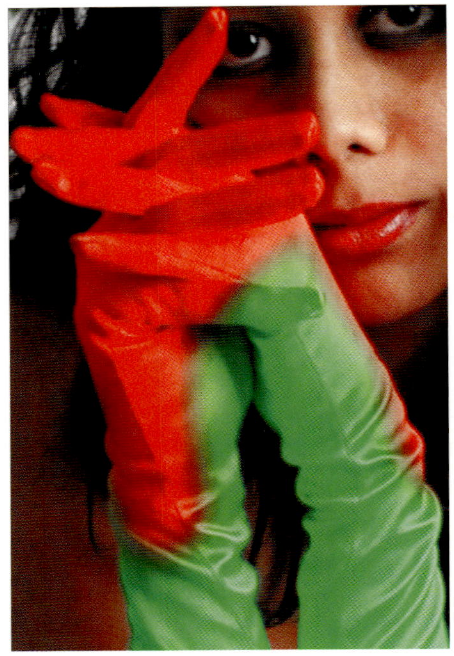

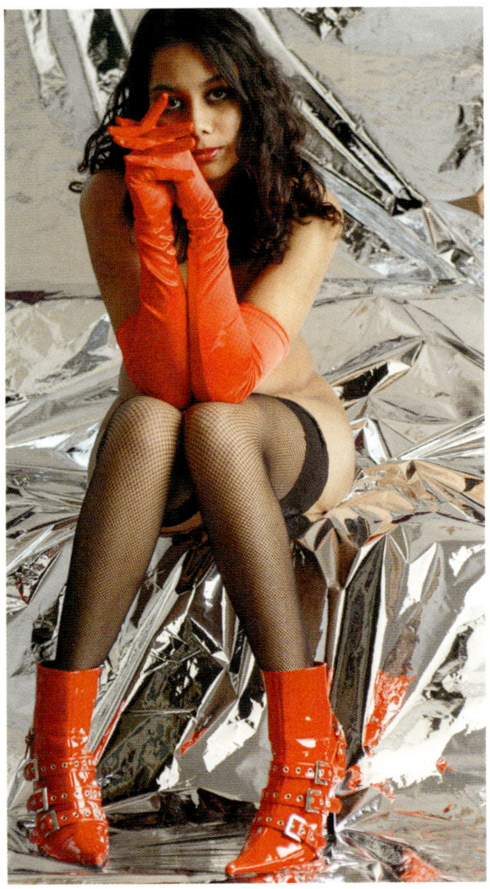

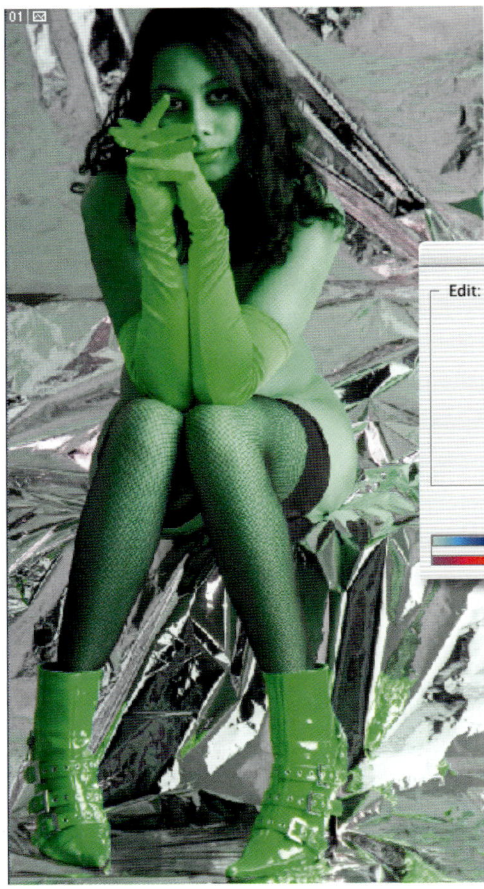

LEFT: After checking the levels of the picture and doing any necessary retouching, I apply a Hue/Saturation adjustment layer. Using an adjustment layer will make it easy for me to change the color of the gloves and boots again, if I want to; for now I'll make them a vivid lime green.

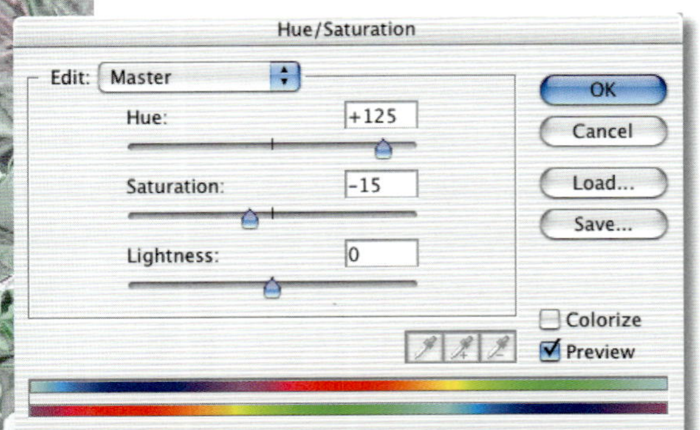

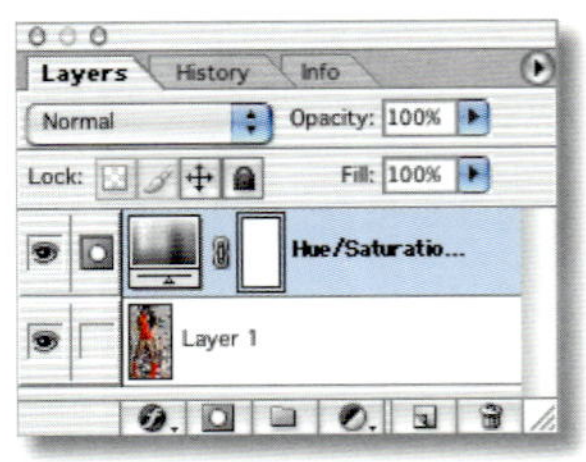

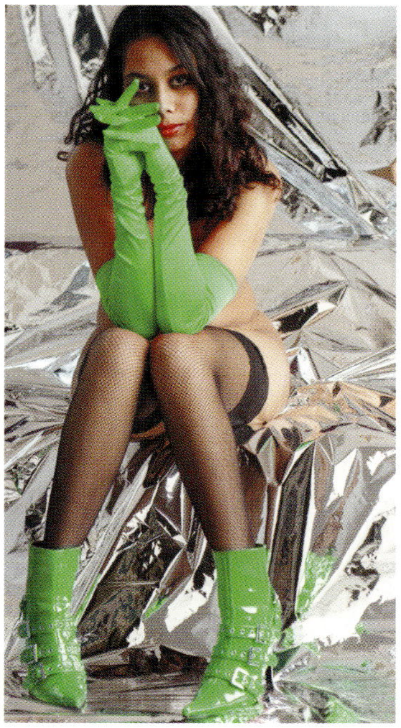

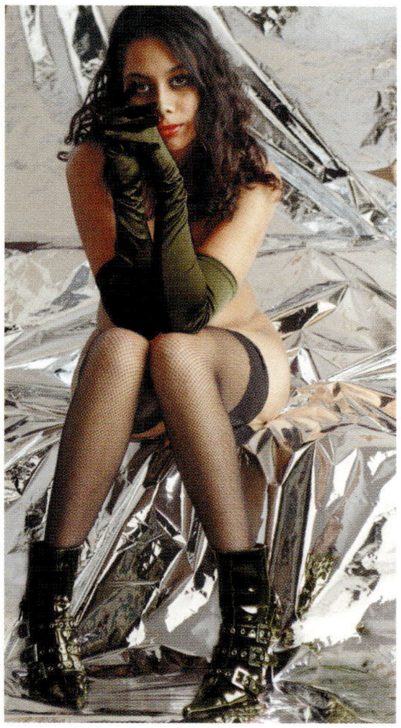

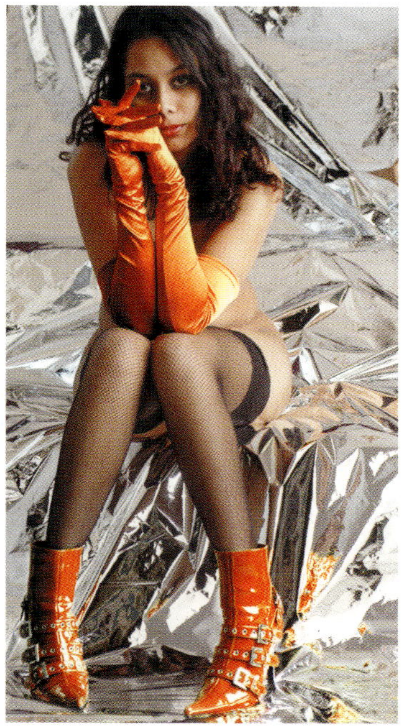

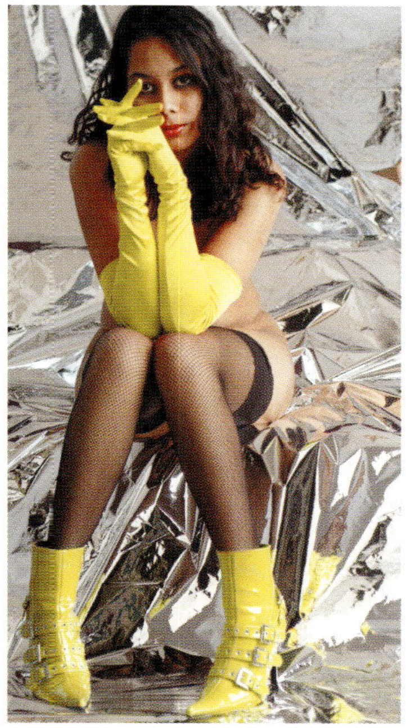

OPPOSITE PAGE, TOP: The next step is to create a layer mask, which we fill with black. This makes it transparent, so we see the original color. Next we set the foreground color to white and start to paint over the gloves and boots. As we do this, the new color appears in the areas we've painted white. It's a delicate process when you're working along the edges of the unmasked areas. In this case it takes some trial and error to work out which reflections are of the boots and gloves, and which of the model. Where I paint out too much, the error's quickly put right by changing the foreground color from white to black and re-painting. I also set the Opacity of my white brush to about 20% and partly masked in the area of Zenith's face close to the gloves, to show their reflection on her skin. Once the mask is perfect, you can experiment by varying the blend mode of the adjustment layer.

ABOVE: This is the same image, with the same adjustment layer, but with the blend mode set to (from left to right) Normal, Multiply, Overlay, and Lighten.

BELOW: Negative images can be created in several ways. In this sequence I've used *Image>Calculations* to create the initial negative image. This lets me control the tonal range better to get a more effective result than by choosing *Image>Adjustments>Invert*. Calculations is a very powerful feature of Photoshop. The image produced in this way has simple, strong lines, but it is a little flat. Adding a Threshold adjustment layer makes it possible to intensify the image. In this example I've used a setting for Threshold which results in a very high-contrast image. However the model's right arm is still noticeably less dark than the rest of her, so as a final step I've burned the arm in. This results in an image that comes close to pure black and white, with very few gray tones. It's suggestive of an etching, recalling the work of artists such as the great English erotic artist Eric Gill.

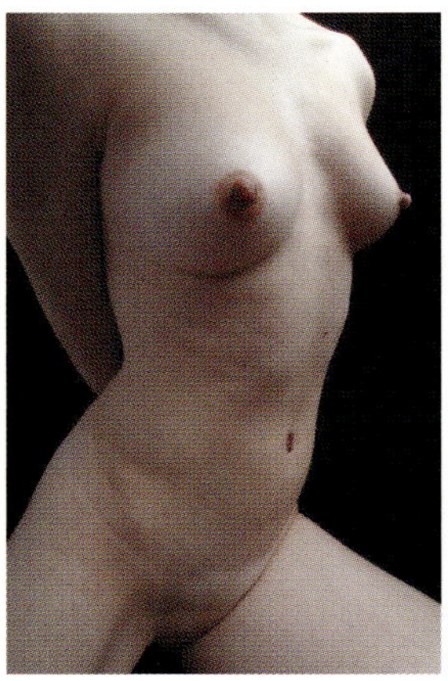

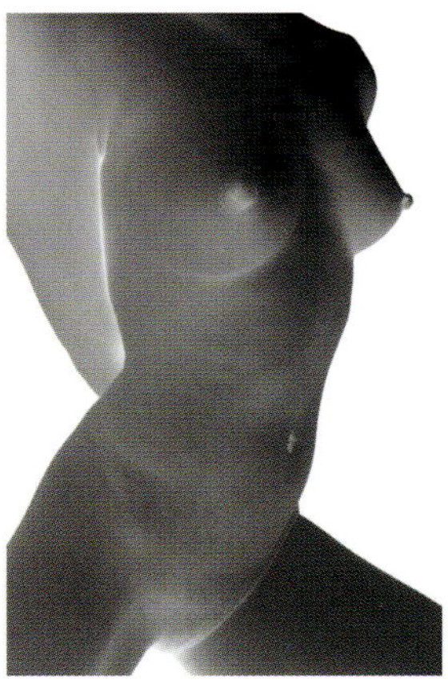

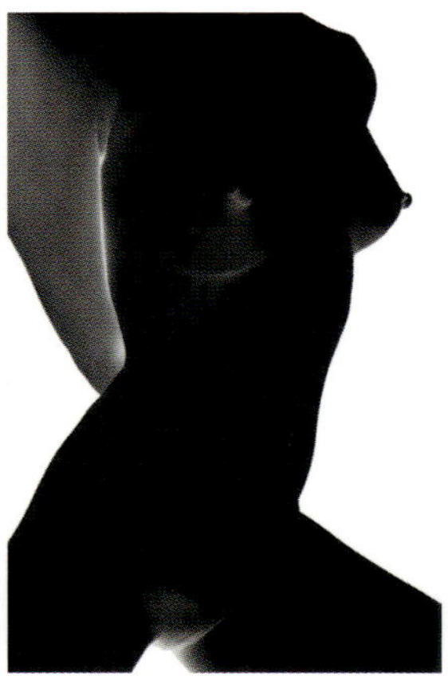

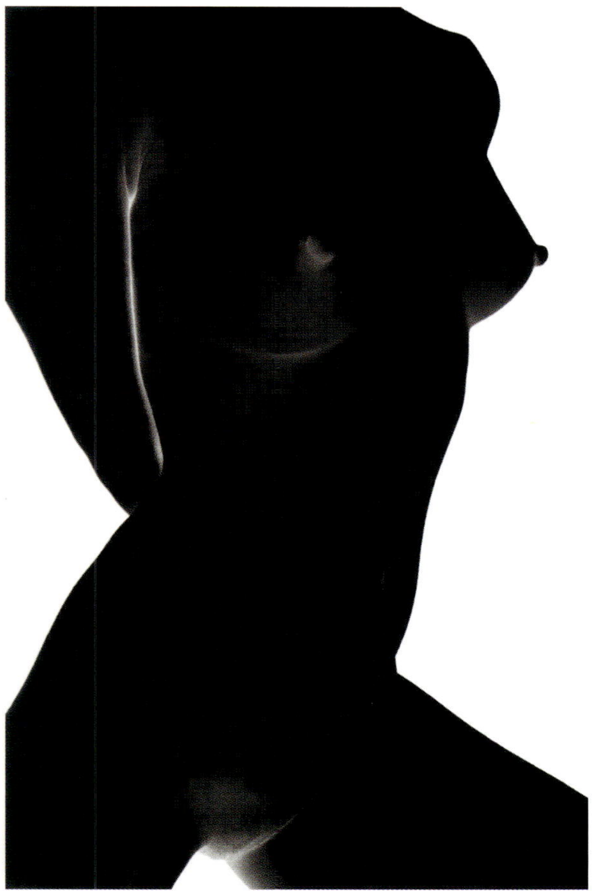

Monochrome

Even today, in the age of color, much of the most powerful nude and erotic photography is still done in black and white. By removing the element of color, monochrome simplifies the image, bringing its essential qualities more immediately to the viewer with a greater emotional engagement and impact.

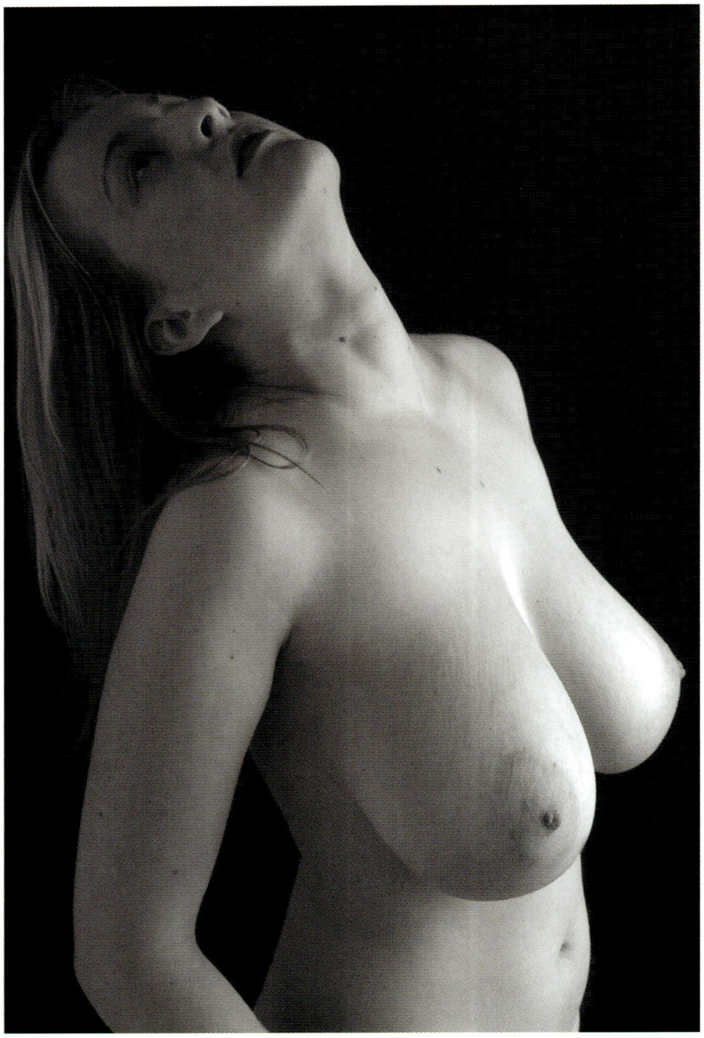

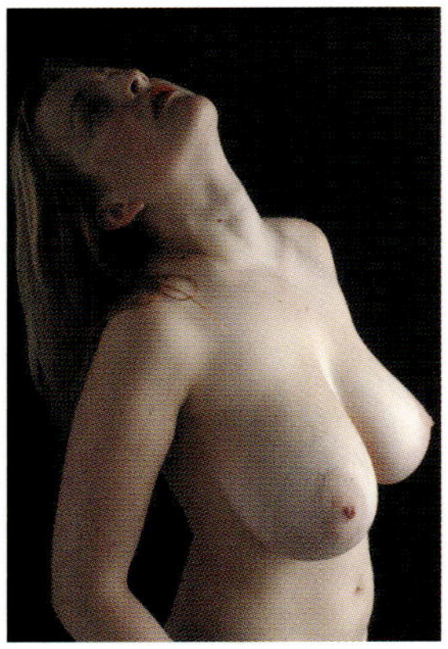

LEFT AND ABOVE: Black-and-white conversion through *Image>Mode>Grayscale*. It's a roughly satisfactory method, but not flexible enough to get a brilliant result.

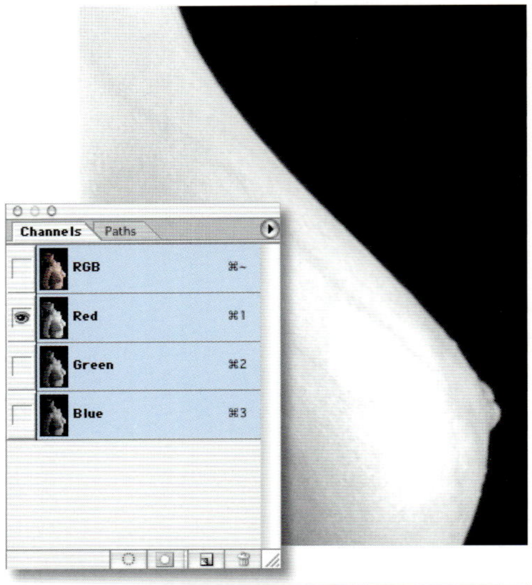

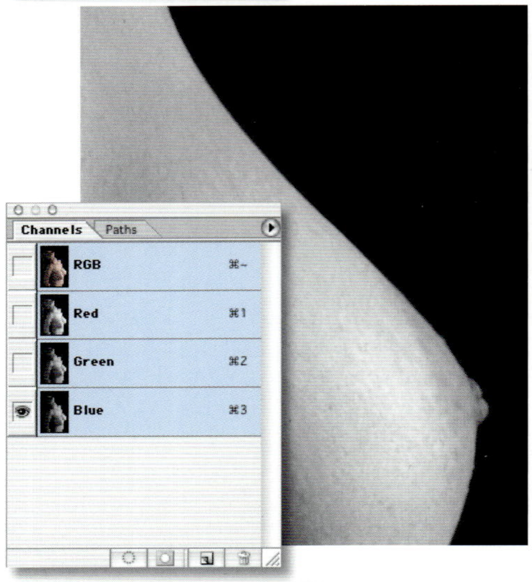

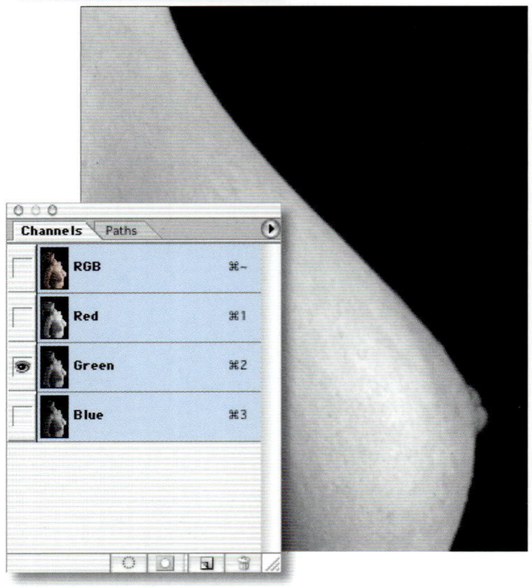

RIGHT: If we compare the monochrome information contained in each channel, we can see big differences. The Red channel makes skin look paler and almost luminous, with less surface texture (but also often makes veins beneath the skin more visible). The Green channel shows more texture and is darker and perhaps more "natural." The Blue channel is noisier, and also often shows marks on the skin more strongly than the other two channels.

Converting to black and white

If your digital camera lacks a black-and-white setting, you can use the computer to convert color images into monochrome. If your digital camera can be switched to black and white it will probably produce cleaner, less noisy results in that mode than you'll achieve using Photoshop's basic conversion tools on color images, but on the downside you won't have a color version to work with should you want one. Luckily, Photoshop has a couple of very flexible ways of creating black-and-white images from color, and these can be used to boost and enhance pictures originally taken in black and white as well.

The simplest methods are the *Image>Adjustments >Desaturate* command and the *Image>Mode>Grayscale* command. Each of these just removes the color information from the image, equally across the Red, Green, and Blue channels, so you don't have much control over the result you get, and you may want to alter it further by using layers and blend modes. You can also convert your image into Lab mode (*Image>Mode>Lab Color*) and throw away the two color channels, keeping only the Lightness channel, but again the result is likely to need further manipulation.

Photoshop has two methods that let us manipulate the channels separately. The first of these is the Channel Mixer (*Image>Adjustments>Channel Mixer*). Once you check the Monochrome box, you can use the three color channel faders and the Constant fader to experiment with different blends until you find what you like best. In general, if the total percentage values of the faders add up to more than 100, you'll find that some areas of the image are "overexposed," but you can get interesting effects by letting one channel go over 100 and compensating by setting another to a negative value so that the total remains 100. For added flexibility, you can also use the Channel Mixer as an adjustment layer (*Layer>New Adjustment Layer>Channel Mixer*).

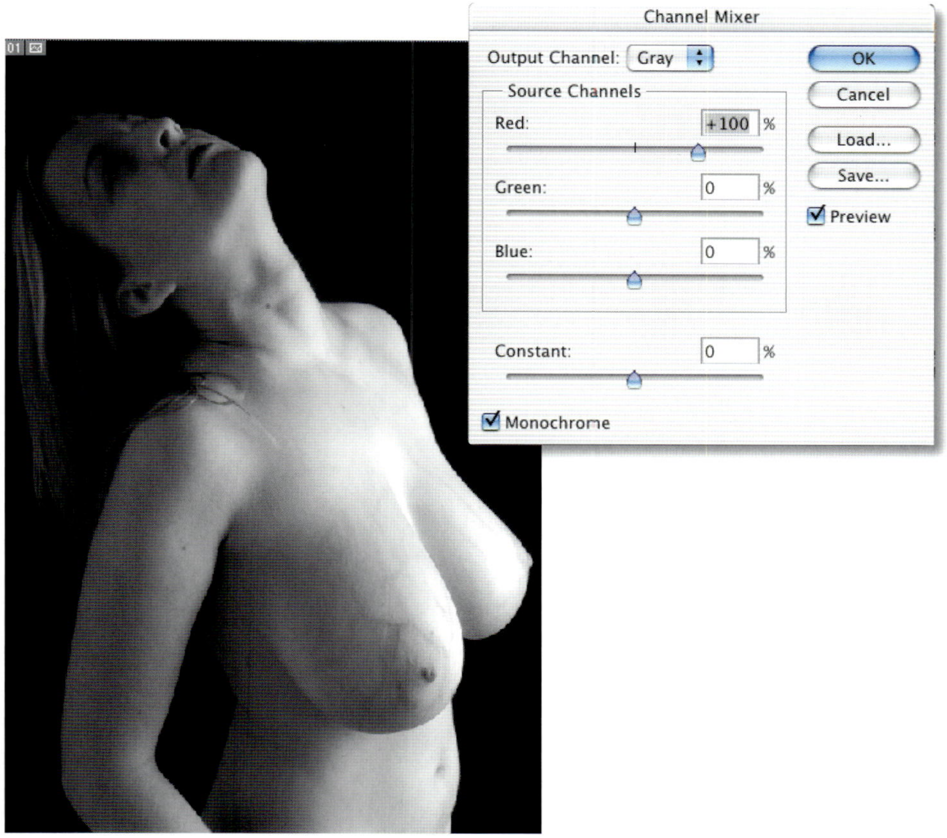

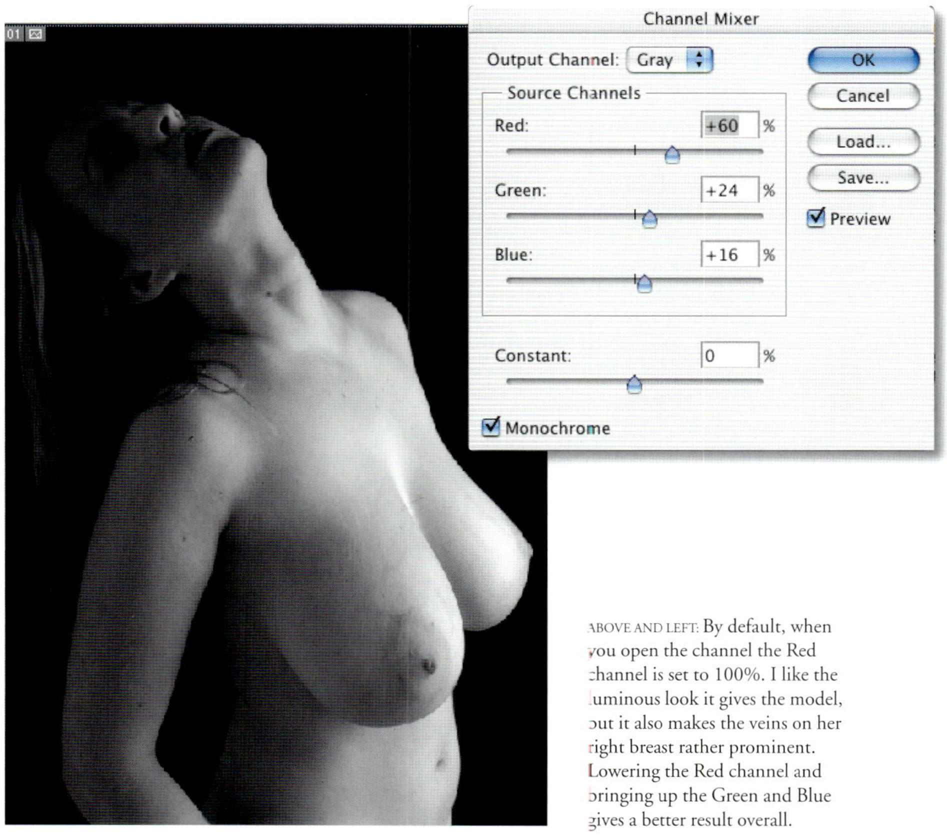

ABOVE AND LEFT: By default, when you open the channel the Red channel is set to 100%. I like the luminous look it gives the model, but it also makes the veins on her right breast rather prominent. Lowering the Red channel and bringing up the Green and Blue gives a better result overall.

The calculated approach

The most interesting and powerful method in Photoshop of converting images to monochrome is *Image>Calculations*. It makes use of layers and blend modes, so it's helpful to have some experience of these beforehand, but don't be daunted by its apparent complexity. Once you're used to Calculations, and appreciate its range and flexibility, you may never use any other method of monochrome conversion again!

After going through the usual procedures of making a copy of the original file to work on, and correcting the levels, the first step is to change the default Background layer to a normal layer, by double-clicking on it in the Layers window. Next, select *Image>Calculations*. Your image turns into a dark, contrasty black and white, and a new window opens with lots of settings to play with.

The best advice at this point is probably just to experiment. Try varying the channels in the two sources, using, for example, Green in one and Red in the other. Note that as well as Gray, Red, Blue, and Green channels in each source, you also have Transparency. (This is why you changed the Background layer to a normal layer—without this the Transparency option is not available.)

While you're at it, experiment with the blend mode and the Opacity. You'll find that a number of combinations are dead ends: for example, if you set Source 1 to Transparency and keep the opacity at 100%, half the blending modes will give a solid white, with none of your image visible. Other combinations will produce a solid black image. Even so, there are endless combinations that do work, which give different results.

When you've found the combination of settings that gives you what you're looking for, change the Results dropdown to "New Document," before clicking on OK. This gives you your black-and-white version in a separate file and leaves the color image unaltered. And when you've found a monochrome conversion you like in Calculations, it's a good idea to make a note of the settings so you can apply them to other images.

Finishing off

When you use a combination such as Transparency, Red channel, and Soft Light to achieve high-key skin tones, you may find that other areas of the picture also become very bright, and need to be "knocked back"—that is, made darker. Fortunately Photoshop's Dodge and Burn tools, which aren't much use on color images, work

BELOW FAR LEFT: The Calculations window, showing its default settings.

BELOW AND OPPOSITE PAGE: Five variants produced with Calculations. The differences are quite subtle. Note the purity of skintone achieved with a combination of Transparency, Red channel, and Soft Light blend at 100% (second from right) and the effect, close to solarization, produced by the Exclusion blend mode.

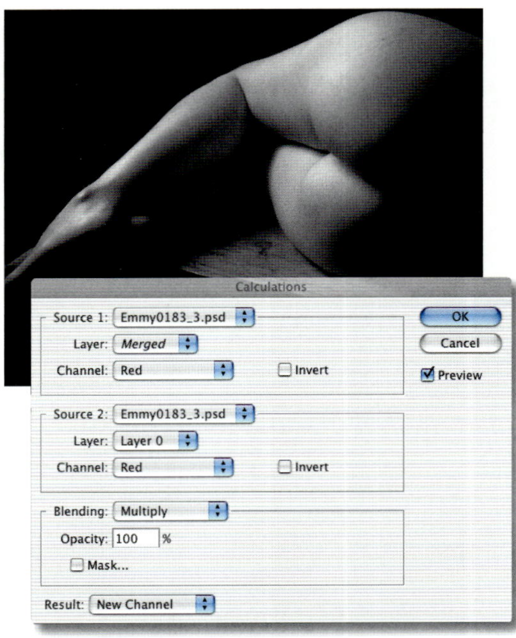

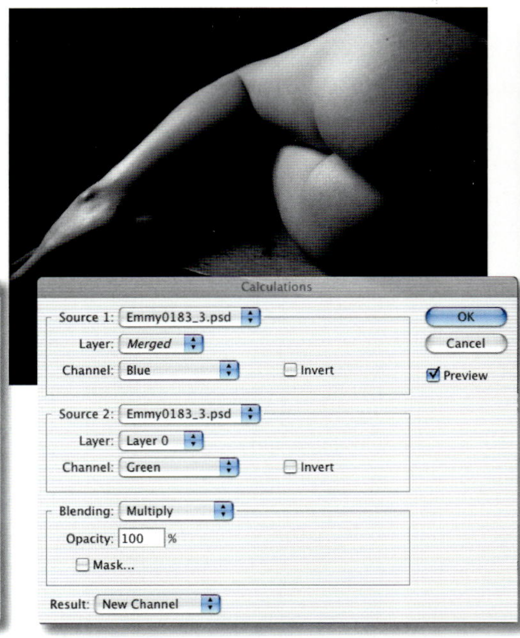

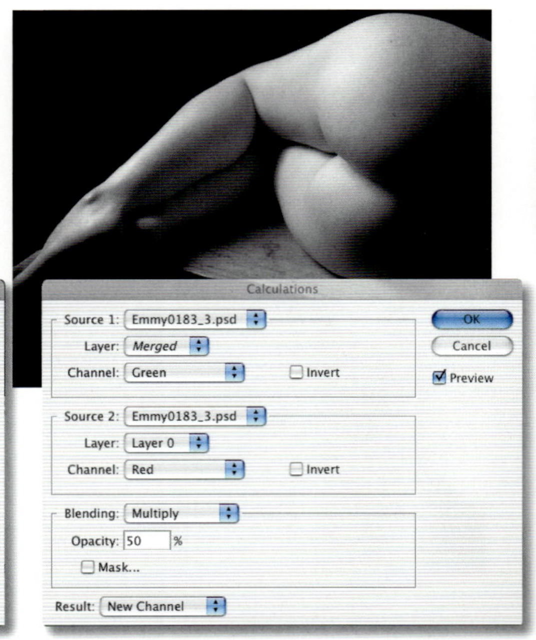

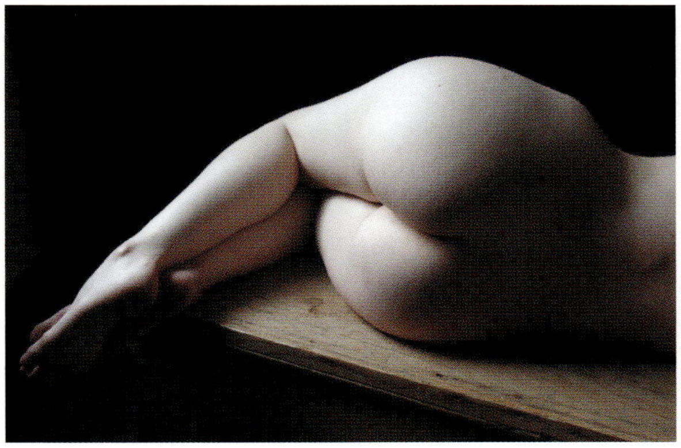

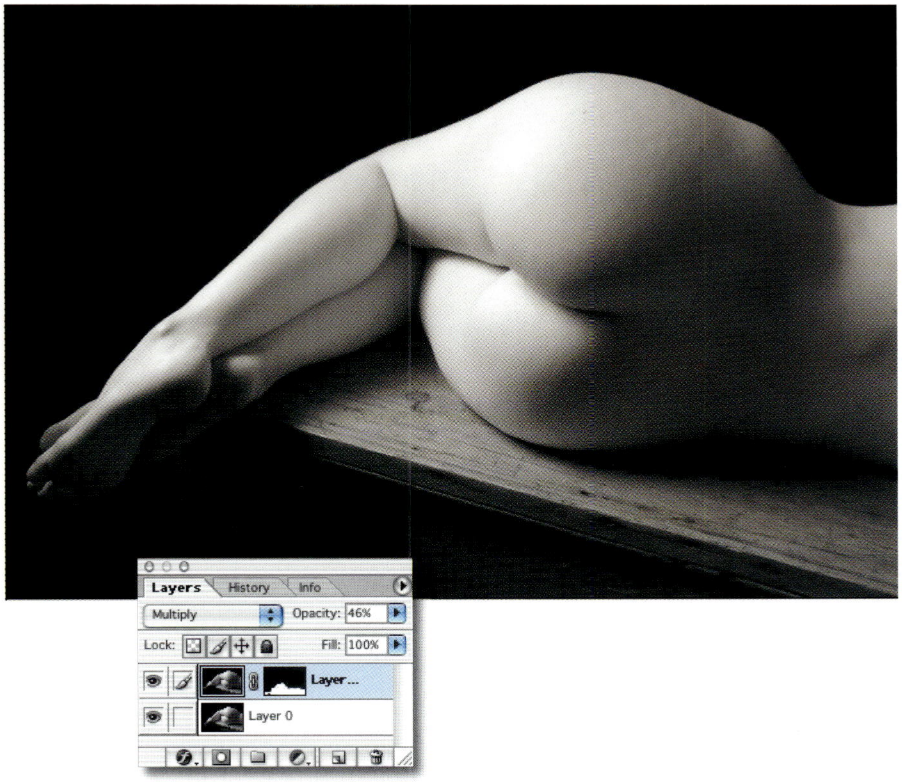

beautifully on black-and-white pictures. You can use the Burn tool to darken small areas. Remember that this is destructive editing: once you've saved and closed the file, the areas you've burned in can't be restored to their previous state. For non-destructive editing of larger areas, such as the top of the box the model is lying on here, you can duplicate the layer, set the blend mode of the top layer to Multiply, then create a layer mask and remove everything except the top of the box from the top layer. Finally, adjust the Opacity of the layer to create the right balance in brightness and contrast between foreground and background.

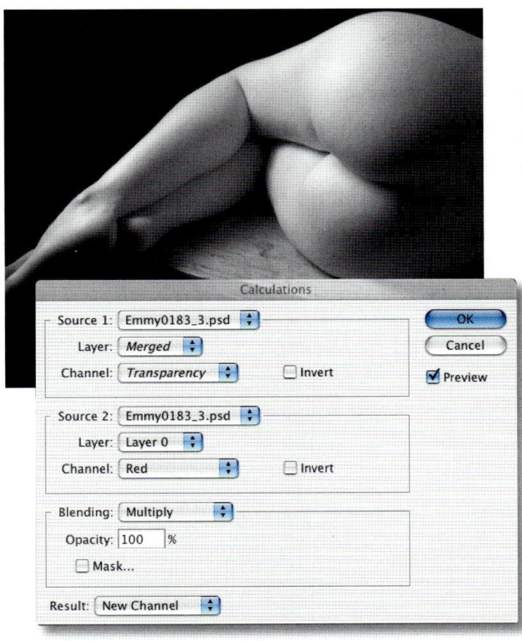

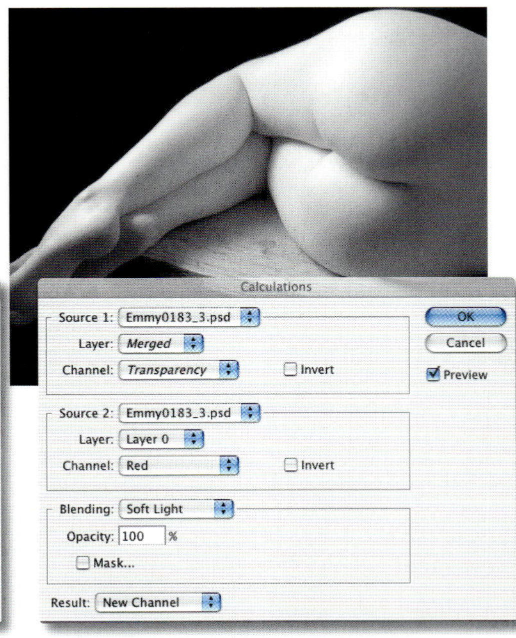

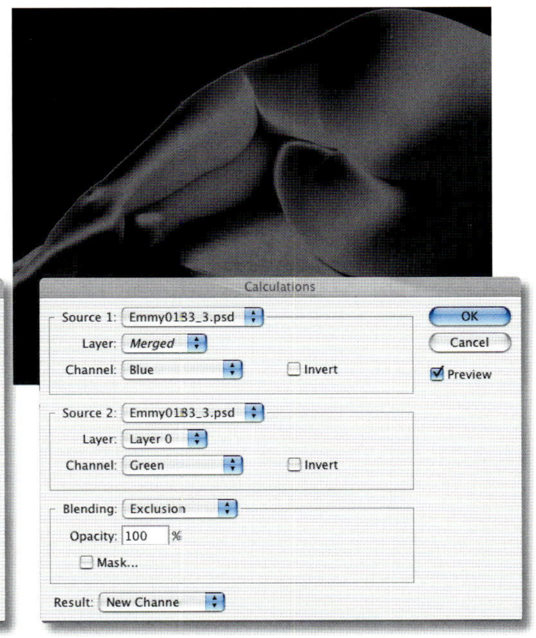

Spot or selective coloring

Digital photographic editing lets you easily remove color from parts of an image (assuming it was shot in color in the first place). By doing so, you can produce a "black-and-white-and-color" picture, sometimes referred to as a "spot color" image. In principle it's easy to do, but there are some points to consider before you embark on it.

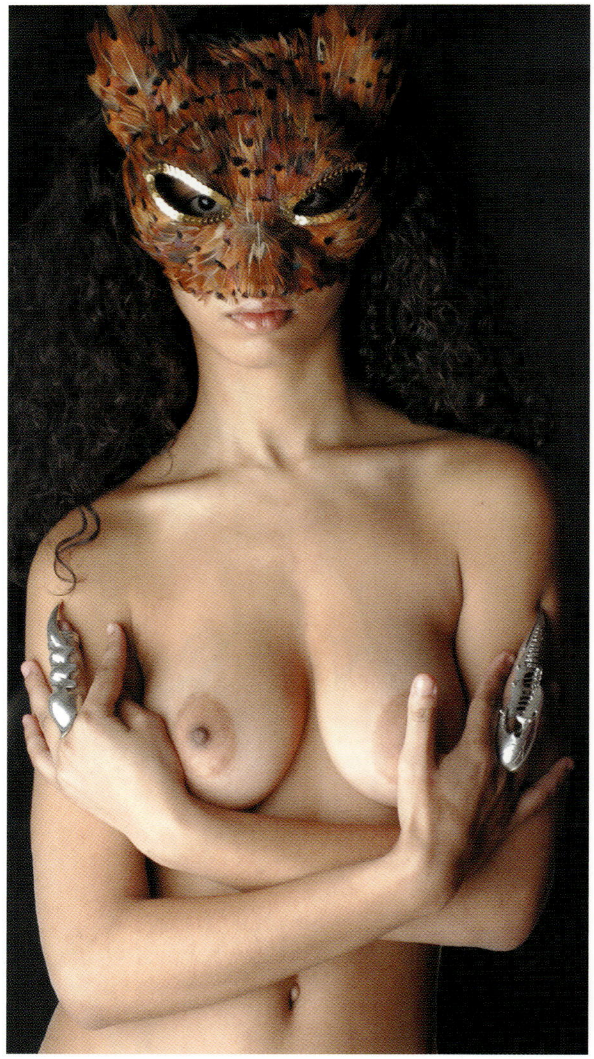

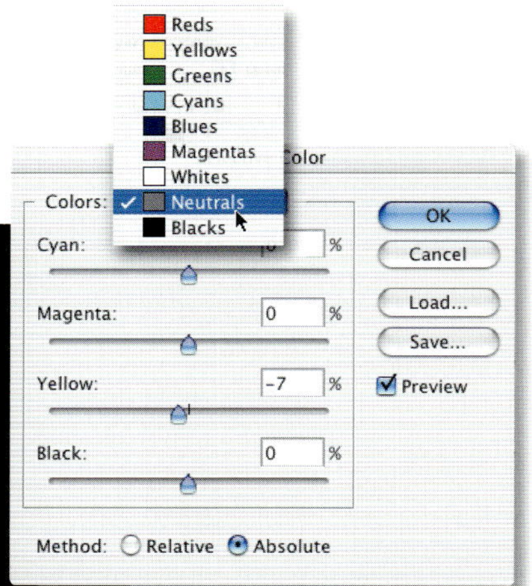

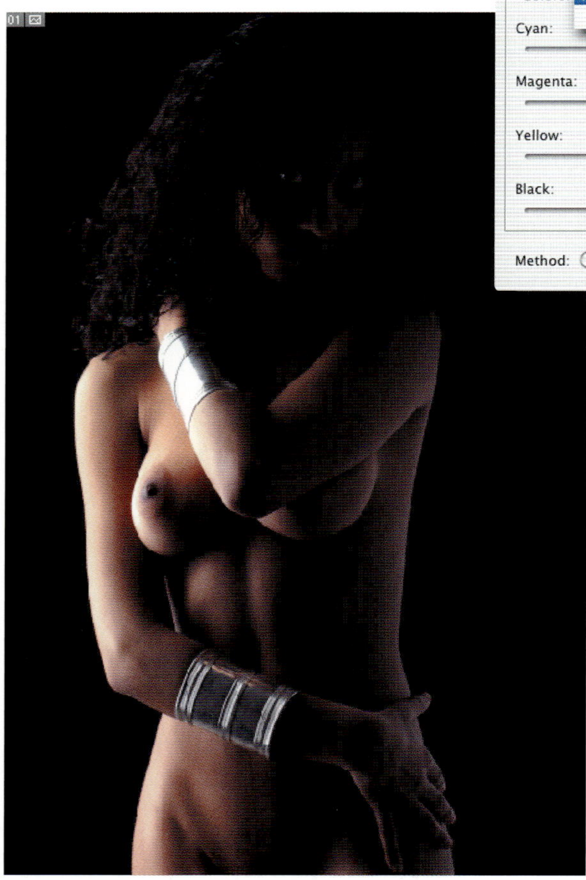

LEFT: Photoshop offers an intriguing tool for shifting color selectively. This is *Image>Adjustments> Selective Color*. It's designed to correct color inaccuracies, specifying which range of color you wish to alter, but it also lets you play with color in "unrealistic" ways as well.

It's possible to create an image of this kind from almost any photograph, so the first question is whether the picture you're thinking about changing will really benefit from the treatment. A quick trawl around the major photographic websites will reveal any number of images in which it's difficult to see a clear reason why the photographer decided to apply this technique. It's also often easy to find images that show poor choices of which elements to retain in color, and which to make black and white. Every summer produces a crop of photographs of black-and-white models wearing brightly colored bikinis! Fortunately the computer makes it easy to carry out a few quick experiments with the picture in order to decide whether the spot color technique will improve it.

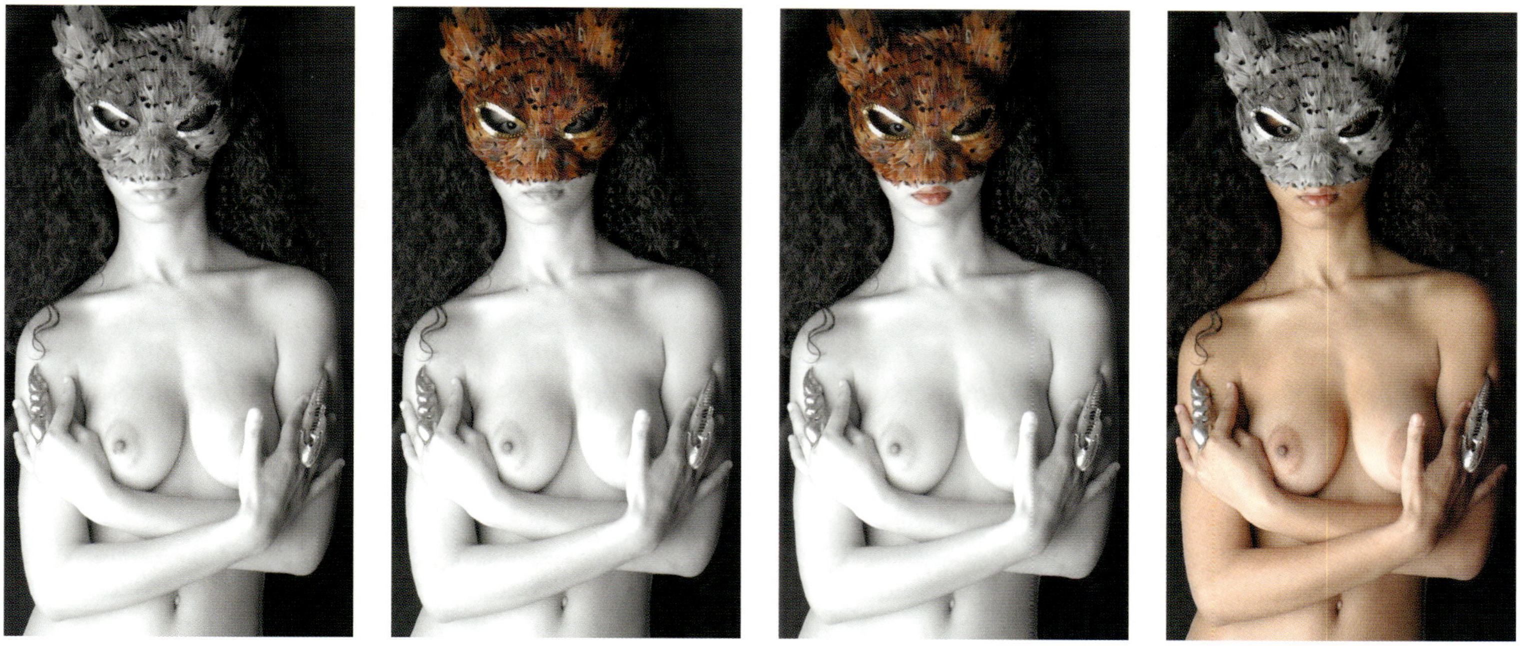

The second point is that, although the trick of doing this is easy to grasp, to do it right, you have to be meticulous in separating the color from the monochrome elements in the image. Again, the Web is host to numerous images in which the edges where the different elements meet are smudged and blurry.

In deciding which parts of the image to treat, our aim is to avoid the obvious. In these examples I've tried out a few different options.

The third version seems predictable, but adding the eyes and mouth to the color area makes the treatment a little unusual. I like the fourth and last version, but compared with the sensuality that's added to the image in the second version when the model's skin is converted to monochrome, the loss of color in the mask in this last version seems to make it rather flat and less exotic: something's been taken away and nothing much added.

OPPOSITE PAGE, TOP: The original image in color.

ABOVE LEFT TO RIGHT: A fairly high-key monochrome version produced with *Image>Calculations*, which is used as the black-and-white layer of the next three images; the cat-mask left in color, everything else monochrome; the mask, eyes, and lips left in color; the model left in color and the mask made black and white.

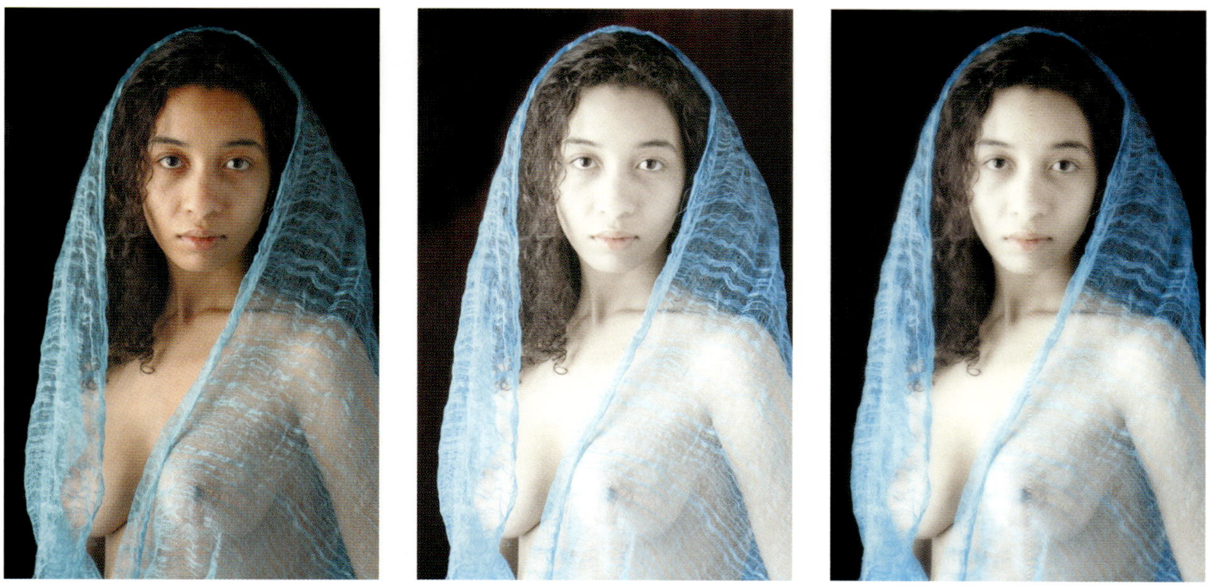

LEFT: Selective Color allows detailed color adjustments. I wanted to give this image a more ethereal feel, by giving the skin tones a paler, glowing look. Selective Color allowed me to reduce the saturation of the model's skin tones, while at the same time boosting the saturation of the shawl. (Note that the skintone under the shawl isn't affected by the change in the color of the shawl.) Finally, I used "Monday Morning," a curiously named filter from Nikon's nik Color Efex Pro! series, to increase the contrast in the image and give it that glow.

Spot coloring from infrared

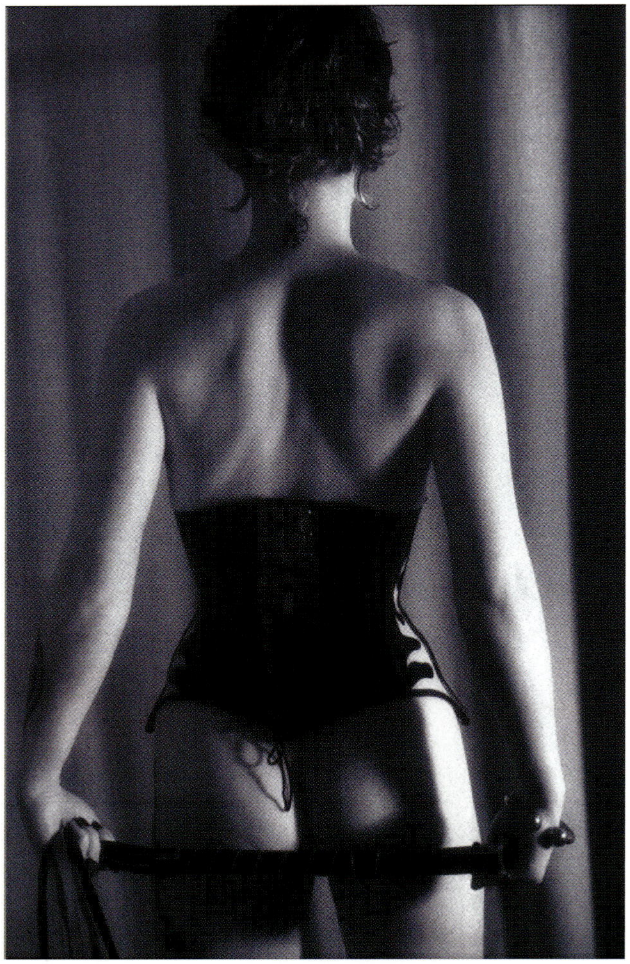

As well as being a very skilled "lightpainter" (see pages 142-143), Dave McAleavy still shoots a lot of infrared film, which he then scans and manipulates in Photoshop. Infrared film produces monochrome images. In *Pillar of Fire* the flame motif on the model's corset is the inspiration for a new digital background. Typical of photographers who use Photoshop at this level, Dave finds that the power of the software means that it's difficult to predict what the result of a new combination of tools will be, so the creative process includes a lot of trial and error.

RIGHT: The swirl pattern completed. Because the infrared image is monochrome, I had to provide the color for the flames digitally.

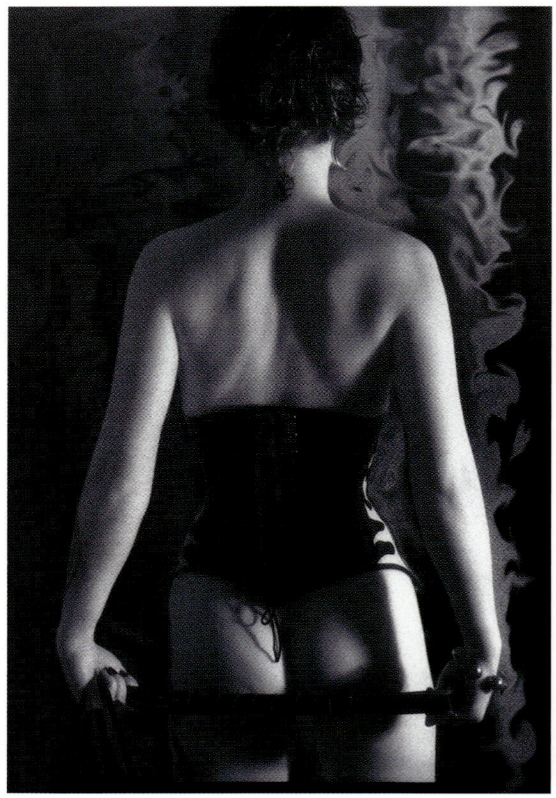

ABOVE: "I began with the original image, an infrared shot, in which the dark, deep purple cloth background, under normal light, turned out a muddy and unappealing gray. But I liked the basic image—the model's pose, the lighting—the slightly 'fetishy' feel, so decided to try replacing the background using Photoshop. I didn't need to do much to the model, so I separated her onto a new layer, and went to work on the background.

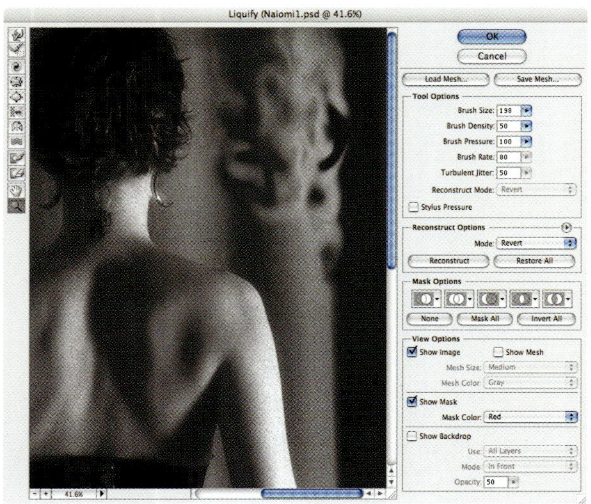

RIGHT: "After much experimenting with Photoshop's Swirl and Pixel Shift, I came up with a background which overall suggested flames, with a 'pillar of fire' on the right, just like the flames on Naomi's corset."

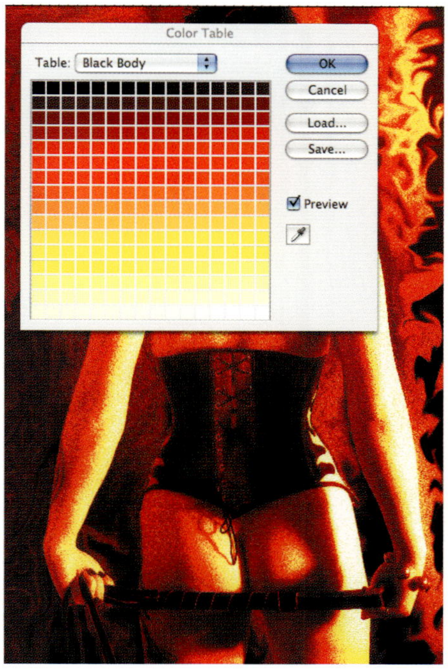

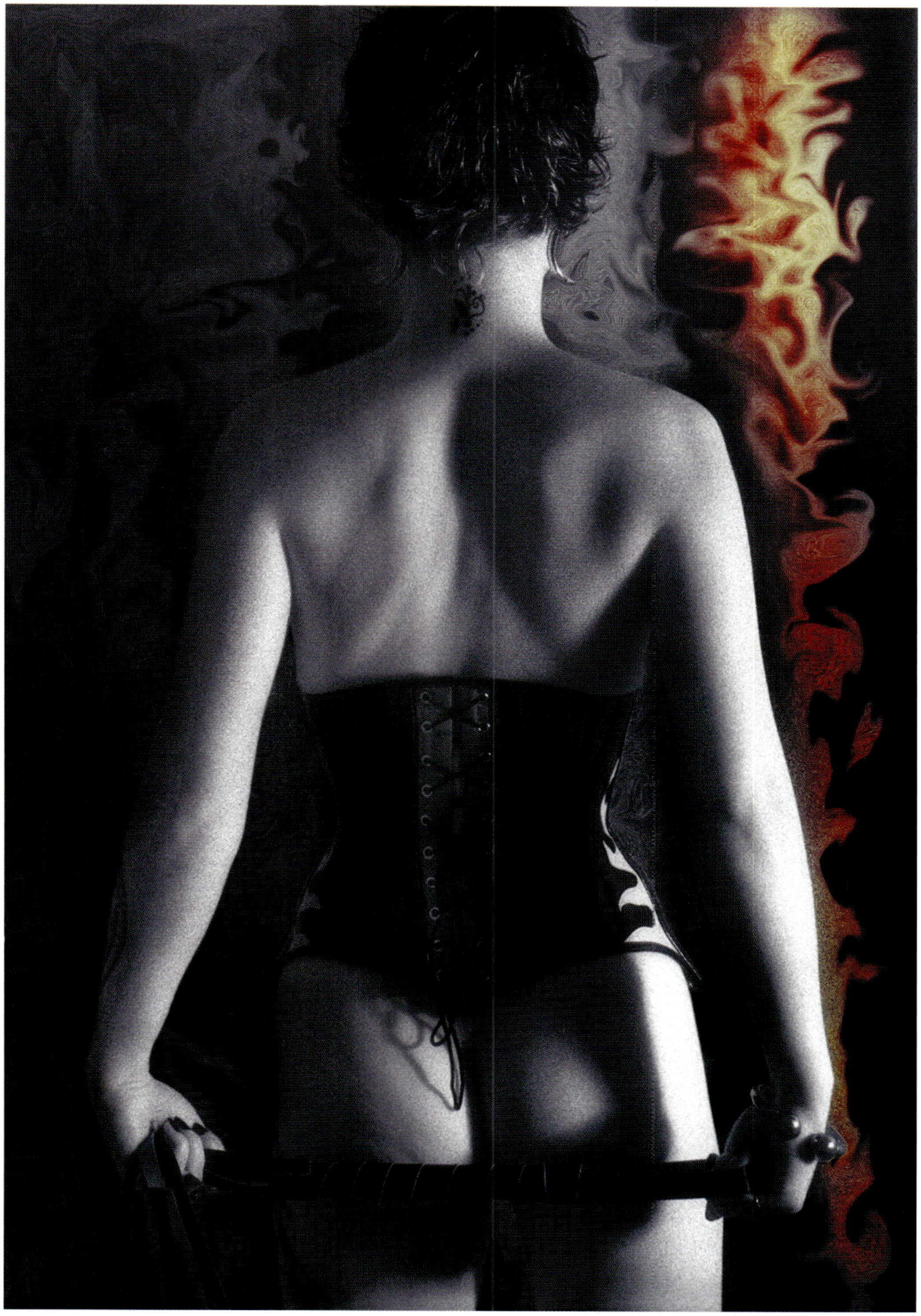

ABOVE: "Within Photoshop's indexed color options there's a palette called Black Light, which mimics the colors a blackbody radiator emits as it is heated—from black to red, orange, yellow, and white. I added this and it worked perfectly for the pillar of fire. Finally, I went back to the corset and lightened the lacing a little, just to make it easier to see, and went carefully over the edges where the model touches the background, to ensure that the join was smooth."

RIGHT: The final product. Note how the "flames" extend all the way across the background, with the "spot" color used only on the border.

Making a spot color image

I'd shot a set of images with model Naomi, exploring the eroticism of boots and stockings. The vivid red and high gloss of the boot suggested the possibility of a spot color image, and I picked the last frame of the set with its tense pose.

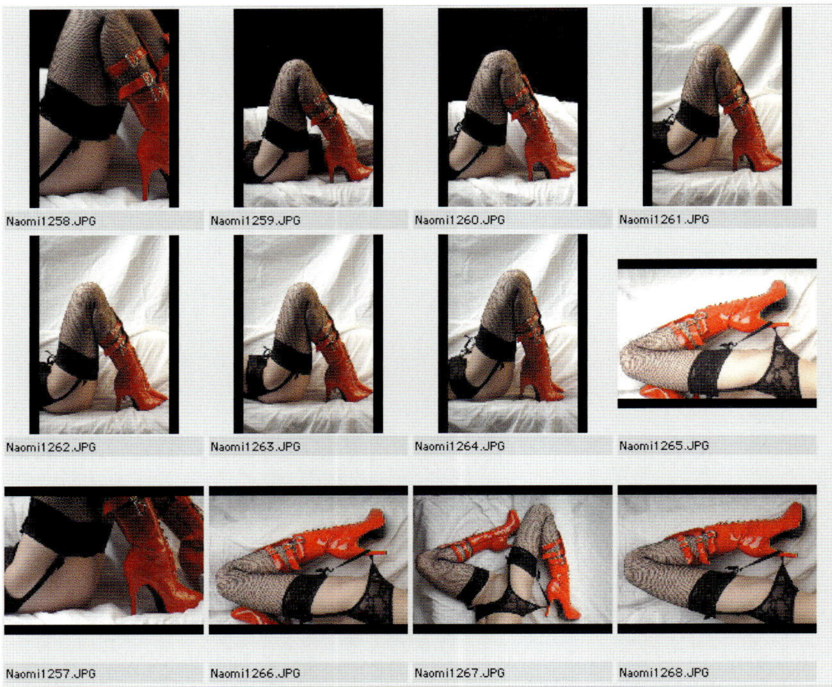

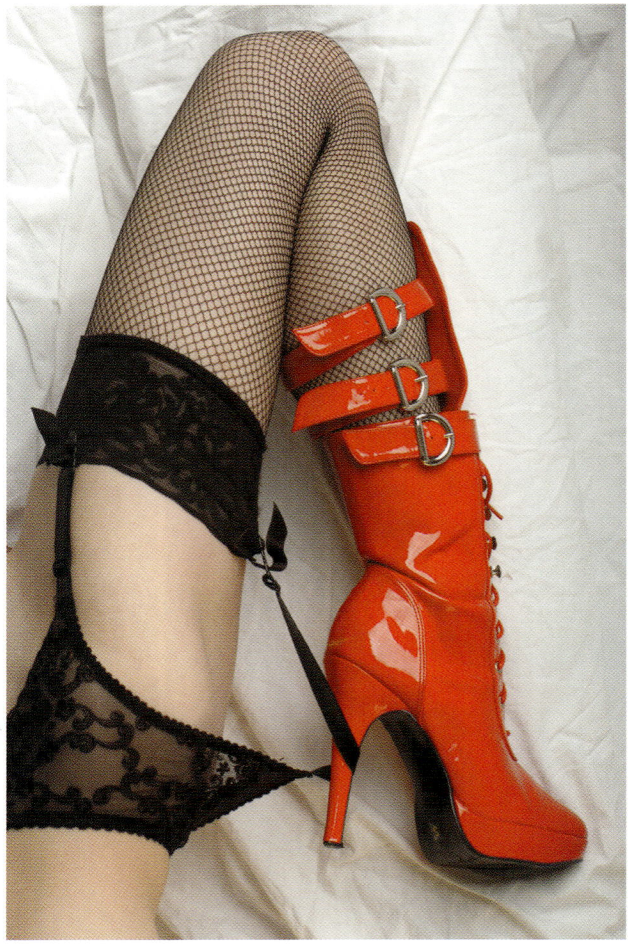

The first step is, as always, to make a copy of the file to work on. Next, we check levels and optimize the tonal range of the image. When that's done we can produce the monochrome version of the image. This is an important step: the impact of the spot color partly depends on having a full tonal range in the monochrome element. If you choose *Image>Calculations* as your method, select *New Document* in the Result dropdown, so that you get the black-and-white version as a new file, and the color version of the image is left unchanged. If you use *Image>Adjustments>Channel Mixer* to create the monochrome layer, you'll need to make another copy of the original file for the color layer.

Whichever method you've chosen, drag the color layer on top of the monochrome layer, and you're ready to go to work.

We've already seen that Photoshop offers non-destructive methods of performing some editing tasks. Some manuals recommend using the Eraser tool for partial removal of a layer, but that's a destructive method. It's particularly unhelpful here because you may want to experiment, removing some parts of the color layer, then putting them back. It's much safer and more precise to use a layer mask. You click on the mask, then paint on the image with black to make the layer transparent. Technically, you're creating an alpha channel, which controls the transparency of the layer: in the alpha

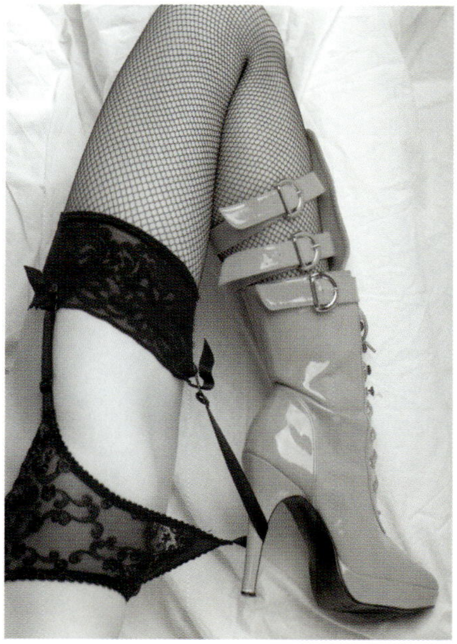

LEFT: The monochrome layer. I decided to leave the mussed-up sheet as is, rather than smooth it out in Photoshop, because it contrasts well with the other textures in the picture.

channel, black is totally transparent, shading through partly transparent grays to white, which is totally opaque. We can clear a lot of the color layer with a broad brush—400 pixels works well here. Then it's a matter of working up to the edges of the boot with smaller brushes, down to three or four pixels in places.

Don't worry if your brush runs over the edges of the boot as you work closer to it: just switch to white in the color palette and paint the edges back in! As you work in more detail you'll need to enlarge your view of the image, maybe working at over 100% magnification to get into all the nooks and crannies. And try out different ideas: I decided that I wanted the boot buckles to be monochrome—it seemed to make them look even more metallic.

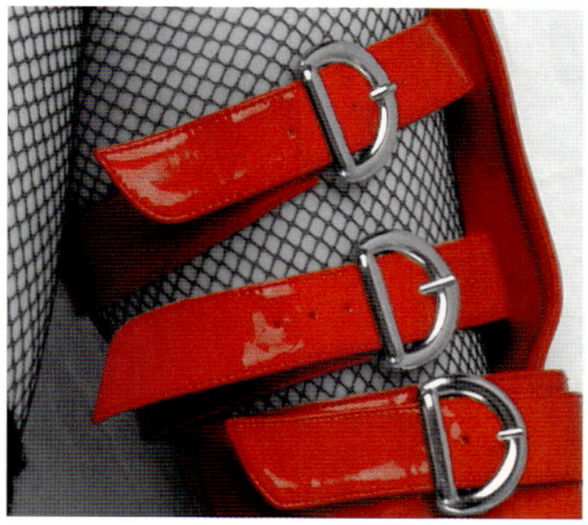

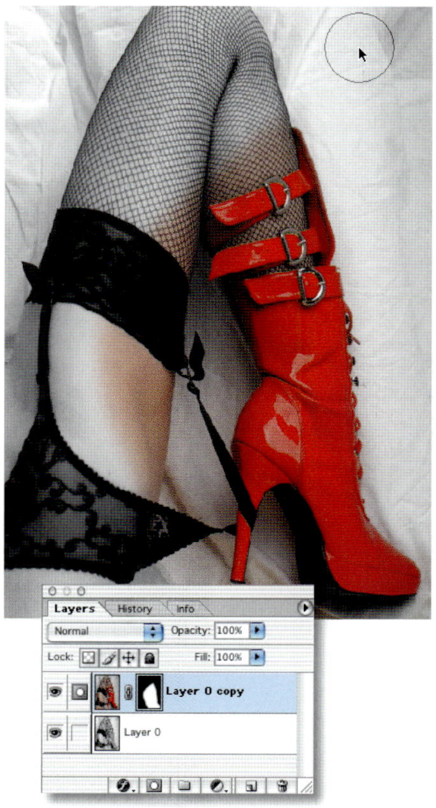

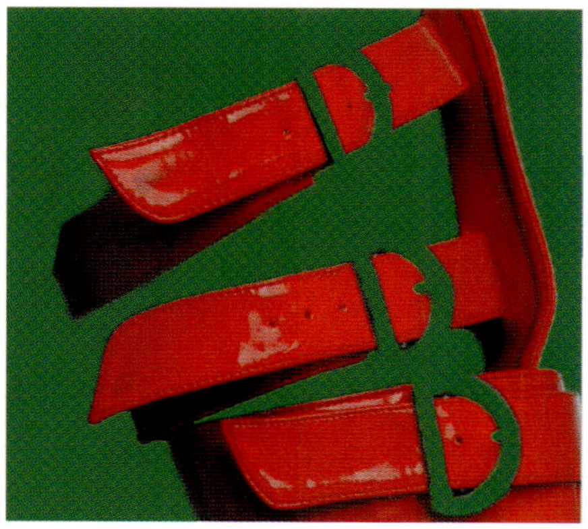

LEFT: Much of the color layer has been cleared with a few strokes of a broad brush. Note how the cleared area of the image is reflected in the shape of the black-and-white areas in the layer mask.

ABOVE & RIGHT: Details of the two layers of the image at 100% scale, and the final result. One striking feature of this image is that it has no clear orientation: it can be hung with the boot heel pointing either up or down.

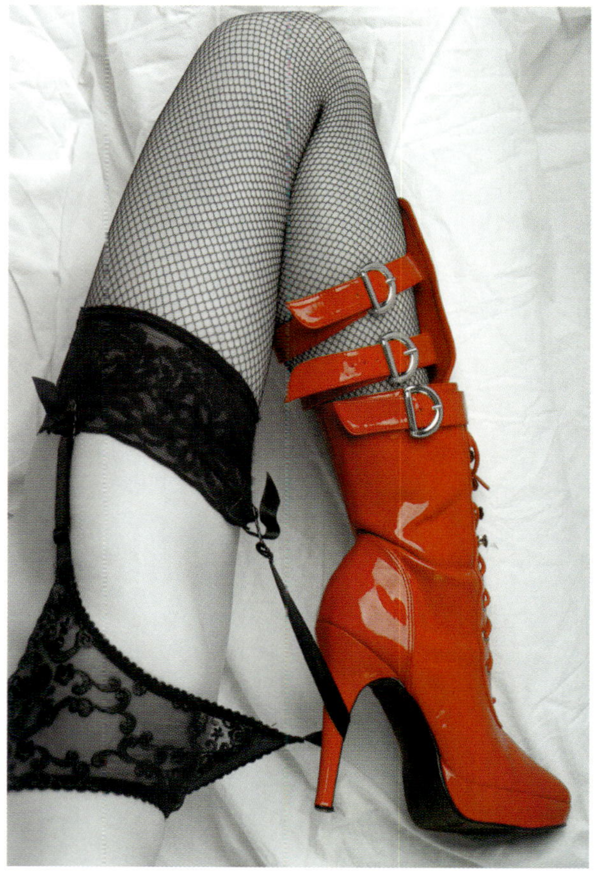

Layers, masks, and blending

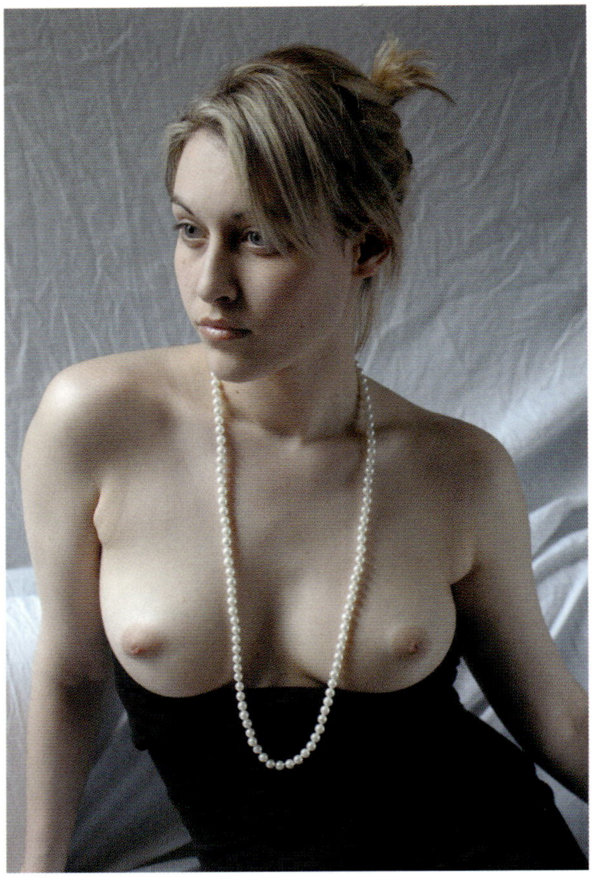

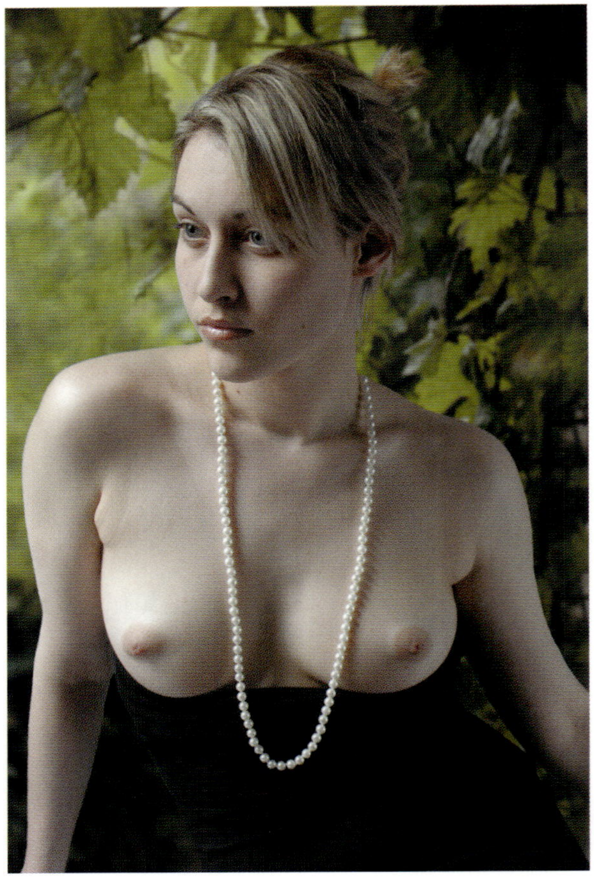

LEFT: Layers and masks are often used to replace backgrounds, moving the model from the studio into a different world. In this example the background was horizontally flipped in order to match its lighting with the foreground.

Now we're at the heart of Photoshop: the ability to bring separate elements into a single image, and to control precisely the way those elements interact with each other. Later on we'll see some spectacular examples of how photographers combine very different shots together; in this section I'm going to work with simpler ingredients, to demonstrate the potential of these features of Photoshop.

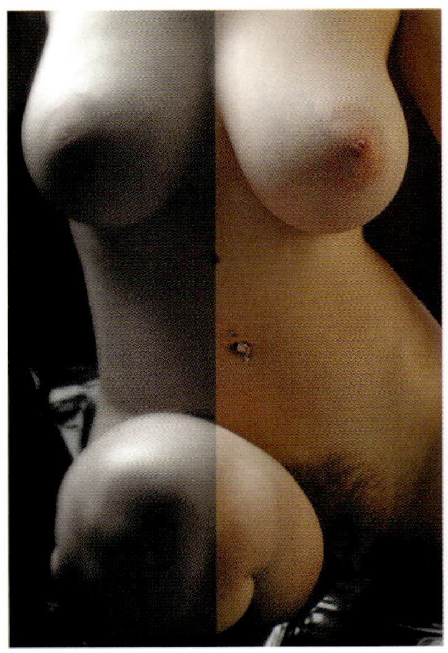

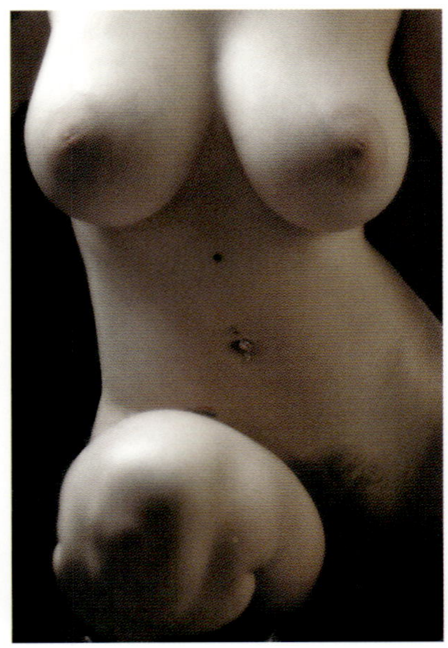

BELOW: In practice, layers, masks, and blends are often used in conjunction with filters. Here the top layer was flattened tonally, by reducing its brightness and contrast, then run through Nikon's nik Efex Pro! "Monday Morning" filter. This added grain, contrast, and blur as well as reducing the color in the layer. Then it was blended in Soft Light mode with the bottom layer, the opacity of which was set to 27%. This reduced the grain slightly, restoring a little of the original color to the image. I also removed the highlights from the background.

RIGHT: Reflections appeal to many photographers, perhaps because they are an equivalent in nature to the photographic process itself. I've separated the reflection from its original, by copying it onto a new layer, and flipped it horizontally. Next I use a mask, which enables any part of a layer to be made transparent, to smooth away any visible edges between the flipped reflection, to make this new version of the image appear natural and seamless. One of the strengths of these processes is that they're non-destructive. The original image is still intact under the flipped layer, and the mask can be endlessly re-edited.

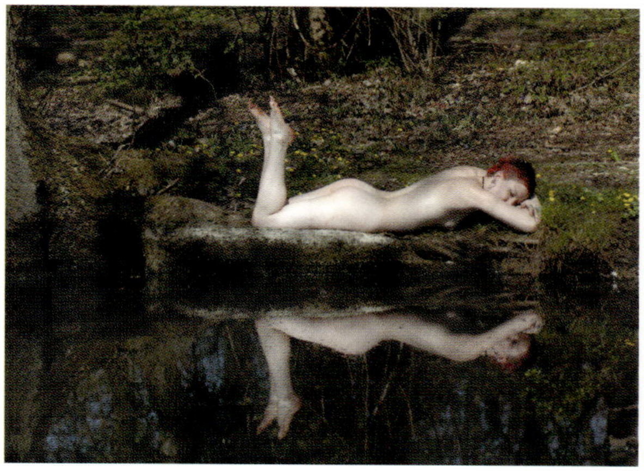

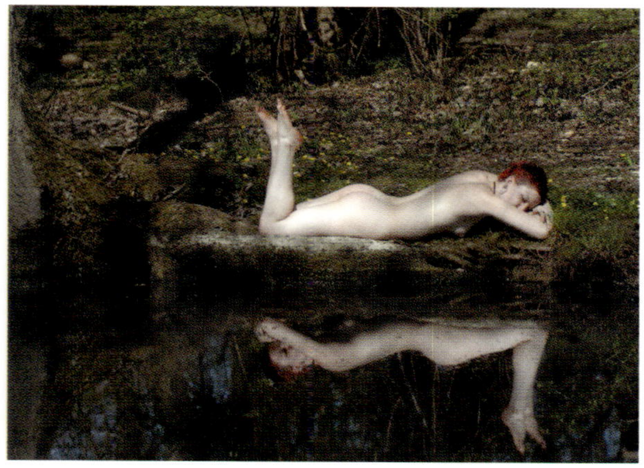

RIGHT: The "flipped" layer by itself, showing its softened and partly transparent edges.

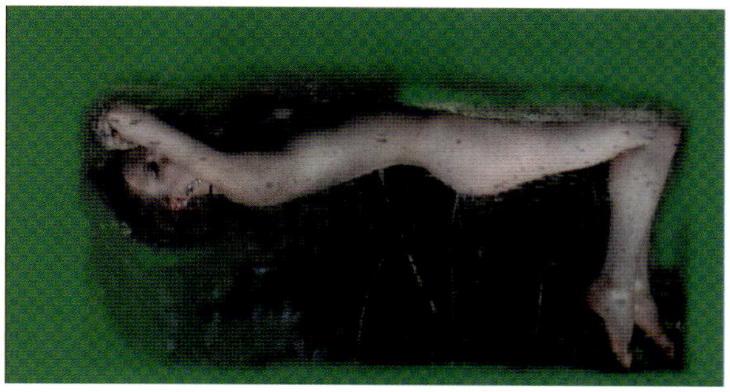

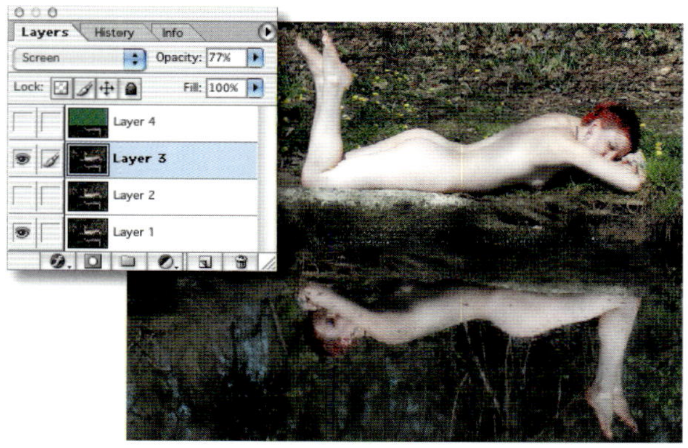

RIGHT: The key technique then is to build up complex images by placing each element on its own layer and using a layer mask to control how much of each layer is visible. We can also create a simple "see-through" effect by reducing the opacity of a layer.

FAR RIGHT: Here I've created a continuous reflection of the woods in a new bottom layer, which is partly visible through the reflection of the model.

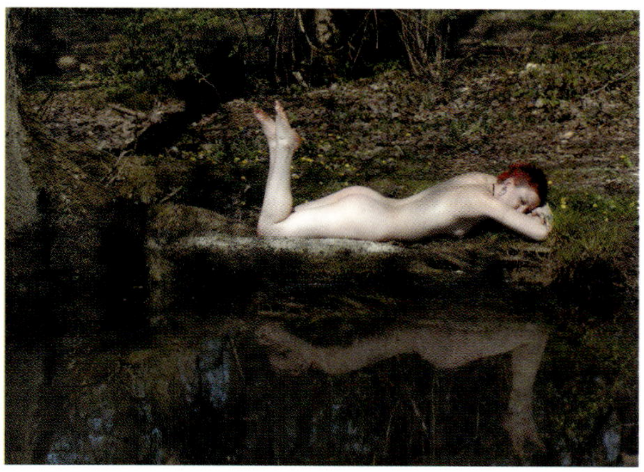

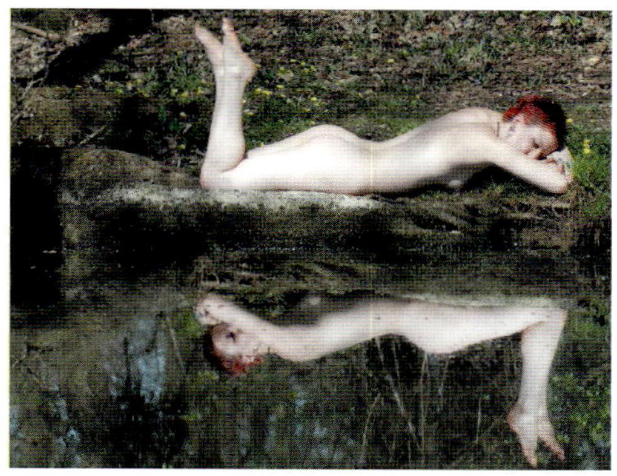

But Photoshop provides a more powerful technique for showing one layer through another. Blending combines the corresponding pixels of two layers according to a set of mathematical rules (explained in more detail in the Photoshop Help). Although a blend applied to a layer only alters its relationship with the layer immediately beneath it, applying blends to several layers will produce a cumulative effect. The opacity of each layer can also be varied. Depending on the blend mode(s) you've chosen, the results you get by varying the opacity of one layer or the other may be very different.

RIGHT: Applied to Layer 3, the Screen blend mode lightens the image. To avoid any highlights blowing out, I've reduced the opacity of the layer slightly. In the next screengrab I've added Layer 4 (the reflection) and applied Screen to it also, thus raising the brightness of the reflection. In the final example I've included Layer 2, but set its blend mode to Multiply, which increases the contrast of the image.

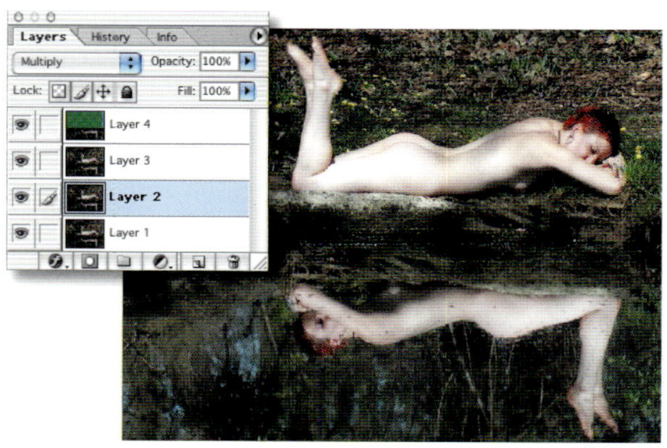

Filters and effects

Photoshop is supplied with a host of filters that can help you to completely change the look of an image. Many other companies also provide filters for Photoshop: a quick search on the Web for "Photoshop plug-ins" brings up thousands of sites. Some artists swear by Alien Skin's Eye Candy range (www.alienskin.com), others by Corel's KPT collection (www.corel.com). I myself make heavy use of the filters in Nikon's nik Efex Pro! set. In addition, Photoshop contains a Filter factory, which you can use to devise your own filters.

Some filters are mainly corrective, intended to make an image look "right." Most of the sharpening and blurring filters come into this category, and their uses are discussed in various sections throughout the book. Other filters are intended to be used more creatively, and we'll also see those in action later.

The problem with filters is, because every Photoshop user has access to the same filters, just applying one "as is" is likely to produce images that look just like everyone else's. So we'll explore some ways of using filters that can give your images a distinctive look. Not all filters have preview windows, by the way, and such windows as are made available are usually too small. When you're trying filters out, you can see what they do more quickly by selecting a small representative area of your image before choosing a filter. The filter will only be applied to the selected area.

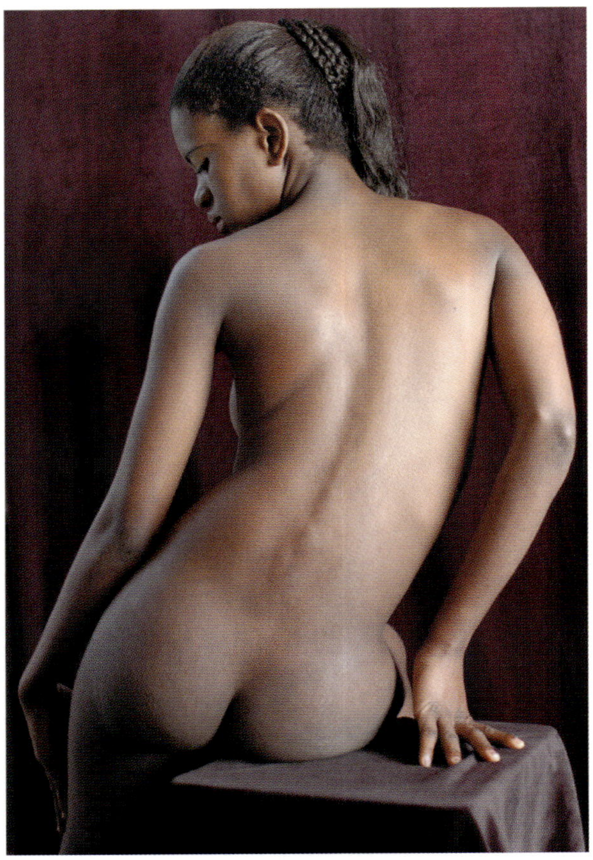

LEFT: This pose derives from the long tradition of painted nudes in Western art and I'll use one of Photoshop's more "painterly" filters, *Filter>Sketch>Chalk and Charcoal.*

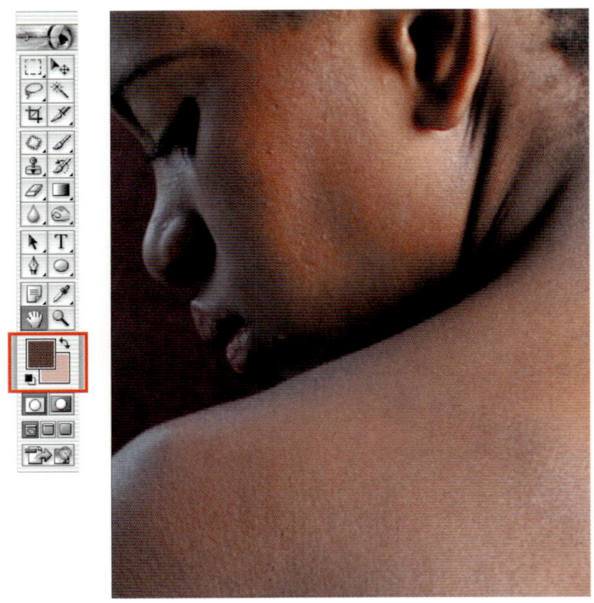

RIGHT: We start by setting the foreground and background colors to a light and dark area respectively of the model's skintones. These colors will form the "chalk" and "charcoal" for the filter. Next we apply the filter, experimenting with its settings until we find a combination that works well.

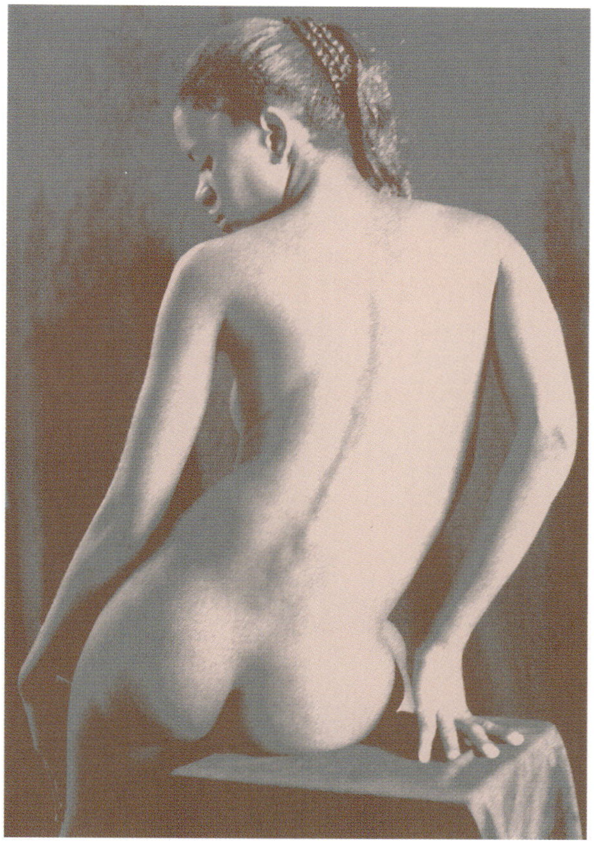

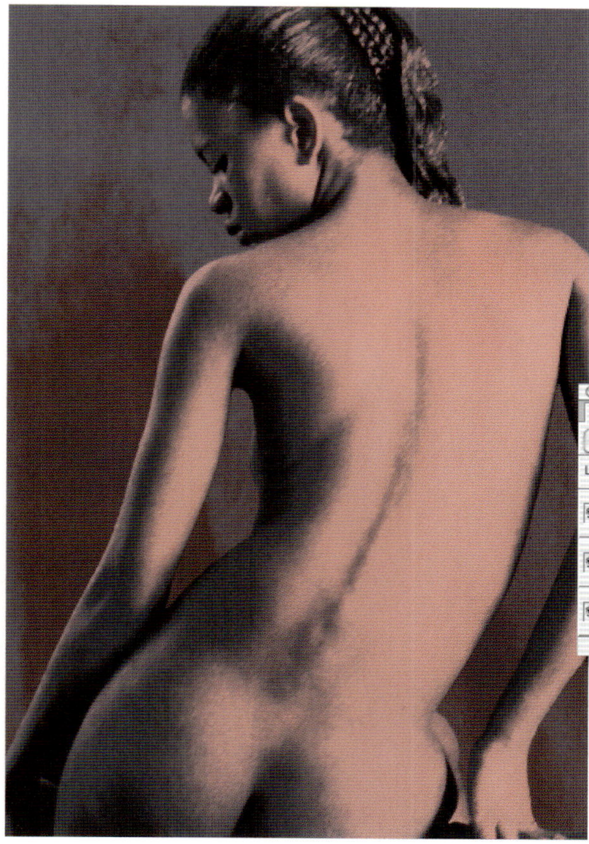

FAR LEFT AND LEFT: So far, so good. But I want to give the image a distinctive look: I'll do that by making the body darker and more contrasty. I make a selection of the model and the stool she's perched on, and copy this to a new layer using *Layer>New>Layer* via Copy. I move this layer to the top, and apply Chalk and Charcoal to it with the same values as before. Now I can experiment with different blends and opacities in all three layers, until I come up with the best combination.

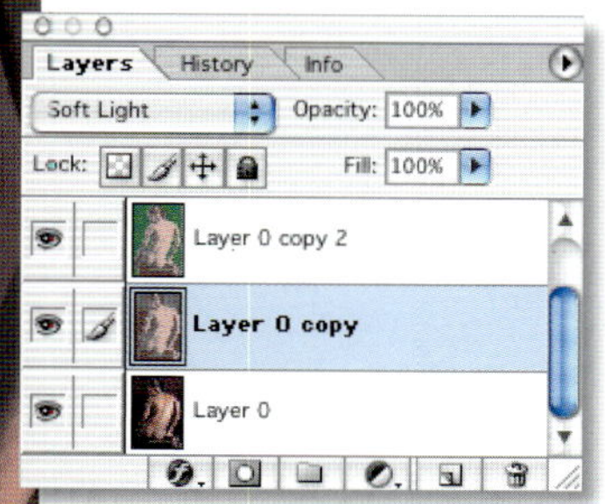

In this case the blend of the top layer (the model without background) is Multiply with 67% opacity; the middle layer is Soft Light at 100% Opacity, and the bottom layer (the original image) is set to 22% Opacity.

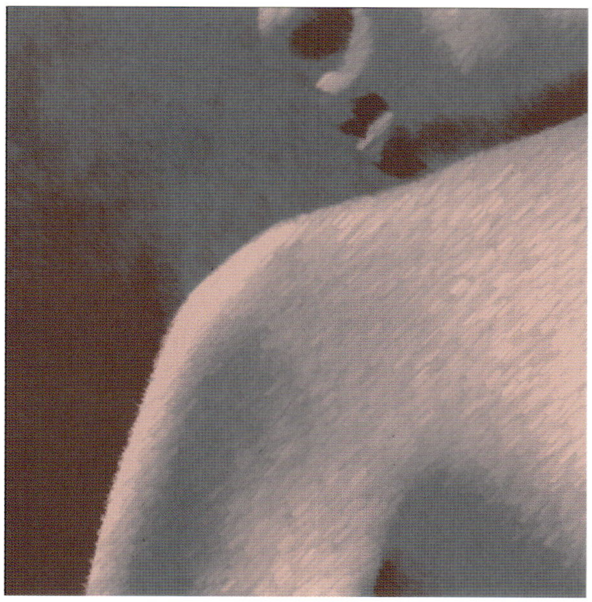

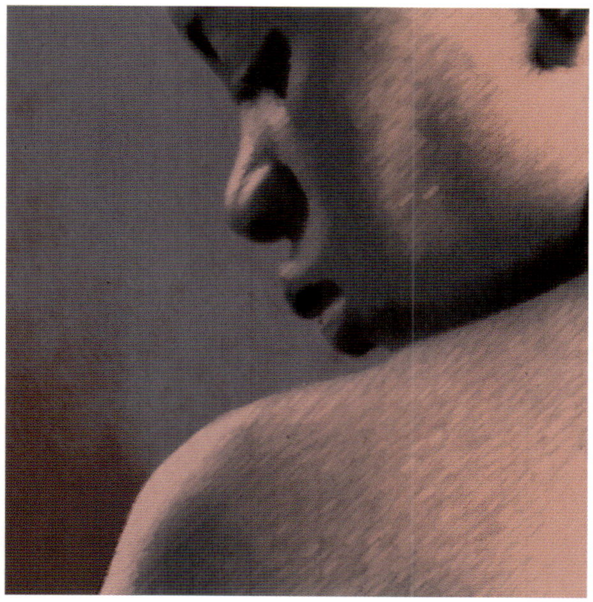

FAR BOTTOM LEFT: Like many of Photoshop's effects that simulate paint, ink, or pencil marks, Chalk and Charcoal tends to produce ragged edges where different colors meet, such as between the foreground and the background. So my final step here is going to be to create an empty layer on top and use the Clone tool to clone the background right up to the edges of the model, thus eliminating that jagged edge, but keeping a little of the dark outline. While I'm at it I'll remove the shadow beyond the right side of her torso.

LEFT: Before doing this I need to check that the Clone tool is set to Use All Layers; and I need to be certain that I've set the blend mode and opacity of each layer exactly to where I want it to be. The Clone tool will use the combined color of all the layers as they now are. If I alter any of the layers after carrying out this step, the outline I've created with the Clone tool will appear as a halo against the altered background.

Classic techniques

A number of Photoshop artists have dedicated their talents to recreating techniques from an earlier, more experimental age of photography. Several of these techniques are quite effective in erotic photography, partly because they refer back to the work of the pioneering artists who took photography and used it to explore the new worlds of sexuality that were opening up at the time.

Line and Lith

Line images are images from which almost all gray tones have been removed, leaving virtually a pure black and pure white image. This was a favorite technique for posters and record covers in the 1960s.

You can create a similar effect by converting a color image to monochrome to begin with, then using the controls in *Image>Adjustments>Brightness/Contrast* to crush the gray tones and achieve the best conversion of the image. *Image>Adjustments>Threshold* carries out the same process. You may find that you need to fill in some parts of the image, for example to complete any outlines that have been burned out in the conversion process.

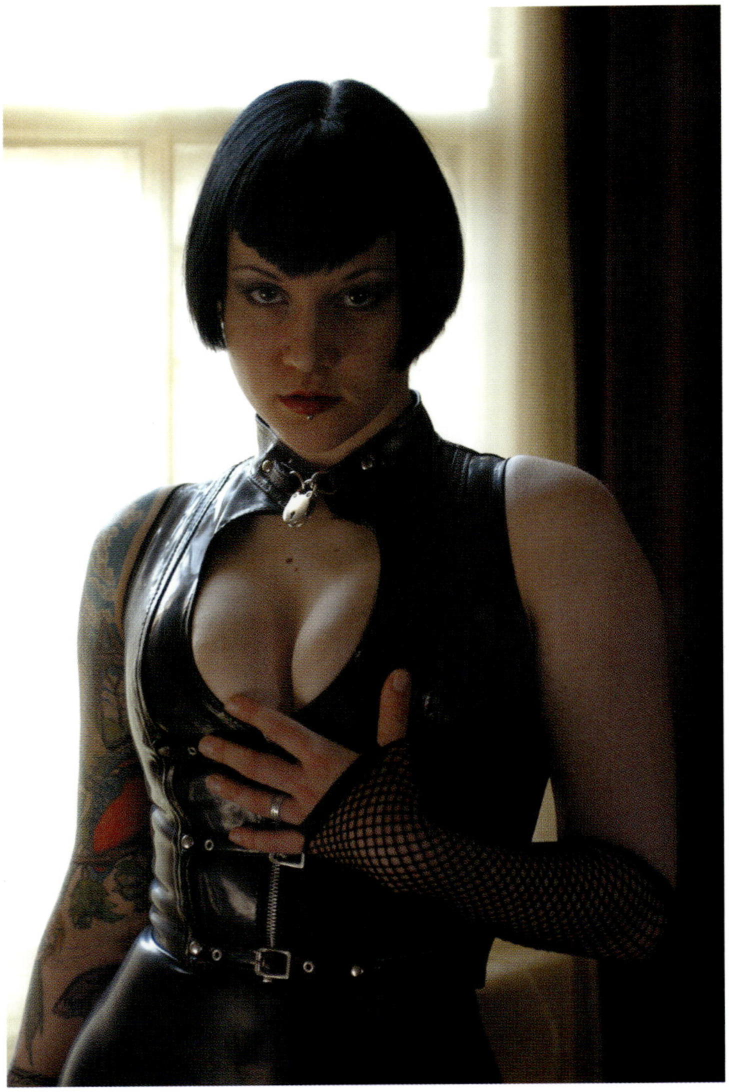

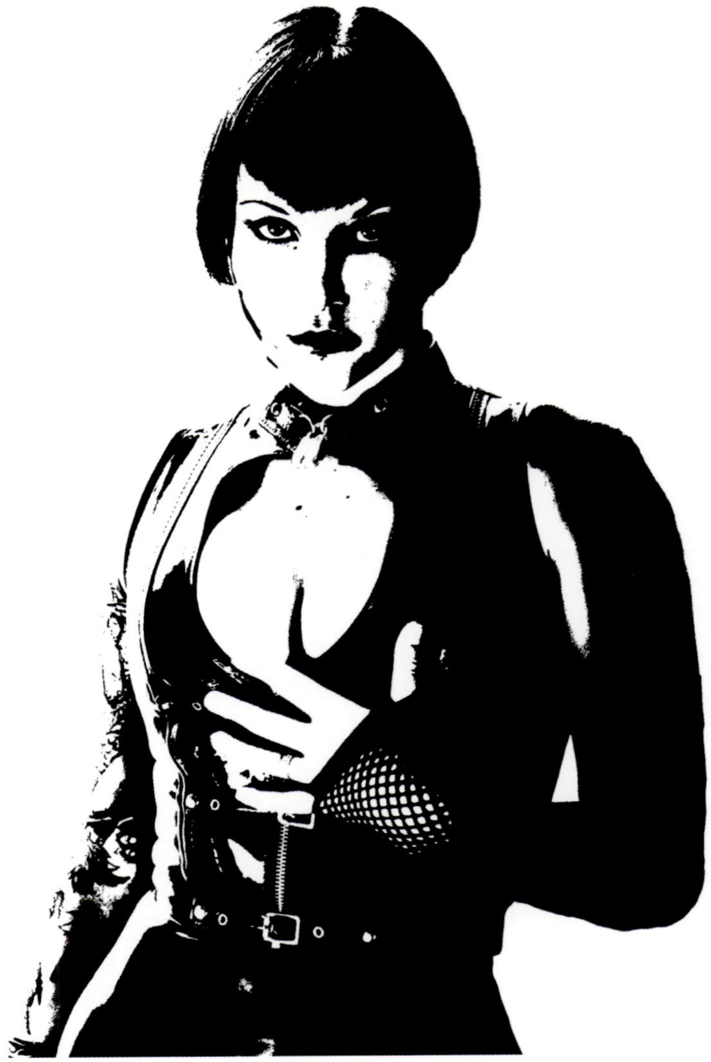

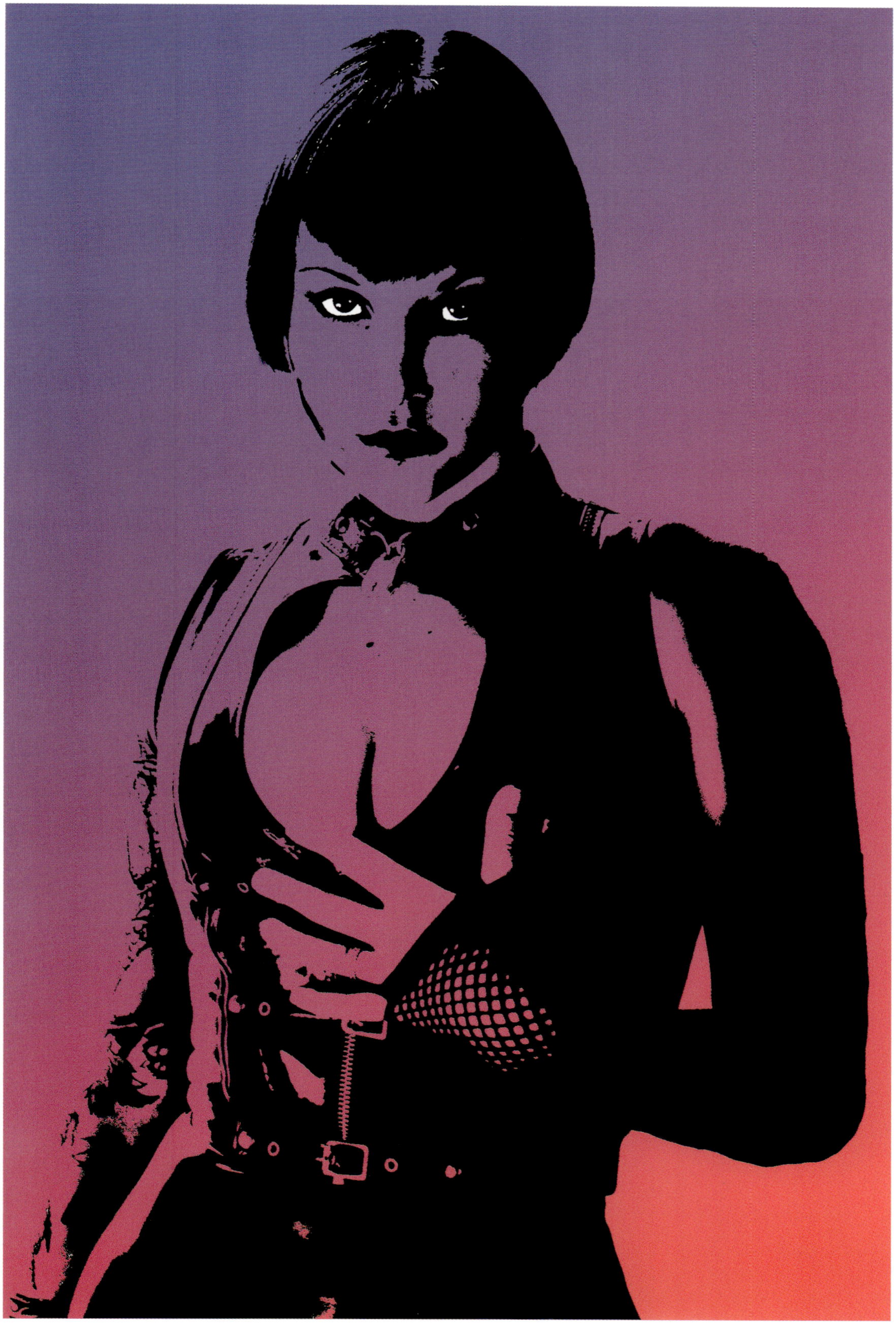

ALL IMAGES: Before converting this image I needed to take out the dark area of the background on the right. The best settings for the image overall left the right side of the model's jawline undefined, so I sketched it in with a small-diameter, hard-edged black brush. Once you've created the monochrome image you can manipulate it further by, for example, selecting the white areas and filling them with a color gradient for that retro 1960s look.

Gum bichromate

Gum bichromate photography is an early photochemical method that doesn't make use of the silver compounds which are the basis of standard photographic processes. It involves the use of gum arabic, which has been made photosensitive, in combination with watercolor pigments. The effect is to paint over a monochrome image with a specific color for each part of the tonal range. You can achieve very similar effects digitally, applying color to the image with a digital brush—an unsual experience for a photographer!

Repeat this process, selecting and copying the midtones, then the low tones. (Selecting three tonal levels worked in this image, but you could have more, or maybe just two.) I kept the Fuzziness setting at about 80. At each step save the selection you've made (*Select>Save Selection*). In this case I found it easier to get the low skintones by selecting the solid black area, adding that selection to the high and midtone selections by using *Select>Load Selection...* and checking the *Add to Selection* button each time, then using *Select>Inverse* to get the low skintones.

You can now go to each layer in turn and paint in it using any brush and colors you choose (I found that for this image a Spatter brush with variable pressure and muted colors worked best). The effect of the Fuzziness setting is to enable colors to overlap each other. Using a brush rather than simply filling each layer enables you to experiment with texture and density in the colors as you paint them on.

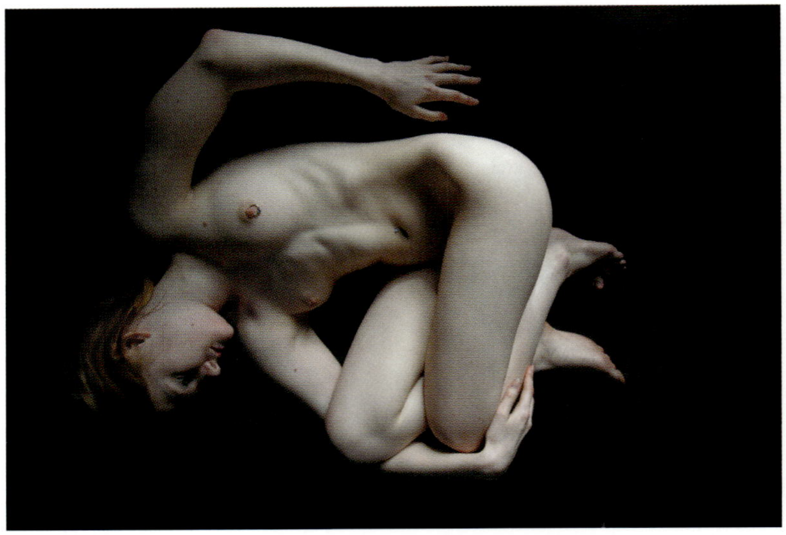

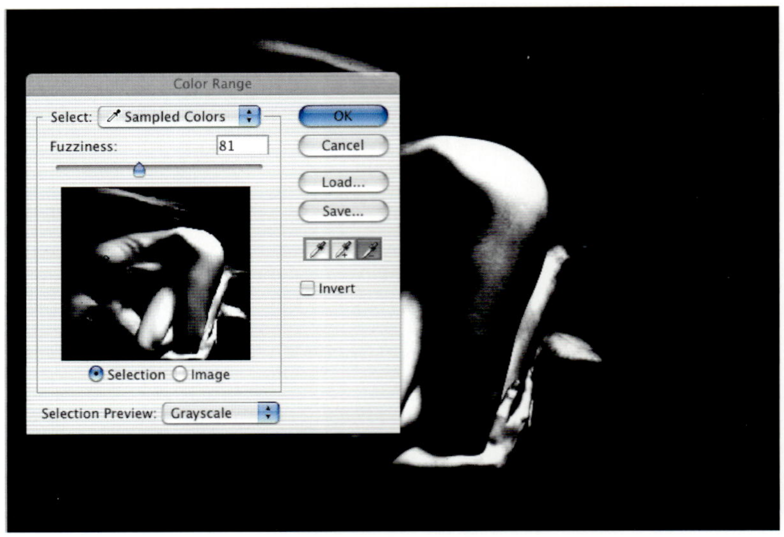

ABOVE: Using Color Range to select the highlights. We begin by converting the image to monochrome, but keeping it RGB (i.e., if you made the conversion using *Mode>Grayscale*, you'll then need to use *Mode>RGB* to recreate the the color channels.) Use *Select>Color Range...* to select the high tones of the image. Then use *Layer>New>Layer* via *Copy*, to copy that part of the image to a new layer.

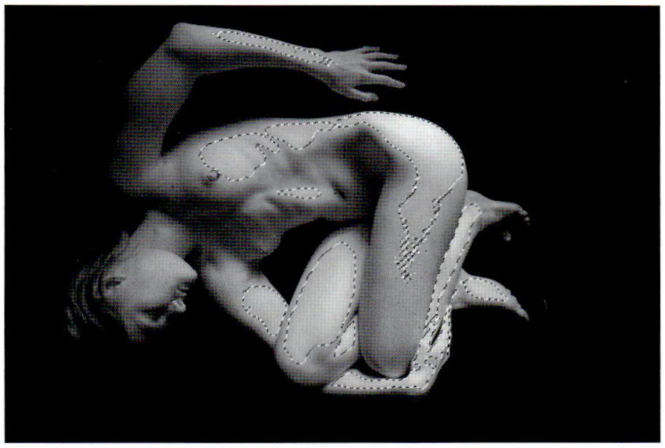

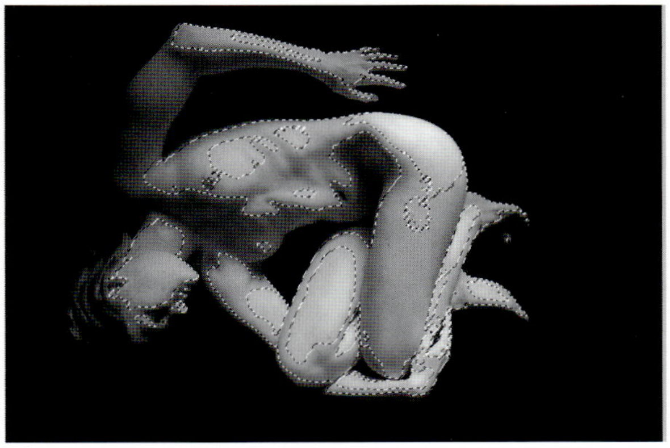

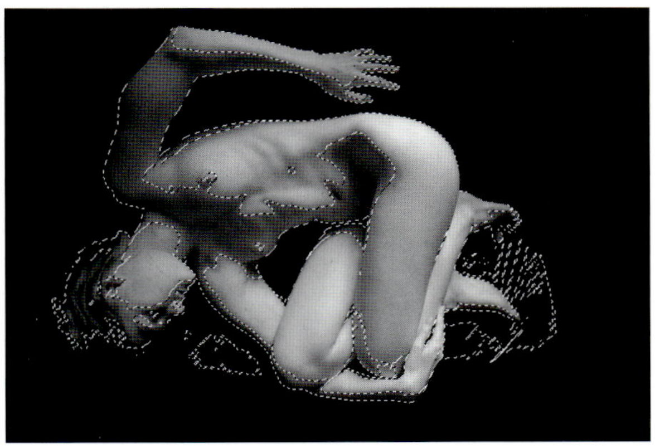

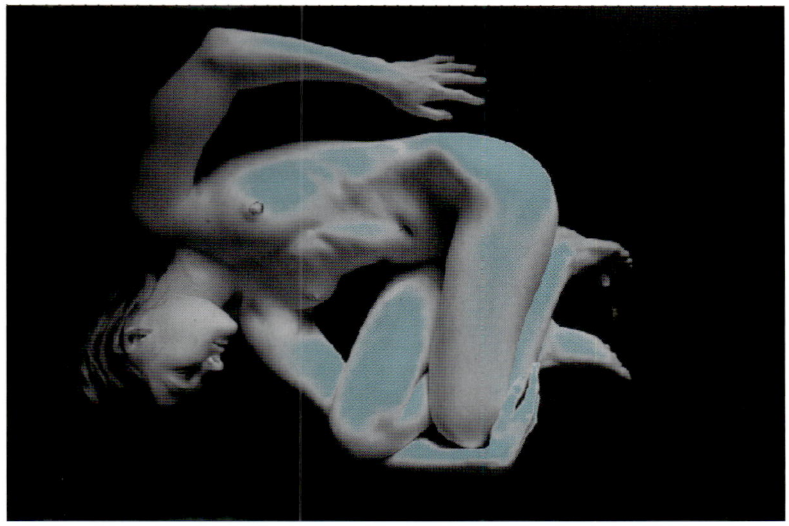

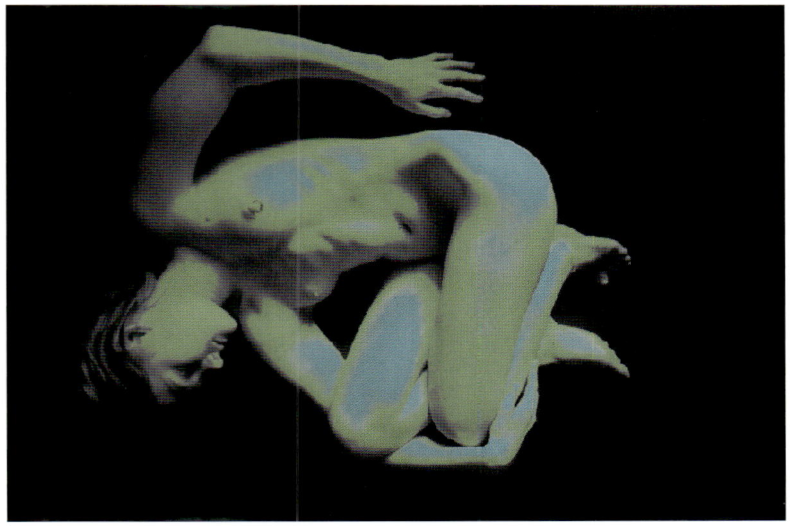

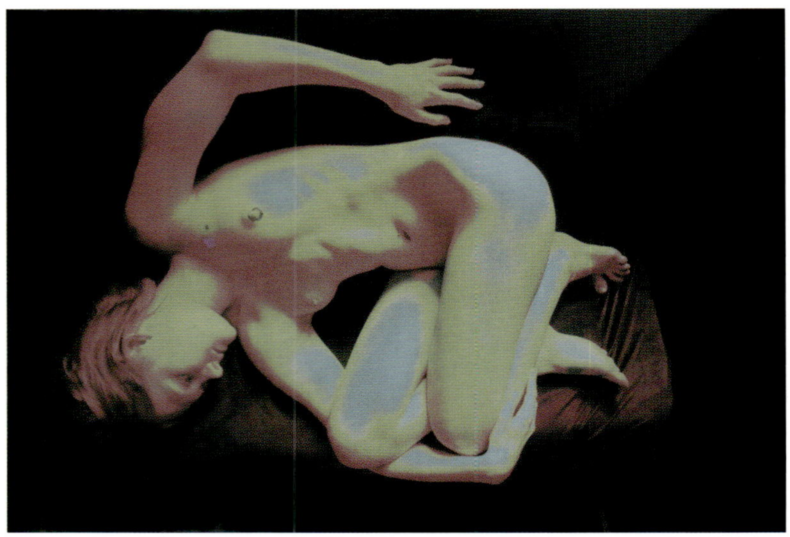

ABOVE: Selecting three tonal ranges.

RIGHT: Building up the color. Because you have each color on a separate layer, you can adjust their opacity to get the right balance and blend between them. If you've reduced the opacity of the color layers, try inverting the bottom (monochrome) layer. You can also use *Image>Adjustments>Hue/Saturation* to vary the layers.

Sabattier effects

In chemical photography, the Sabattier effect is a partial reversal of tones that occurs when film or paper is re-exposed to light during development. This re-exposure affects different tonal levels differently; in black-and-white photography some of the best-known examples are in Man Ray's so-called "Rayographs," with their typical hard black or white edges to areas where there's a strong change in tonal values.

Sabattier effects are notoriously difficult to replicate in the darkroom (no two prints ever come out the same), but on a computer they can be effectively simulated, and are much more easily controlled. They're achieved by using a Curves adjustment layer, shaping the RGB curve downwards to form a catenary curve.

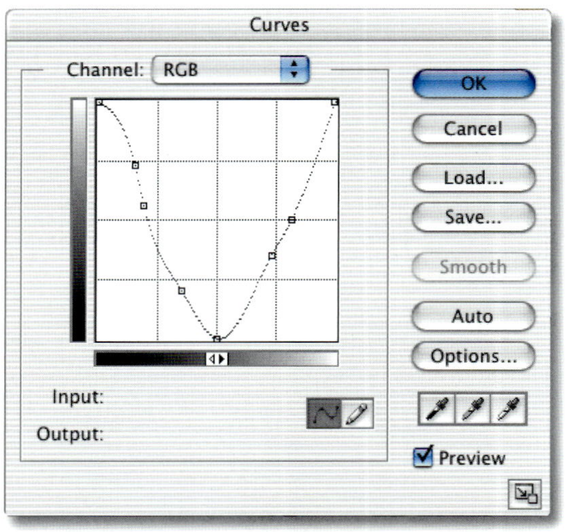

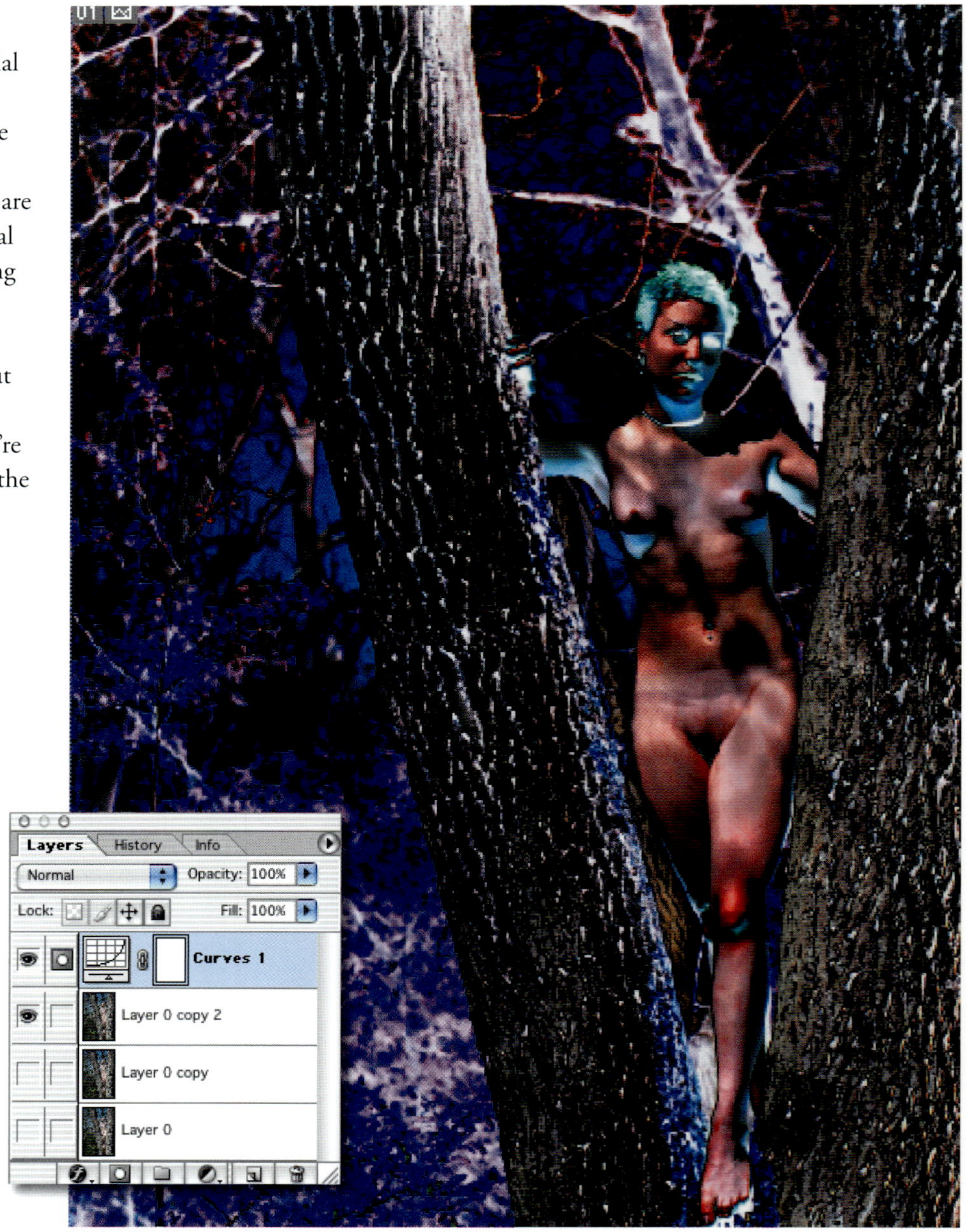

ABOVE: In this example I've created a curve whose lowest point is fairly central, but you can experiment by reshaping the curve more irregularly. You can also experiment with the Red, Green, and Blue channel curves separately. (When you've found a good set of Curves, you can save the settings to apply to other images.)

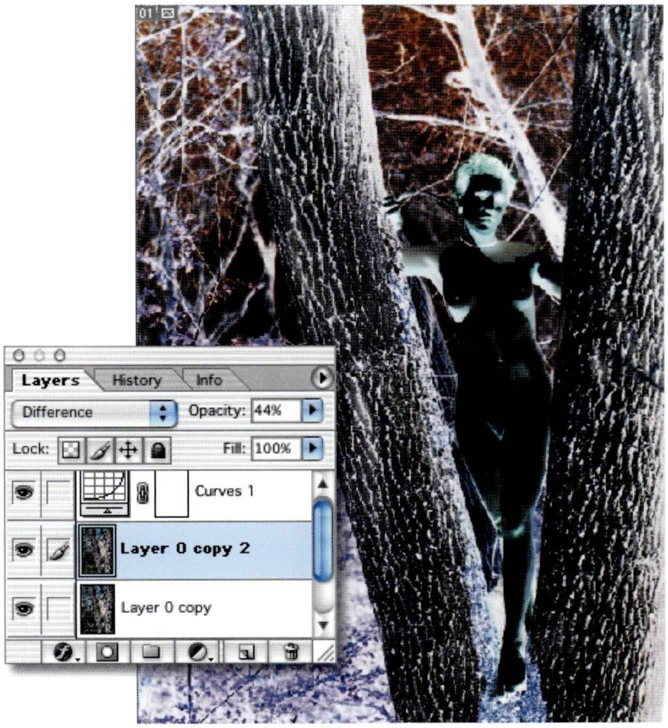

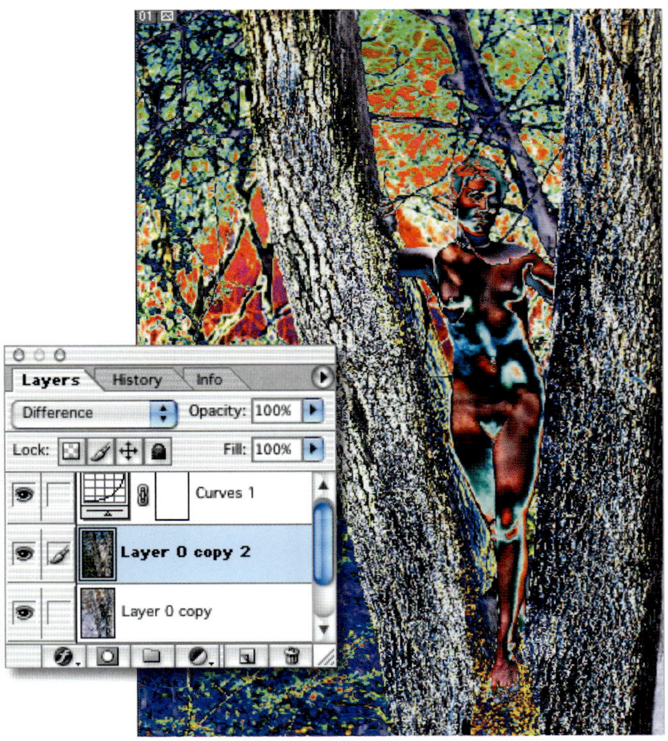

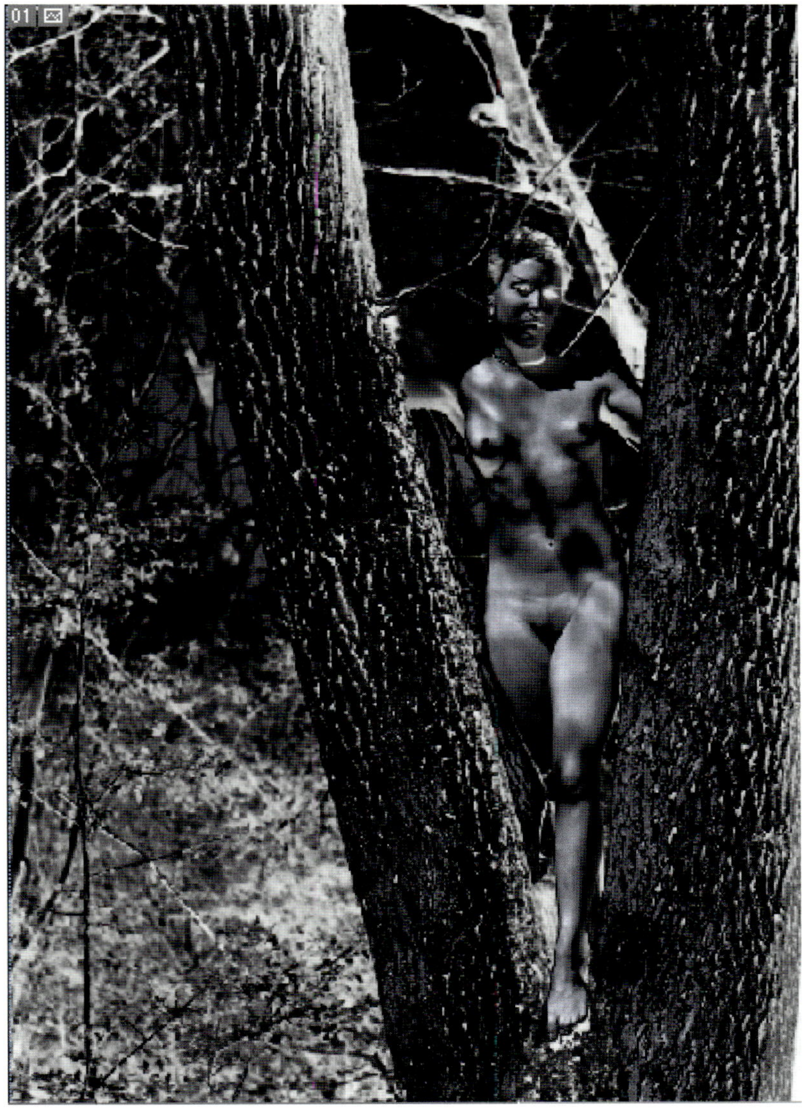

ABOVE LEFT AND LEFT: Sabattier effects work well with multiple layers. In particular, the Screen, Difference, and Exclusion blend modes produce striking effects. To use Difference you may need to reduce the opacity of the top layer, or Invert (make negative) the layer beneath it (or both).

ABOVE: You can also create Sabattier effects with monochrome images, again experimenting with the use of inverted layers. (All these examples were produced with the same Curves settings.) You'll often notice that small shadows or highlights (such as a catchlight in the model's eye) turn into very noticeable hotspots or black blobs when you apply any of these treatments, so a certain amount of tidying up of the image may be necessary.

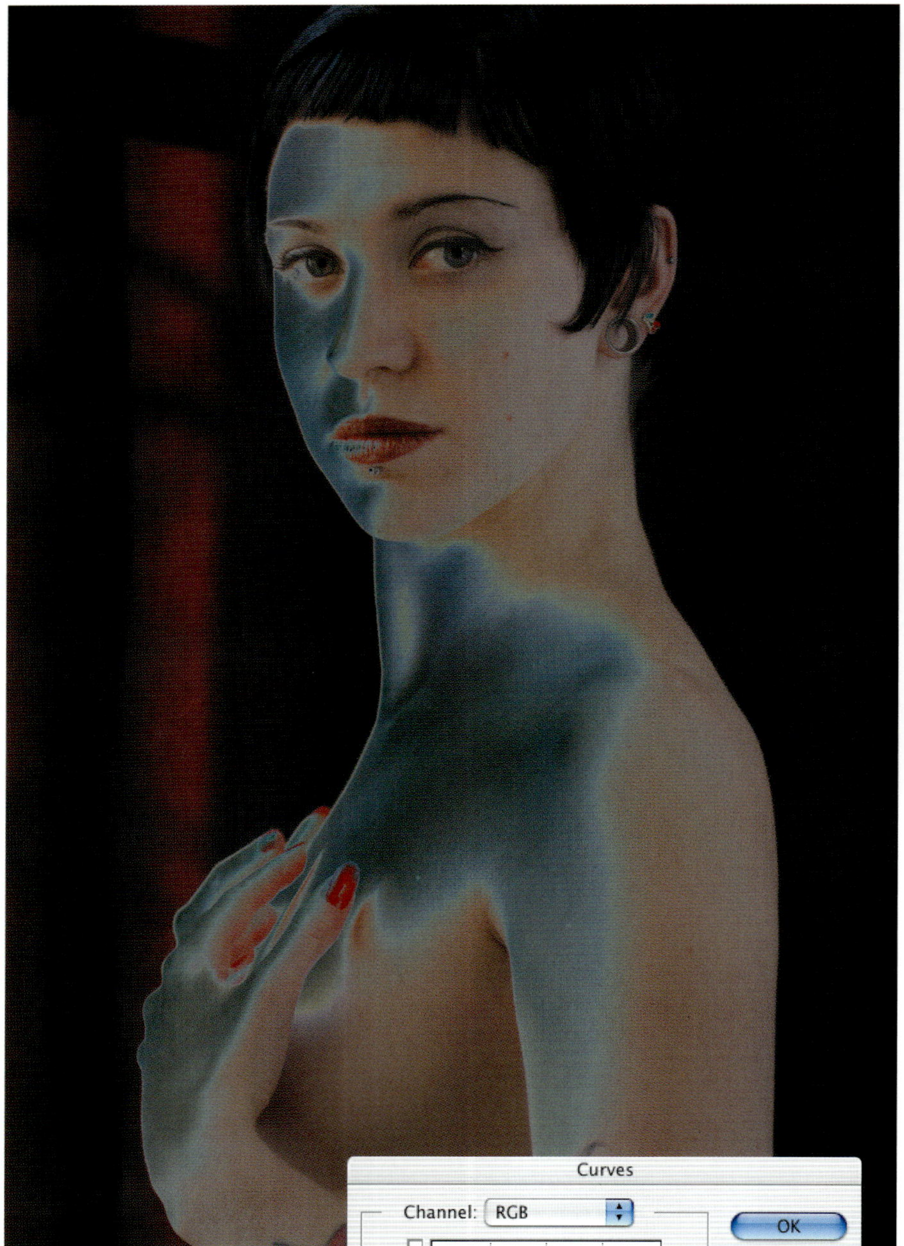

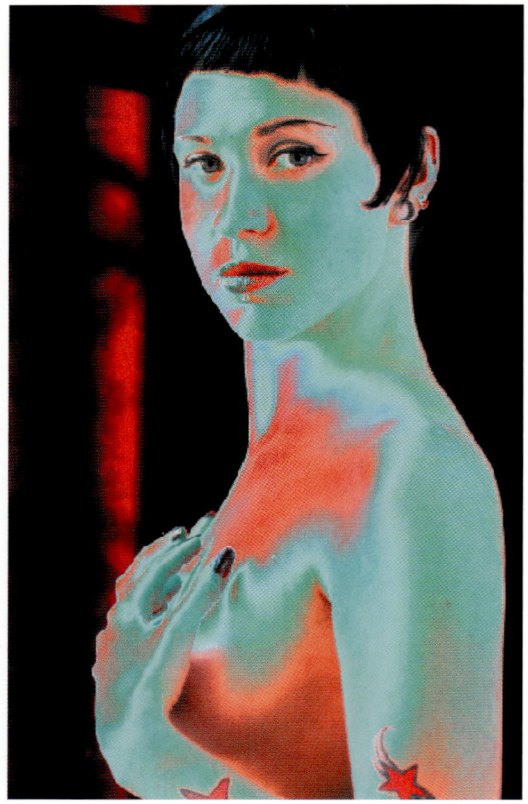

THIS PAGE: Using Curves to achieve solarization effects.

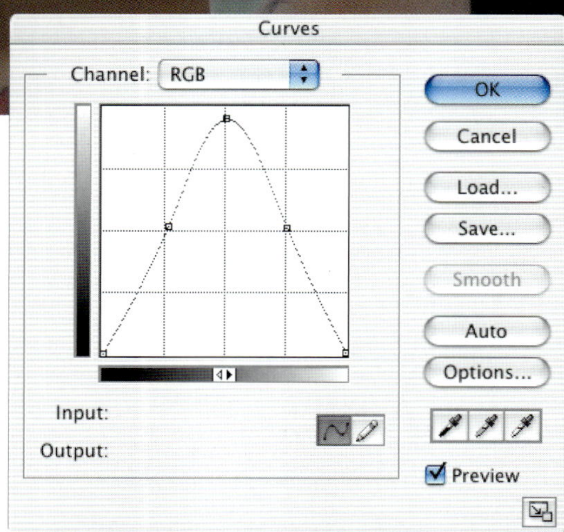

Solarization

In digital photography, solarization has come to refer to a set of effects that overlap with Sabattier. Photoshop provides *Filter>Stylize>Solarize,* but you can't adjust its results, and it tends to produce very flat images.

On the other hand, if you use Curves, but this time shape the curve upward, you'll produce brighter, punchier solarization effects, which you can control and vary. Inverting the base image produces different results.

While color solarization is interesting to play with, its effects tend to be unpredictable, with tiny adjustments to the curve(s) making a big difference to the image. Solarization seems to me to come fully into its own with monochrome images, where the riot of rather random color we've seen in the last few examples is subdued by the simplifying effect of black and white.

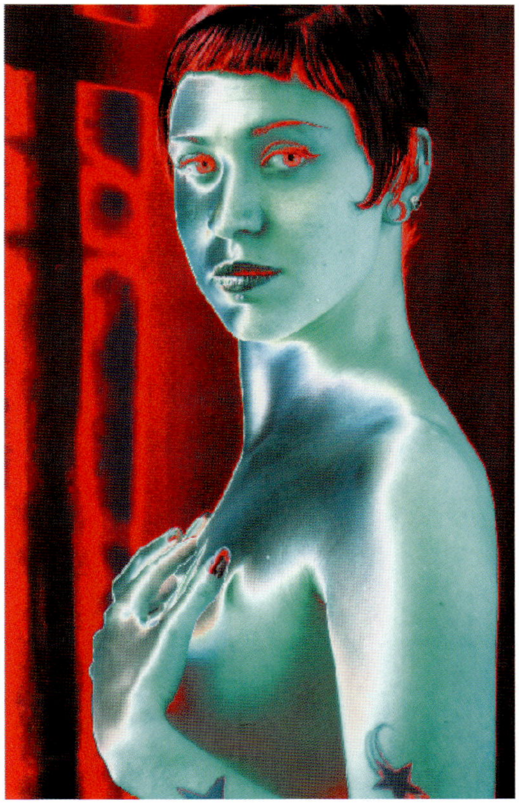

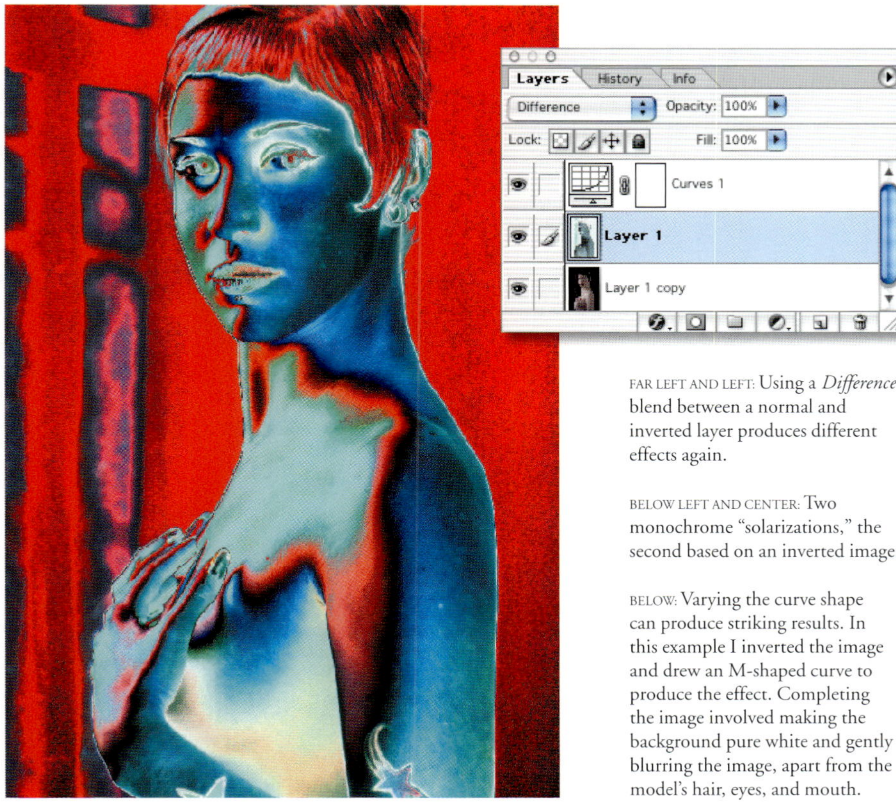

FAR LEFT AND LEFT: Using a *Difference* blend between a normal and inverted layer produces different effects again.

BELOW LEFT AND CENTER: Two monochrome "solarizations," the second based on an inverted image.

BELOW: Varying the curve shape can produce striking results. In this example I inverted the image and drew an M-shaped curve to produce the effect. Completing the image involved making the background pure white and gently blurring the image, apart from the model's hair, eyes, and mouth.

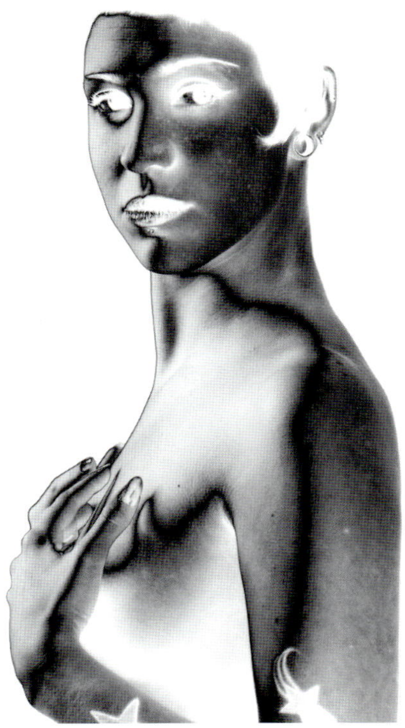

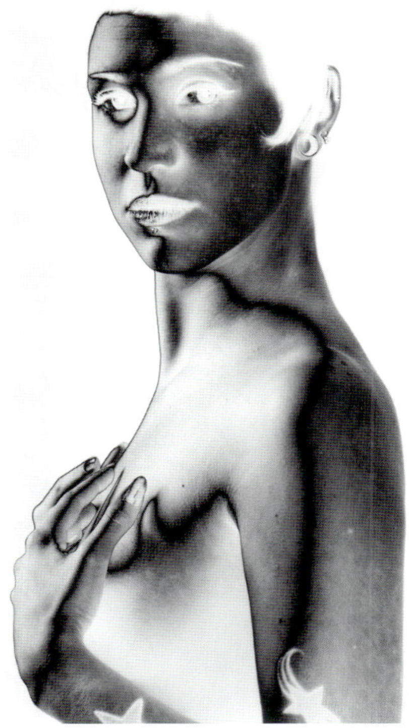

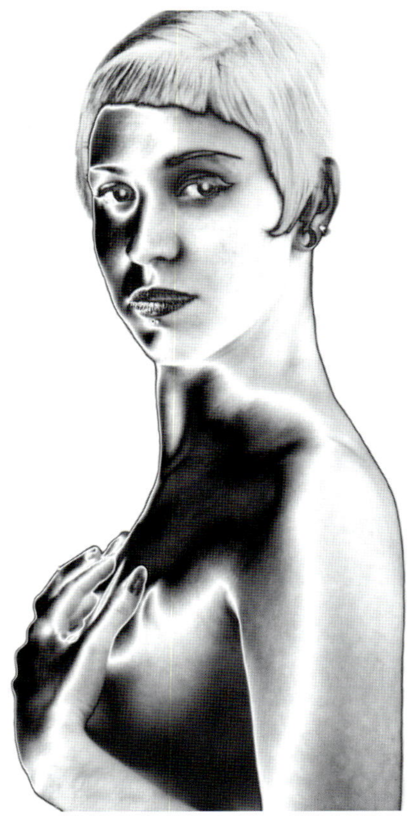

Showcase

Just as physical attraction between people is impossible to put into words—we can't explain why it's there, it just is—erotic photography is not something that can be categorized neatly and put into a box. All our desires and fantasies are unique, so an image that one person will find arousing may leave the next completely cold.

The images in this showcase section represent a broad range of approaches to the genre by a number of photographers from different parts of the world. They share the common ground of working with one or more models of either sex, but there the similarity ends. This is an area of photography above all others where the photographers' individuality and ideals are as exposed as their subjects.

The techniques employed to create these images differ widely, too. For some, the digital aspect of their work is confined to scanning a conventional print with basic adjustments for color and contrast. Others have embraced the editing process, conceiving the entire production from start to finish in advance, with many separate images and hours of work with layers and masks behind the final result. This section of the book explores the background of each image and reveals how it was achieved. The aim is to provide inspiration and to reveal the extraordinary and diverse talents that abound in this genre.

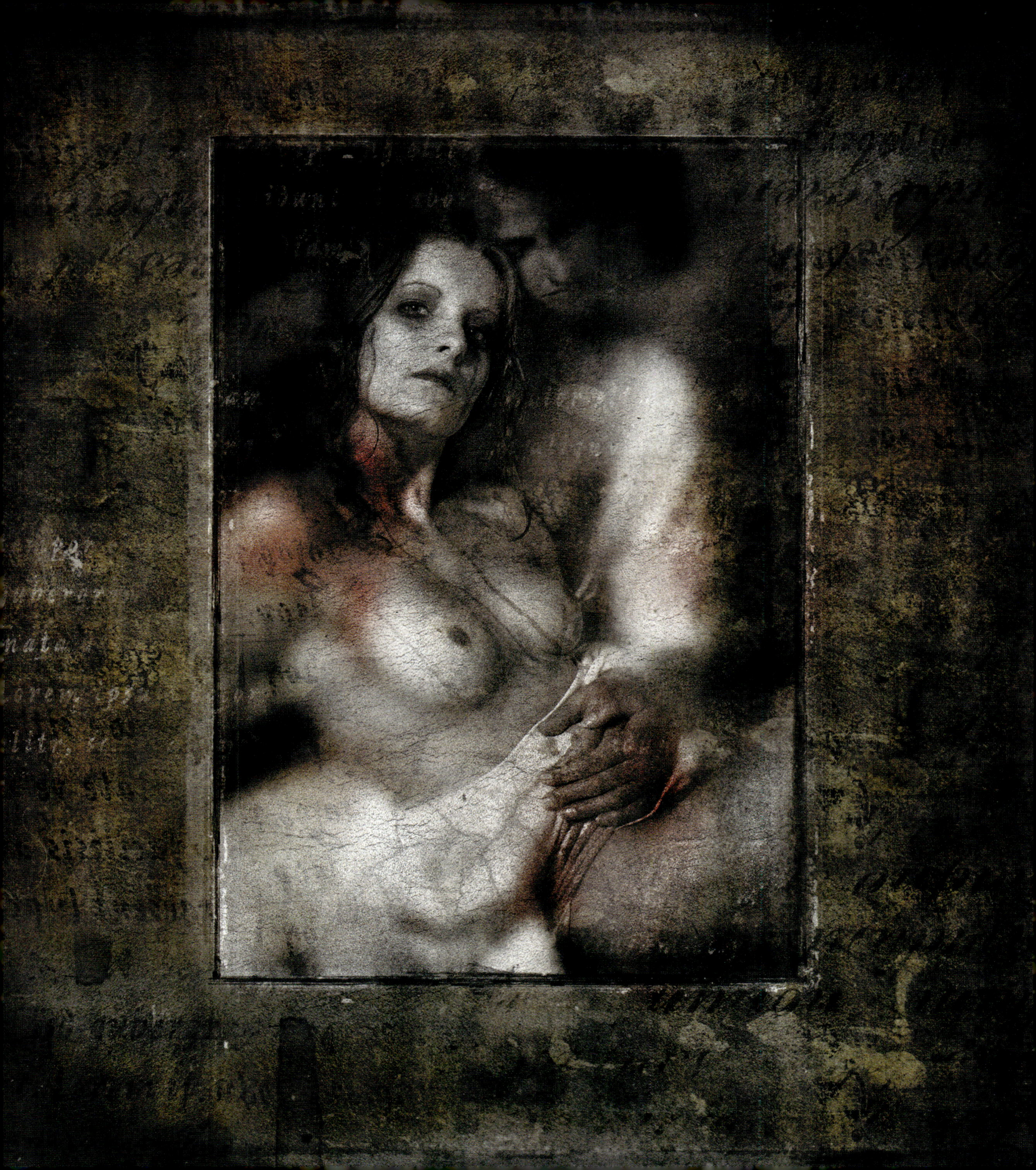

Charly B

A photographer for over 40 years, Charly B describes photography as his passion rather than his profession. Erotic imagery is his specialty, shot both on location and in the studio, and recently he has embraced digital techniques as a way of adding a further element of fantasy to his work.

BELOW: Photographed in natural light in an outdoor location, the original shot had a background that was too cluttered and distracting with all the detail of the tattoos. Charly used Motion blur in Photoshop on this area, ensuring that the blurred effect followed the direction of the bricks. The result echoes the colors on the body in a complementary way and adds interest without dominating the bold composition.

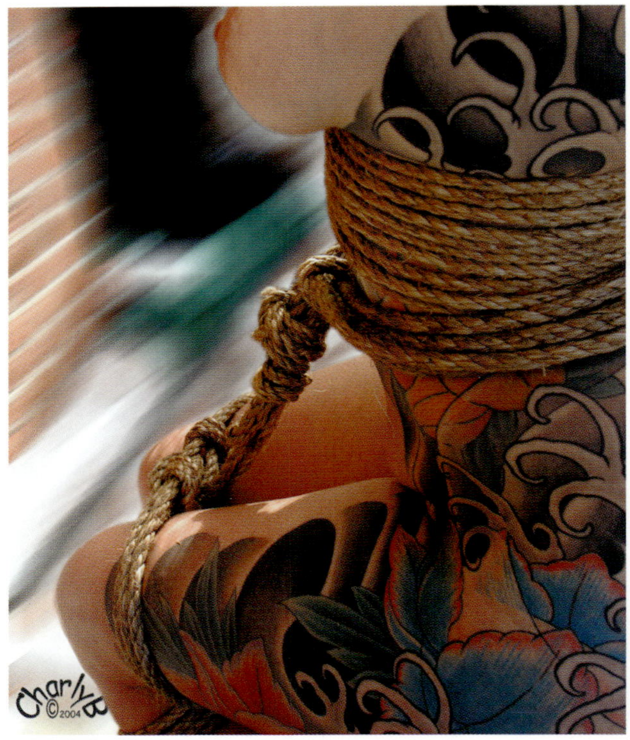

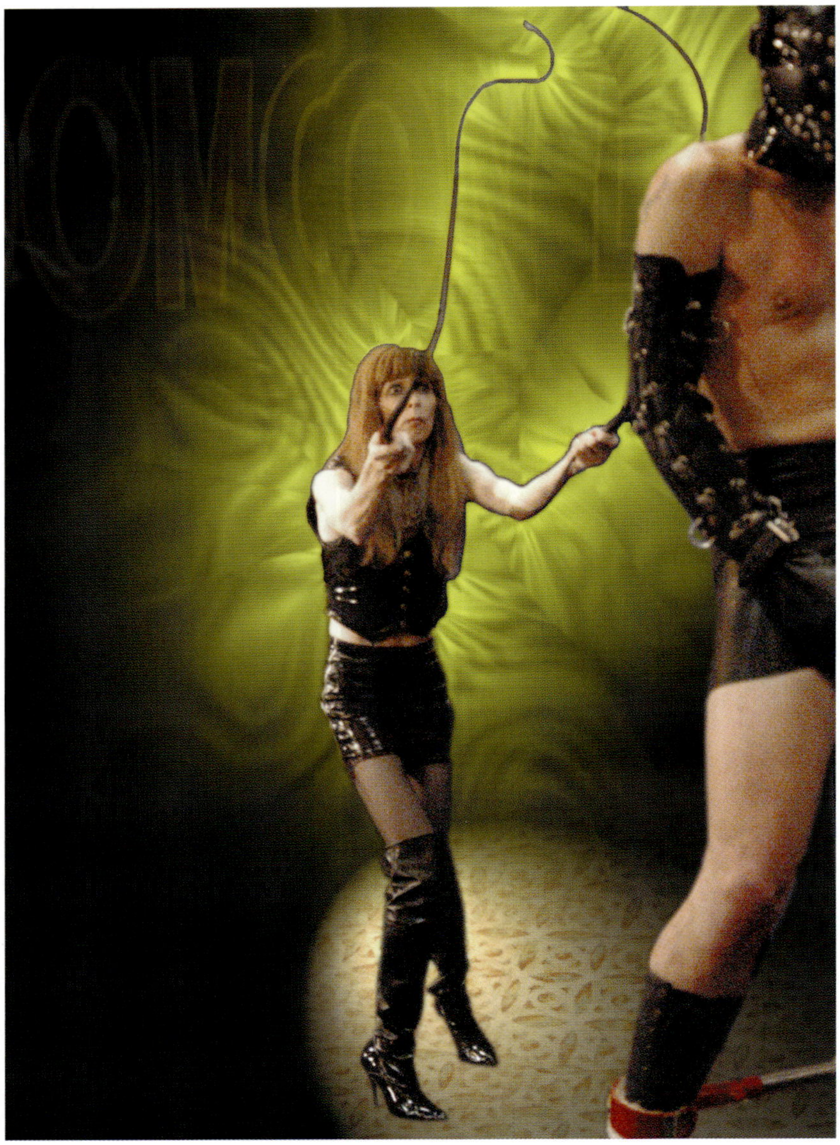

LEFT: This shot was taken live at the DomCon 2004 event in Hollywood and, because Charly had no control over the setting, the original was too distracting and messy. "The mistress, who promoted the event, and her slave, were cut out from the original picture and put on a transparent layer," he explains. "The next layer had the DomCon banner, which I had to piece together as I didn't have a clear shot of it. Below that was the carpet from another photograph, and with it the spotlight from Photoshop's Lighting Effects filter. Controlling the ambience associated with the filter essentially blocked out everything else. Then the corona from the Eye Candy plug-in was placed around the mistress, with reduced opacity to allow the banner to show through."

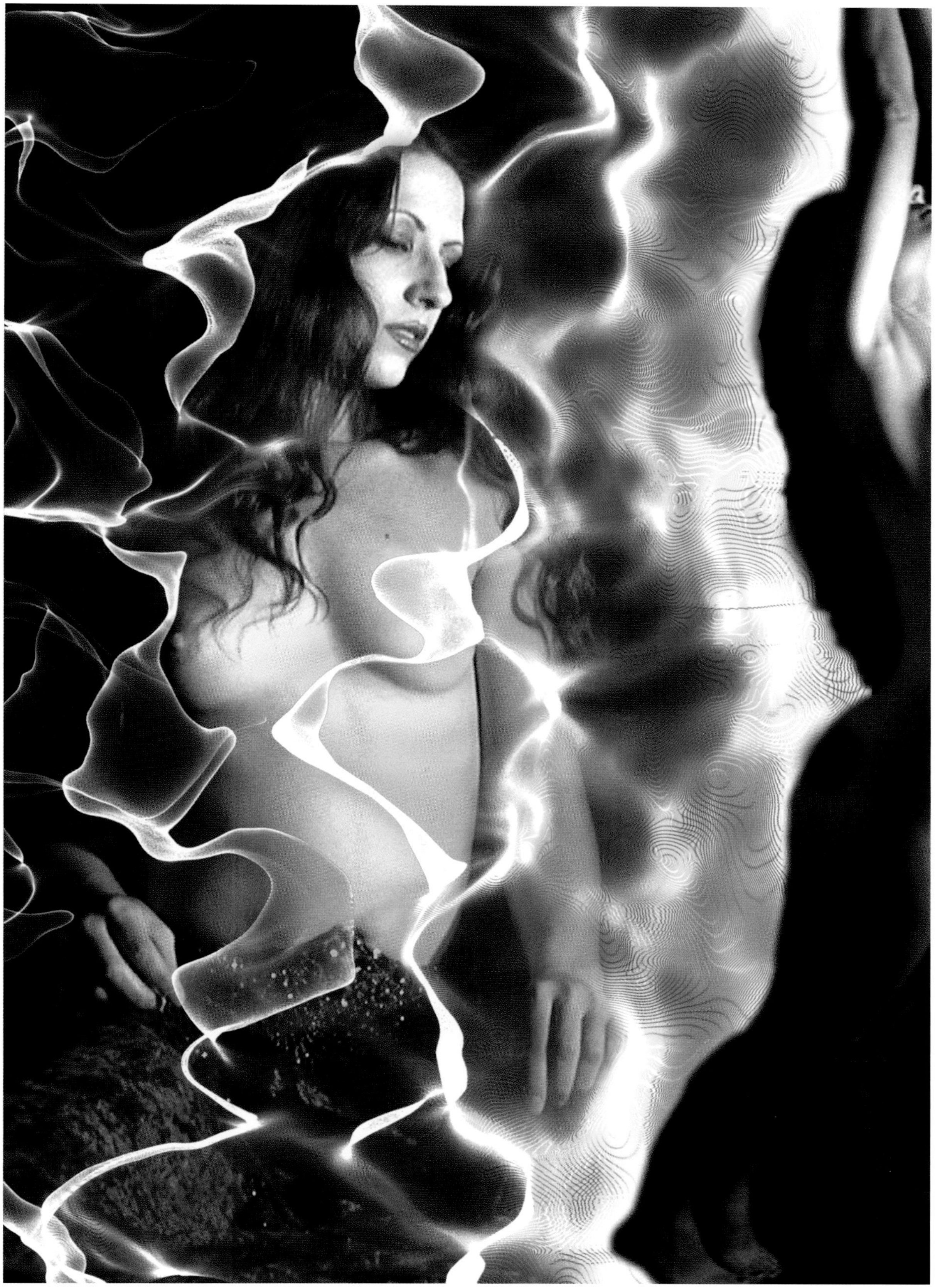

LEFT: "This image started out with the arched pose of Lena Ramon, one of my favorite models," says Charly. "The original shot was cut out in Photoshop, feathered, and placed on a transparent layer. Then the image was selected and the selection moved just inside the actual image to eliminate any halo effect. The smoke is from Eye Candy, a Photoshop plug-in that can be manipulated to fit in with any situation. This was placed over the bottom layers to create an image of neverending motion."

G. W. Burns

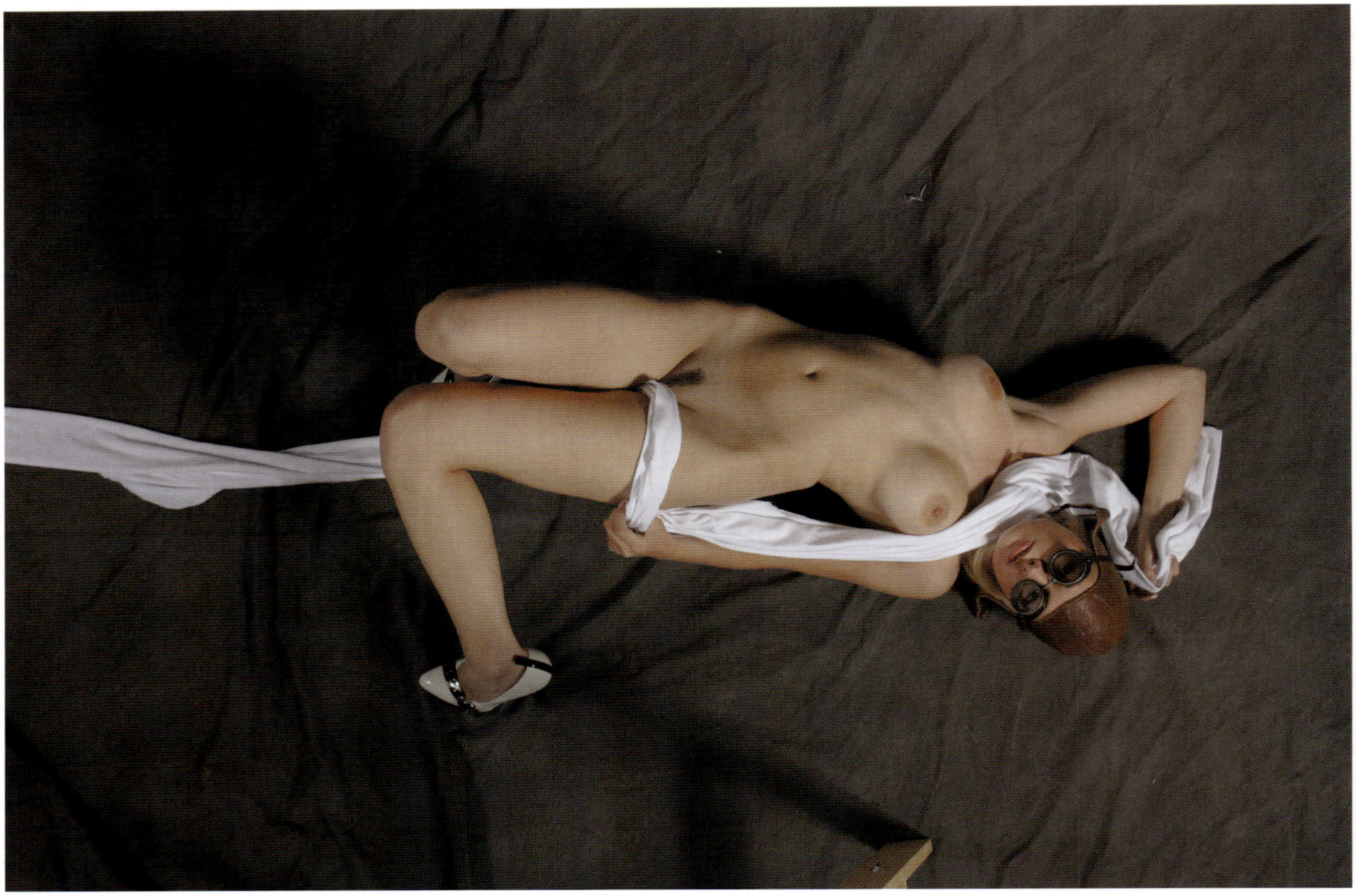

G. W. Burns has been working with Photoshop for around three years, producing images that have been exhibited and published in magazines such as *FHM*. He often goes on location, photographing landscapes, textures, and details that can be used as backgrounds. Merging these with shots of models to create a mood and tell a story is a challenge that he particularly enjoys.

ALL IMAGES: "The image *Damned If You Do* was one of those that evolved after the shoot," explains Burns. "I shot *Penthouse* centerfold Martina Warren in my studio, against a plain background, and the original idea was to merge this image of her onto another shot of an old World War I biplane. When I went to the hangar later, I found that the logistics of it prevented me from getting the angle I had intended, so I was forced to ad-lib. I thought it might be fun to have her falling out of the sky, and the addition of the ocean with sharks swimming below just seemed to compound her already precarious predicament. The image is made up of three layers: Martina, the clouds, and the water, with sharks merged into one. Lassoing the desired items and blending them together is rather easy when you have images that work together. I like to shoot models lying on the ground while I am perched on a ladder from above as it gives you a lot of flexibility in what you can do with them afterwards. It is always a good idea to smooth out any lines from seams and to use the opacity level to help blend any merged images."

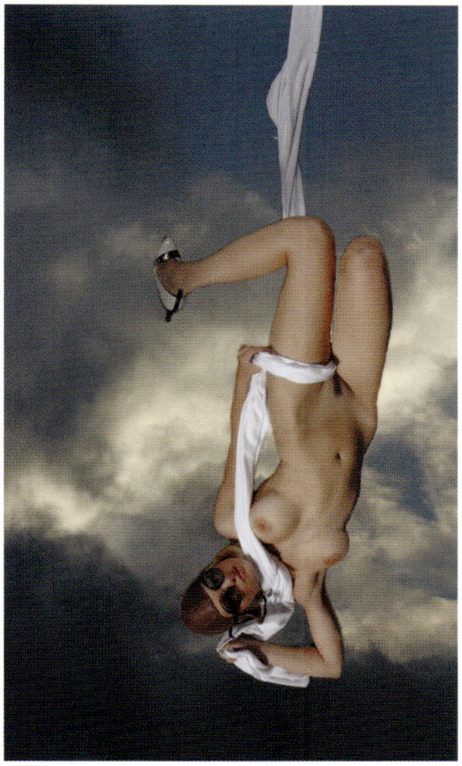

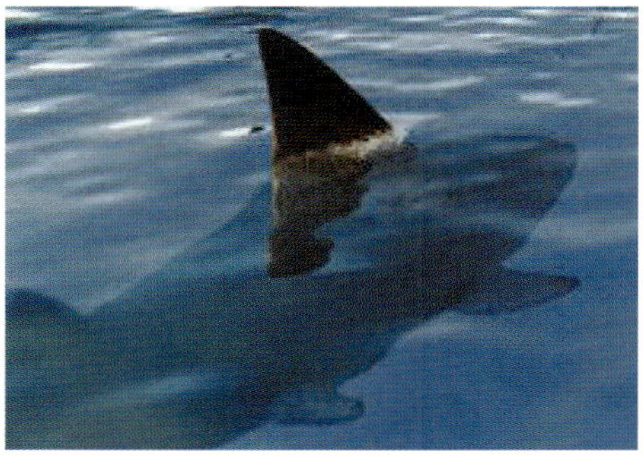

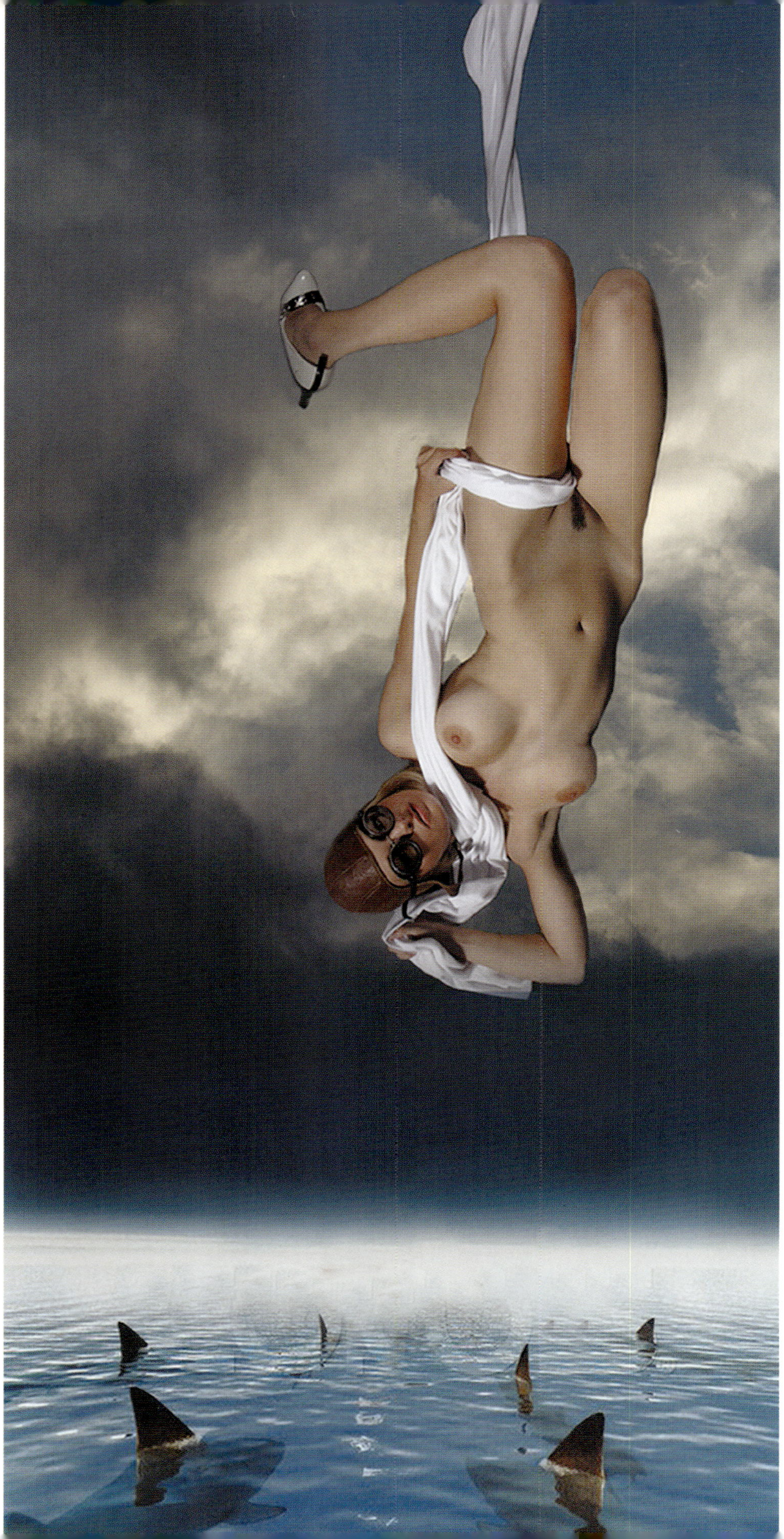

G. W. Burns

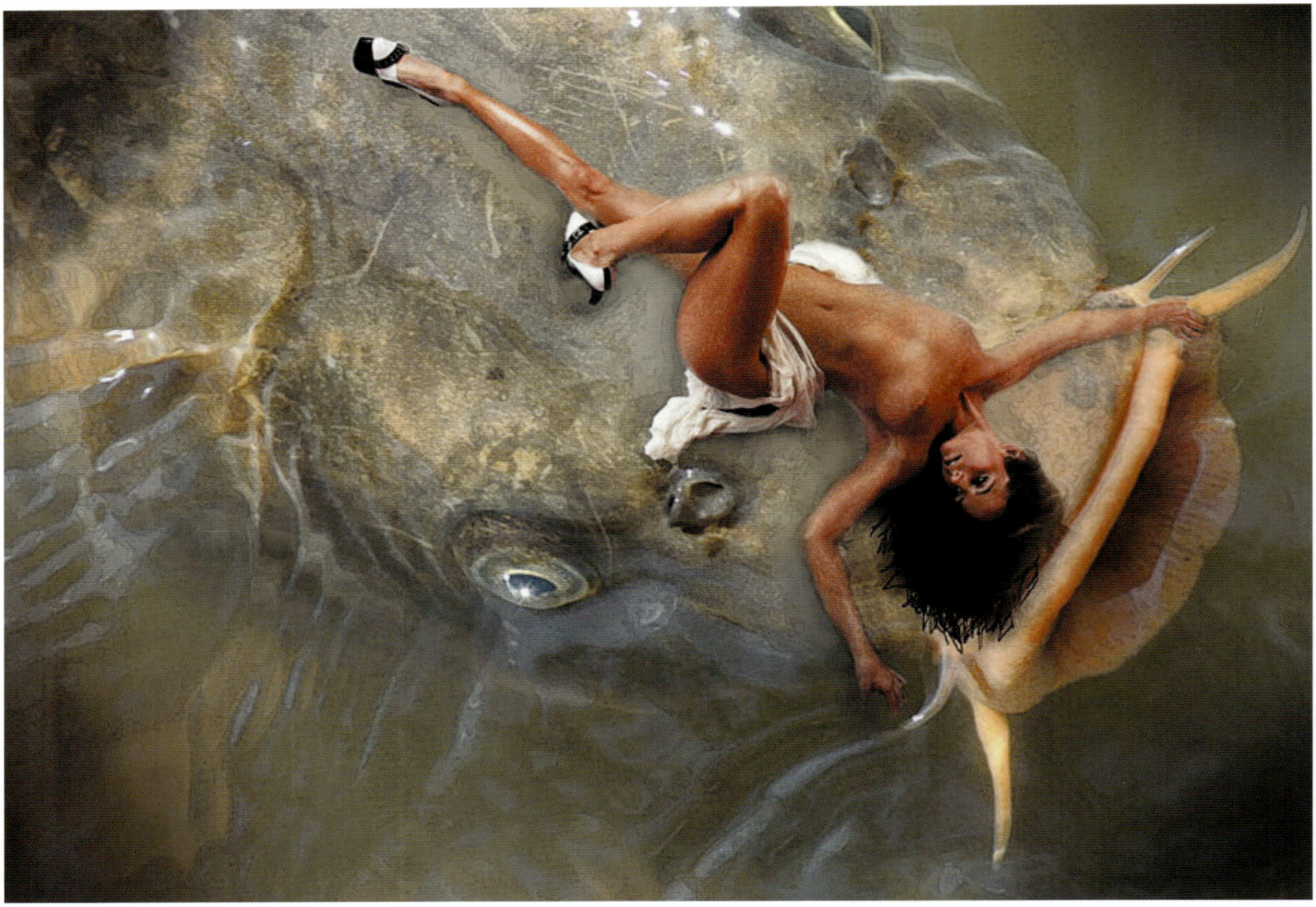

ABOVE AND RIGHT: "There are certain images from one's childhood that linger long into your adulthood," comments Burns. "I remember Captain Ahab in *Moby Dick* entangled in the harpoon line on the back of the great beast. So when I took the image of Angela Marie on the floor of my studio, I was suddenly struck with the similarity of the pose and thought it might make a cool picture. Remembering that I had shot some Japanese koi in the Missouri Botanical Garden just a few weeks earlier, I thought one of them could serve as my modern day Moby Dick. After layering the two images together, I used a Photoshop filter from Flaming Pear called Aetherize to get the dramatic, wild colorization. Like any layering technique, smoothing out the seams so that they blend together can be a time-consuming affair, but well worth it afterwards."

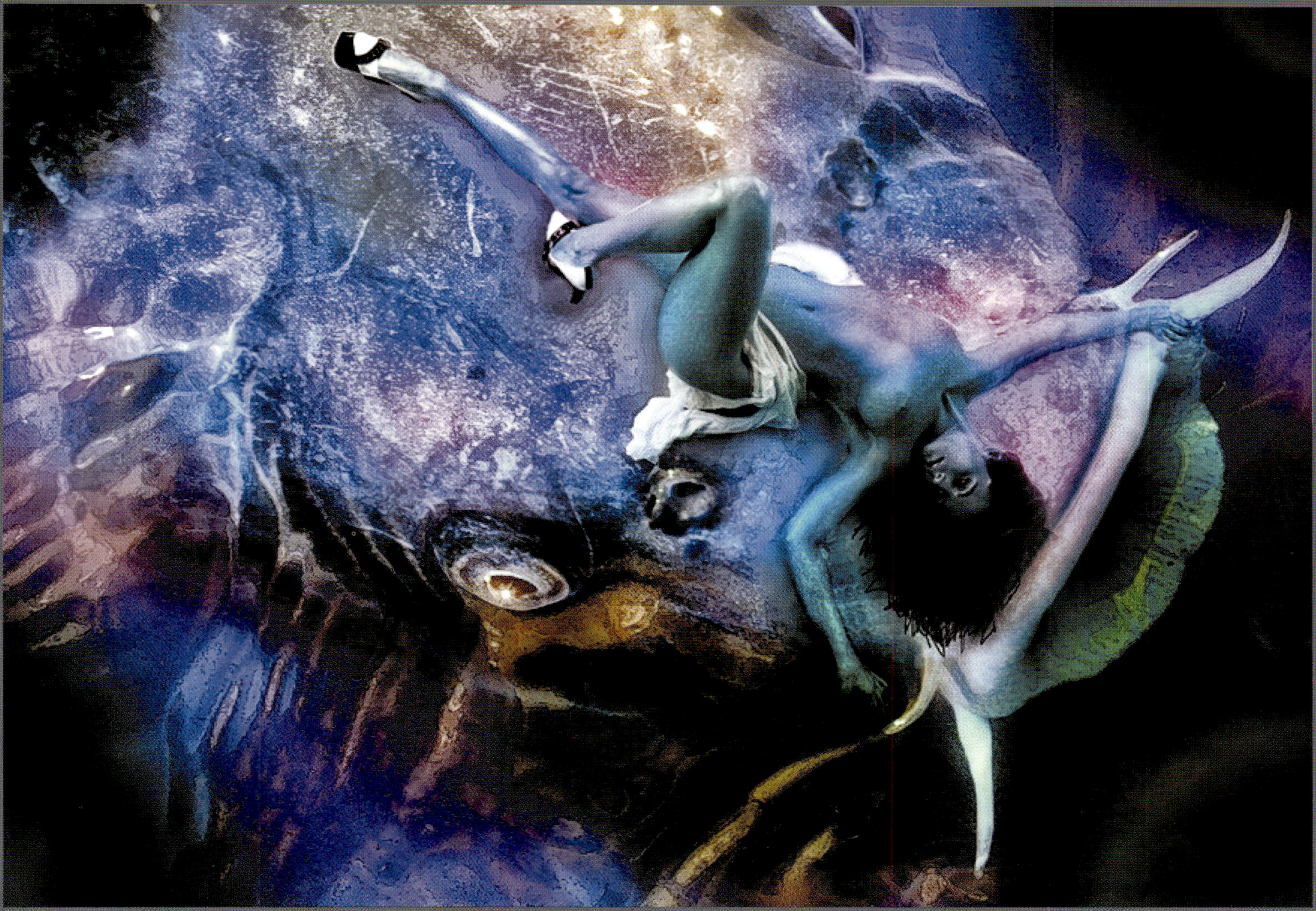

G. W. Burns

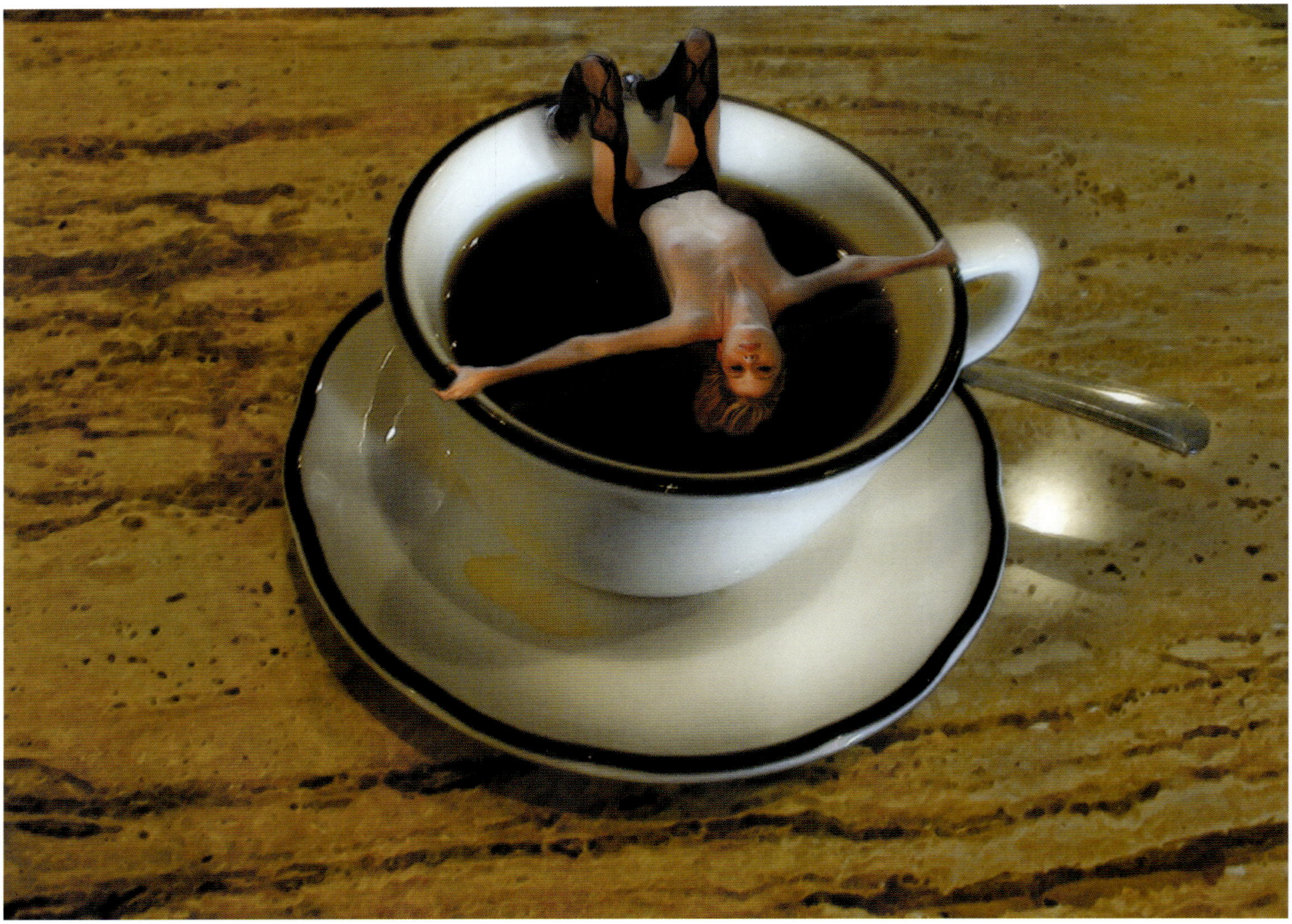

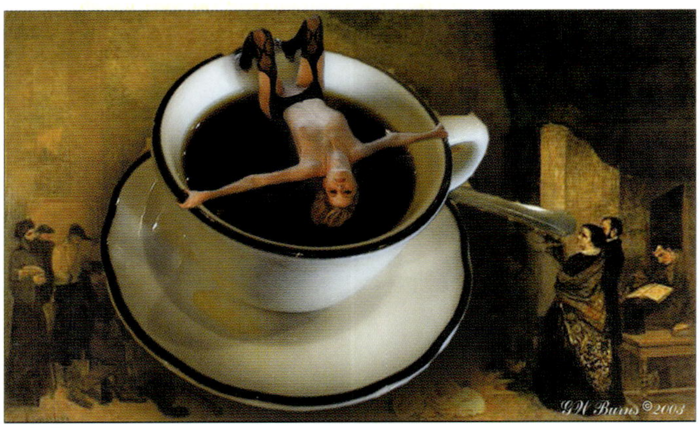

ABOVE AND LEFT: Once again, this image, entitled *Not Your Average Cup of Joe*, started out with a studio shot of a model lying on the floor, and photographed from above. Burns had quite different plans for it in the beginning, though, as he explains, "I had the idea of having Dixon hanging precariously over the mouth of an active volcano. Of course, finding an active volcano that I could photograph proved to be an impossible task. One morning, while I was pondering what to layer her over, sitting there right in front of my computer was my cup of coffee. Sometimes serendipity is a photographer's best friend. After several layers and adding the Degas painting underneath as a background, I emerged with a rather fun image."

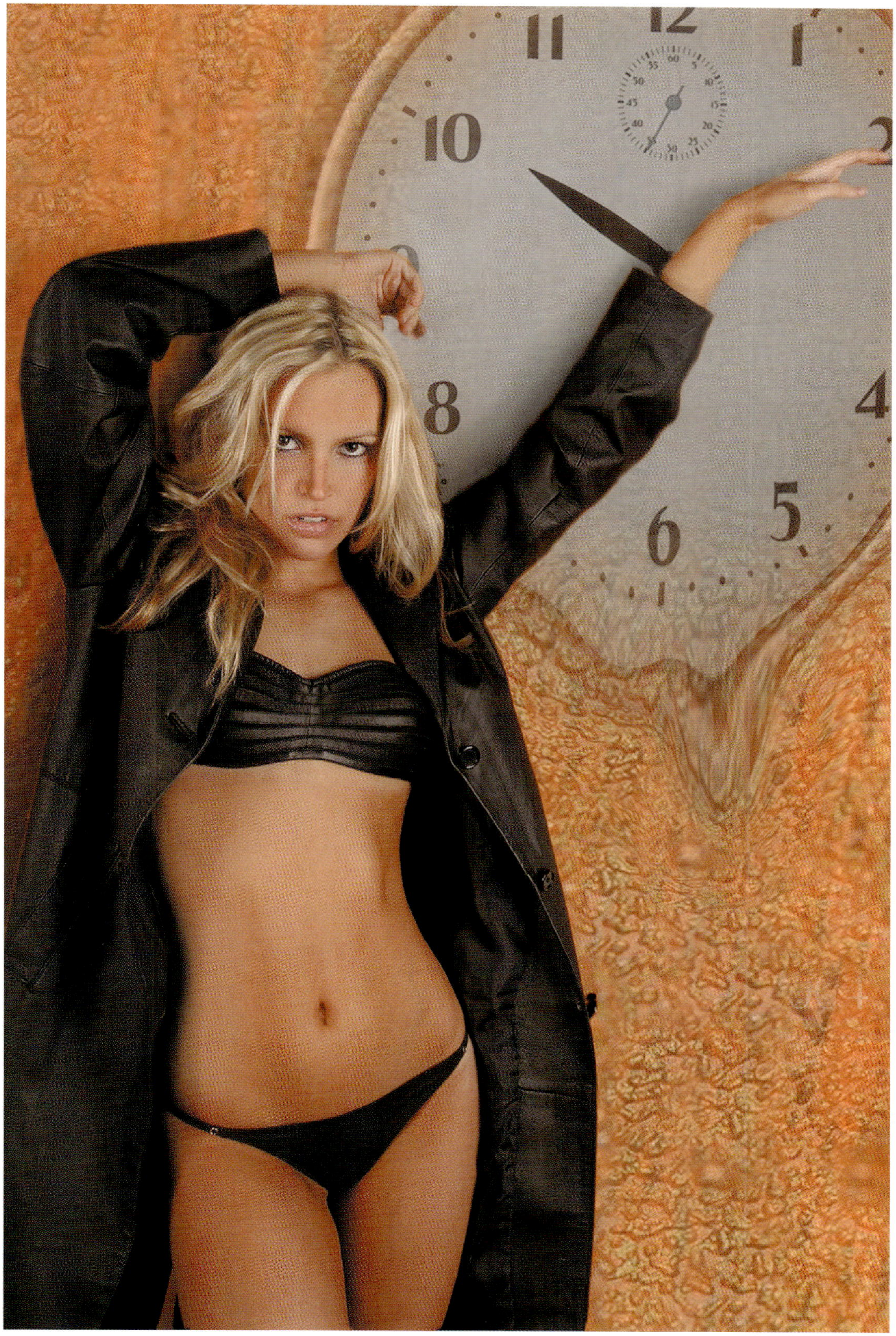

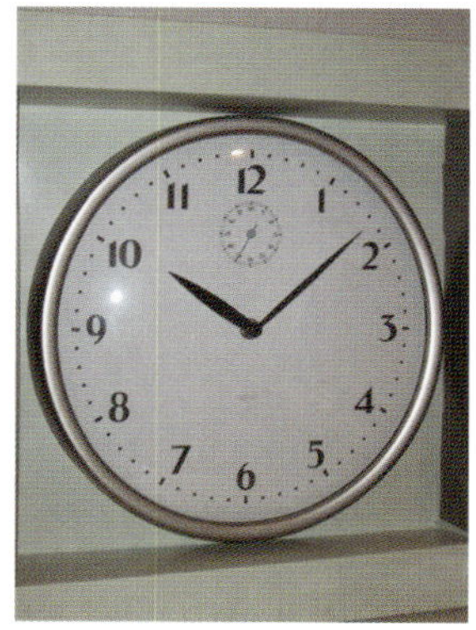

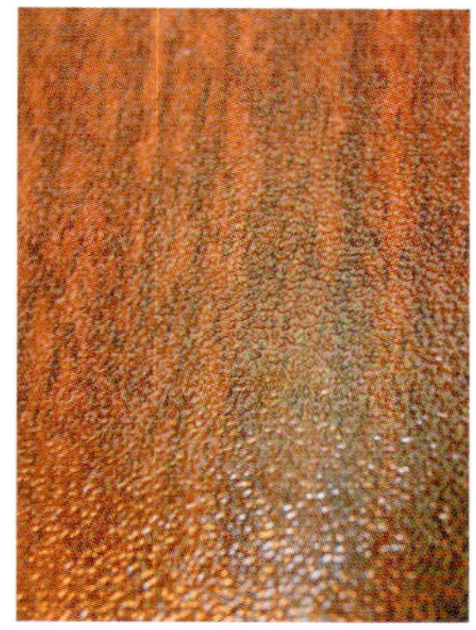

THIS PAGE: "This image was actually one of those that took shape after the shoot," says Burns. "I had painted one of my walls in the studio a bright orange, and after taking some images of Abriana against it, the classic book and movie title, *A Clockwork Orange*, seemed like a cool idea to run with. After cleaning up the shadows and slight imperfections of the original photo, I layered a texture on the back orange wall and faded the opacity so that they blended together. I then added the clock and used the Liquify tool to make it appear as if it were melting. Once again the opacity was faded so that the underlying layers bled together. I had to make a duplicate of the image and lasso Abriana from the original so that I could paste over the composite. Before doing this, though, I airbrushed her shadow over the composite image to create depth, and then added the pasted image from the original. A little cleanup with the Cloning tool around the pasted images improved the seams. Voilà, *A Clockwork Orange!*"

Derek Caballero

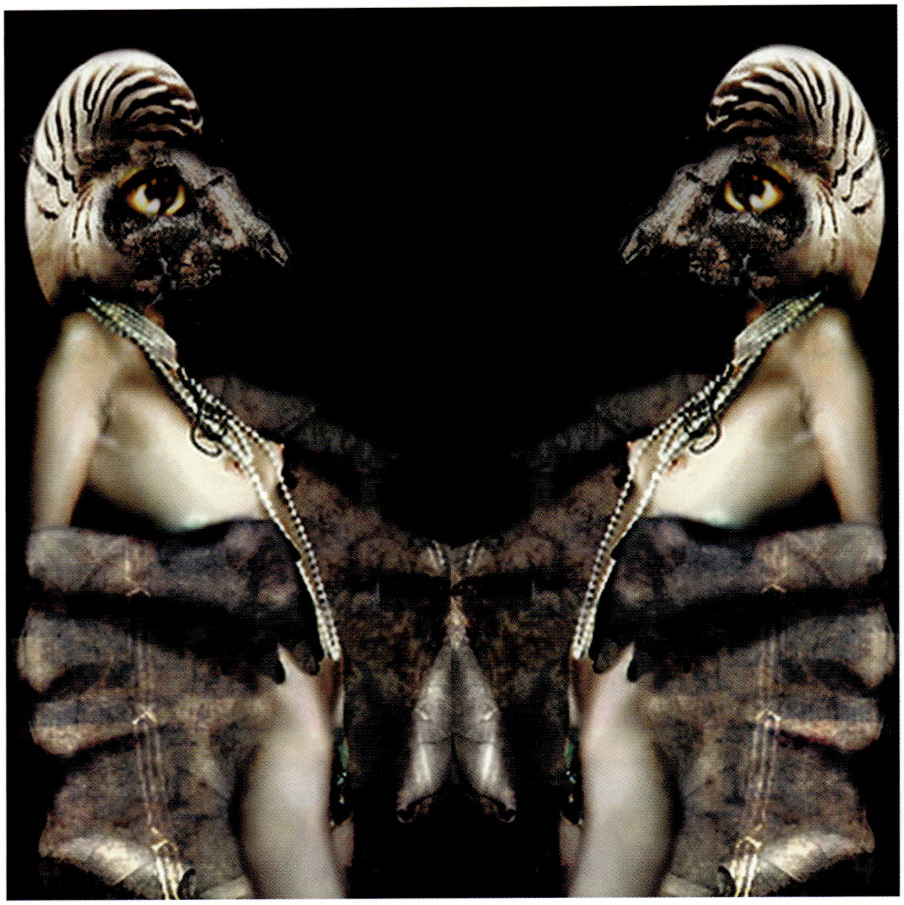

LEFT AND BELOW: *Sabe* is a fantasy figure, "a tribute to female power," explains Caballero. "The helmet of a tiger's skull represents sensuality and strength, and the eyes gaze into the future, seeing all and remaining calm." The body of the model, including the pearl necklace, was photographed in soft, ambient light, and Caballero then found an image of a saber-toothed tiger's skull he felt would work as her head, and suit the body posture. "I layered the head on to the body and used the Burn mode to create additional density. The skull looked too obvious, so I added the nautilus shell, using Dodge, Burn, and Eraser to make it look like an extension to the skull. The eye belongs to a friend of mine and was cut, pasted, and layered into the skull to give human feelings to the fantasy figure. By that stage, I had had enough work so walked to a café, finding a beautiful leaf on my way. That was my fabric draped over Sabe's arm, with a metal sunglasses case overlaid in Burn mode to add more texture. The curves in the leaf were produced by shading and blurring it slightly into Sabe's leg as if it were connected. I call this kind of pixel blurring 'welding.'"

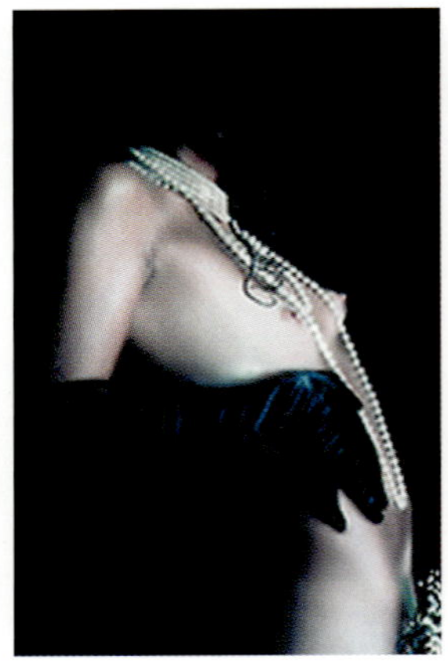

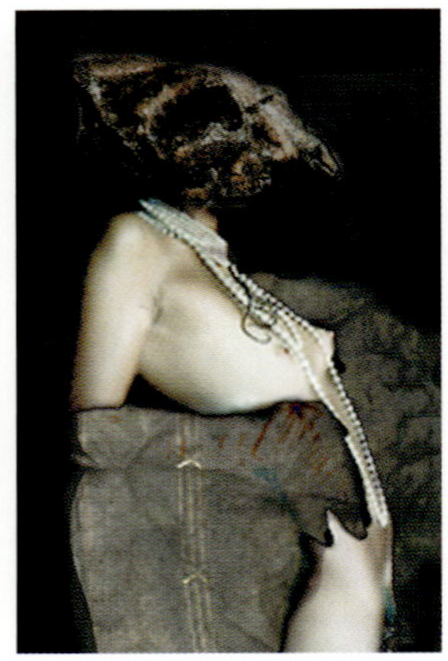

Derek Caballero is a relative newcomer to digital technology but now uses it in preference to film for much of his personal and commissioned work. He uses the digital camera to create painterly images, even before he manipulates tones, contrast, and colors in Photoshop, using broad strokes like a painter on canvas rather than a technician. He was an award winner in the digital, beauty, music, and wedding categories in the 2004 Lucie Awards.

OPPOSITE PAGE, BOTTOM: The image started off as a nude portrait of a model, whom Caballero gradually transformed and partially clothed, drawing from his stock of bone and fossil images and the Dodge and Burn tools in Photoshop. He first created the "cloak" by finding a bone photograph and curving it to the right shape. To give the cloak more weight, he duplicated it and blended the two layers together, carefully erasing and burning to blend the two together. Then a textile pattern, in the form of an image of a seashell fossil, was added in Burn mode, and the cloak was lengthened with fossilized clam shells.

Next the model's hair drew Caballero's attention: "It was purple and punky in style, and I wanted a more regal red," he says. "I worked on two separate hair pieces by carefully erasing from the center of the hair and adding to it with another layer of hair, doing this dozens of times until it looked natural. To add drama and mystique, I produced a rim light around the figure, created with the Diffused Glow filter." Finally, he reduced contrast with Curves adjustment and added a faint texture of grain.

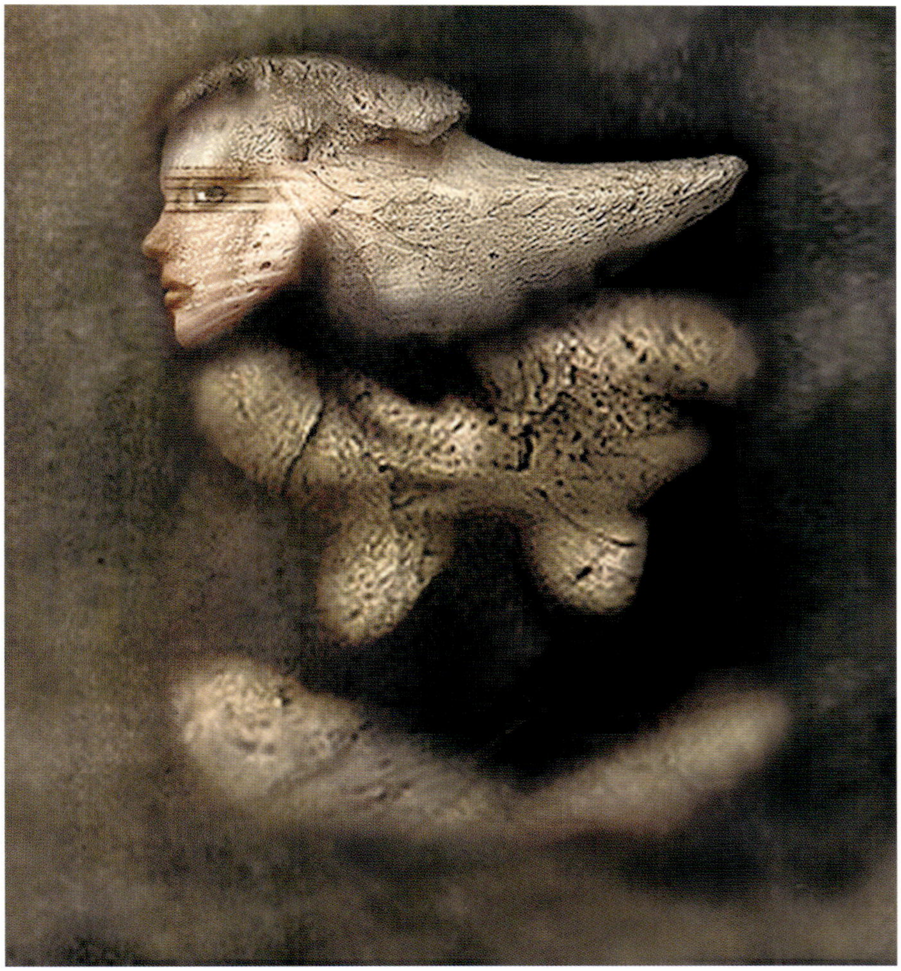

LEFT: *The Disembodied Yoga* grew from a concept of the separation of the mind from the body, with the fossil representing wisdom and timelessness. To bring the carved appearance of a statue to the image, Caballero began with two photographs. The first was a profile of a bald girl looking sideways at him, lit with a 650-watt lamp to create a hard light around her face. The body shot was a different model, leaning over with her legs crossed, lit with a Mole Richardson studio light with a Fresnel lens. The images were combined and then overlaid with a photograph of a rock, enlarged until it looked like very porous stone. For the head, he used a fossil of an animal claw and overlaid it on top of the profile of the face. Setting Opacity to 60 per cent, he was able to erase parts of the fossil away, so that it appeared to be an extension of the girl's head; then he dodged and burned to create shadows and highlights. "The entire piece didn't come together until I shadowed between the head and torso, thus creating the floating body sections," explains Caballero. "To remove the density around her, I added a layer of texture to wrap the outer edges of the entire image. Finally, I played with color variations until I found the final palette."

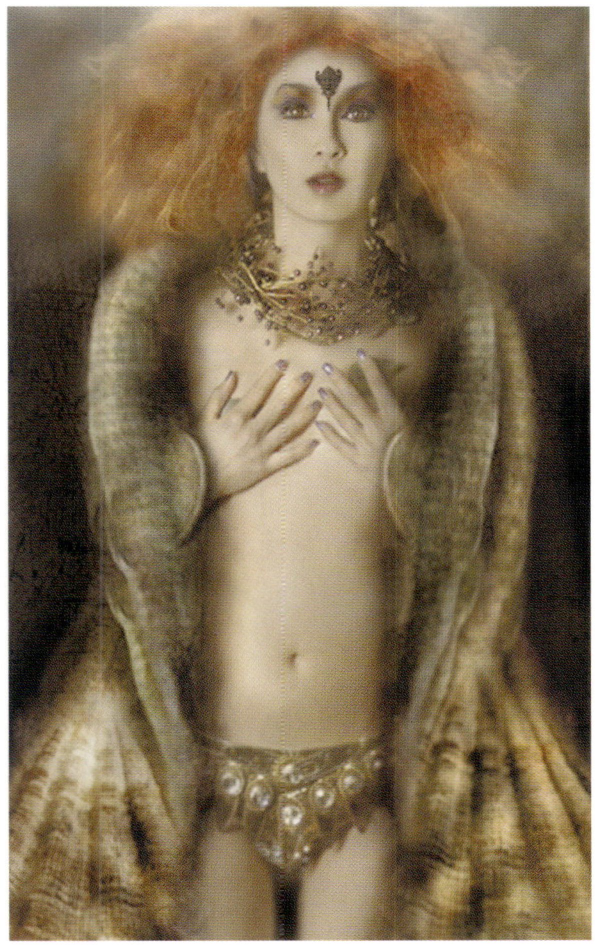

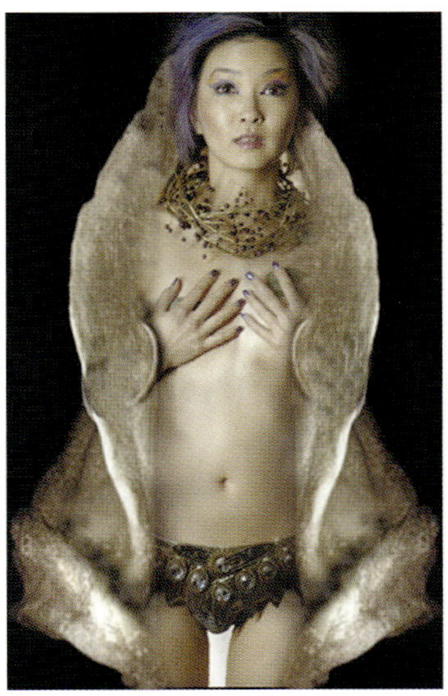

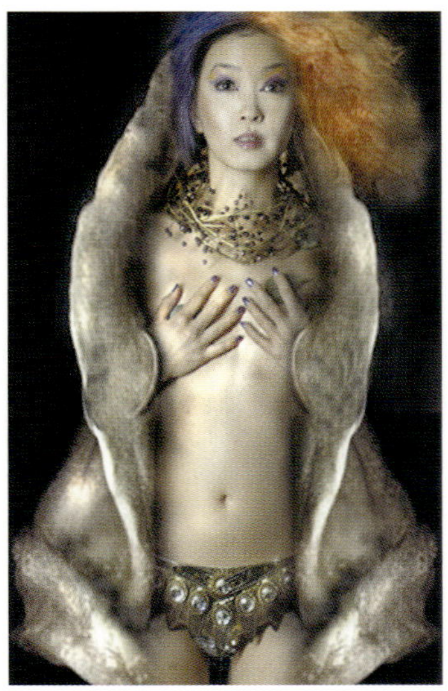

Derek Caballero

BELOW: *The Mermaid's* erotic values lie in the look, the pose, and the costume of the model, but the lighting and the color cast add to the atmosphere and nautical theme. Much of the work was done during the initial shoot in the studio. Caballero used a Nikon D100 camera with the light provided by a Kino Flo, which has a slightly green cast, mixed with tungsten, which gives a yellow one. The final color blend was set in Photoshop using the yellow and green Curves. "I also wanted to focus more attention on the model's face, and so I really carved the light away from her cheeks with the Burn tool," he explains. "The shadow of the pearls was burned for drama and the pearl headdress highlighted with the Dodge tool to add depth to the face. I thought that her expression needed to be more sexy to fit with her posture, so I bloated the lips ever so slightly with the Liquify filter. The last highlighted accent was to the beads that drape her body. I carefully dodged specific beads to kick up the brilliance of the jewelry. Once complete, I pulled down the Curves slightly to add to the contrast and pop up the colors."

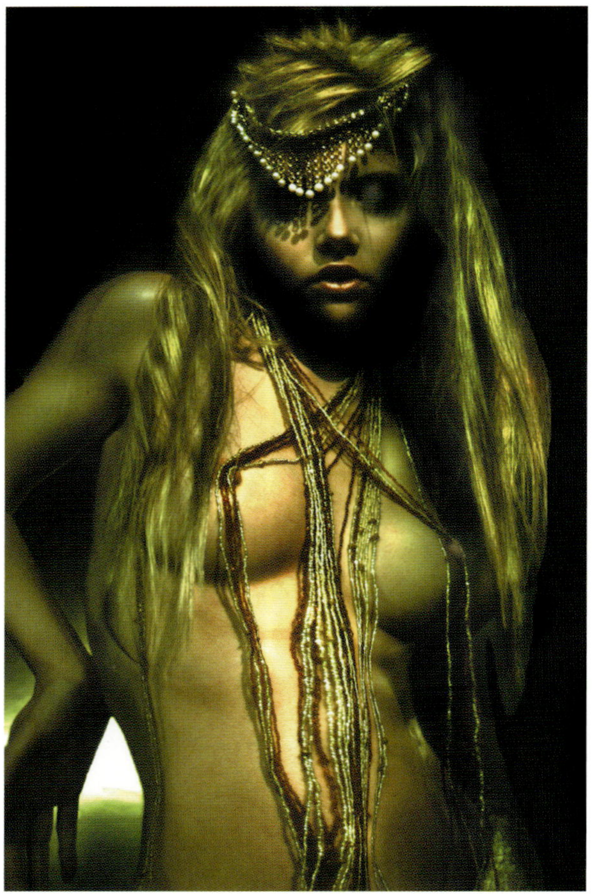

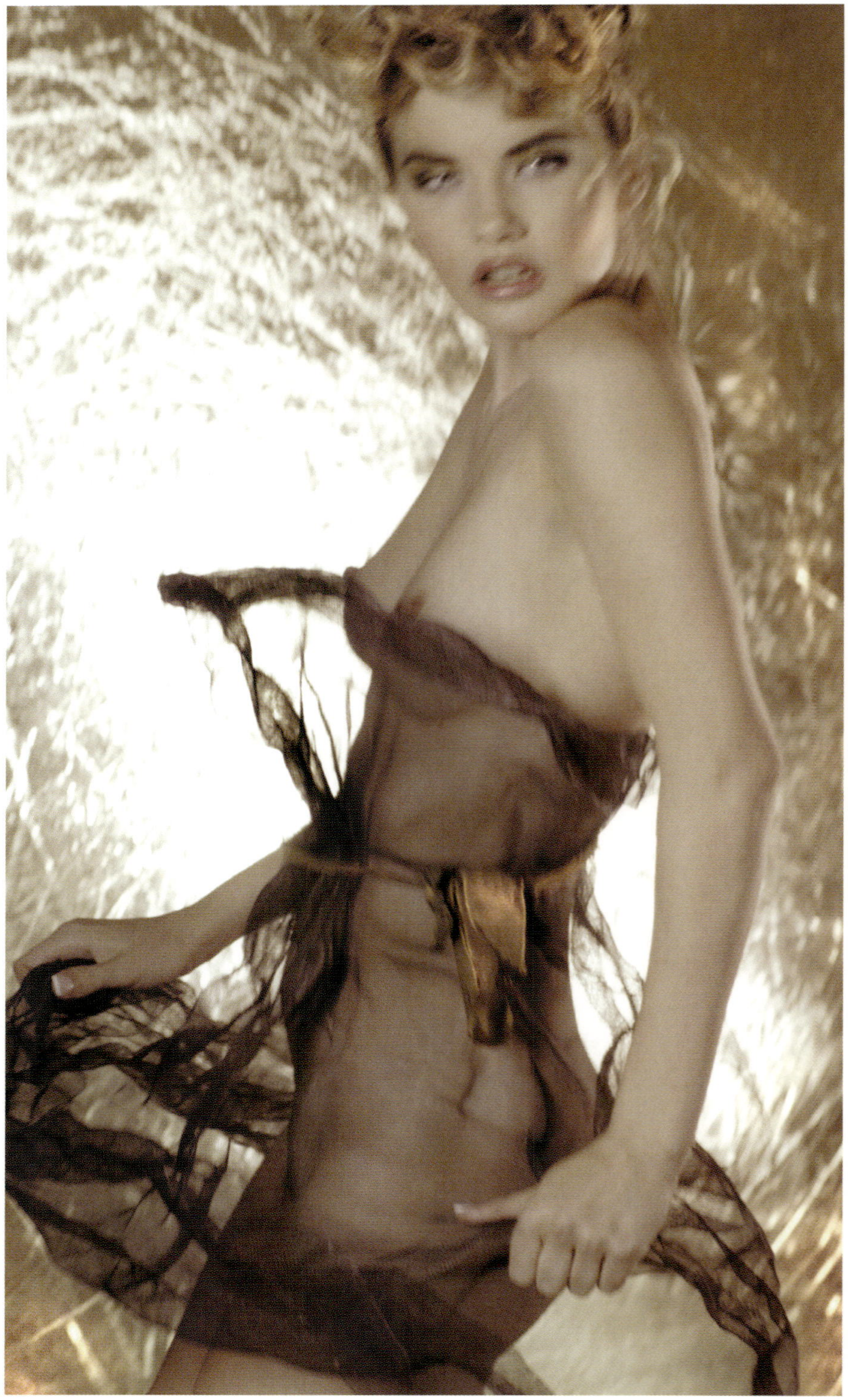

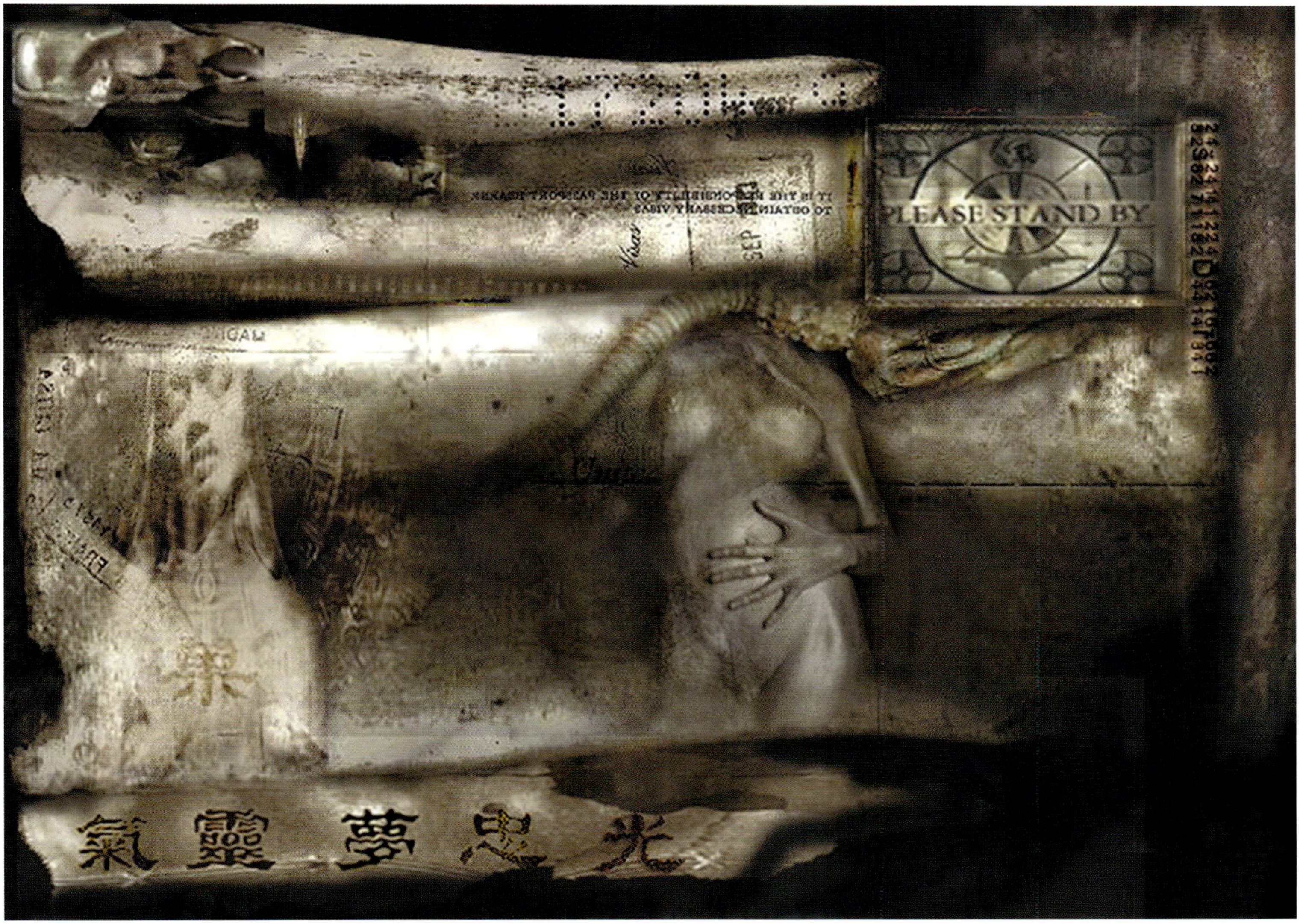

LEFT: *The Dance of the Screen Dress* was very much a collaboration between photographer and model. She danced during the shoot to the music of Massive Attack, and a slow shutter speed allowed some of the model's movement to register. Caballero designed the dress along the lines of erotic club wear, and this, too, inspired the mood of the image. He used a Nikon D100 camera, a Kino Flo as his main key light, with a reflector made by Wescott as the background. Very few refinements were needed afterward. The hair was highlighted piece by piece with the Dodge tool, and the eyes and ribbon were given the same treatment. The last adjustment was to warm up the image by adding a touch of magenta, red, and yellow.

ABOVE AND RIGHT: Caballero builds his images painstakingly, adding each element piece by piece and saving at every stage. This one took him well over 60 hours to complete. "My idea was to create a digital replica of what would be my HD TV theater in my new house," he explains. "My palette was an array of organic shapes, urban decay, erotica, and spirituality."

His starting point was the "wall" of the room—a bone duplicated, downsized, and stacked one on top of the other. He then added numerous other elements, including a fresco image of an Asian Madonna, an image of a headless body, manipulated to look like a statue, and a TV set, surrounded by an old picture frame. The scanned seal of his passport, a piece of metal for texture, a fossilized sea urchin, and various pieces of artwork were also individually added to get this extraordinary result, which could be described as a piece of digital sculpture.

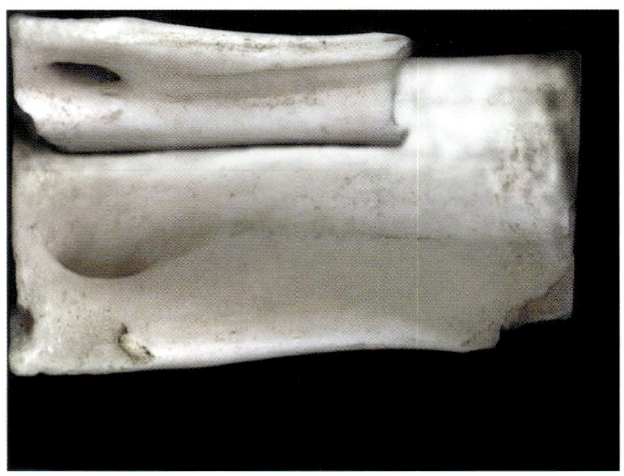

John Campbell

John Campbell began shooting black-and-white photographs in the early 1970s, while a university student in his home state of Louisiana. Since then, he has pursued various professional and academic interests, garnering advanced degrees in philosophy, theology, and psychology. His interests and practices in spirituality and mysticism shape his vision and inform his images. John is the owner and primary creative director of PhotoGecko Studios and Gallery in Austin, Texas.

ALL IMAGES: These three very subtle, impressionistic images were all created on different occasions, using the same lengthy process and a combination of traditional and modern techniques. Originally, they were shot with Polaroid type 55 film in a very simple 4x5 zone plate camera under daylight-balanced studio floodlights. This camera is like a modified pinhole camera, but whereas the latter has an infinite depth of field, or focus range, a zone plate camera throws everything slightly out of focus, with interesting effects. These effects are enhanced by the long exposure time of one to two minutes, which was a requirement of the slow ISO 50 film under the lighting that Campbell used. "Polaroid type 55 yields a positive —which I use for checking composition and exposure— and a negative transparency," he explains. "I break all the rules with the negative transparency. I do not, for example, immediately clear the antihalide coating with sodium sulphite, as the instructions would have me do. I merely hang the transparency on a wire and leave it for days at a time, allowing the emulsion to warp, warble, split, and burn—creating the types of effects seen in the images. Occasionally, I even leave the remnants of the film's

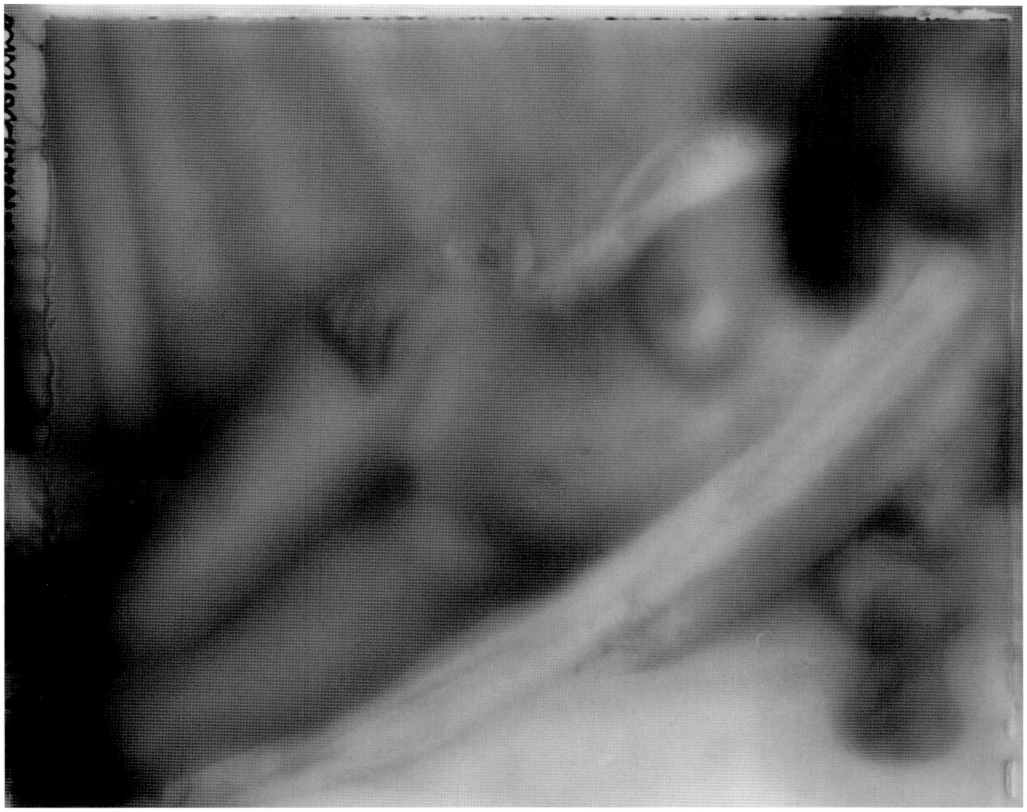

protective paper wrapper on, which causes it to adhere to the negative. Eventually—I've waited for anything from 24 hours to two weeks—I soak and clear the image in the sodium-sulphite solution and get my first real look at the results. I then scan the image as a 16-bit (1,600 dpi) image file and make adjustments using Curves, Levels, and various other tools in Photoshop. I can then print the image using various pigment or dye-based inks onto a variety of high-quality papers. I sometimes reverse the image and print to large transparency sheets for negative printing on hand-coated stock, such as platinum, palladium, and albumen, or POP stock, such as Centennial POP."

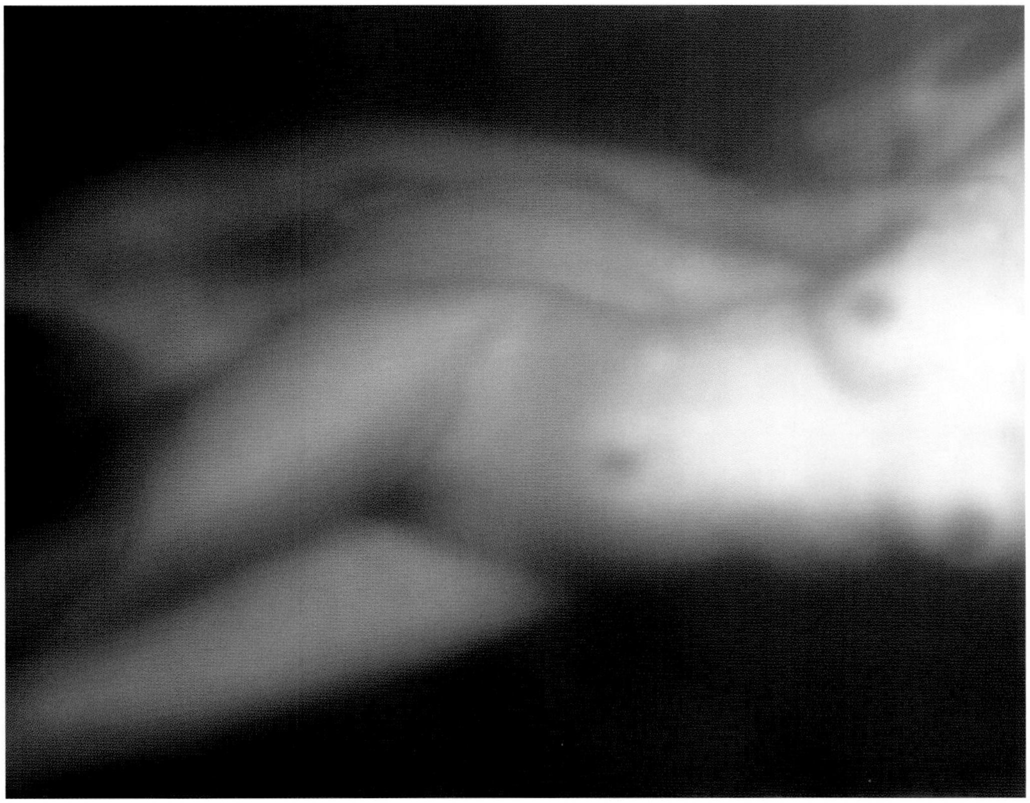

John Campbell

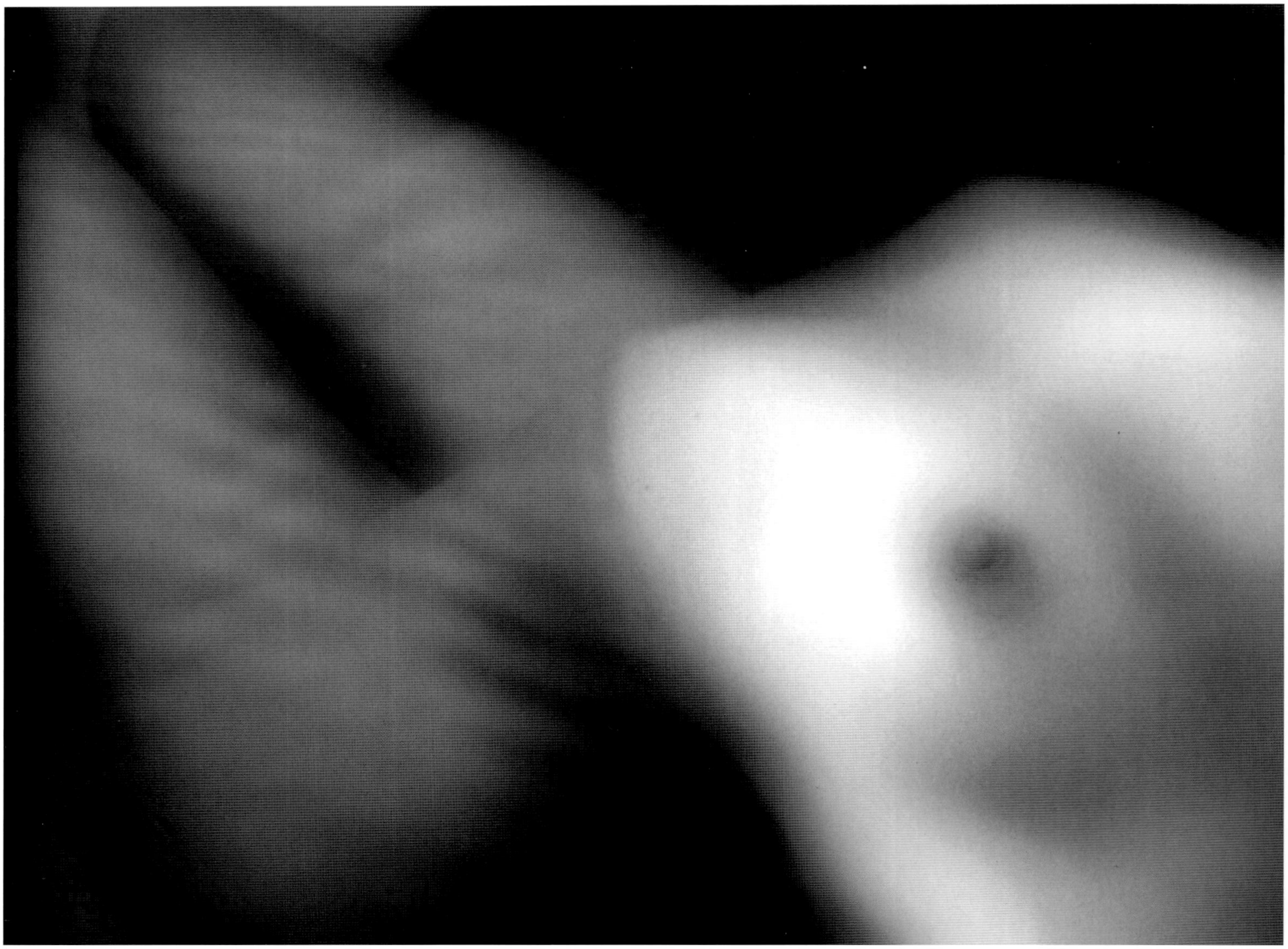

ABOVE: Things don't always go to plan during a photo shoot, but sometimes images that would have barely seemed worth printing can be transformed with imaginative use of editing techniques. This was originally shot with Campbell's 4x5 zone plate camera, which gives the soft-focus effect distinctive in his work. The ambient light was very low, and so he used two flash units to light the model as she leaned back over a chair. "One of the flash units failed to fire during the shot, resulting in the dark lower region of the model's body," he explains. "I was intrigued by the emerging form, however, so I superimposed a water shot over the original image in Photoshop. I then masked part of the water from the model's form, down to the darker portion of the original image." The result is a wonderful play of light and shade, which emphasizes the form of the body.

RIGHT: "This shot of my wife was taken with a conventional medium-format camera in very low available light, using Bergger 100 ISO film, processed in Pyro," says Campbell. "The lengthy exposure, something around one-and-a-half seconds, created unusual effects in this and other images in a series that I took. I enhanced the balance and contrast in Photoshop."

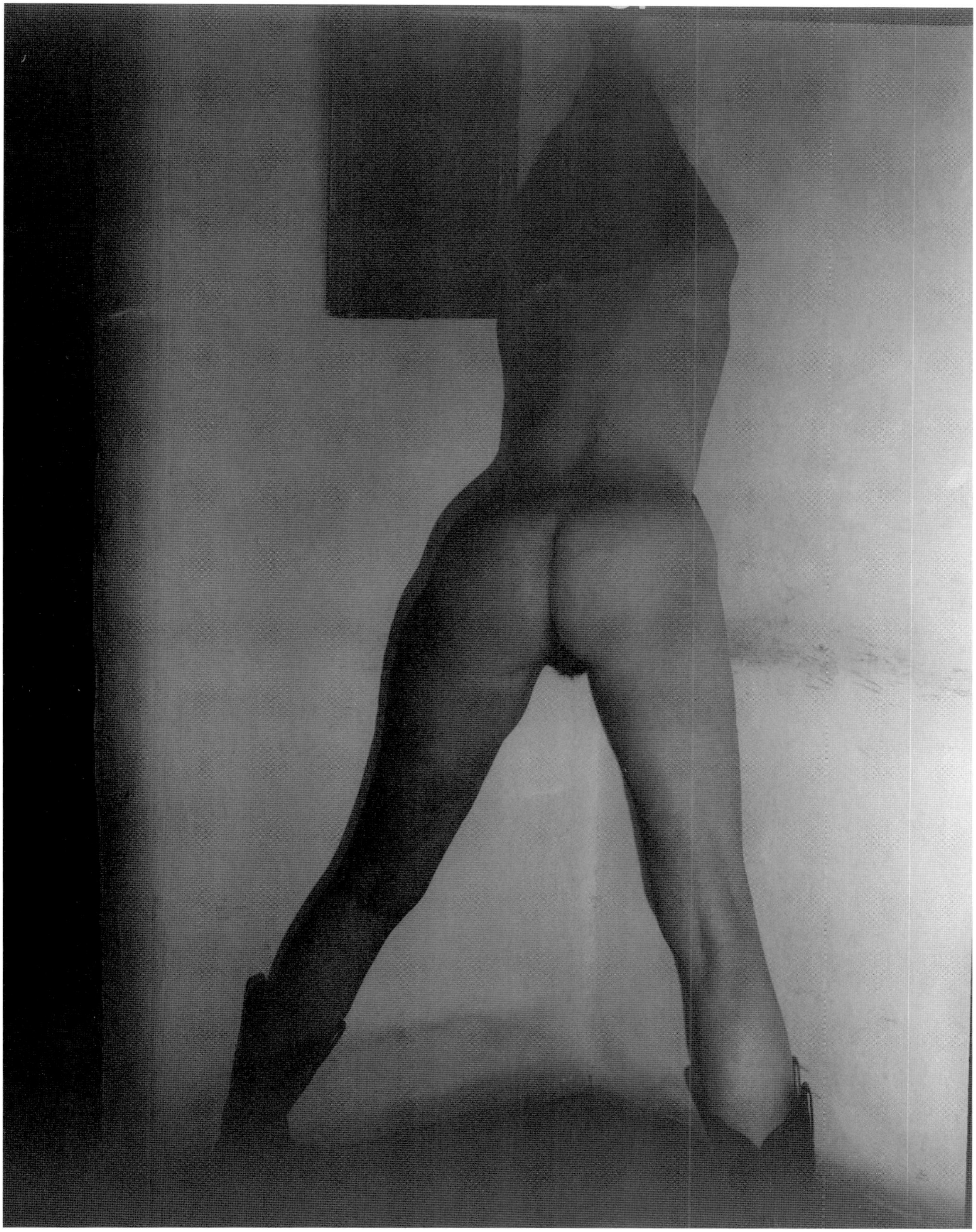

Matt Conrads

Born and raised in Germany, Conrads worked there as a photojournalist before moving to the US in 1996, where he finds many of the unusual and dramatic locations he loves to incorporate into his images. He has a strong background in Photoshop, but he uses it purely to add finishing touches to his original photographs.

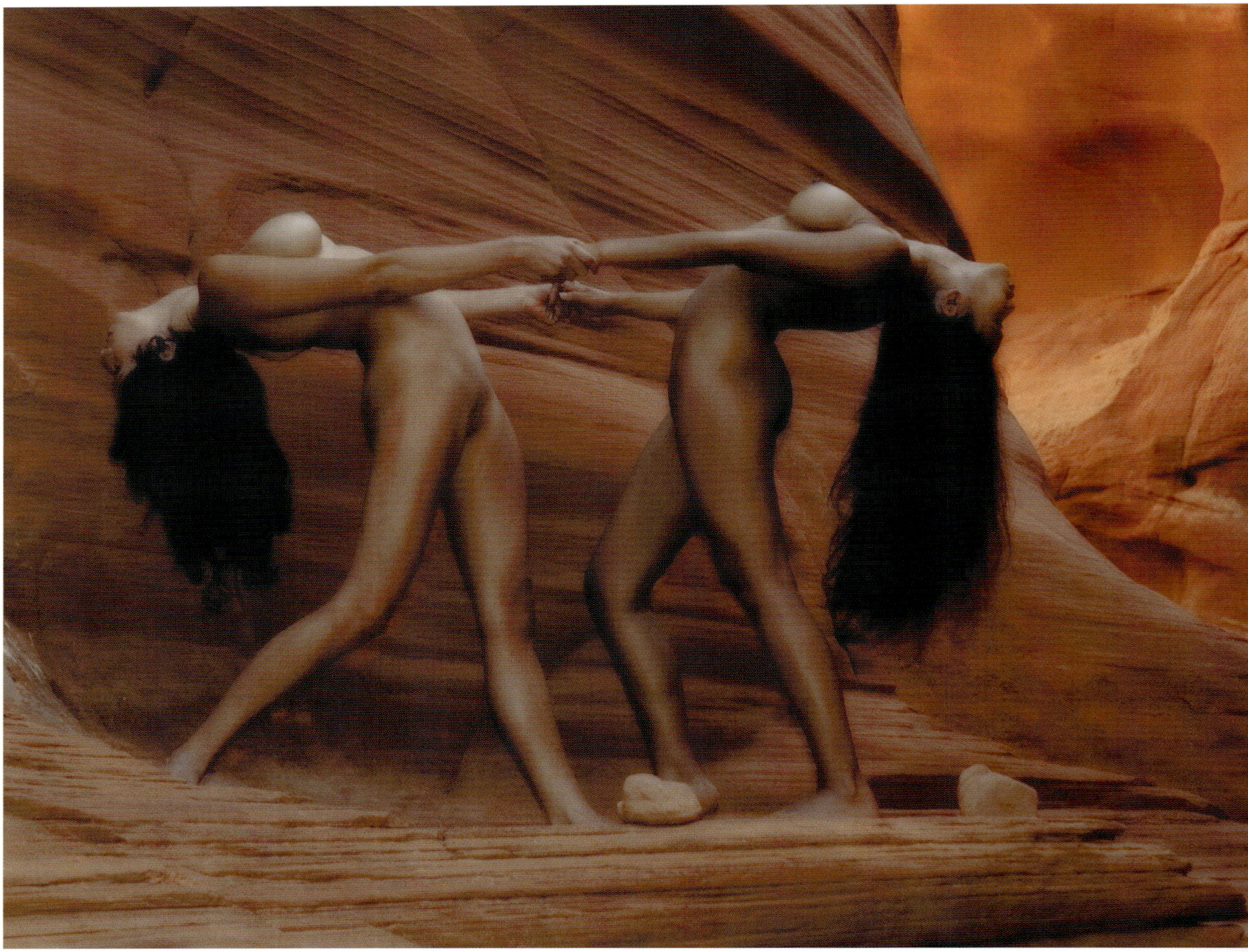

LEFT: Conrads had a vision of this image firmly in his mind before heading on location with two models to the stunning Antelope Canyon in northern Arizona. He knew that the amazing texture, shapes, and lines of the rocks would complement the curves of the models' bodies in this pose, and that in early morning, the soft but directional light was perfect for emphasizing the forms of both the models and rocks. The only alterations he made to the image were tweaking the colors and smoothing out the models' skin.

RIGHT: Taken during the same shoot in Antelope Canyon. The eye contact, pose, and costume of the models makes this a much more overtly sexual image. Conrads made more adjustments to it in Photoshop, too, to give it more of a sultry and mysterious atmosphere. He smoothed the skin tone of the models considerably to contrast with the roughness of the background. He also used many layers with different blending modes and additional light and color overlays to achieve a soft-focus effect similar to Vaseline on the lens at the time of shooting.

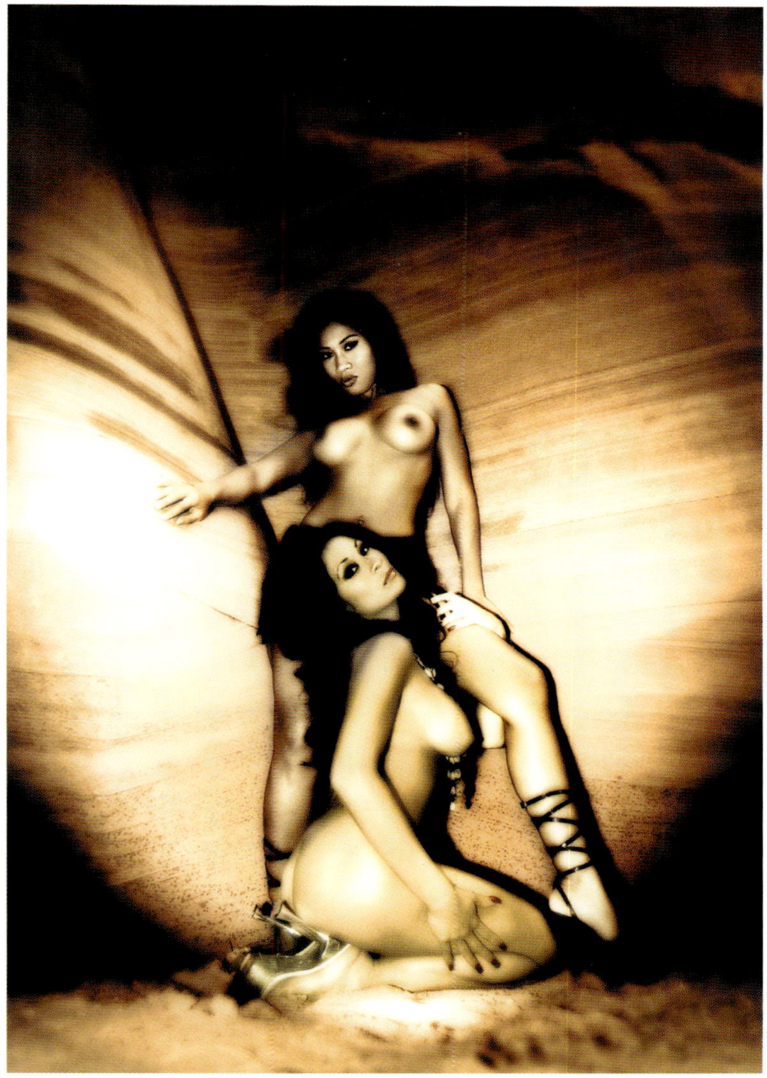

RIGHT: Combining a "straight" shot of a model with a different background is a fairly straightforward technique that can be extremely effective. It is most successful if the pose and lighting of the portrait are planned in advance to complement a chosen background, as they were here. The look in the model's eyes gave Conrads the idea for this composition. She was photographed in the studio against a white background and then superimposed onto a shot of an Egyptian pyramid that he had in stock. A warm color overlay enhanced the overall mood of the final image.

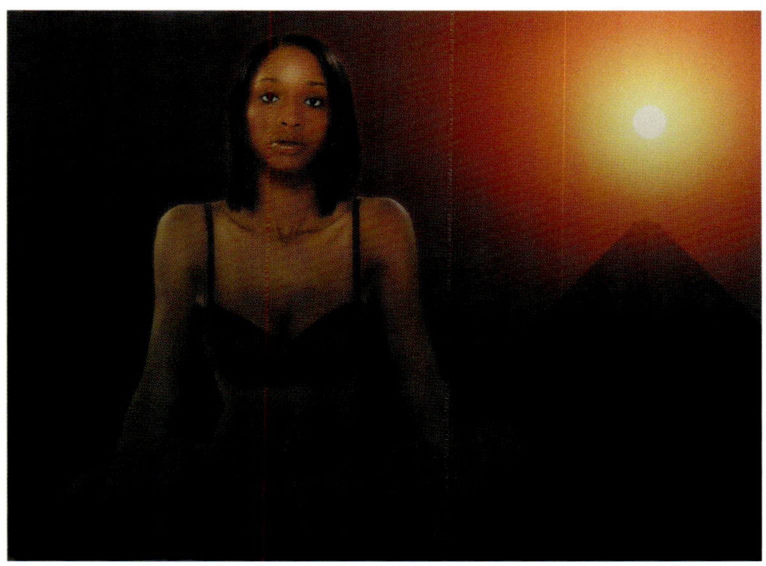

Matt Conrads

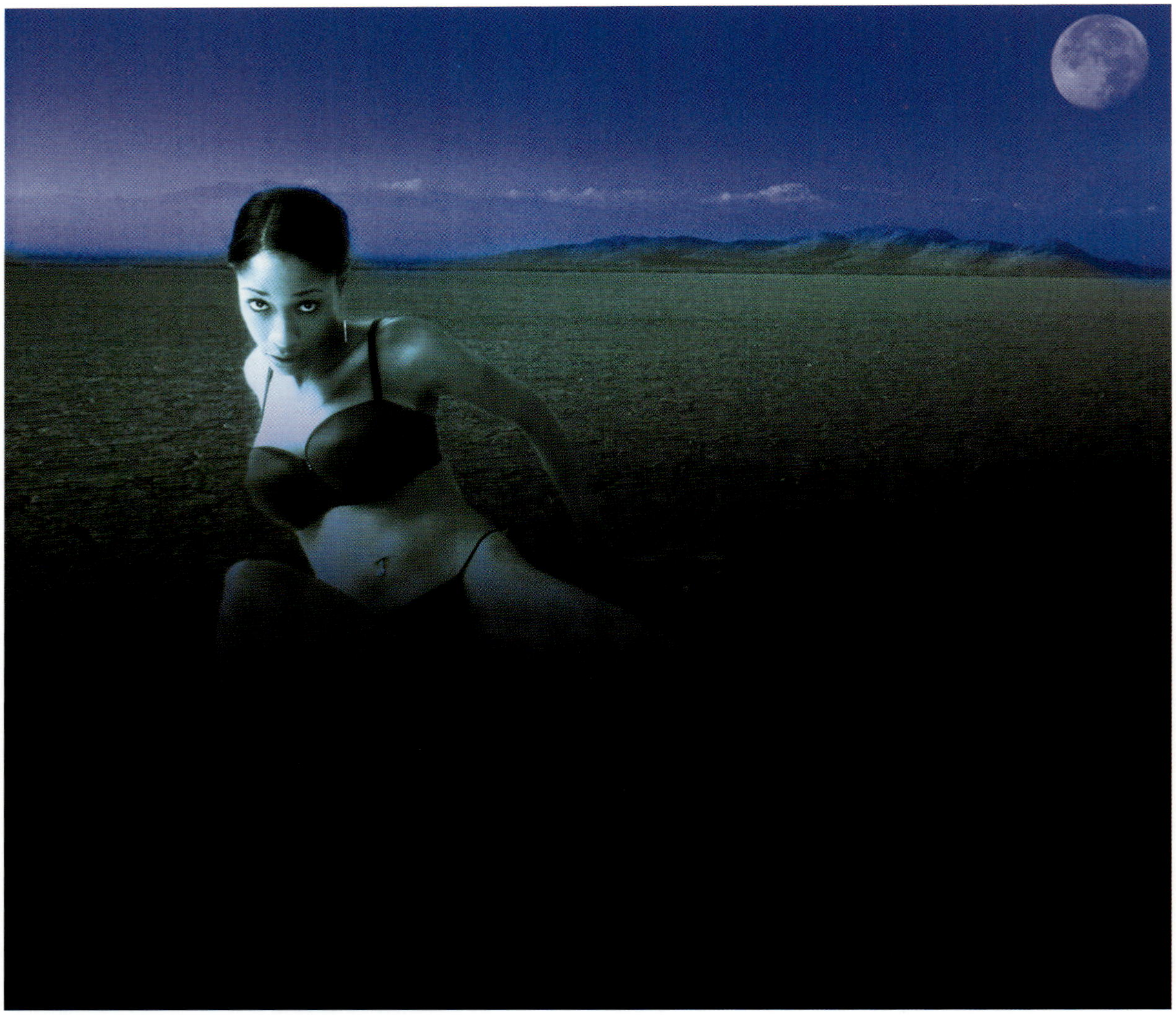

LEFT: Conrads takes every opportunity when he's traveling to collect landscapes for stock, which can later be combined with studio shots of models. If he doesn't have a suitable background himself, he draws on the resources of a stock agency. The background here is a dry lake in Las Vegas, toned in Photoshop with a blue duotone. The model was photographed against a neutral background, and the two images merged seamlessly together. "I used a variety of layers in different blending modes from Luminosity to Multiply to Overlay. A gradient fill makes the foreground a little more obscure, and a cooling filter gives the composition the final look," reveals Conrads.

RIGHT: You wouldn't know it, but the original shot was taken on location out in the desert in Arizona. "It's not quite the place for that kind of outfit," admits Conrads. "On the other hand, this is a perfect example to show that digital photography has no boundaries. If photographers are willing to jump the fence of their own backyard, they will discover that there is a whole world of unlimited options out there. With the help of a stock photo of an old wooden door, the scene was brought into a different dimension."

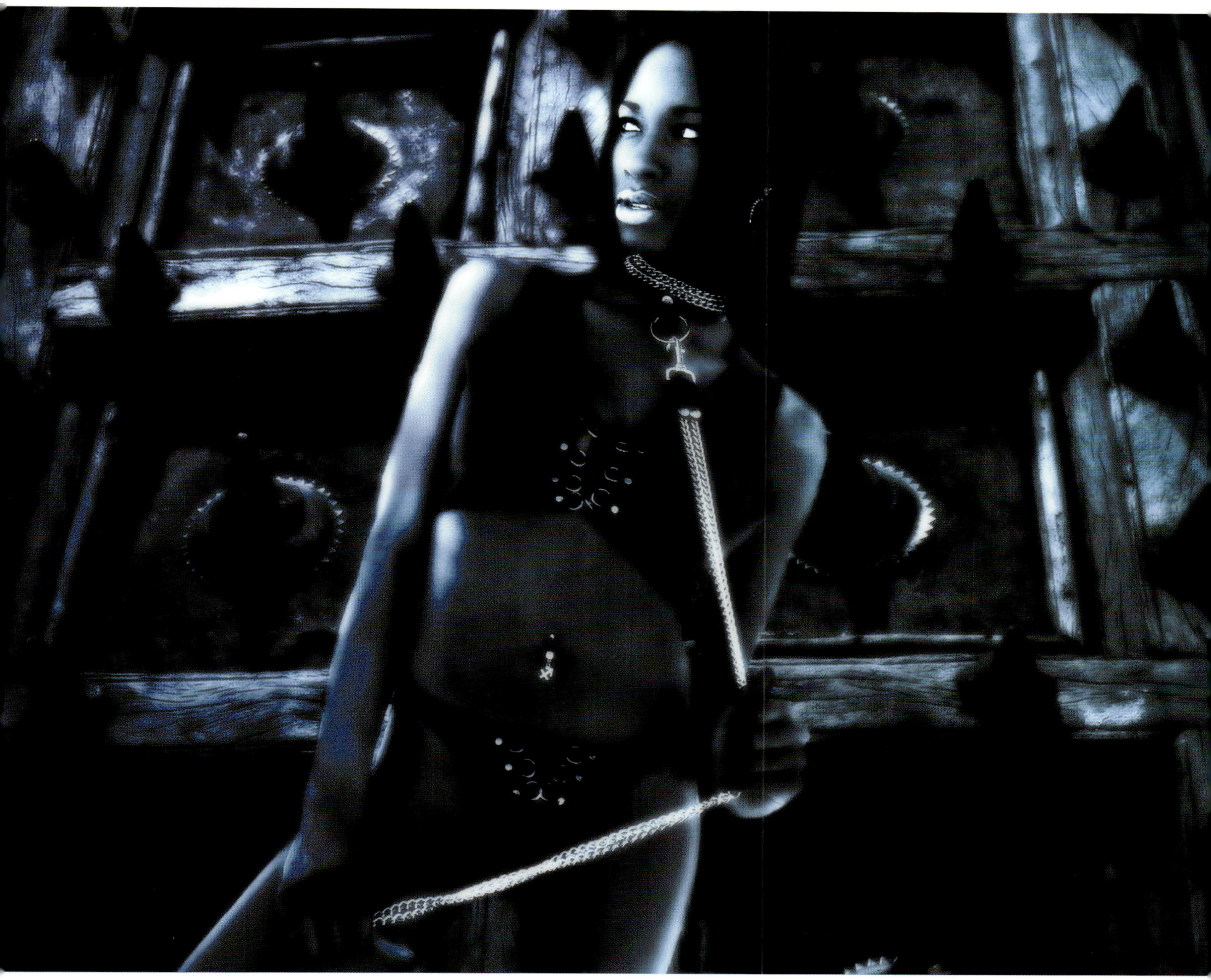

Matt Conrads

RIGHT: Conrads photographed the African-American model in his studio against a brown background. "Shooting someone on a background that is almost identical to their skin tone seems a strange thing to do," he concedes. "The pictures actually turned out nicely, but after working on some of them, I had the idea to make a drastic change in Photoshop. A few adjustment layers later, the model's skin appeared to be gold. The major enhancements were made on an adjustment layer for selective color. That technique works really well on dark skin tones."

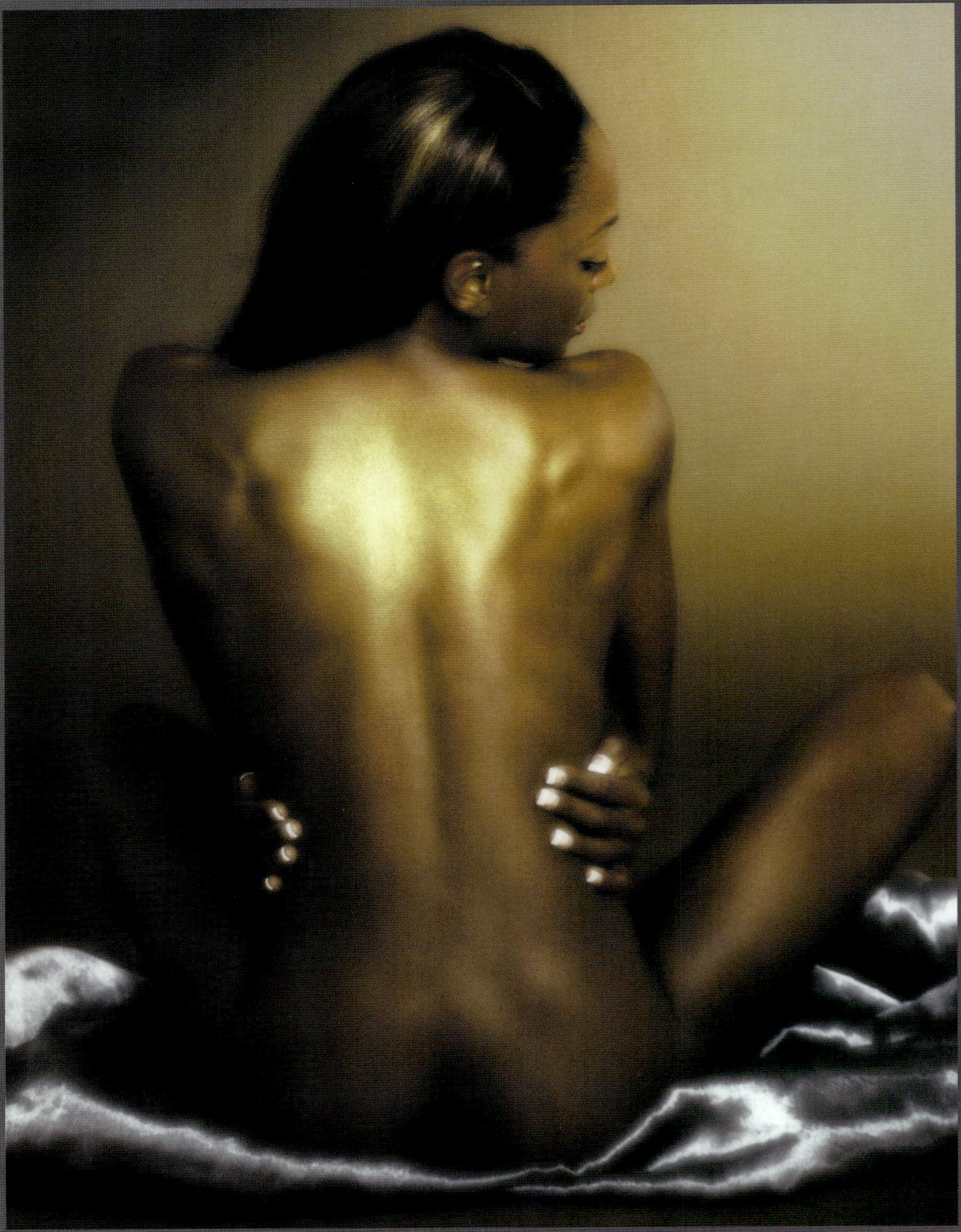

RIGHT: "Photographers who shoot a lot in the studio will all, at some point, run into a similar situation—they have plenty of really nice pictures, but they all look kind of alike," says Conrads. "Adding interest to a shot is fairly easy, as long as it was shot on a neutral background that is not very difficult to knock out. Once the model is separated from the background, the possibilities are endless, especially if you are signed up with a stock agency where you are bound to find something suitable." This was originally shot with bright strobe flash, and Conrads chose a similarly well-lit background with areas of highlight and shadow that match the model. Background color was also important, to pick up the model's jewelry. While the setting may not be believably real, it does give the portrait an appropriate lift without distracting attention away from the subject.

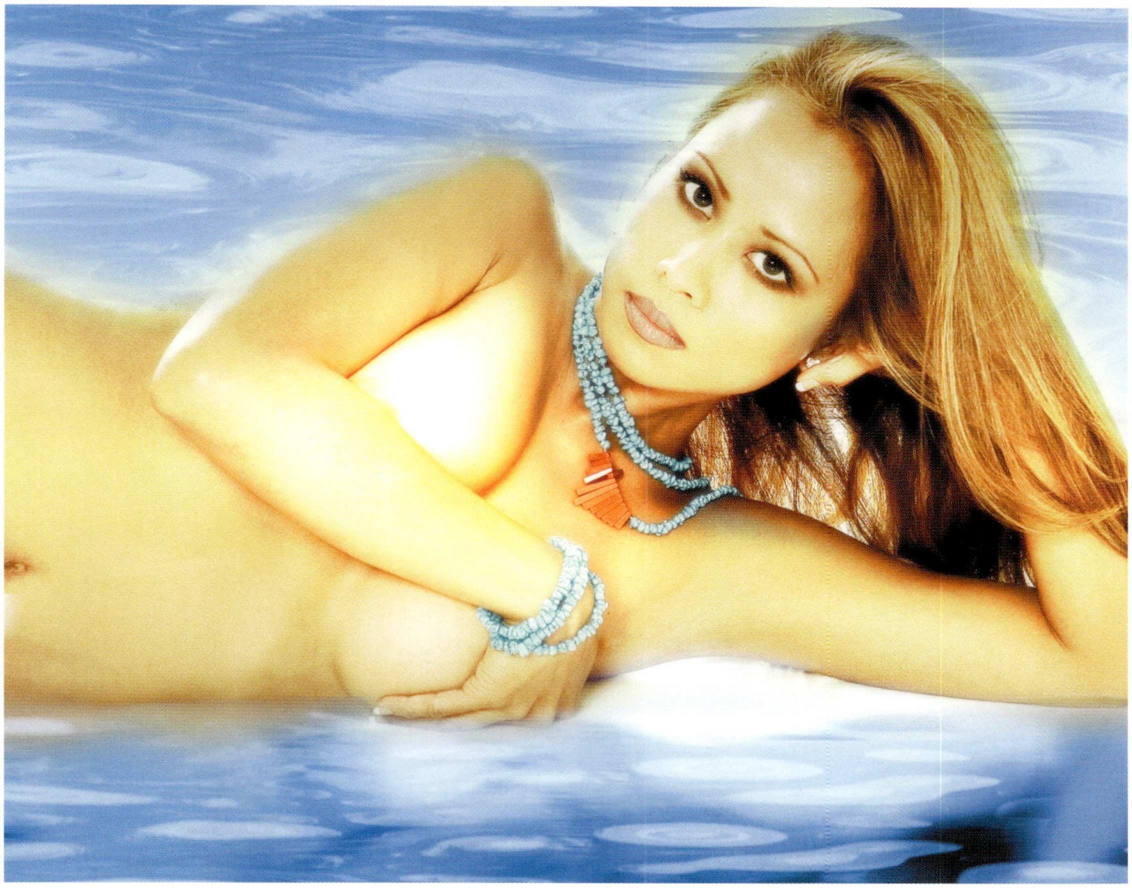

RIGHT: This montage of several different images, digitally combined, started out as something very different before Conrads let his imagination rip, as he explains. "The original photo was shot in the dunes between Yuma, Arizona, and San Diego, California. That's the place where they filmed some scenes for *Star Trek*. But that was not what gave the inspiration for this. Actually, it was more the publicity surrounding Saturn in the summer of 2004 due to the spacecraft mission. Although the color blue usually stands for coldness, this image implies the opposite."'

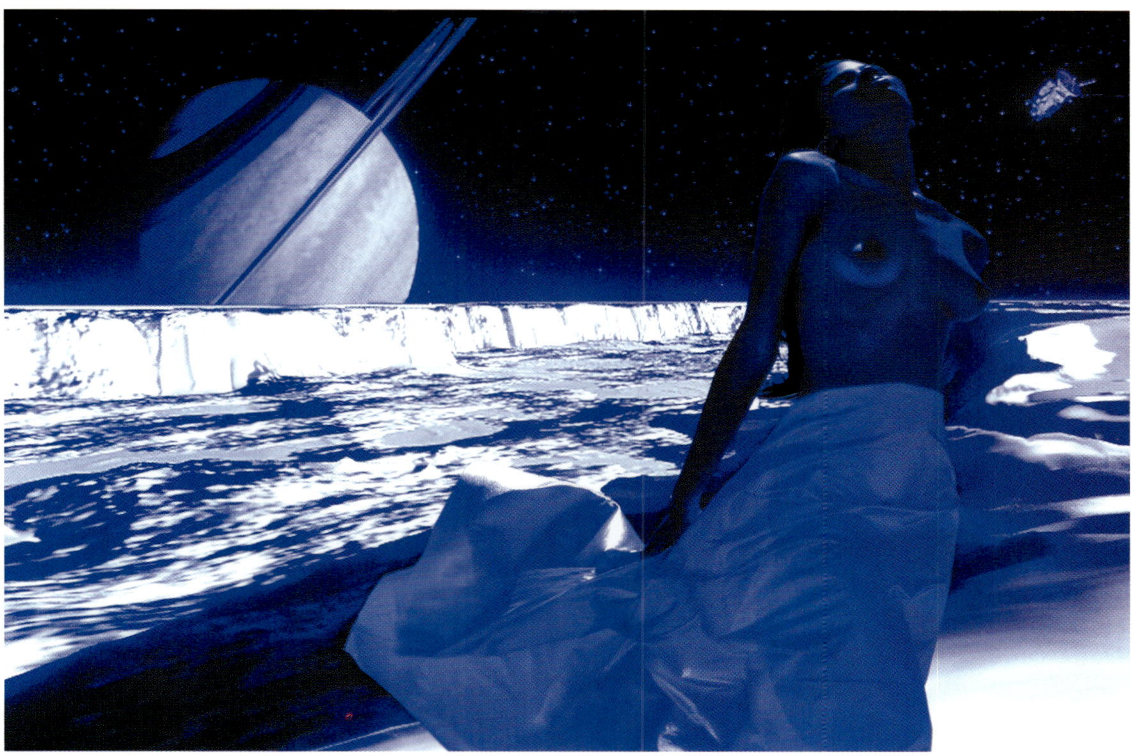

Matt Conrads

RIGHT: While digital techniques can rarely work sufficient magic if the initial lighting, pose, and composition are weak, it can do wonders if it is only the background that lets an image down. This shot was taken in a backyard that Conrads says was simply not designed for a photo shoot. "It was the typical location that many hobbyists might be confronted with on a permanent basis," he says.

"There was an untrimmed palm tree and a very unphotogenic wall behind the model that made this shot look anything but appealing. The solution I found was to make a copy of the background layer and distort it with a strong Motion blur. By applying a layer mask to the blurred picture on top of the original, the underlying picture was then revealed by painting with a black brush over the layer mask."

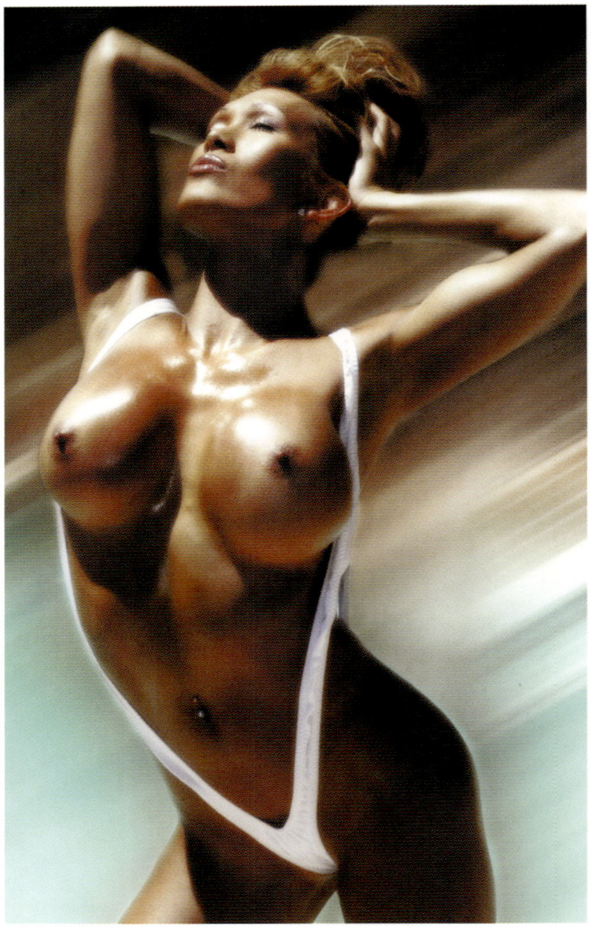

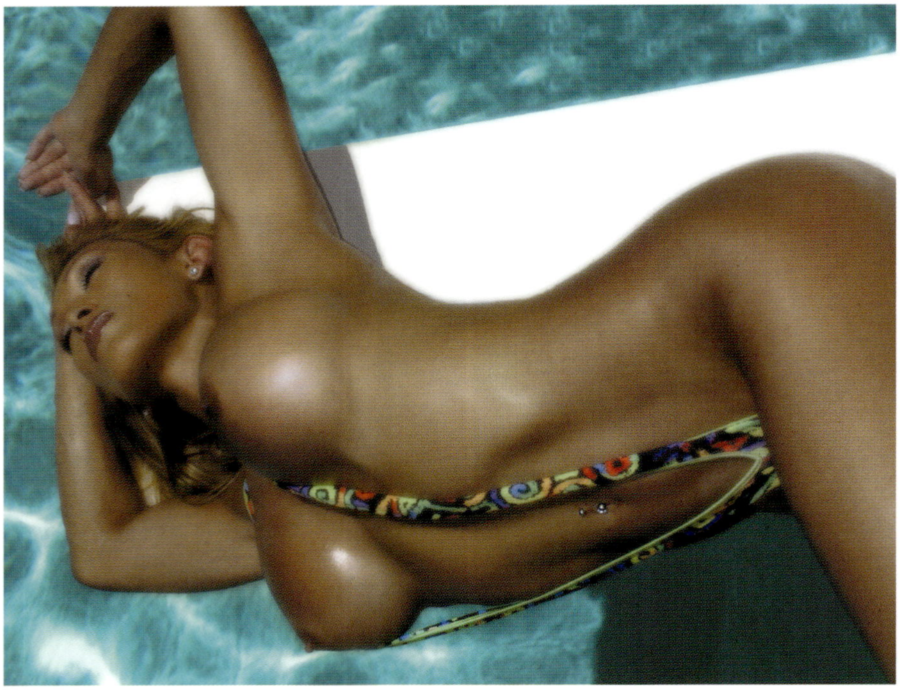

LEFT: "This image of a Polynesian model was not looking very promising during the shoot," recalls Conrads. "The location was just not working as there was something distracting in the background whichever way you looked. There were no other options that day, though, so I had to think of a way to work round it. I had the idea of shooting from an extreme angle, with the model lying on the high dive board and myself standing on the stainless steel handrail, trying to keep my balance. On the computer, the image was rotated 90 degrees counter-clockwise, the skin tone and the tint of the water optimized in an adjustment layer and, voilà!, a picture that looks like a million dollars, shot in a far-from-perfect environment."

RIGHT: Conrads started out with a shot of the model lying on a mirror and, although happy with that, he decided it would look even better if he could make it seem like her reflection was in sea water. After the water was layered on top of the image, the blending mode of the water layer was changed. Usually this is Overlay, but sometimes Pin Light or Vivid Light look better. Finally, the underlying picture was partially painted back by applying a layer mask to the water layer and painting with a fuzzy black brush on the layer mask, thus revealing what lies underneath.

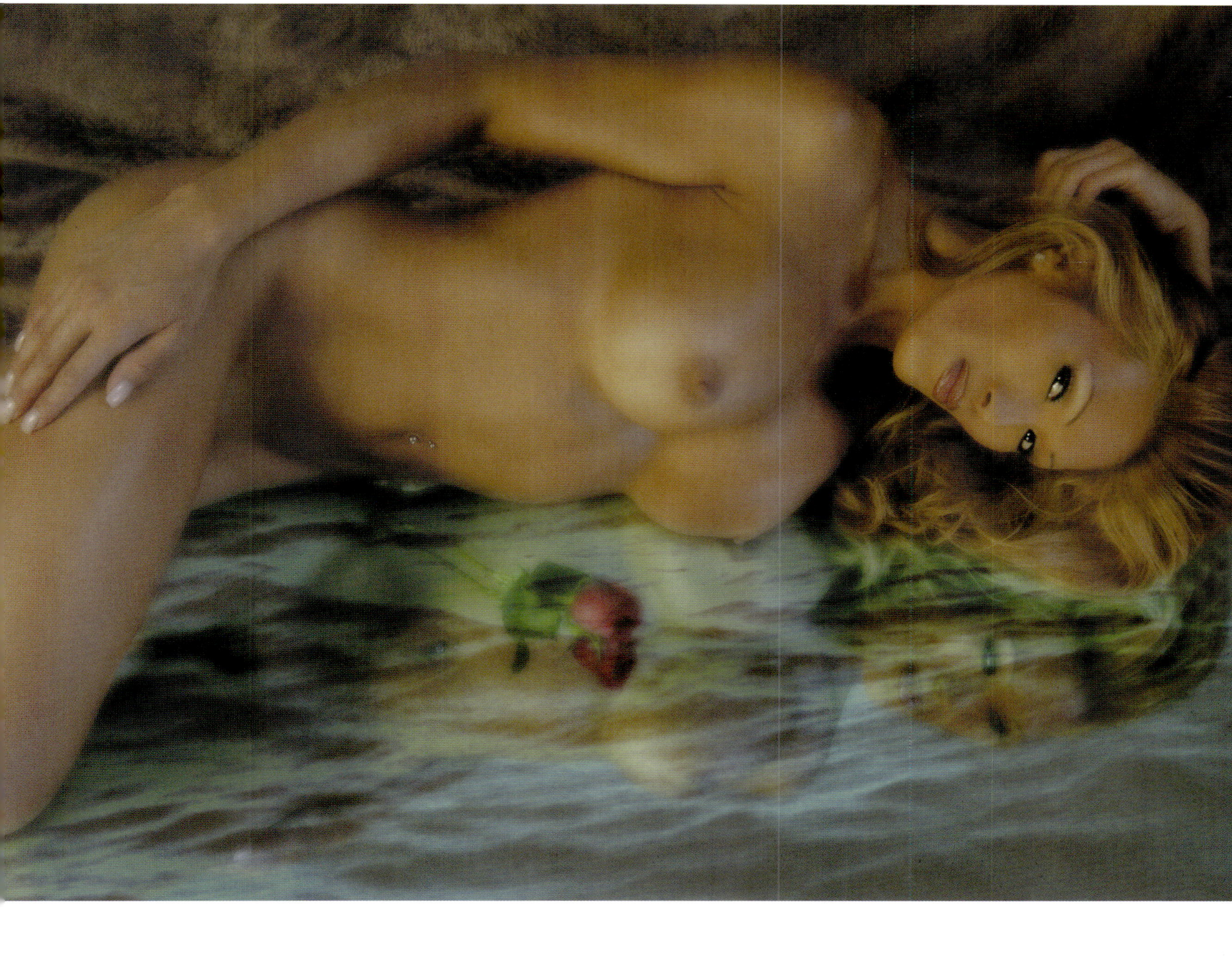

Heather Dellinger

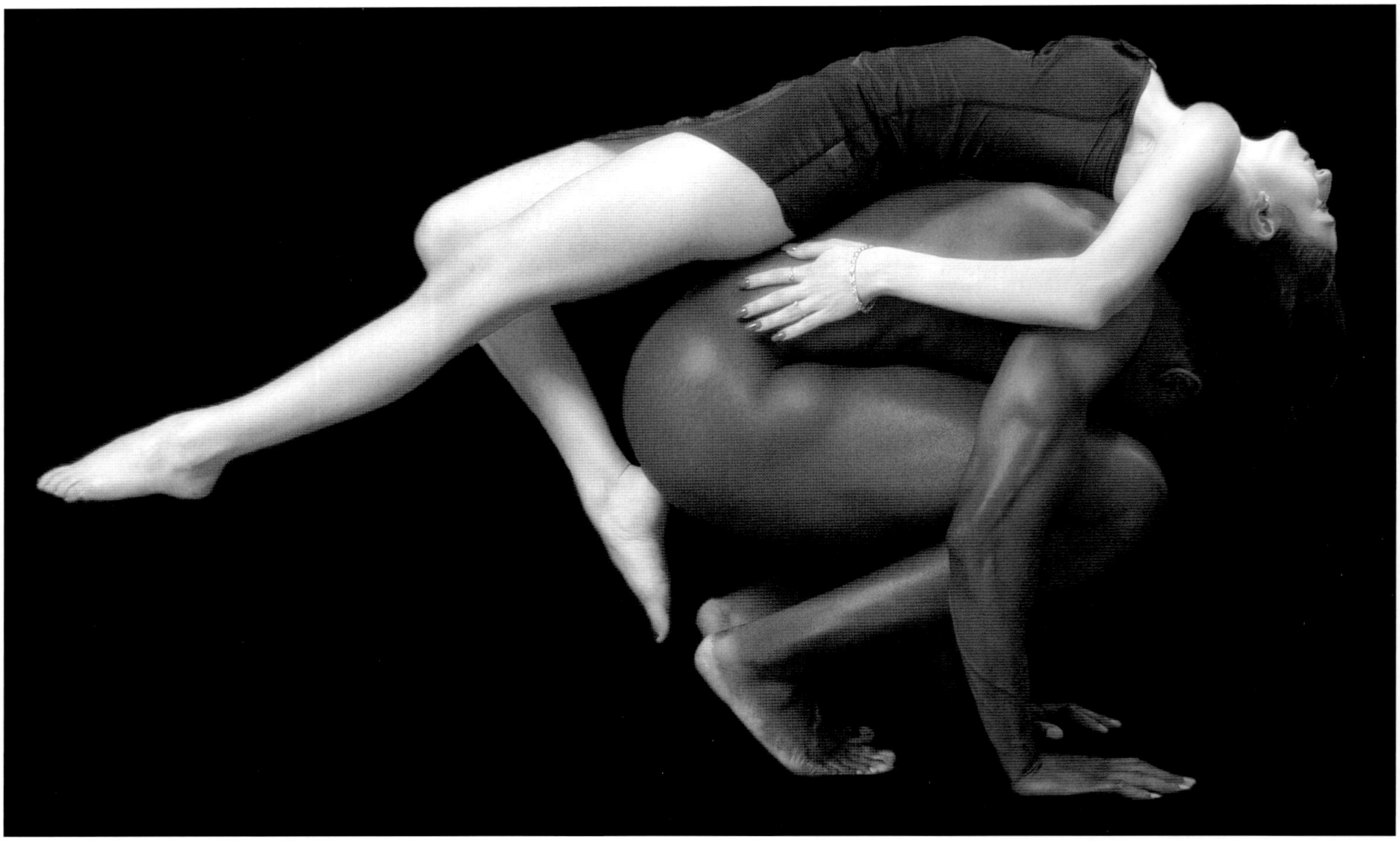

Heather Dellinger's interest in photography began when she tried out a class as a sophomore at college and discovered she had found her niche. In 2002 she signed up with an online photographer/model-posting site and hasn't looked back. Based in Chicago, her work encompasses fashion, glamor, and editorial photography, using digital tools to subtly enhance traditional photographic elements of light and shade.

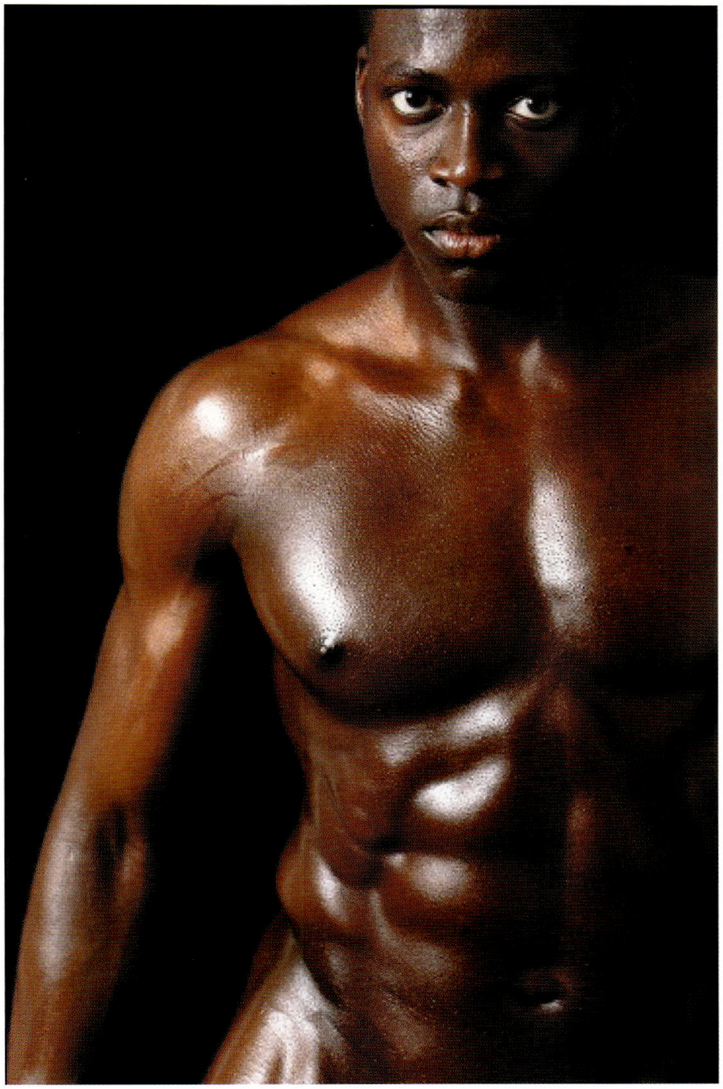

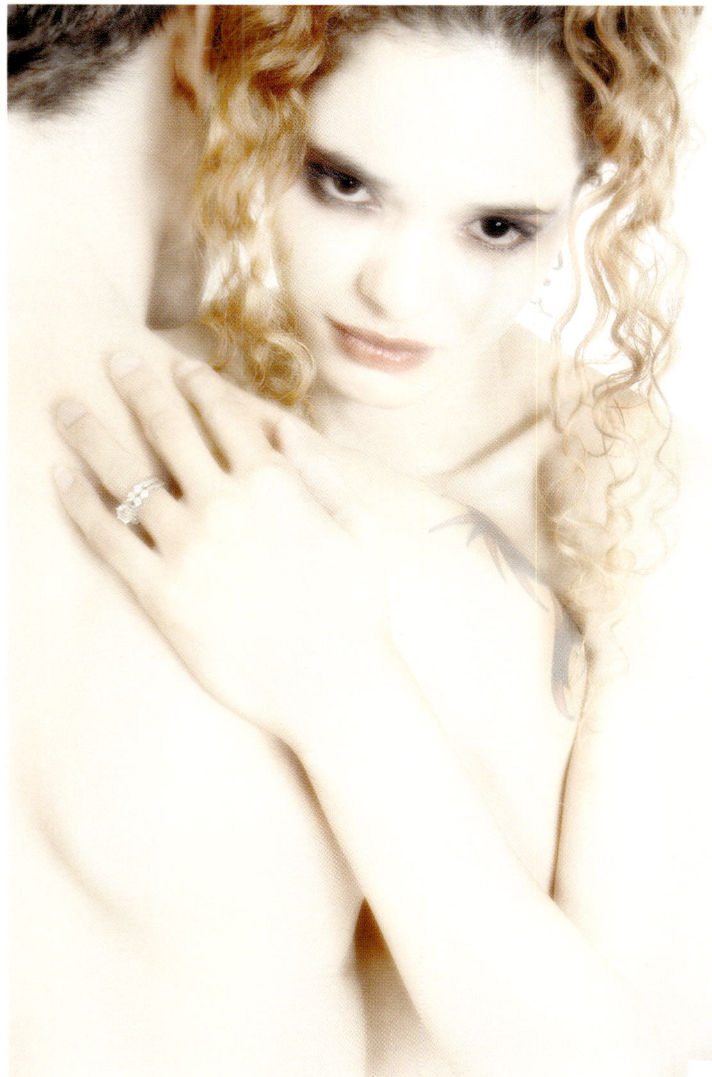

OPPOSITE PAGE: This image aims to be both erotic and disquieting in terms of the pose and the implied relationship between the two models. "Adeoye came to me wanting fitness shots but the idea of straight 'fitness' didn't really appeal to me, and I wanted to achieve something more imaginative and sensual," explains Dellinger. "There's something dance-like about the pose, with both bodies linked through formal elements, like the alignment of Magdy's right leg and Adeoye's feet. Although the image was shot in color, conversion to monochrome was the best way to maximize the contrast between them."

ABOVE: "Here I wanted to bring out the intensity and confidence of the model's eyes and gaze, as well as emphasize his amazing muscularity and skin tone," says Dellinger. "I used a strong strobe light with umbrella from the side so the shadows would accentuate the curve of the muscle. The flash head was positioned to catch both eyes clearly." The asymmetrical crop, framed in the camera rather than in post-production, is characteristic of a lot of Dellinger's work and helps to give this shot its impact.

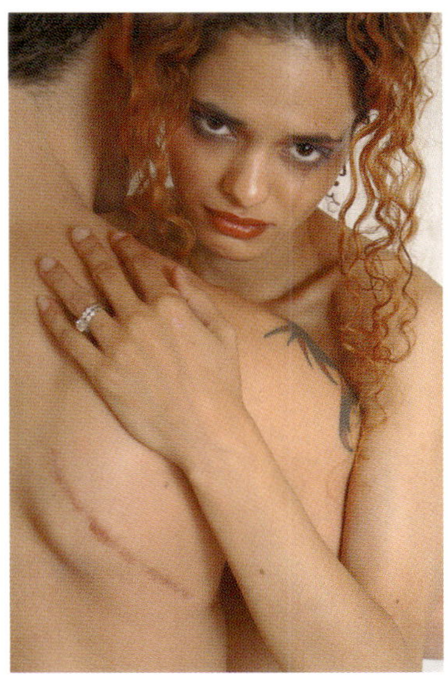

ABOVE: "To me this photo represents a sense of loss," comments Dellinger. The lighting came from a single strobe with white umbrella on the right but Heather decided a hi-key effect would enhance the picture, giving the softer, more dream-like quality of the finished image (above). First using the Healing tool in Photoshop to dispense with the male model's scar, she lightened the whole image, did a Diffuse Glow (low grain) and then used the Burn tool around her hair and his tattoo. The eyes were intentionally left dark as Dellinger felt they were the most expressive part of the picture.

Heather Dellinger

RIGHT: Dellinger's main aim with this shoot was to capture the suppleness and elegance of model Ulrika. "She trained as a gymnast, which made it possible for me to set her in off-balance poses like this one. Throughout the entire shoot we were testing the limits of poses," Dellinger says. "This picture encompasses the grace and elegance that we were trying to achieve through the flow of the fabric and the curve of her body." Editing in Photoshop involved lightening the overall image, increasing the contrast, and then putting a light glow over it. Some cloning was also done to extend the backdrop onto the floor, resulting in the finished shot on the right.

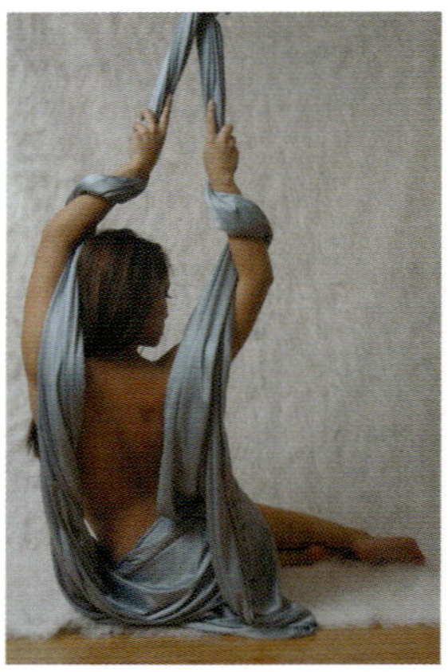

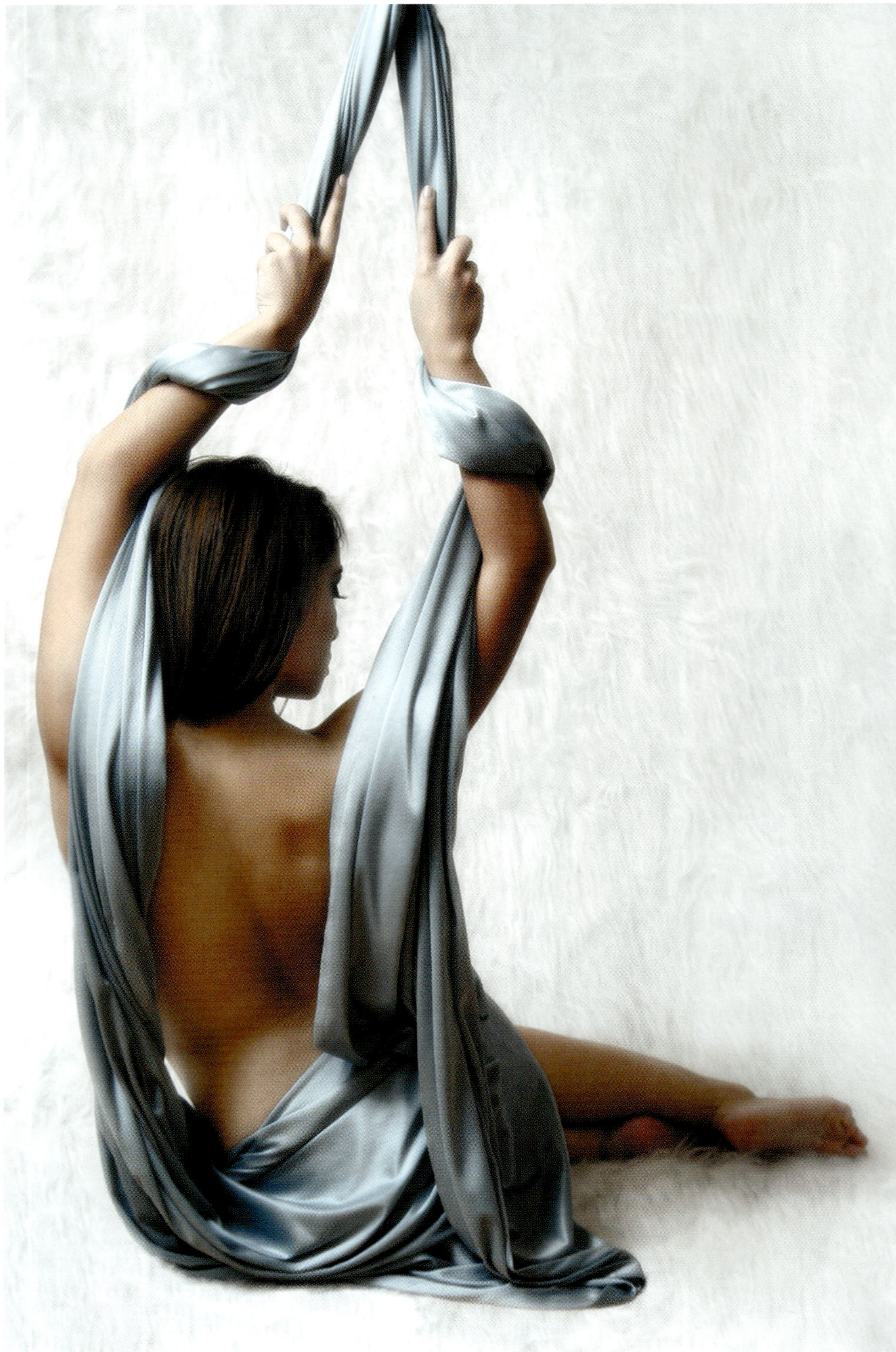

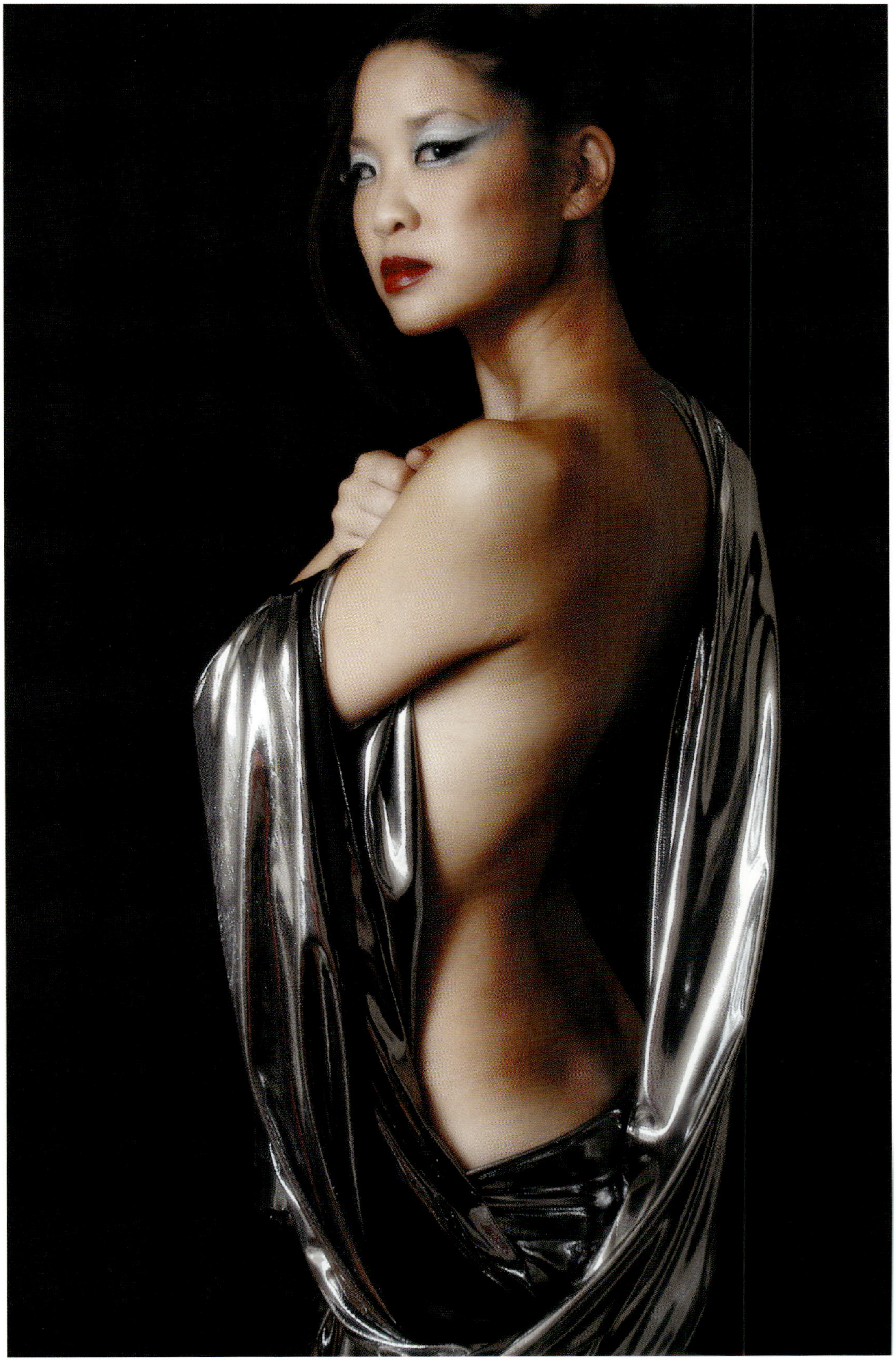

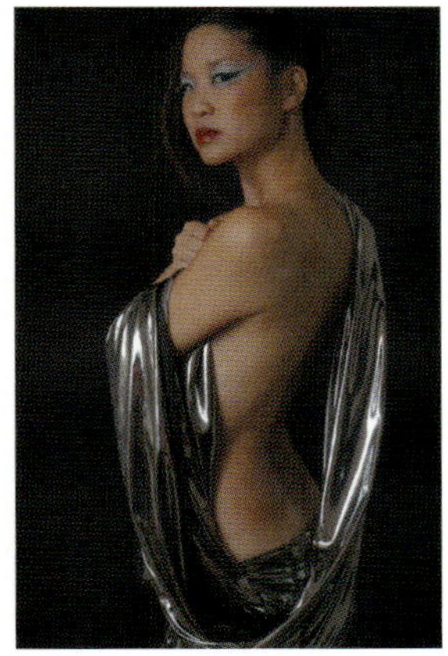

LEFT: In this subtly erotic portrait of model Christine, Dellinger was interested in the way the fabric draped around the body and glistened in the light. "I tried to emphasize Christine's pure elegance through her posture and in the way I framed her statuesque figure. I feel the photos leave the viewer with a real sense of her grace. I tossed a strong diffuse glow on the image, darkened the background to black, and highlighted her make-up slightly."

Christopher Donovan

Christopher Donovan's digital montages vary considerably in mood and tone, from the soft and painterly, to graphic and defined. He always plans the image from start to finish, aiming to shoot every part of it in sequence and within the same environment to help maintain realism.

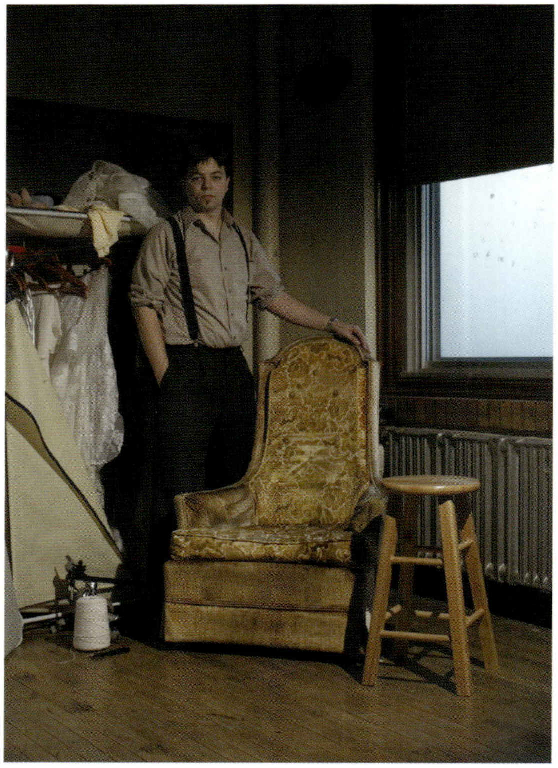

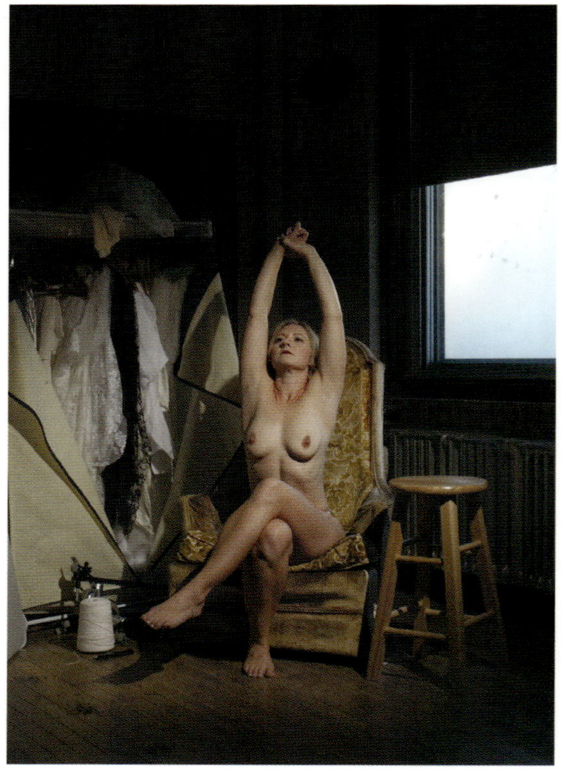

ALL IMAGES: This unconventional self-portrait with a disembodied model required much thought and planning to complete the various stages and make the end result so startlingly real-looking. Donovan's starting point was to photograph himself alone by the chair, which serves as the background. He then shot the other elements in the sequence they are shown here, including a shot of the empty chair to allow him to mask out any areas lost to unwanted shadows in the other shots. The different elements were combined in Photoshop using layers and masks. "These are the two things you really need to be good at in Photoshop," he says. "The layer mask is fantastic because it is not destructive, so you can continue to add or remove a part of one picture on layer A to or from a picture on layer B at any time." Donovan also uses layer masks to control color by using Hue/Saturation adjustment layers. For the final image here, the Hue/Saturation layer was colored with a low-saturation warm tone and then the opacity adjusted to create the desired effect.

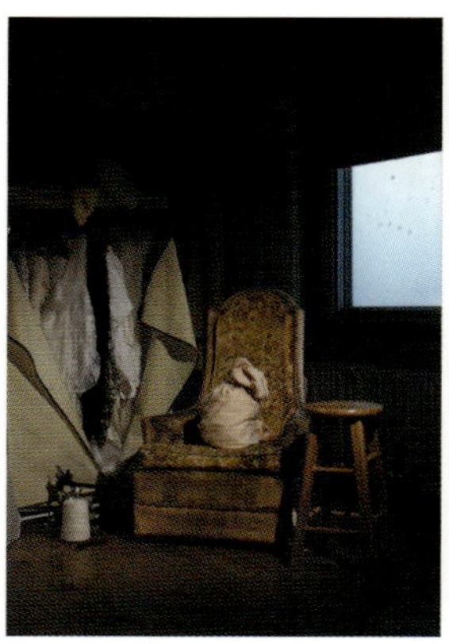

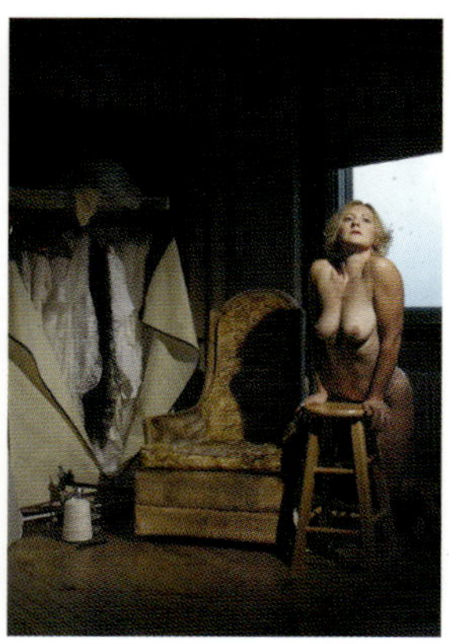

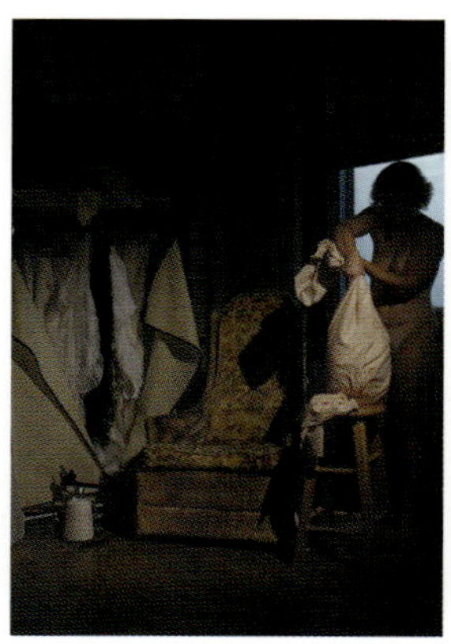

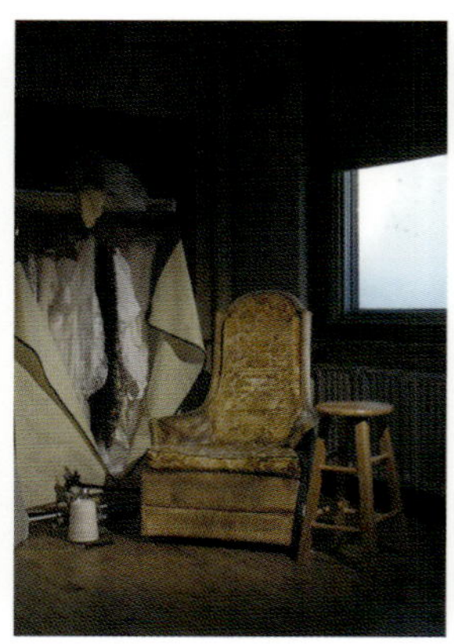

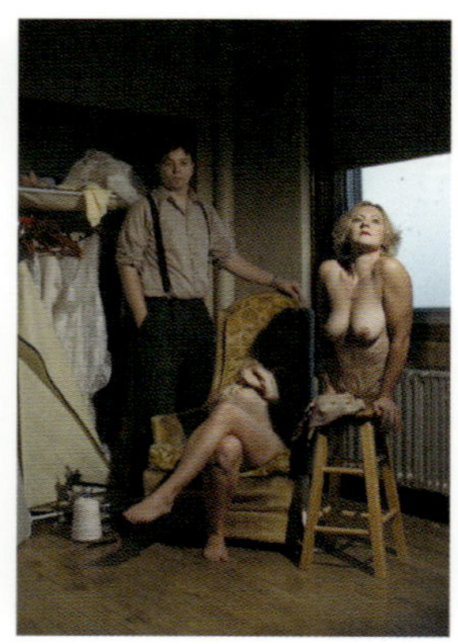

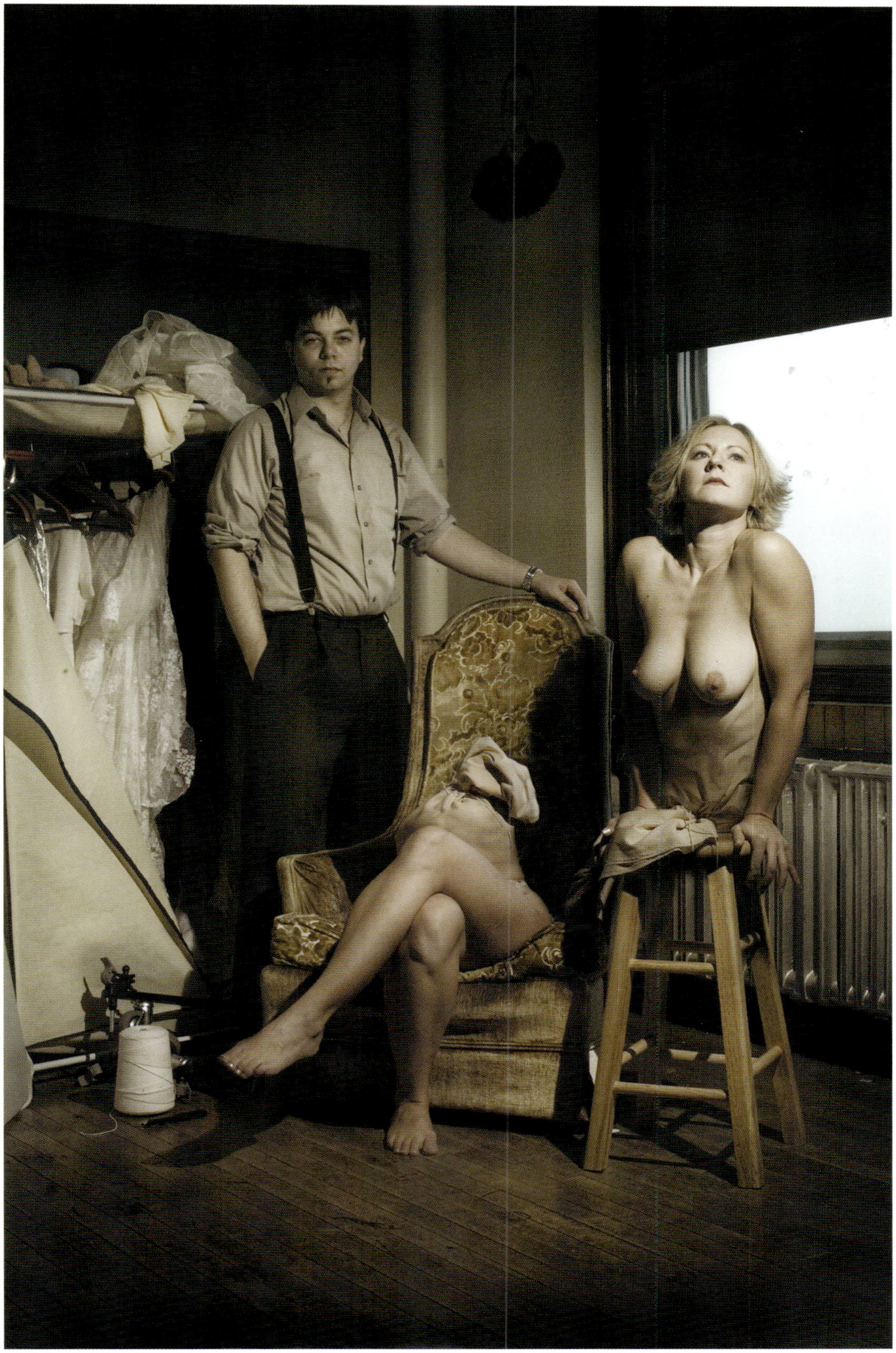

Christopher Donovan

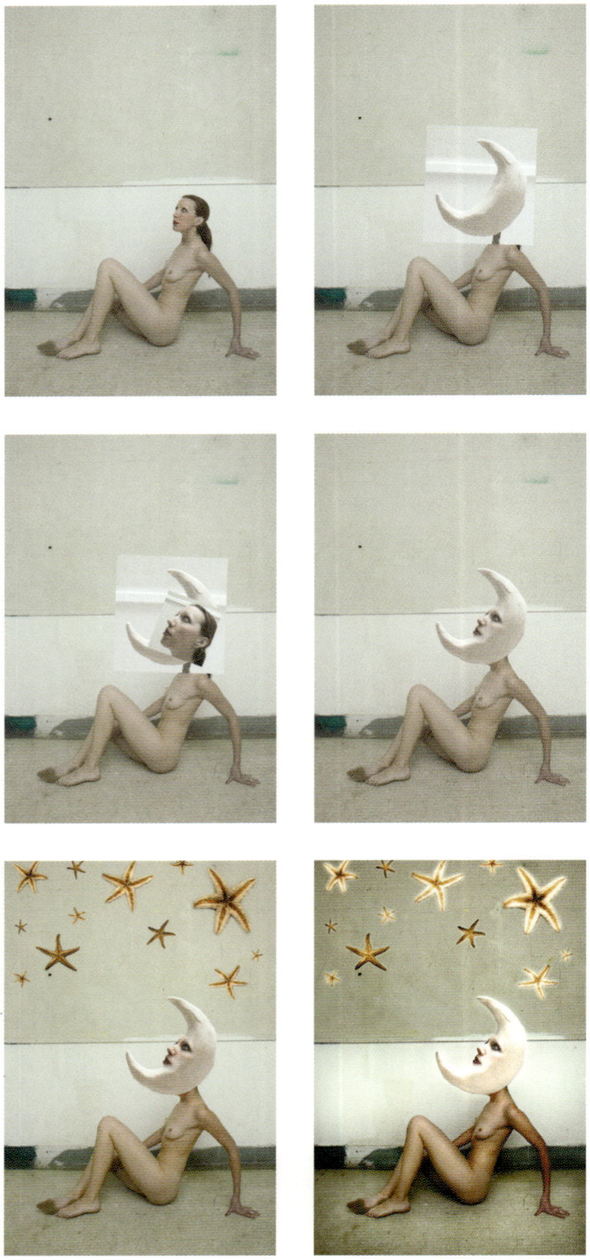

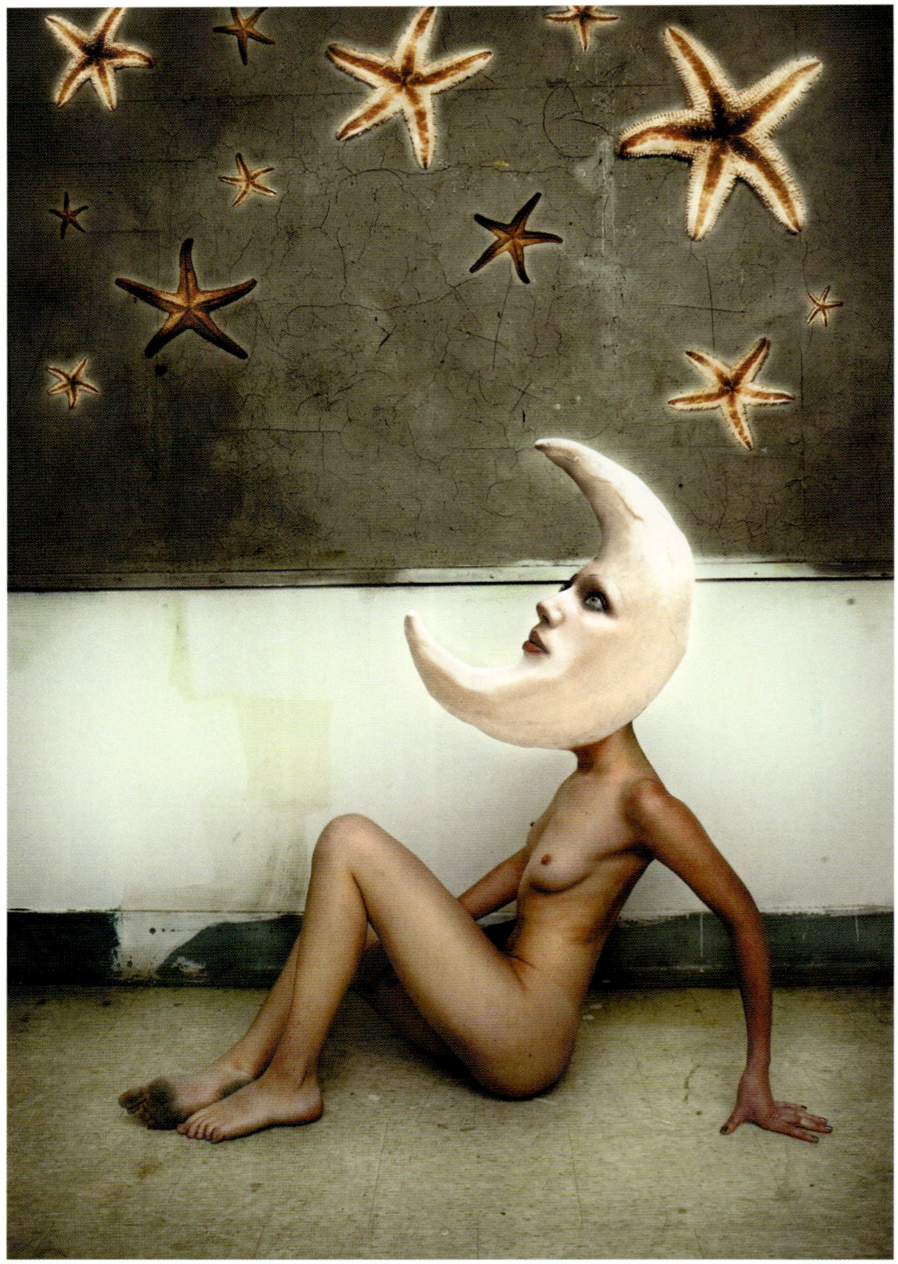

THIS PAGE: None of Donovan's montages happen by accident. Before any shots are taken, he goes through a careful planning process to work out exactly what the digital steps will be to give him his final result, which is usually unrecognizable from the preliminary photo. "All my images are sketched out first," he says. "I will hunt down something like the starfish, if they are on the sketch. But also, if I find something interesting that has a lot of texture or general creative possibilities, I'll hang on to it to use later."

This composition began with a straightforward shot of the nude model against a very plain and somewhat shabby-looking background. Slowly, via many layer masks, the transformation took place. Firstly, the moon object was superimposed onto the model's body and then a close-up of her profile was added on top of this. The moon was brought to the fore again to reveal only the enlarged eyes, nose, and mouth, then scans of dried starfish were layer-masked into the scene. Highlights and shadows were emphasized by masking in Curves adjustment layers. The final image had more of these layers, mostly in the top half of the image. Hue/Saturation adjustment layers were also painted in using layer masks to increase or decrease saturation in certain areas.

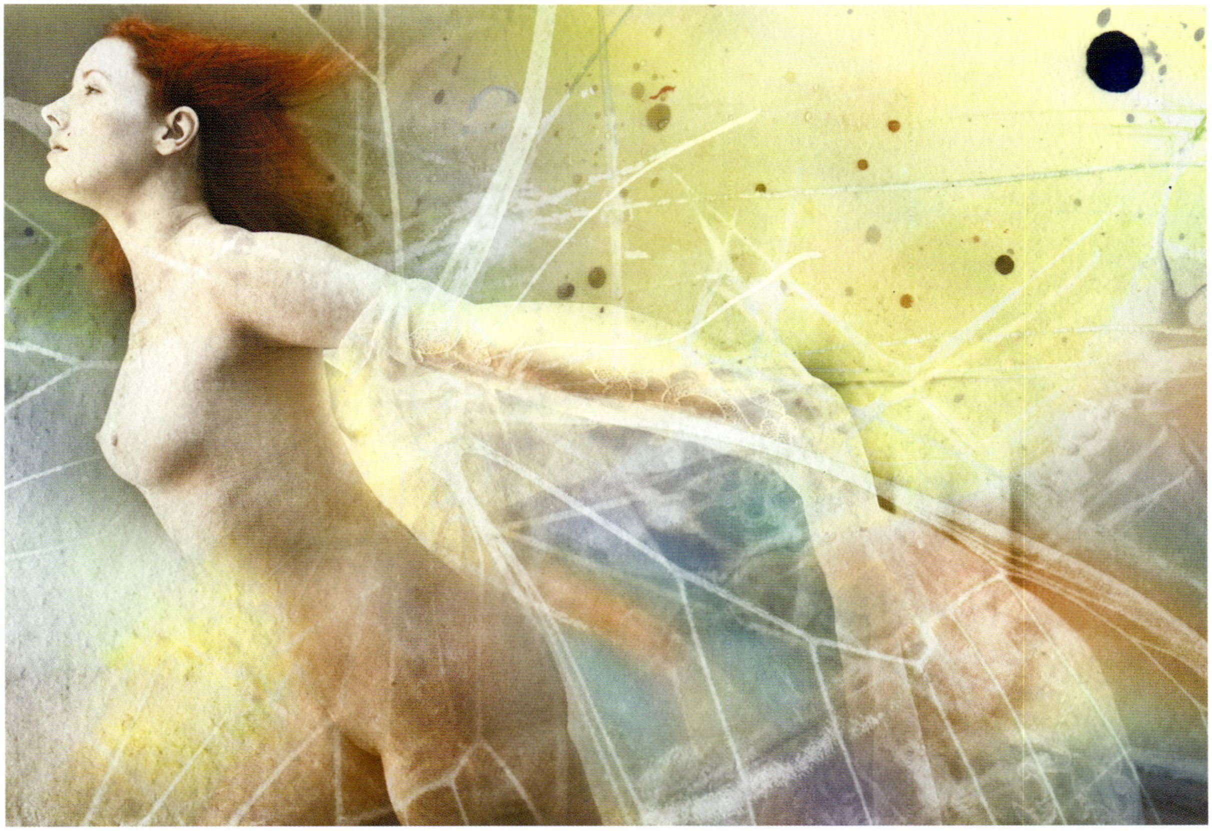

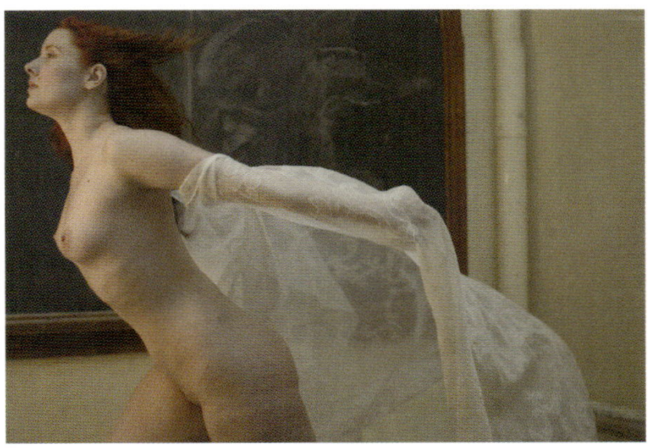

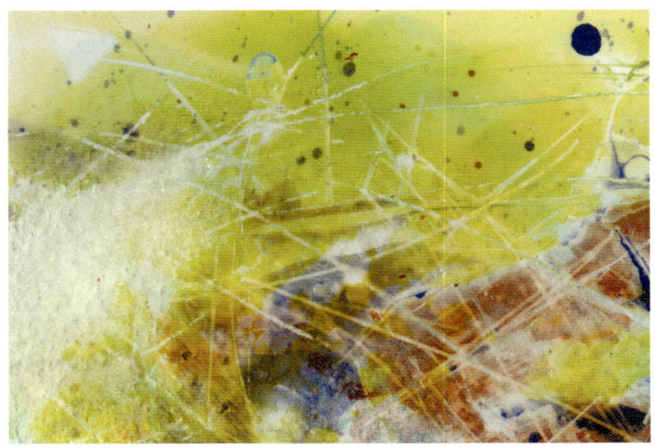

THIS PAGE: Donovan had in mind a colorful butterfly when he planned this image, and the model, Justine, posed with a piece of fabric flowing behind her for the wings. The original shot was combined with a painting and a scan of textured watercolor paper. The paper and painting were duplicated using blending modes and layer masks for the desired effect. Hue/Saturation and Curve layers were also used with masks for further control, and then watercolor effects added with the program Corel/Procreate Painter as a final touch.

Christopher Donovan

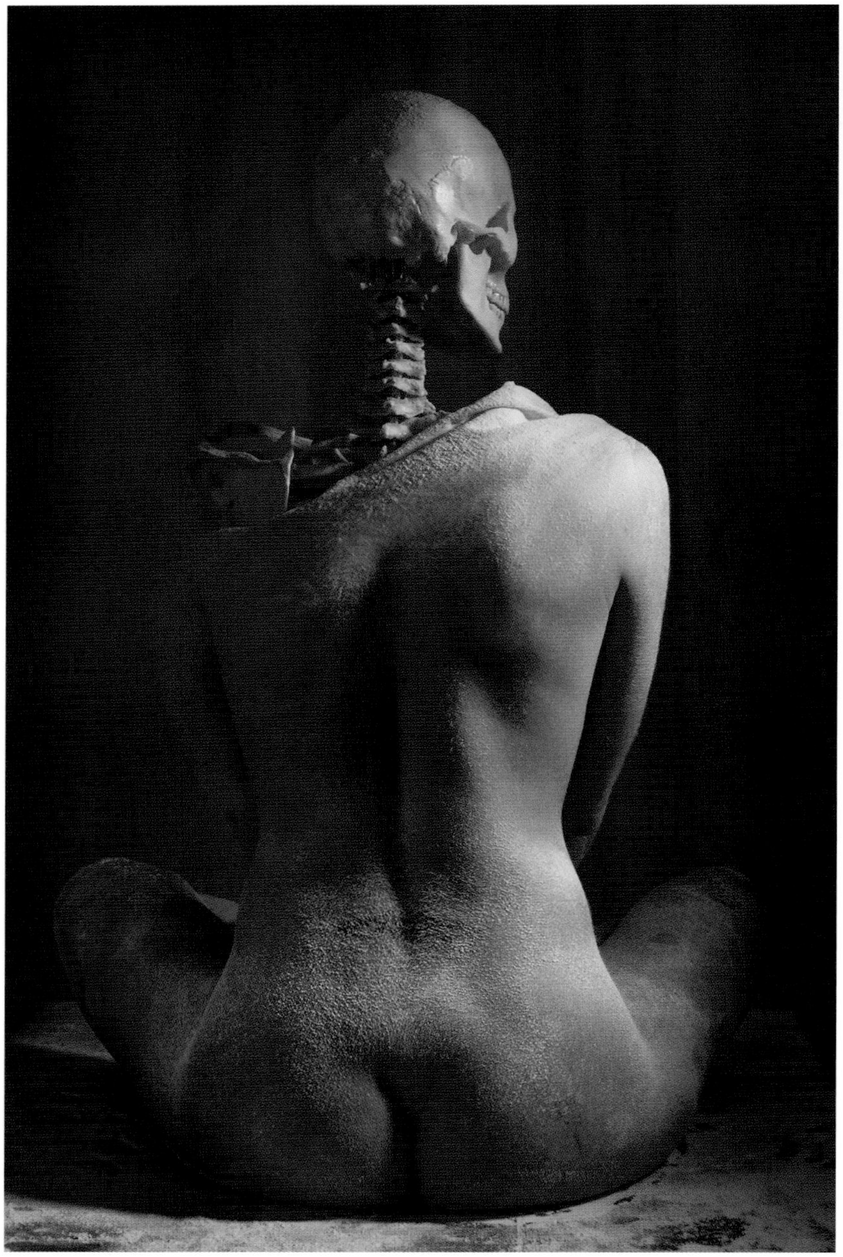

THIS PAGE: This is one of Donovan's more straightforward montages—at least in its execution—with only two elements layer masked together. Nevertheless, attention to detail was important, especially in taking the original photographs. "I always try to shoot everything in the same environment, as it helps to maintain realism," he says. "When creating a montage, consider your lighting, camera perspective, depth of field, sharpness, and film or noise grain. When shooting a model and combining him or her with an object or landscape, shoot the object or scene first. Then have it available as a print out or on a laptop to help you work out where they fit in."

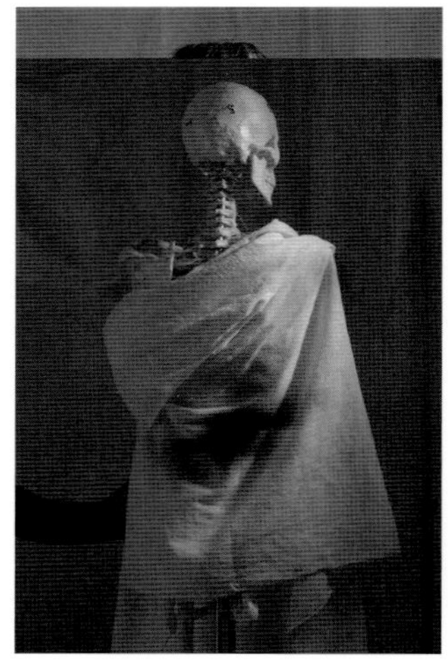

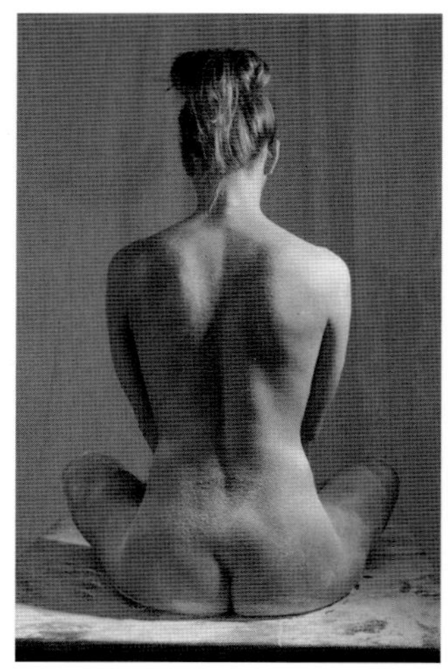

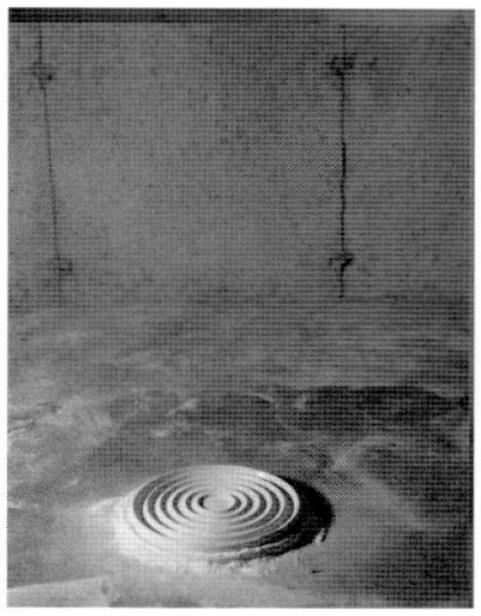

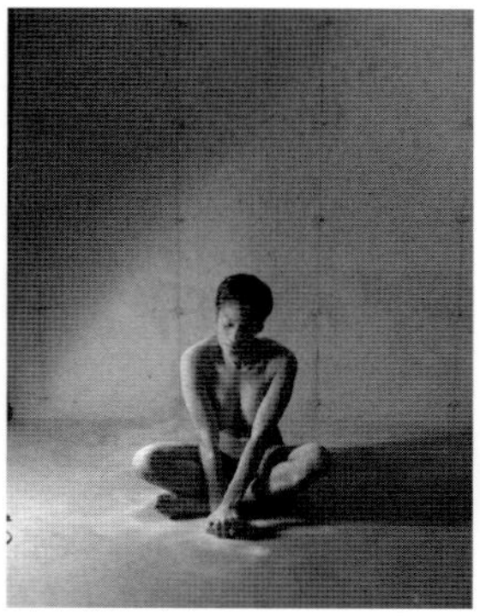

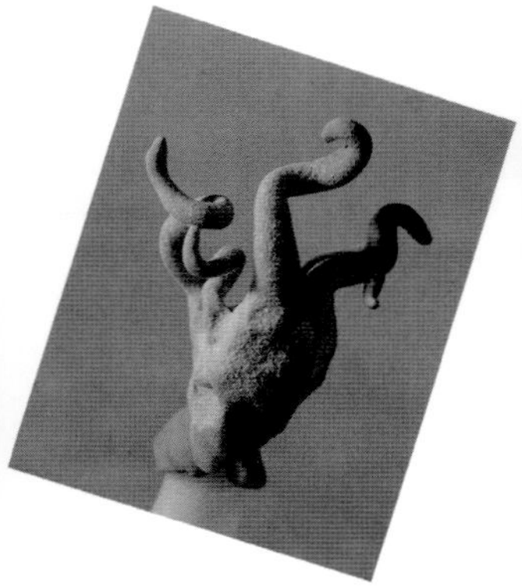

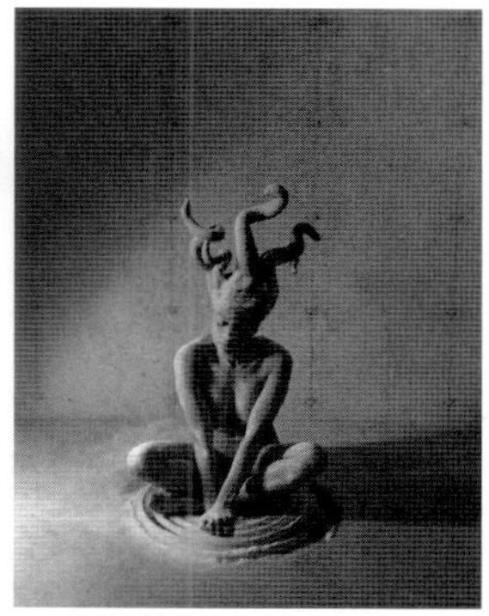

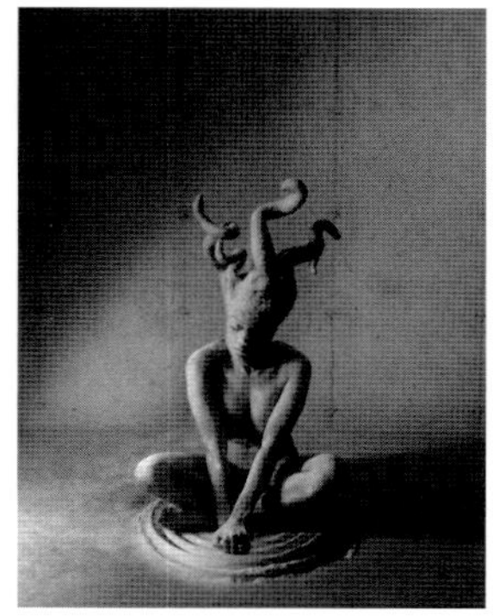

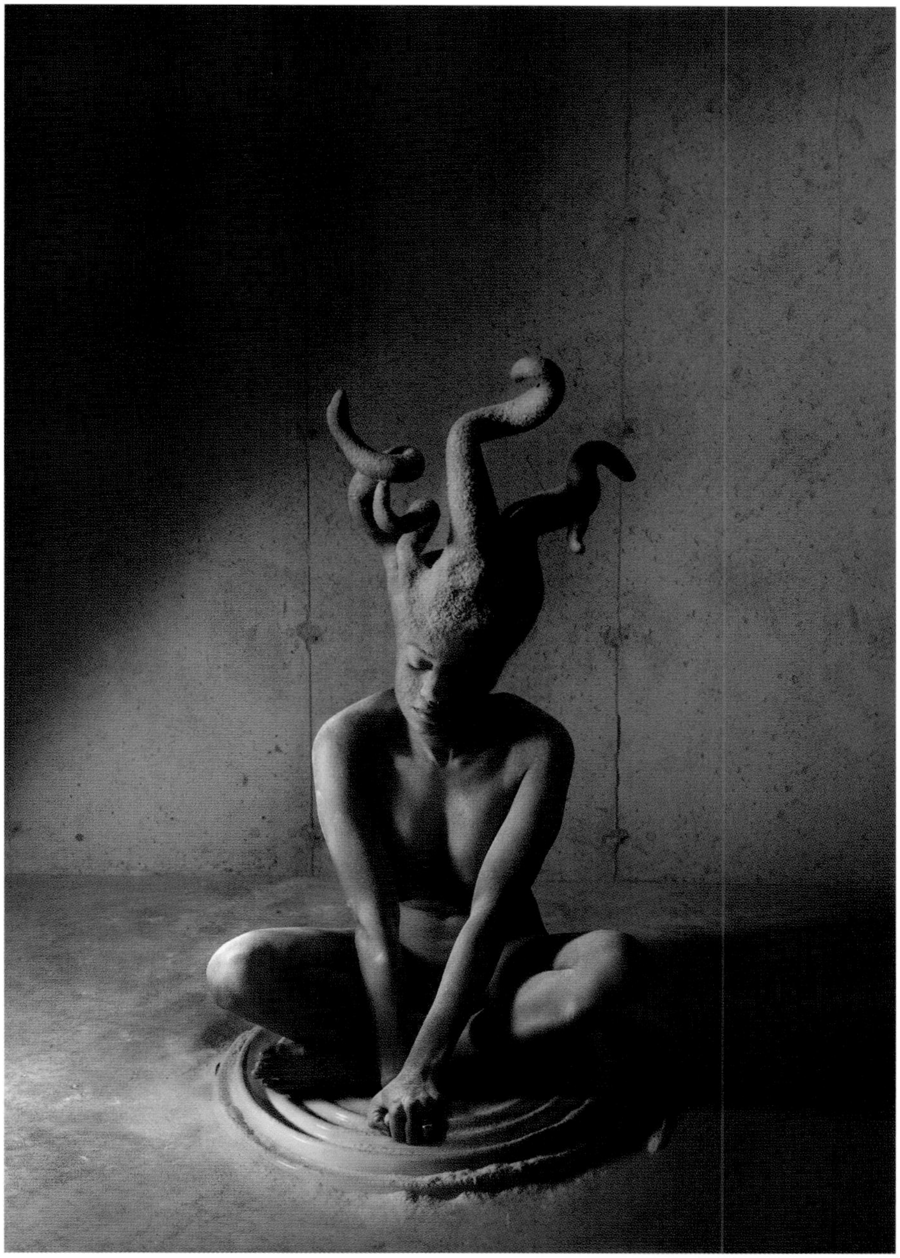

THIS PAGE: Three different images were photographed in the same cell-like environment and combined in five stages to produce this strange fantasy figure. The model, tentacles, and circular "plinth" were combined with layers by dragging a new image layer to the document and clicking Add/Remove Layer. By masking in Curve adjustment layers, highlights and shadows are emphasized to produce a near-complete image. As a final atmospheric touch, some color was added. "I use layer masks to control color by using Hue/Saturation adjustment layers," explains Donovan. "By coloring with any given hue, you can adjust the color of your image easily with a permanent undo—by which I mean the layer mask."

Christopher Donovan

ALL IMAGES: Donovan's imagination and patience know no bounds when it comes to creating complex images like this. As you can see, there were many stages involved, beginning with a nude shot in the studio, with a plain background, and even lighting. Donovan gradually layered in the other elements, including a photo of sky and sections of various tree and foliage images. The sun was created in Photoshop from a simple circle, with Gaussian Blur added and Hue/Saturation layers applied to create the desired colors. The crinkled texture, like a piece of canvas, actually came from an old tea bag that was scanned and added using various advanced blending modes. The final image looks convincingly like a watercolor painting by an old master due to Donovan's skills with the Corel/Procreate Painter program.

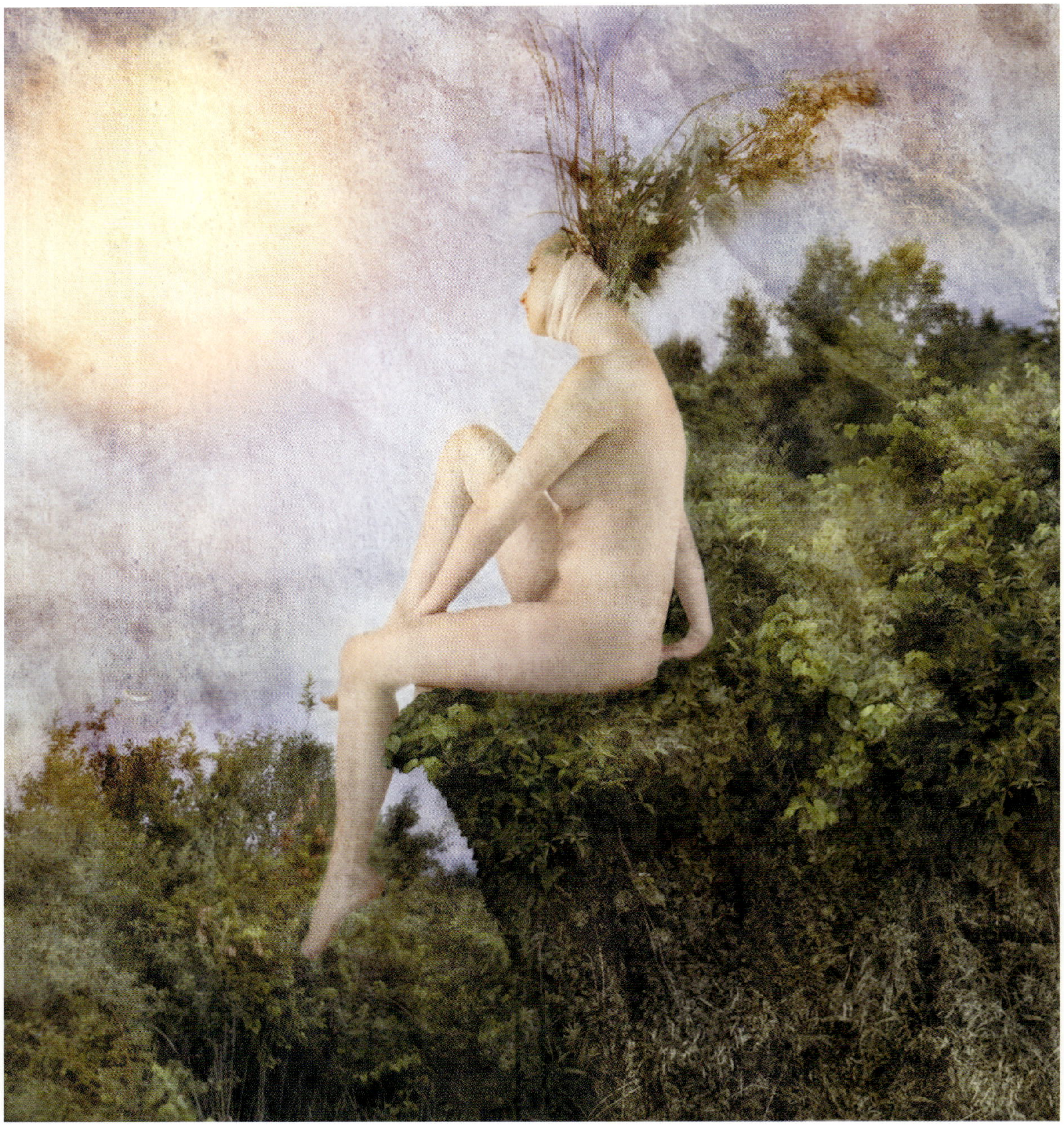

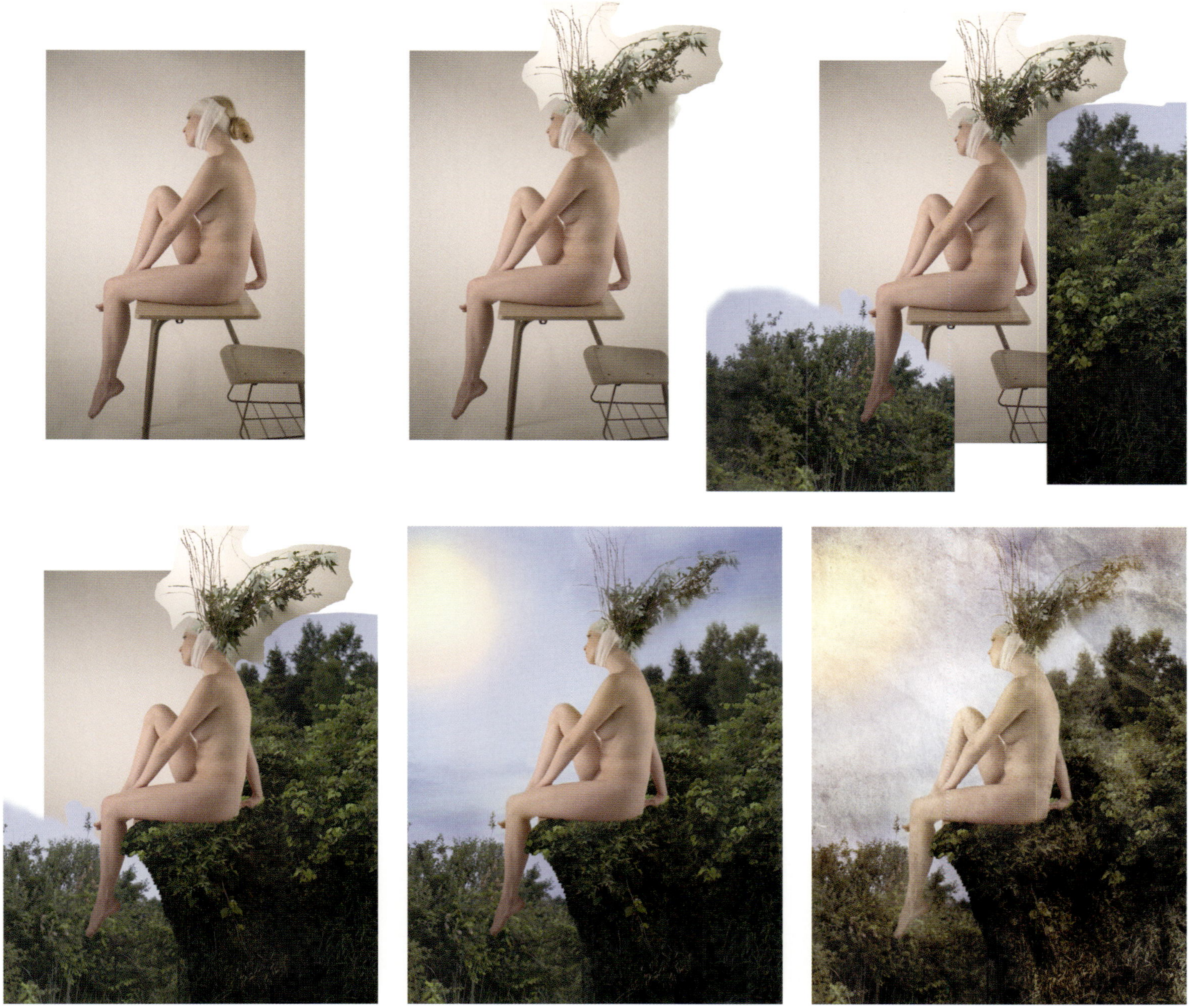

Christopher Donovan

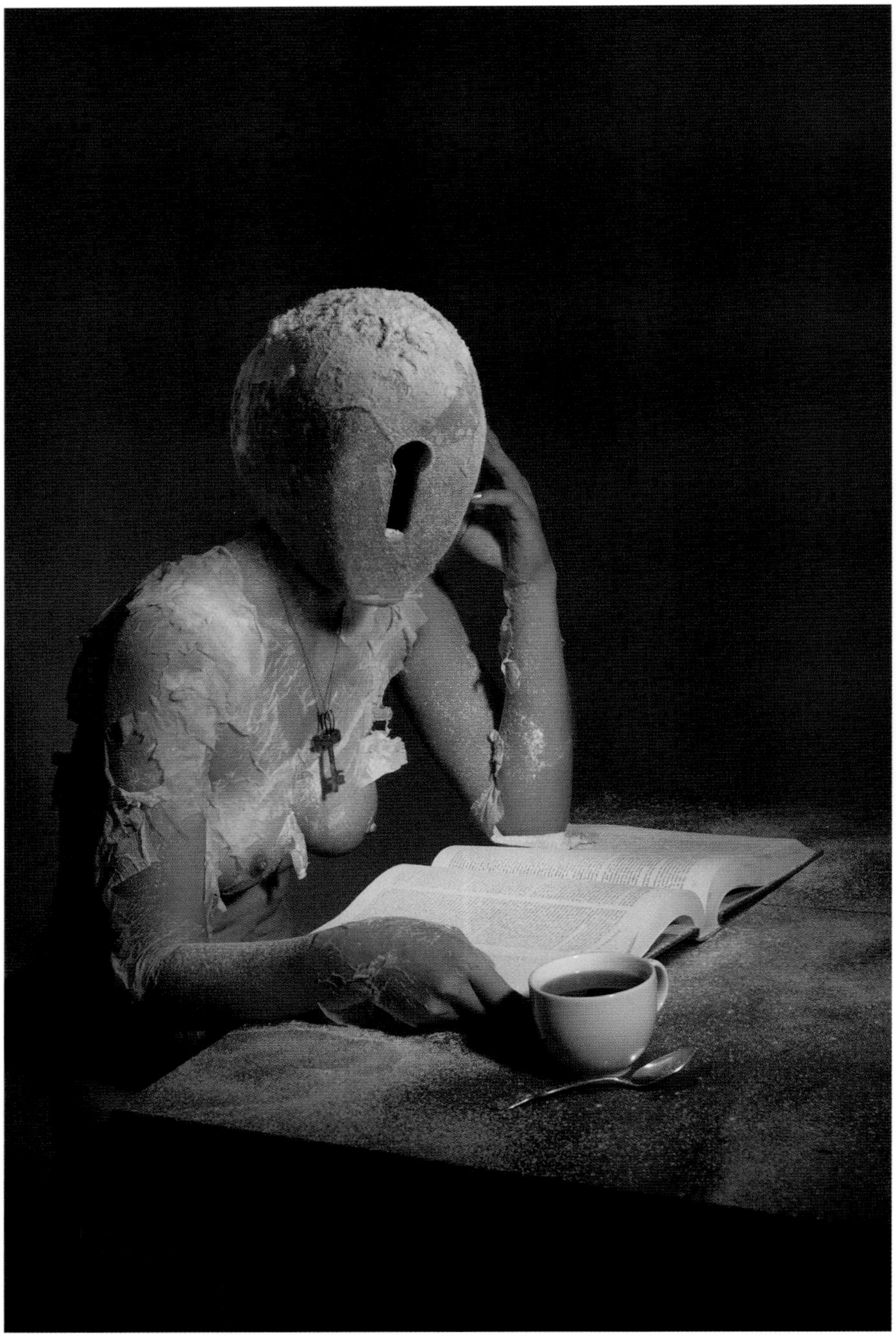

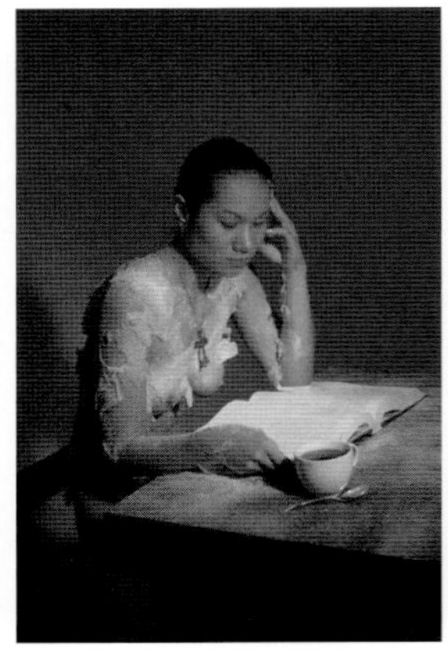

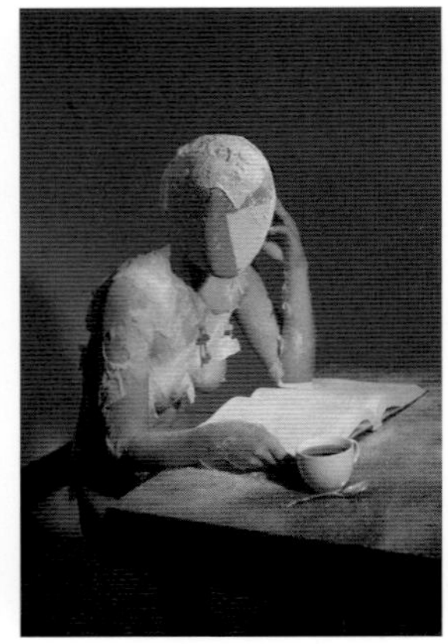

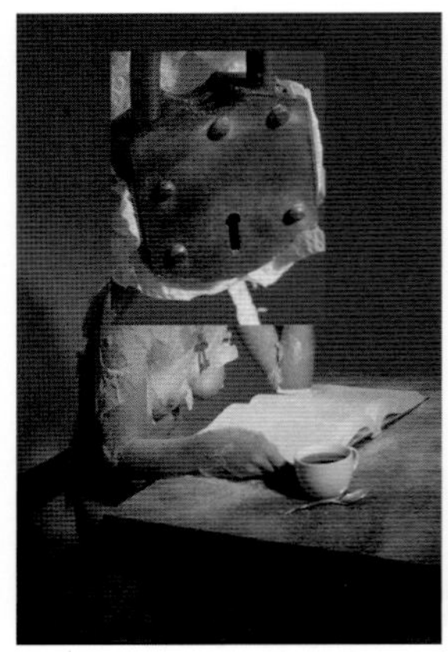

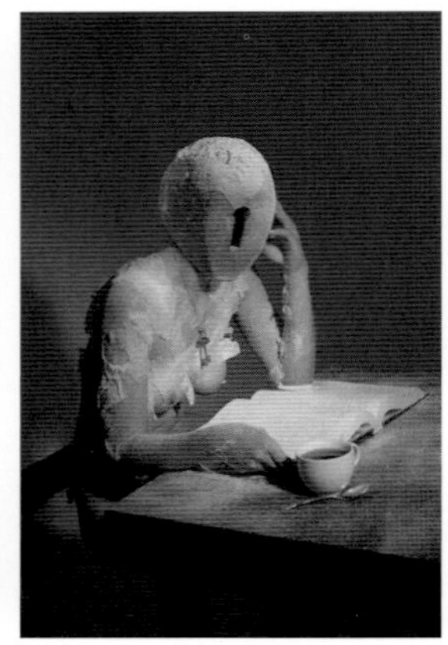

THIS PAGE: "My images don't come from strange dreams, drug use, or an unhappy childhood," says Donovan. "They come from a creative perspective on reality—just imagining 'what if?'" In this image the innocent and very "real" activity of reading a book with a cup of coffee is alarmingly de-humanized by the blank head with a lock replacing the features. The texture on the skin and "head" add to the slightly creepy atmosphere, as does the background gloom. Again, layer masking was used to add the head object and image of an old padlock, and then Curve layers adjustments were made to add appropriate shadows and subtle tones in selected places.

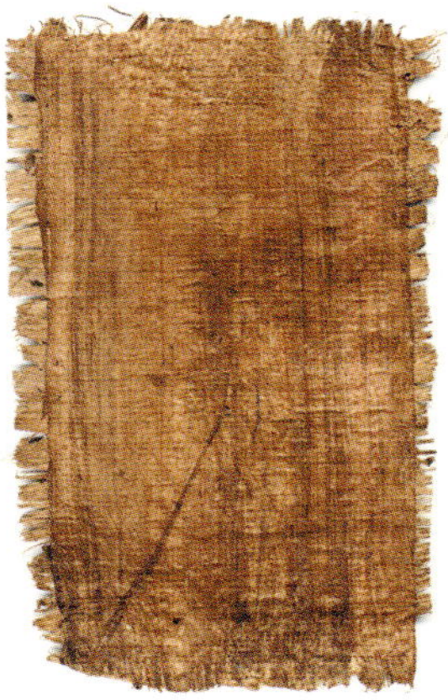

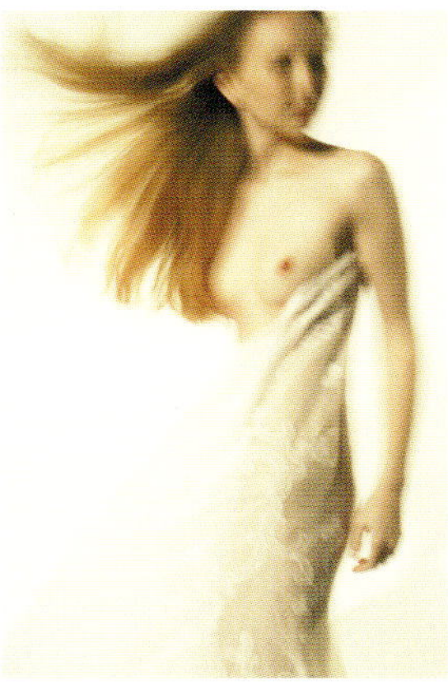

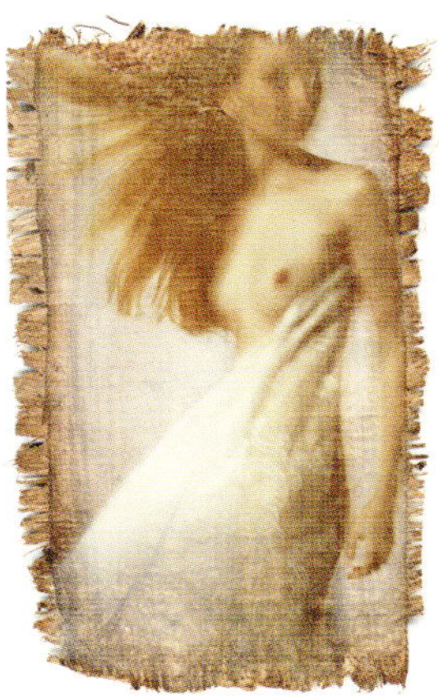

THIS PAGE: Donovan has a collection of textures, like this piece of bamboo paper, that can be scanned and used when an appropriate image comes to mind. The initial photograph was taken in the studio, using an industrial fan to blow the model's hair and a slow exposure for deliberate blur of her movement. It was no accident that Donovan chose a red-haired model. He knew that it would blend perfectly with the color of the bamboo paper. These were combined using blending modes, as he explains. "Open the blending options by double-clicking on a layer, and there you can not only adjust the mode—Screen, Multiply, and so on—but also blend the properties of two layers. If you move these sliders, you can adjust the degree to which the highlights and shadows will blend. Hold the Alt key while you are doing it, and you will notice that the arrow of the slider will divide into two and allow you to create a much smoother blend."

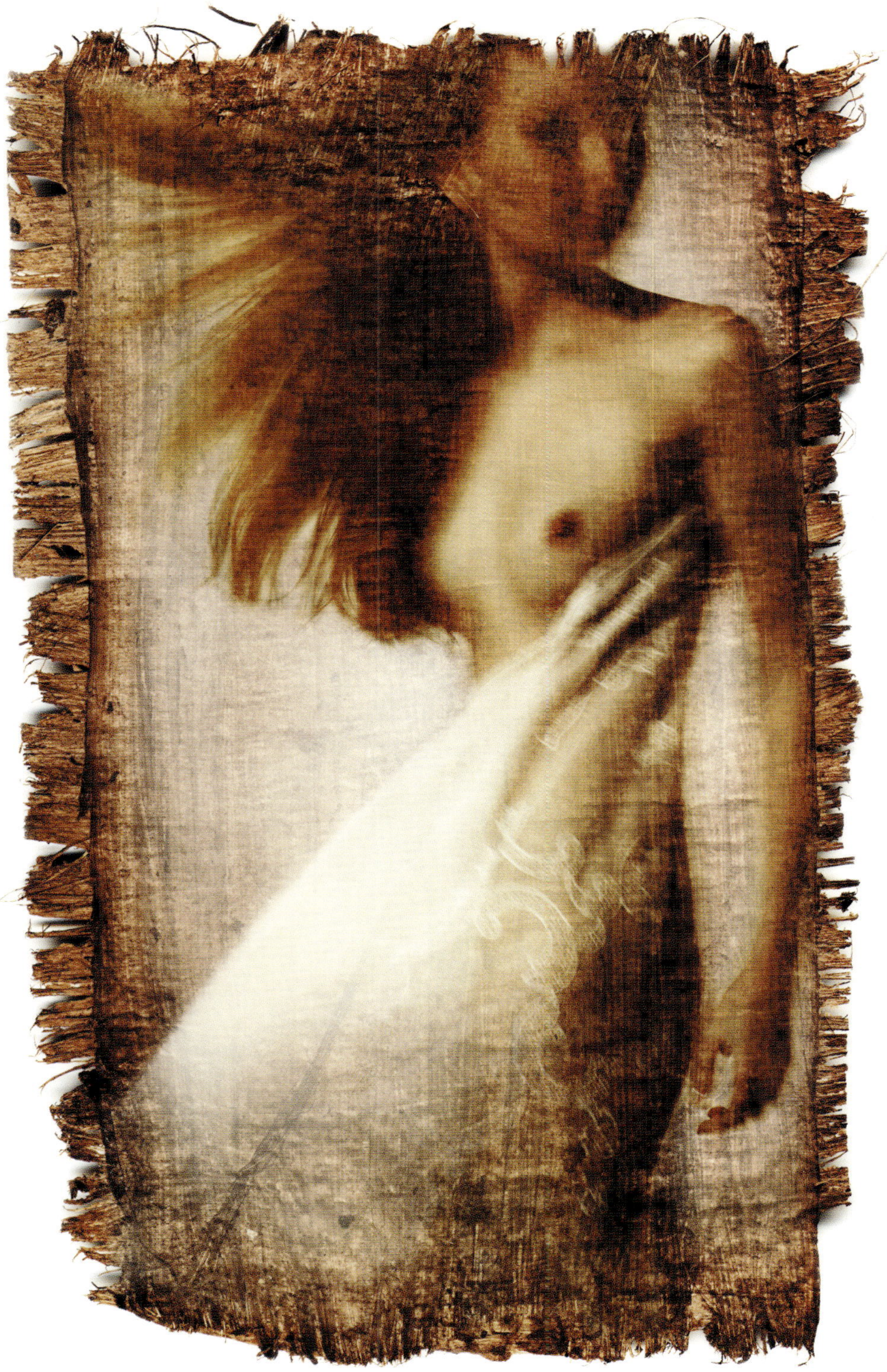

Christopher Donovan

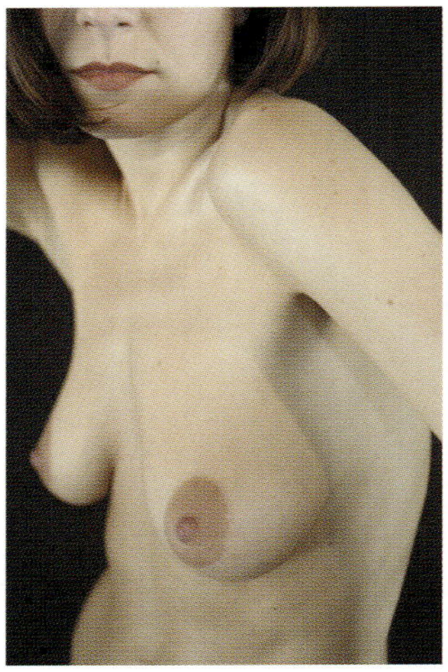

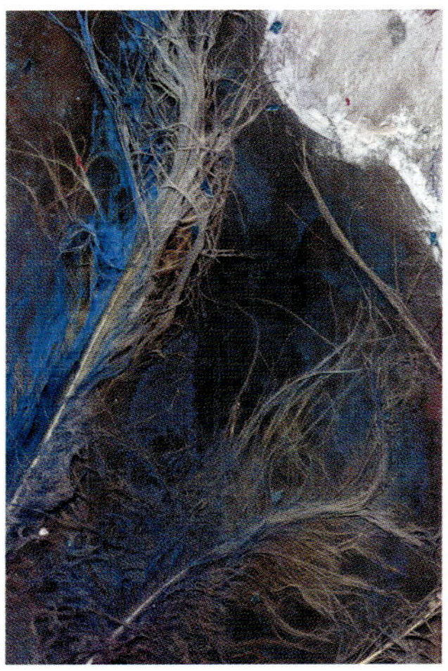

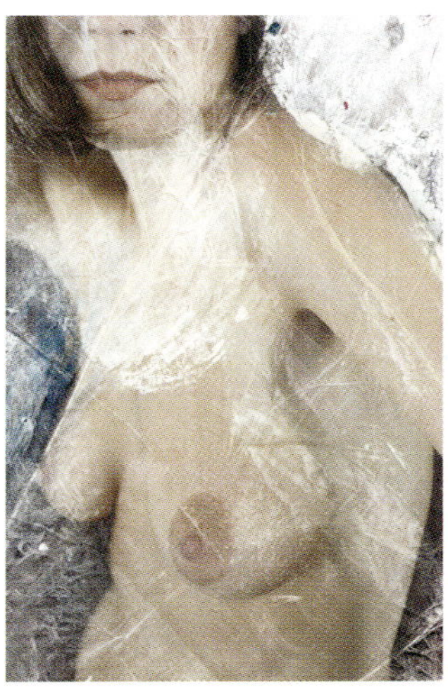

THIS PAGE: A scanned painting was the inspiration here. Donovan combined it with the model, using various blending modes, advanced blending settings, and layer masks. The composition and pose of the model are simple but strong, almost like a classical sculpture. As such, the photo lends itself to this kind of digital treatment much more than if it had been overly complicated.

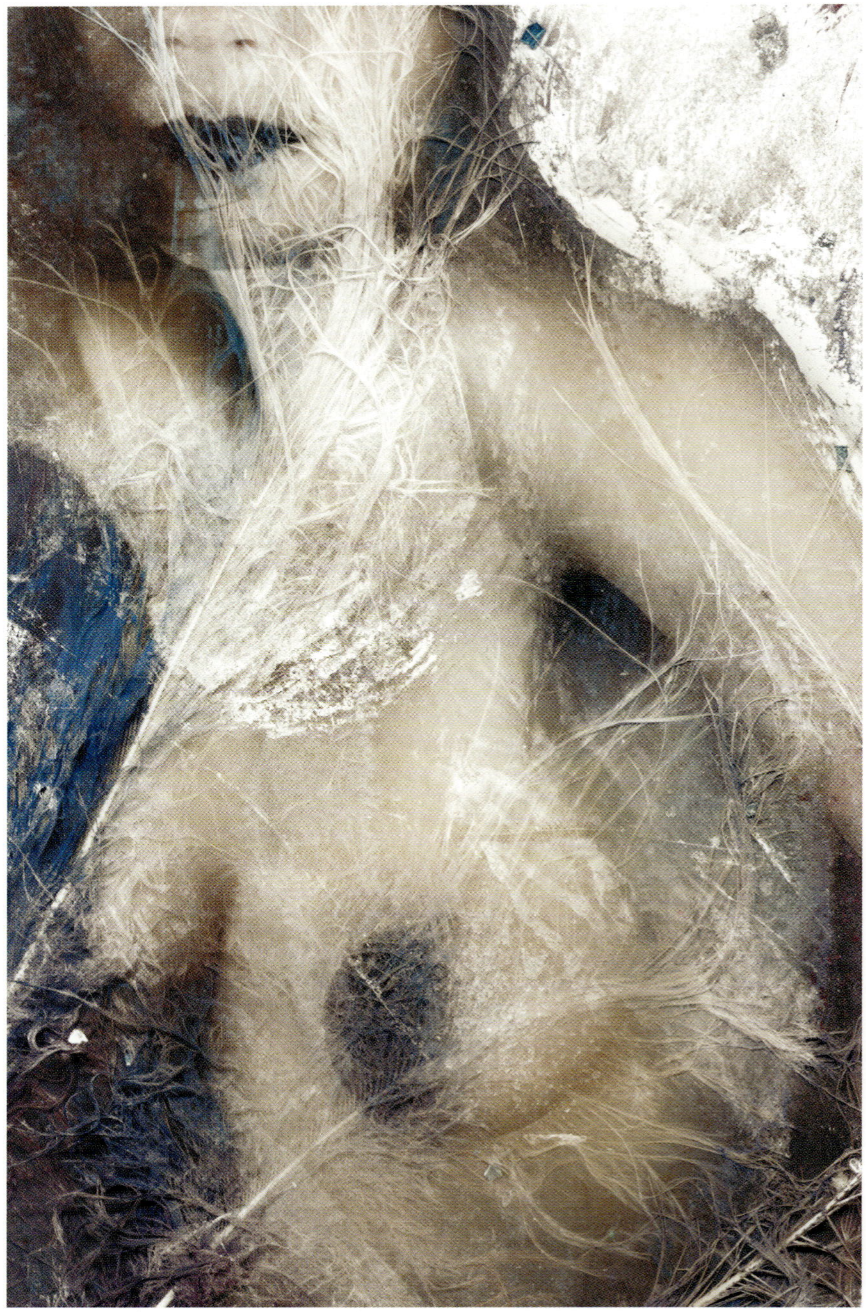

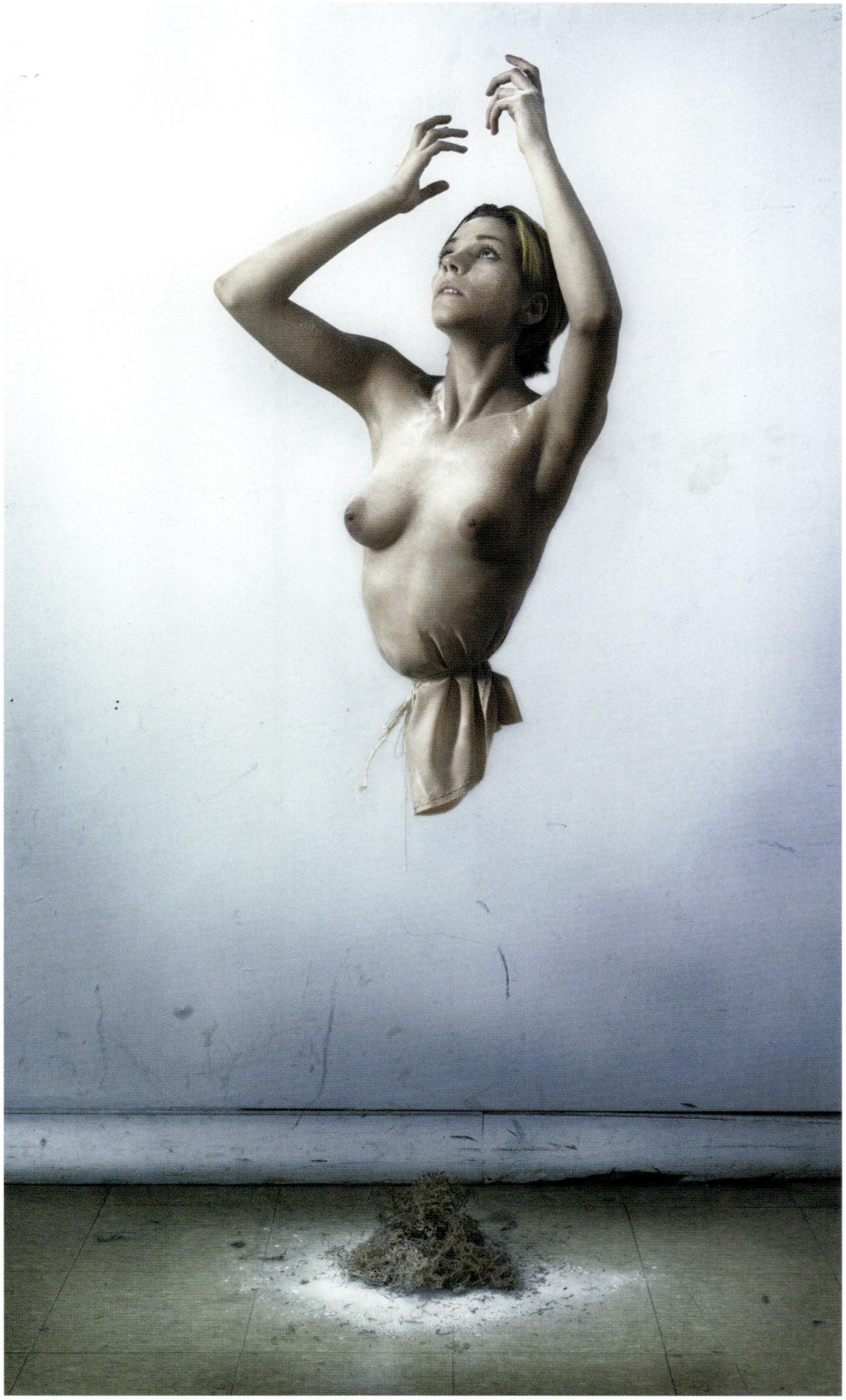

THIS PAGE: Donovan chooses not to reveal the concepts behind his images, preferring to leave it up to the viewer's imagination to interpret them. Could this figure be rising up to an afterlife, leaving her ashes behind? That's actually dried moss and flour on the floor, with the model then photographed in the same spot and with the same lighting. The third element, fabric filled with cotton and tied with string, was also photographed in the same way. The three were layer-masked together and the final image colored with Hue/Saturation adjustment layers. The white glow around the figure adds to the otherworldly effect.

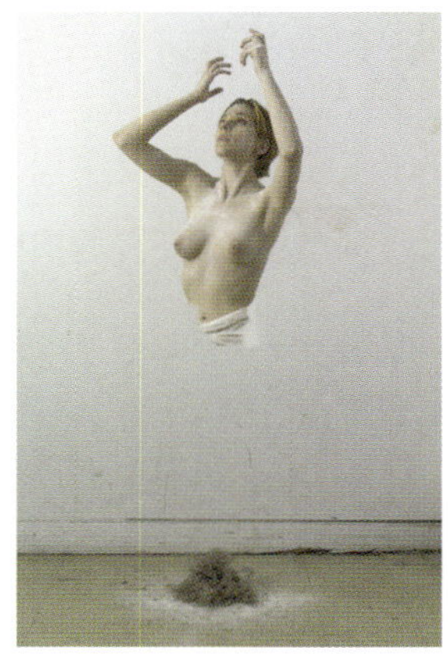

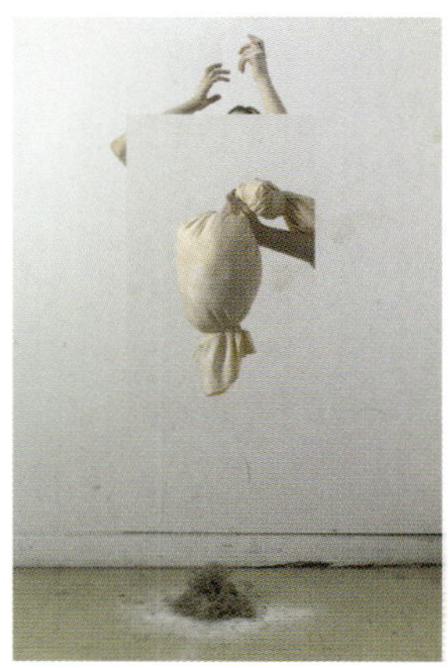

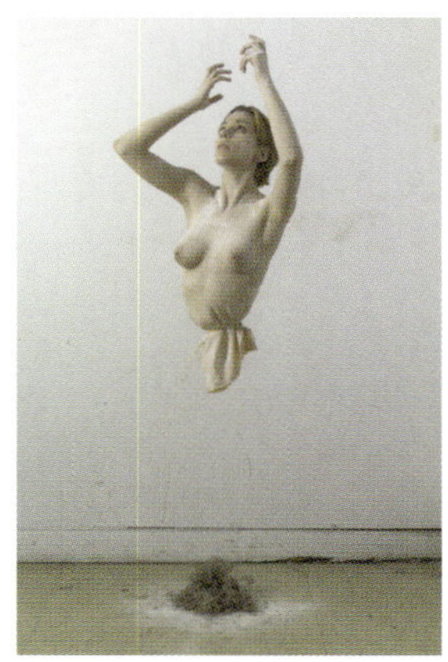

Christopher Donovan

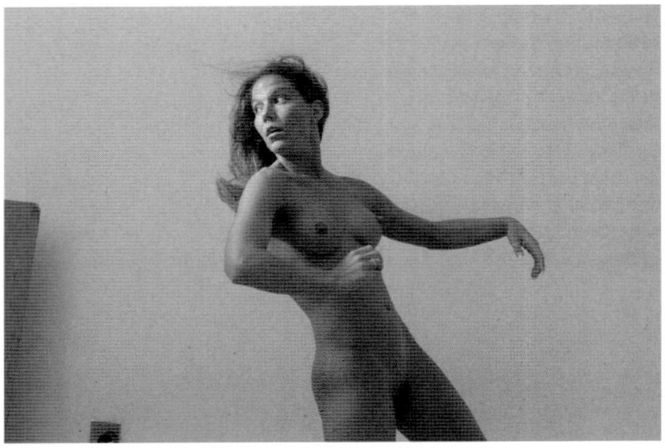

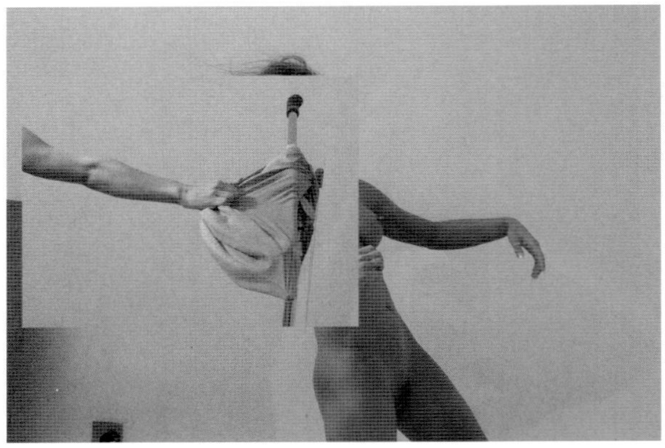

THIS PAGE: This image demonstrates just how important it is that Donovan has a clear vision of the way his work will take shape. The model's pose was directed precisely, so that she really looks as though she is being grabbed. The "loose skin" was cleverly constructed using fabric attached to a metal pole, then pulled by an assistant, ensuring the folds were in the right places before being photographed. The two elements were then combined and the image cropped to give the alarmingly realistic final effect.

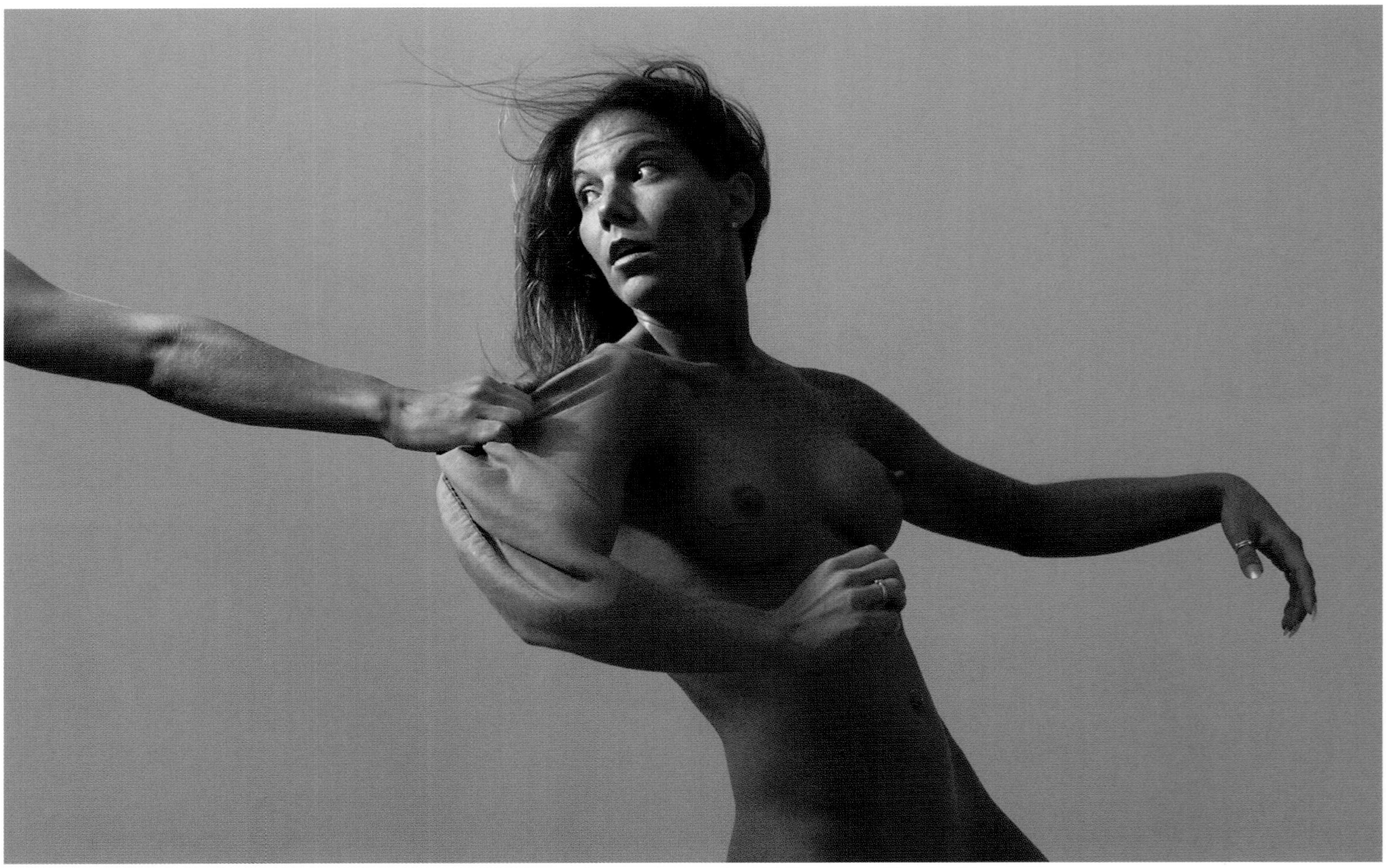

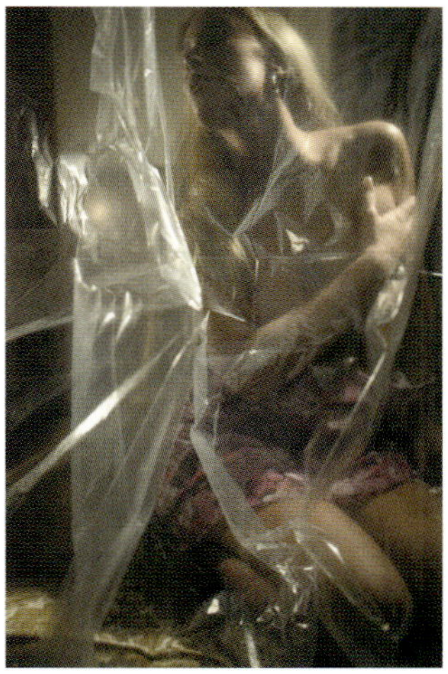

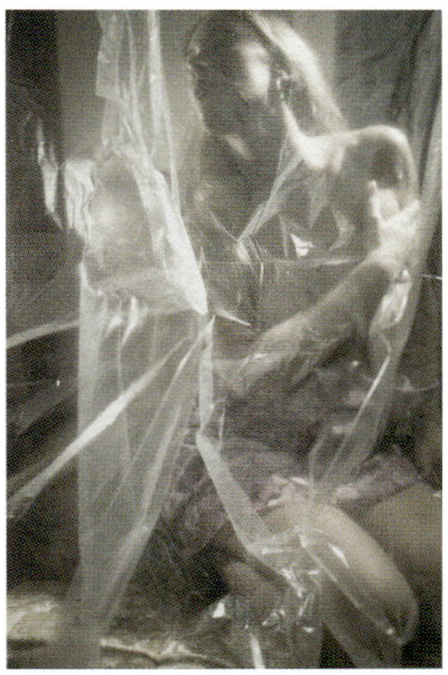

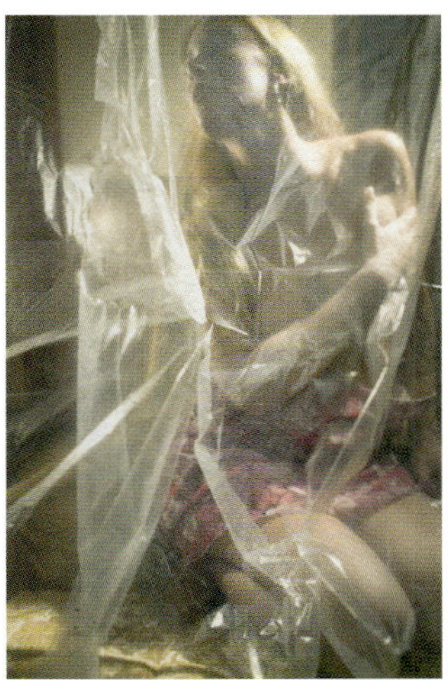

THIS PAGE: This photograph was originally taken in fairly low and contrasty light and it doesn't look too promising at this stage, with the model wrapped in and partly obscured by a plastic sheet. Once it was lightened with Curve adjustment layers, you can see it begin to take shape as more of the model's features are revealed. Donovan then set to work with the Corel/Procreate Painter program. "I'm still new to this, but I use it from time to time to add painterly effects," he explains. "I find it has better brushes than Photoshop, though I only use a few of them and I do so subtly, otherwise I find it difficult to create realistic images. Here, the Sponge brush added texture, and then I smeared it with Watercolor brushes."

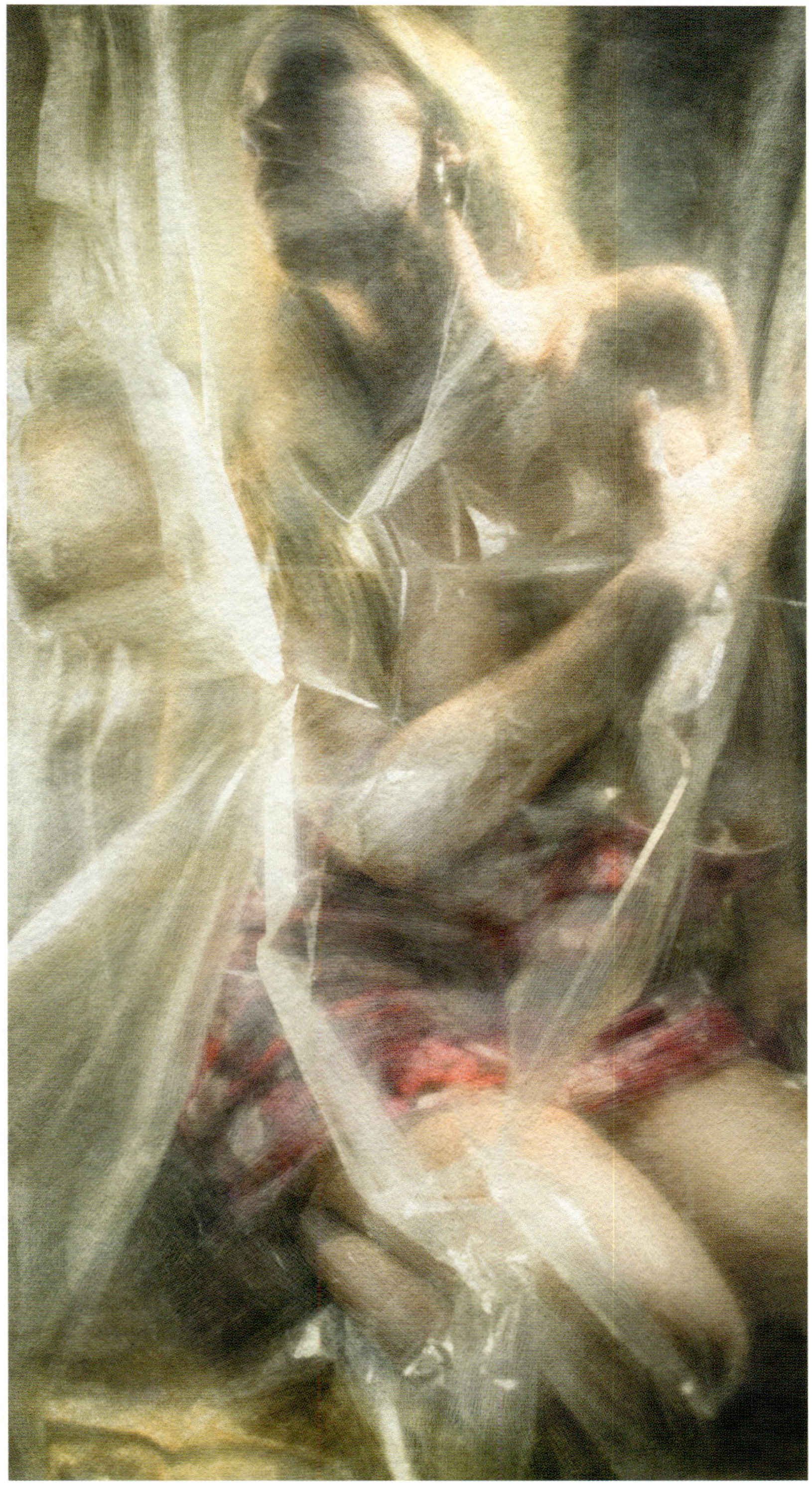

Steve Gatlin

Steve Gatlin has viewed and documented the world through his lenses for as long as he can remember and shot just about every style of photography imaginable. While some of his wedding and portrait work is photographed in digital, his true passion is still working with film, which he processes and prints in his own darkroom.

His current body of work is from an "experiment in light and motion" called *The Beauty Project*. It is a series of images shot at night in various outdoor locations. By working in the dark, Gatlin is taking the concepts of "light-painting" and combining them with the nude human form to create visions of beauty.

All of the shots are made on Kodak T-Max 100 film and processed and printed in his darkroom. For the purposes of website exhibition, the pictures are scanned from the negatives and manipulated only for proper exposure. This is always limited to brightness and contrast, and dodging and burning.

"Everything you see in one of my shots can be printed by hand in my darkroom just as it can from a digitized version on one of my websites. There is no manipulation beyond what is exposed on the film."

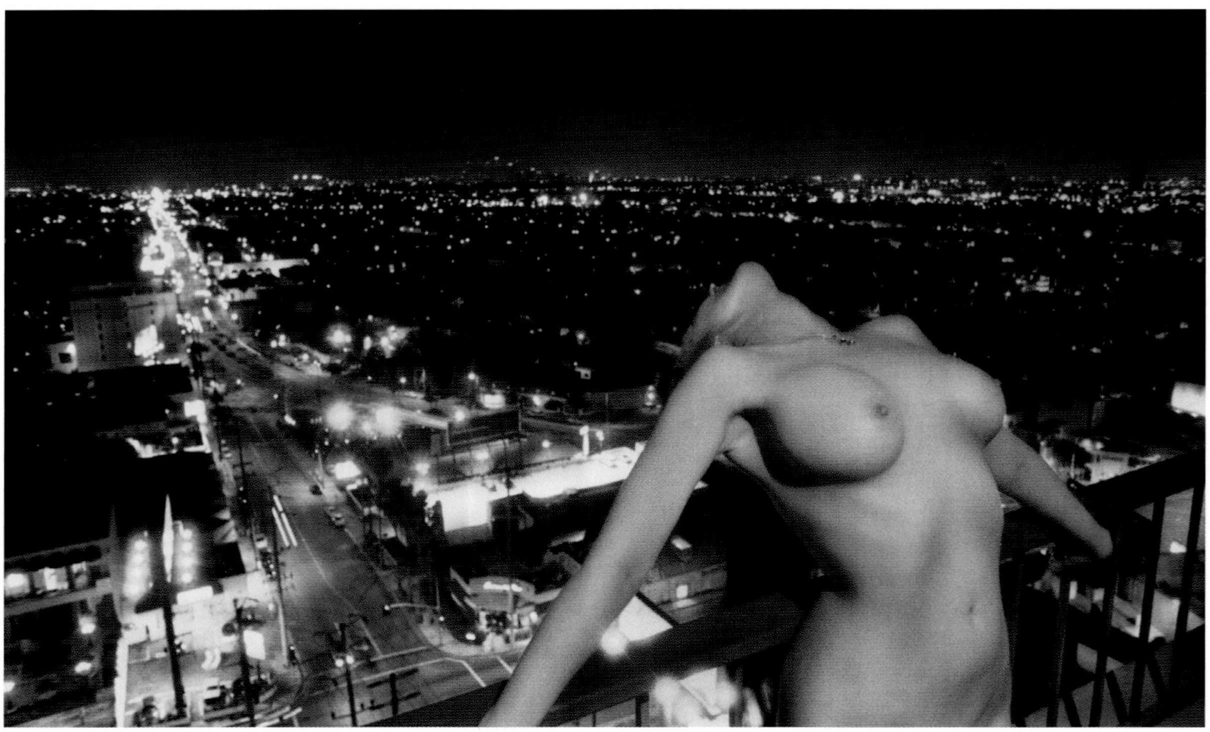

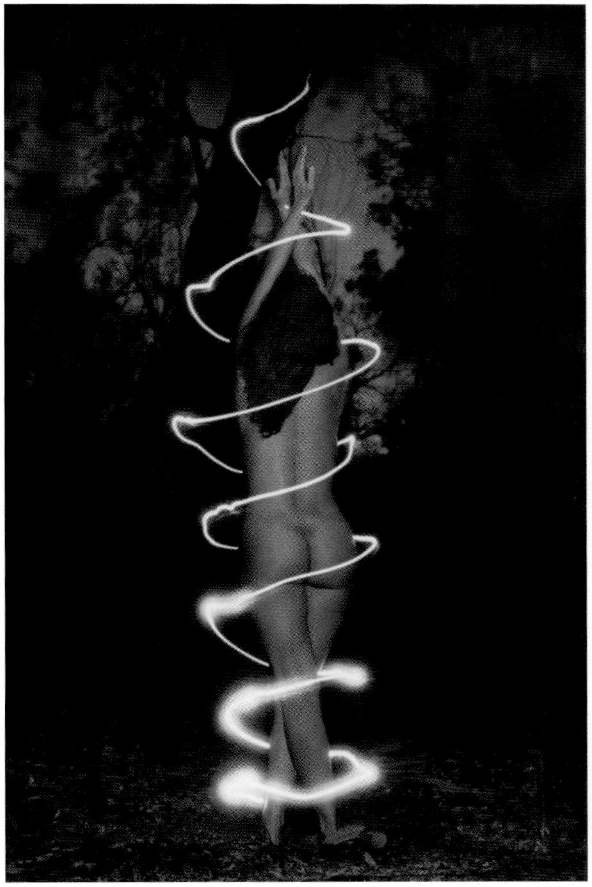

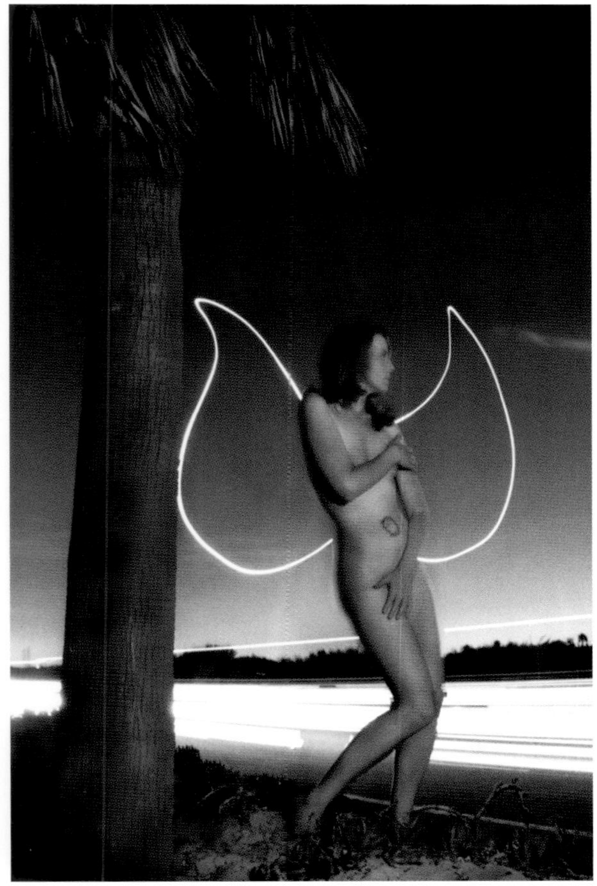

LEFT: This picture, entitled *Bent City*, was set on the rooftop of the model's apartment building in Hollywood, California. It overlooks the renowned Melrose Avenue, and one can see the car lights and night-time hustle and bustle of the Hollywood scene below. "The top of this building was a photographer's dream as one side contained a lit-up pool and deck area and the other, where this shot was taken, was dark and secluded," he explains. "This allowed me to use a variety of 'light-painting' techniques using the city of Los Angeles as a backdrop. For this shot I asked the model to grab onto the guardrail and lean as far backward as she felt comfortable doing. Once in position, she was required to hold still for three shots. I decided a 5-, a 10-, and a 15-second exposure would do the trick. At the end of each exposure, I would cast light from above using a handheld flash. I usually vary the direction of each flash illumination so that I can see different shadow effects. This particular image was taken with a 10-second exposure, and the flash illumination was from above and slightly to her left. Photoshop manipulation was only needed for standard dodging and burning."

ABOVE: Gatlin had worked with this model a couple of times before taking this shot, both in fairly public outdoor locations. "We decided to take a break from that and headed off to a dark wooded park to get this shot. The privacy made it easy to work and explore different ideas of 'light-painting.' For this shot, I asked her to hold position while I moved into the frame. Because it was dark, I was able to stand beside her without being exposed to the film. With a small flashlight, I started at her feet and passed it around her body, moving upward until I passed her hands and streaked the light into the air to finish. Then, before the end of the exposure, I moved back behind the camera and illuminated her with a handheld flash. We tried 10 different variations, and this was the best finished shot. Again, a digital version of dodging and burning was done, producing the same results as would have been achieved in a darkroom.'

ABOVE: "*Fallen Angel* was a concept I had in my head before the shoot and had discussed with the model as we scouted for the perfect location," Gatlin explains. "Because of the close proximity to moving cars and people, I wanted to make sure that she felt comfortable being out in a public situation in the nude. I needed an area where I could capture moving cars as well as keep her dimly lit because I would be running into the shot to draw the angel wings and didn't want to burn myself into the film. As it turned out, we found the perfect spot alongside a public parking lot in Huntington Beach, California. There were no street lights, which allowed me to position her in a reasonably dark area alongside a palm tree. "After we discussed the technique I'd be using, I had her hold position as I began the exposure. I ran into the shot and, using a small flashlight, drew a set of angel wings behind her. Then I moved back behind the camera and illuminated her with a flash to complete the shot. It takes an average of 15 to 20 seconds to complete a shot like this. I usually attempt at least five different variations to ensure that at least one looks right. The key is to imagine the frame of your shot as you're "drawing" in mid-air and try to keep within it while maintaining smooth, fluid movements." This image was taken on Kodak T-Max 100 film, the negative scanned, and dodging and burning tools used to fine-tune the areas of light and dark.

Steve Gatlin

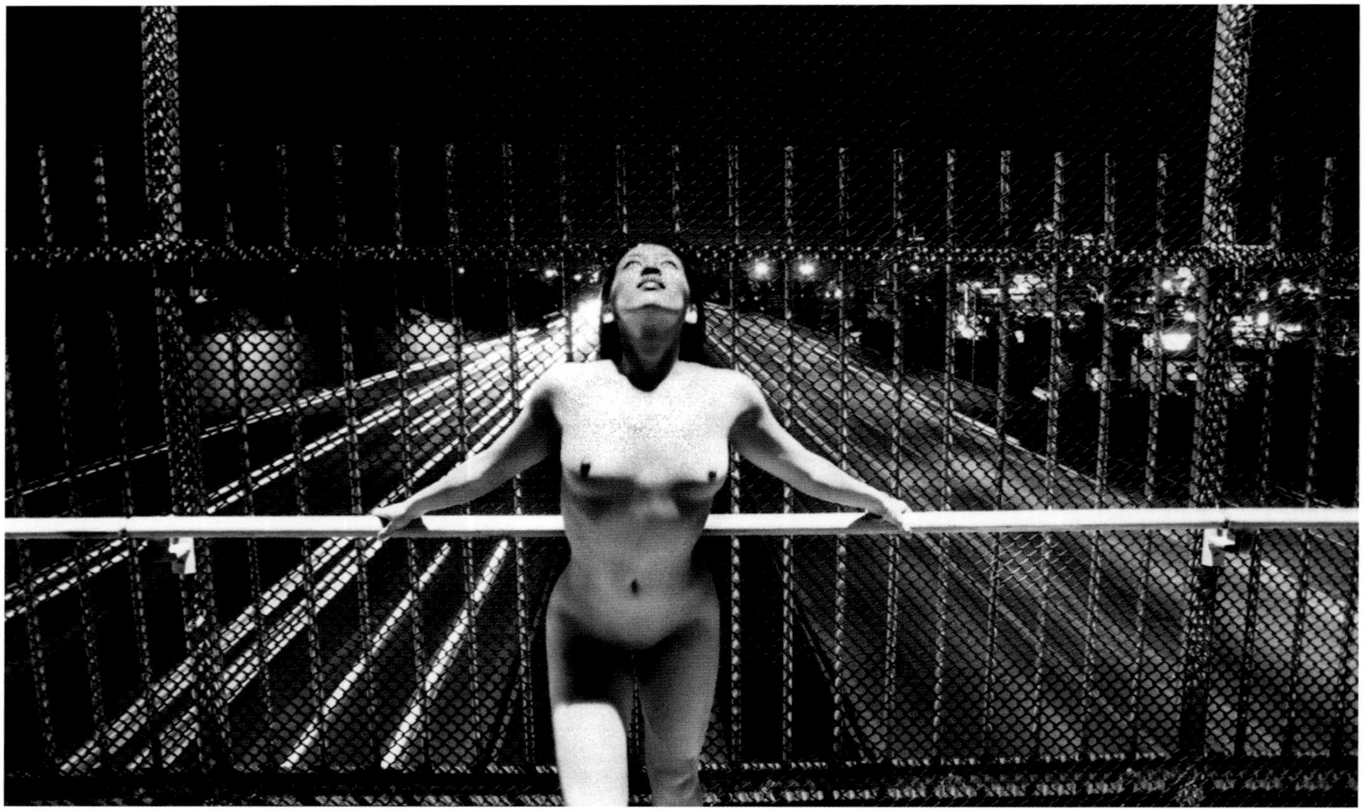

OPPOSITE PAGE: This "painting with light" technique requires a totally dark setting so that the photographer can move into the frame to use the flashlight during a long exposure, without himself registering on the film. It also requires the model to stay perfectly still so that the lines of light "drawn" around her will record in the right places. For this shot Gatlin began with the flashlight at the model's fingertips, and then swept the rays of light toward the camera. "Once I felt I had sufficient lights, I popped the model with a handheld flash and ended the exposure. Although I was doing several light-painting shots at the time, this one is the only one of this style I attempted. Photoshop manipulation was used only to dodge and burn various parts of the image."

ABOVE: "This was shot on an overpass near downtown San Diego. It was for pedestrians only, which made it relatively easy to watch for people approaching," Gatlin recalls. "I positioned the model so that she stood in the center of oncoming and passing traffic below to give symmetry to the image. The overpass had street lamps above so I felt that a handheld flash would not be needed, as it would 'burn' the subject too much." It isn't easy to judge the correct exposure for night-time shots like this, so Gatlin tried three different shutter speed settings of 5, 10, and 15 seconds to increase his chances of one being correct—in this case, 5 seconds.

RIGHT: Rather different in style from Gatlin's other images shown here, *Woven* was taken toward the end of a shoot he was doing with these two models. "We were outside on a dark beach in Long Beach, California, which allowed me to use the area behind them as a black canvas. The concept was to play off their similar tattoos and body types to create an image that at first glance would be a mirror image. Upon closer inspection, the viewer would see two different people. I asked them to stand back-to-back and interlock their arms, then, using a handheld flash, I lit them from various angles over the course of six different exposures. Normal dodging and burning in Photoshop was all that was needed to complete the image digitally."

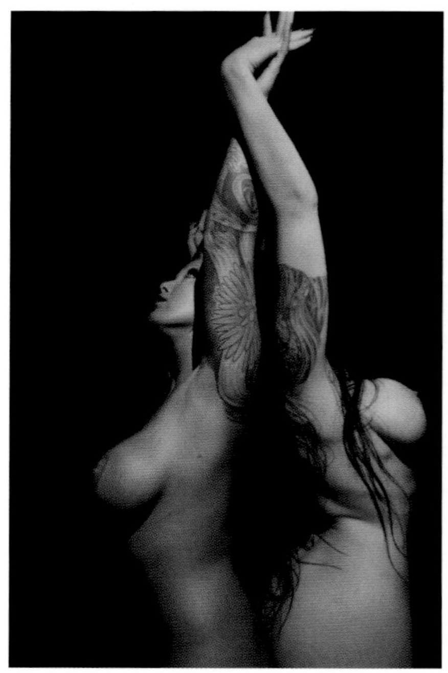

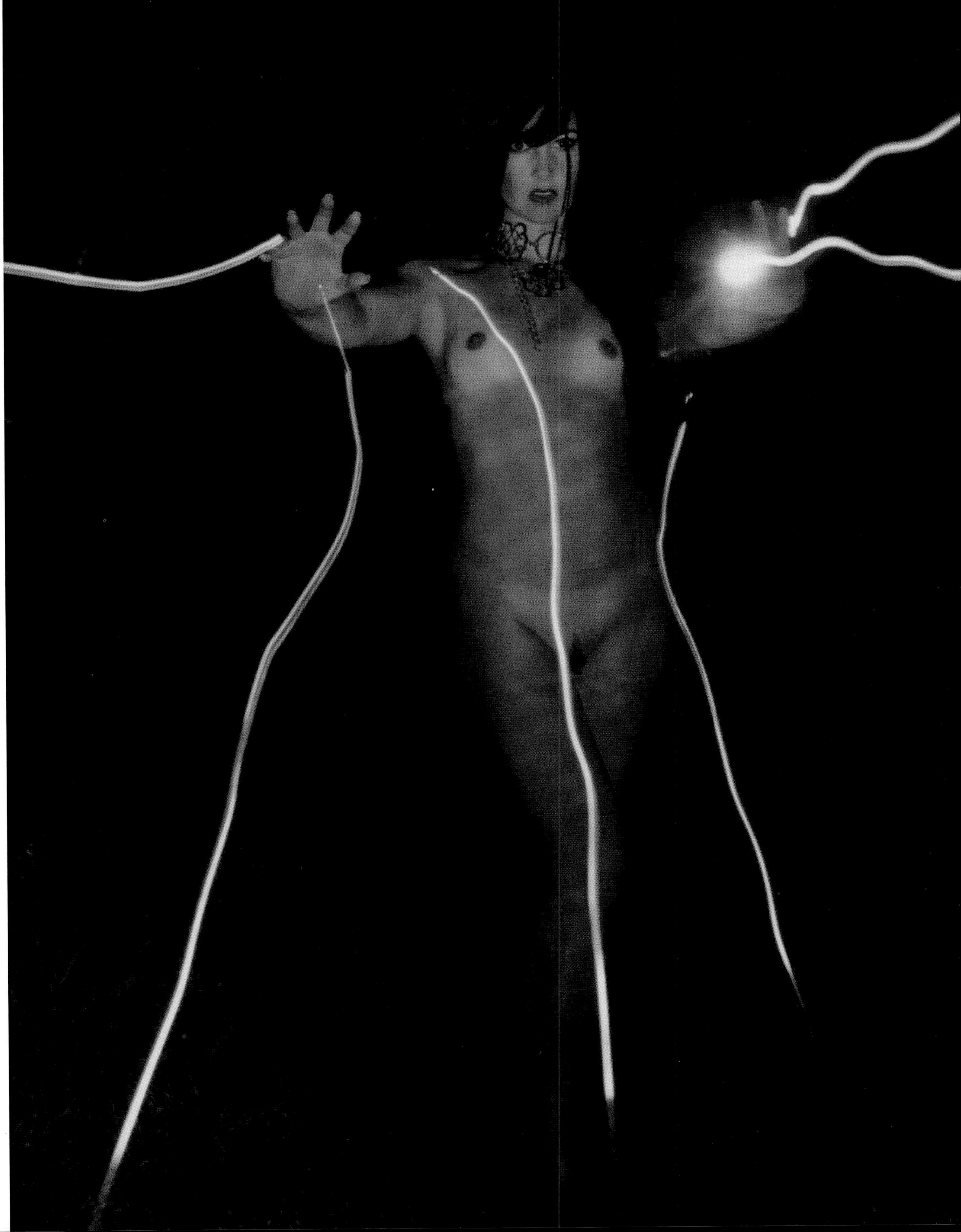

Ed Gordon

Award-winning Irish photographer Ed Gordon is well-known throughout Europe and the US for his portrayals of the nude in the landscape. He shares his skills through events and workshops run from his own studio and overseas locations. His work has been widely exhibited and published, and in 2004 he was the first non-American photographer to win the prestigious *Swimwear Illustrated* award. Gordon has embraced digital technology but prefers to use in-camera techniques to create his images, keeping manipulation in Photoshop to a minimum.

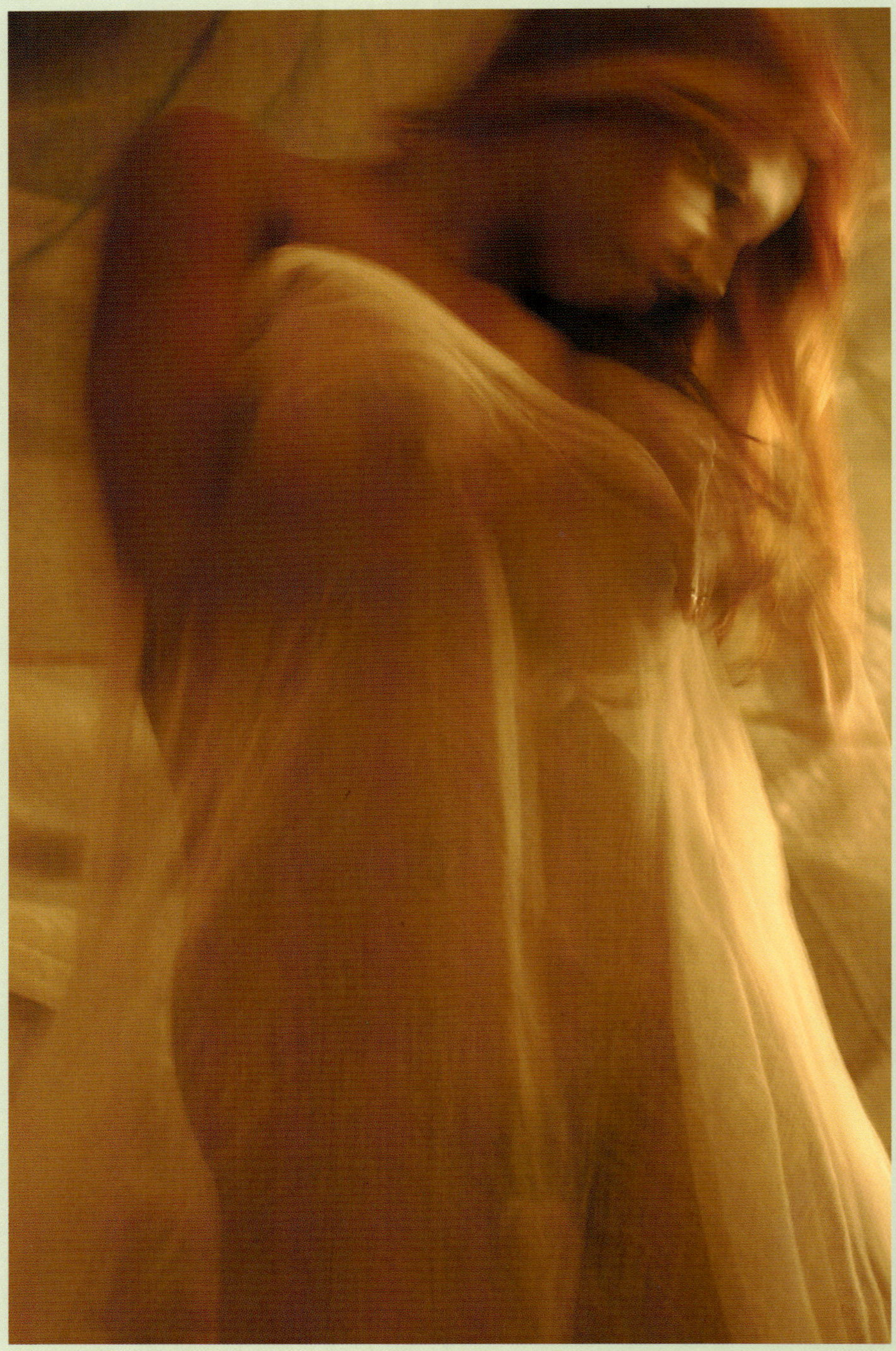

LEFT: Gordon uses a digital SLR camera, the Nikon D100, for many of his images. "The advent of digital technology has been a real boon for both professional and amateur photographers," he says. "The immediacy and control available, plus the ever-increasing image quality, makes for an exciting time for us all." One of digital's chief benefits is the ability to check lighting and exposure on the monitor, which was particularly beneficial for this shot. It was taken indoors with light from a window mixed with tungsten lights to give this orange color cast, creating a sensuous, mellow feeling. The shot was adjusted slightly with Levels in Photoshop for brightness and contrast.

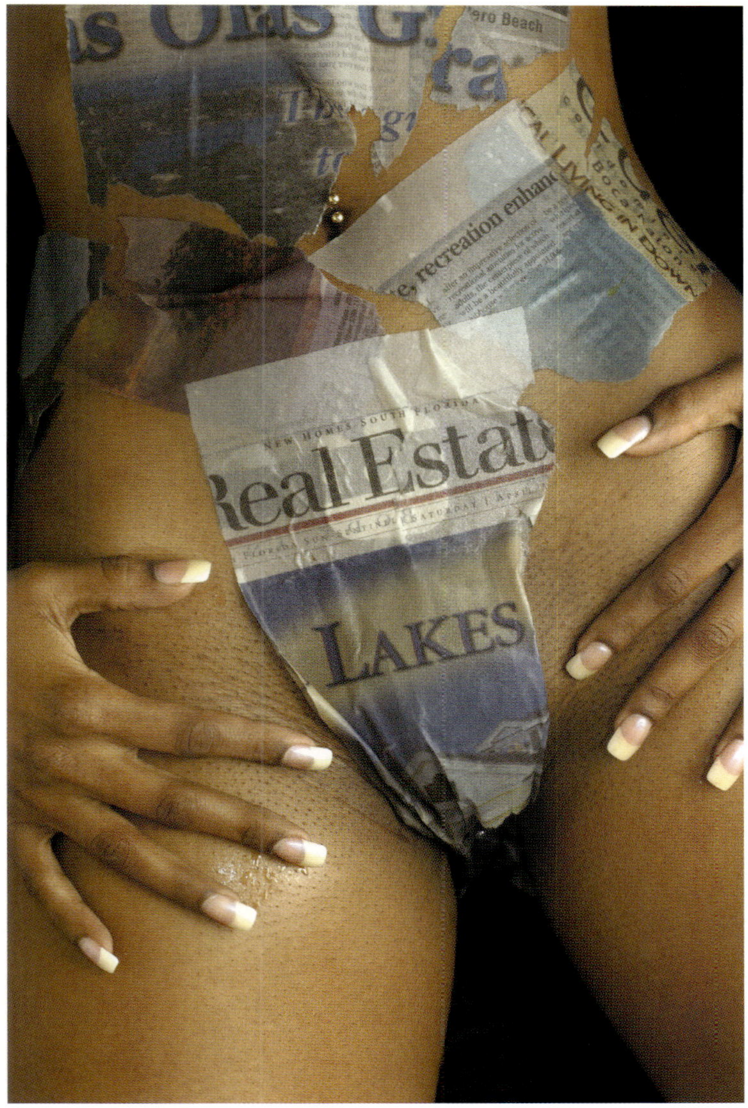

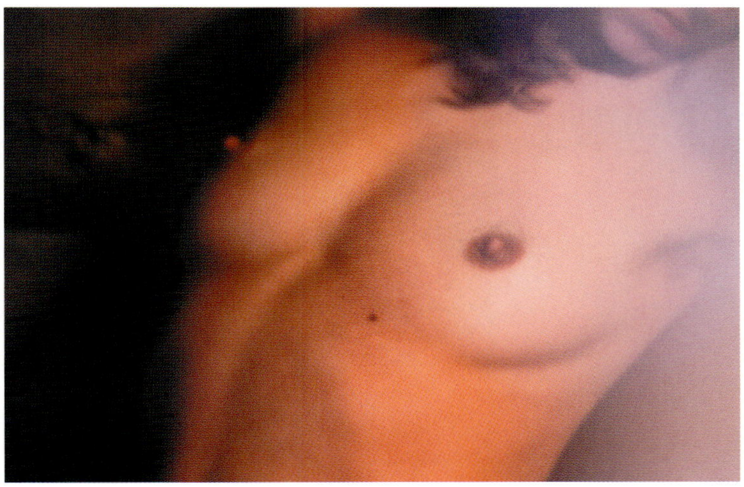

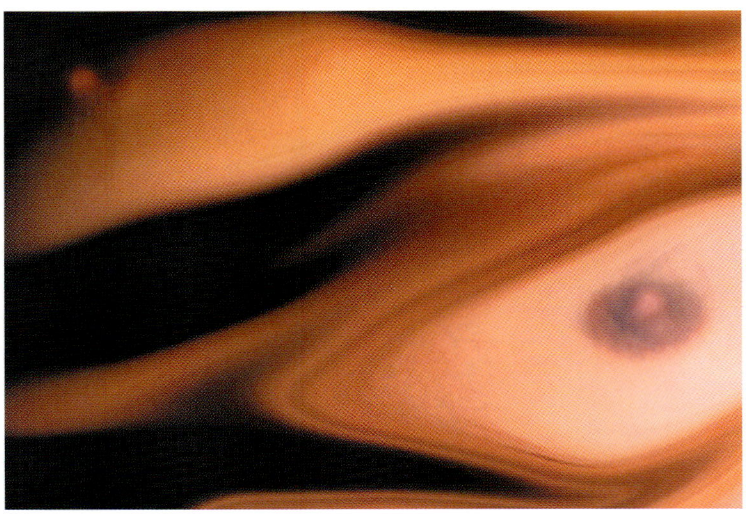

ABOVE LEFT: Gordon feels that despite the power of Photoshop, "a bad picture is always a bad picture," and can't be rescued by technology. Almost all his pictures rely on the basic photographic skills of observing how light describes the subject and uses one's knowledge of exposure and strong feeling for composition to get the image right as the shutter is pressed. This "straight" shot was taken in natural window light, with very thin gauze stretched over the lens to give a dreamy effect.

LEFT: The same shot, but here Gordon decided to experiment with the Liquify tool in Photoshop. The fluid, watery result is very different and much more surreal.

ABOVE: Here the model was draped in newspaper that had been soaked so that it stuck to her body—a simple idea, but a clever one. The cropping and especially the position of the hands give the shot real impact. Gordon used his Nikon D100 camera with fill-in flash bounced off the ceiling to soften the effect.

Ed Gordon

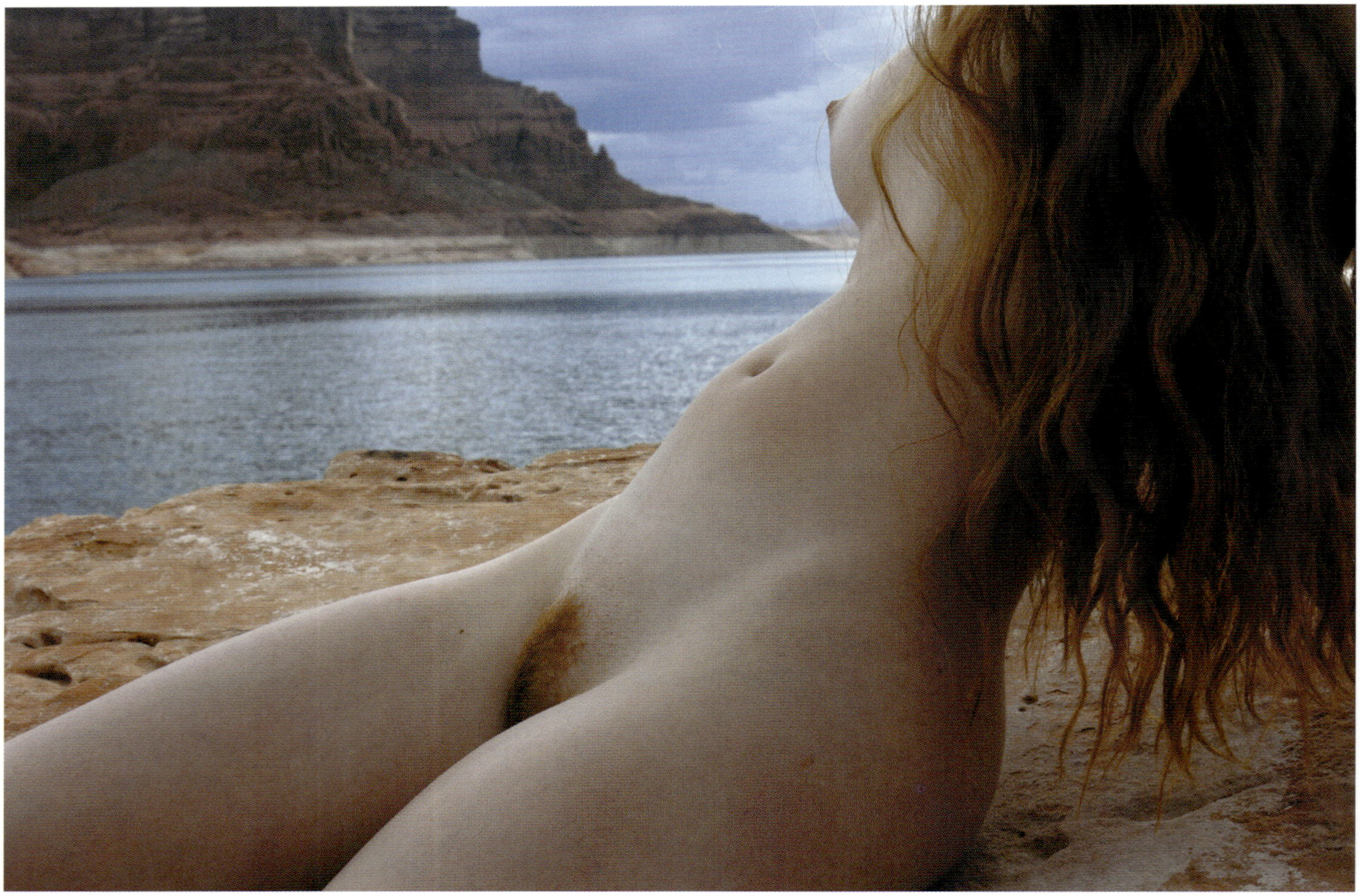

ABOVE: Gordon specializes in shooting the nude in the landscape—a compelling partnership, but a challenge to ensure the nude is in harmony with the environment, rather than an incongruous addition. He has achieved the balance very well here, with the color of the hair echoing that of the cliffs behind, whose jagged texture serves to emphasize the smooth contours of the body. Gordon used a 17mm lens on his digital camera, enabling him to use a small aperture to keep the background in focus.

OPPOSITE PAGE, TOP LEFT: "This shot was taken during an enforced bad-weather break," explains Gordon. "I was teaching in the canyons in Utah and it began to rain heavily. The danger of flash floods is very real in September, and so we had to postpone the planned shoot for that day. Sitting on our houseboat, I noticed rain droplets on the mosquito netting that covered the windows and asked Tara, our New York model, to pose for me. It just goes to show that there is no substitute for opportunity."

OPPOSITE PAGE, TOP RIGHT: The power of this image lies in the models' gaze—four eyes hitting the viewer in an uncompromising way—and their pose, which leaves plenty of room for interpretation. Gordon used a wide-angle 17-35mm lens on his digital SLR with a small aperture to get maximum depth of field, keeping both subjects sharp. Careful composition at the time of shooting meant that no cropping was required afterward, only fine-tuning of the brightness and contrast.

OPPOSITE PAGE, RIGHT: Harsh frontal lighting is usually avoided for portraiture, but it can work extremely well for the nude because shadows help define the contours of the body. Here, the light also gives the impression of heat on the skin, contrasting with the refreshing coolness of the water.

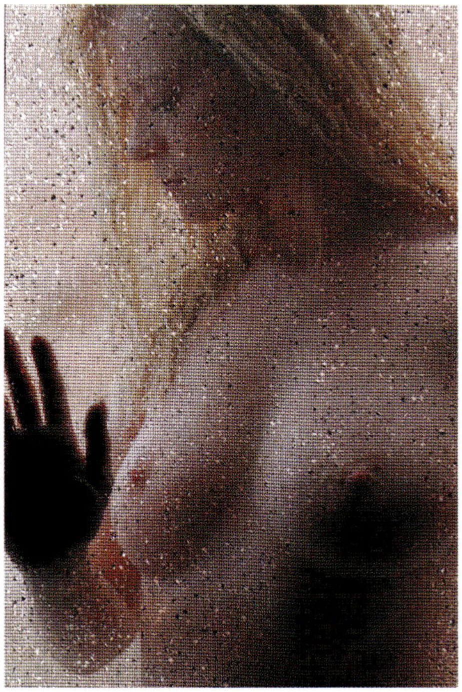

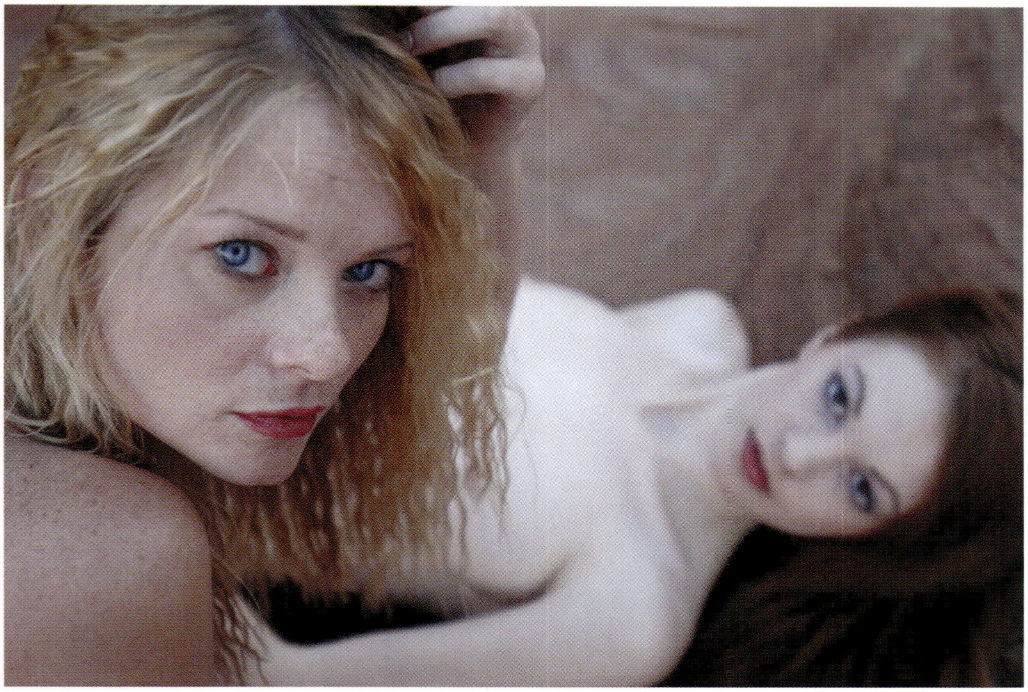

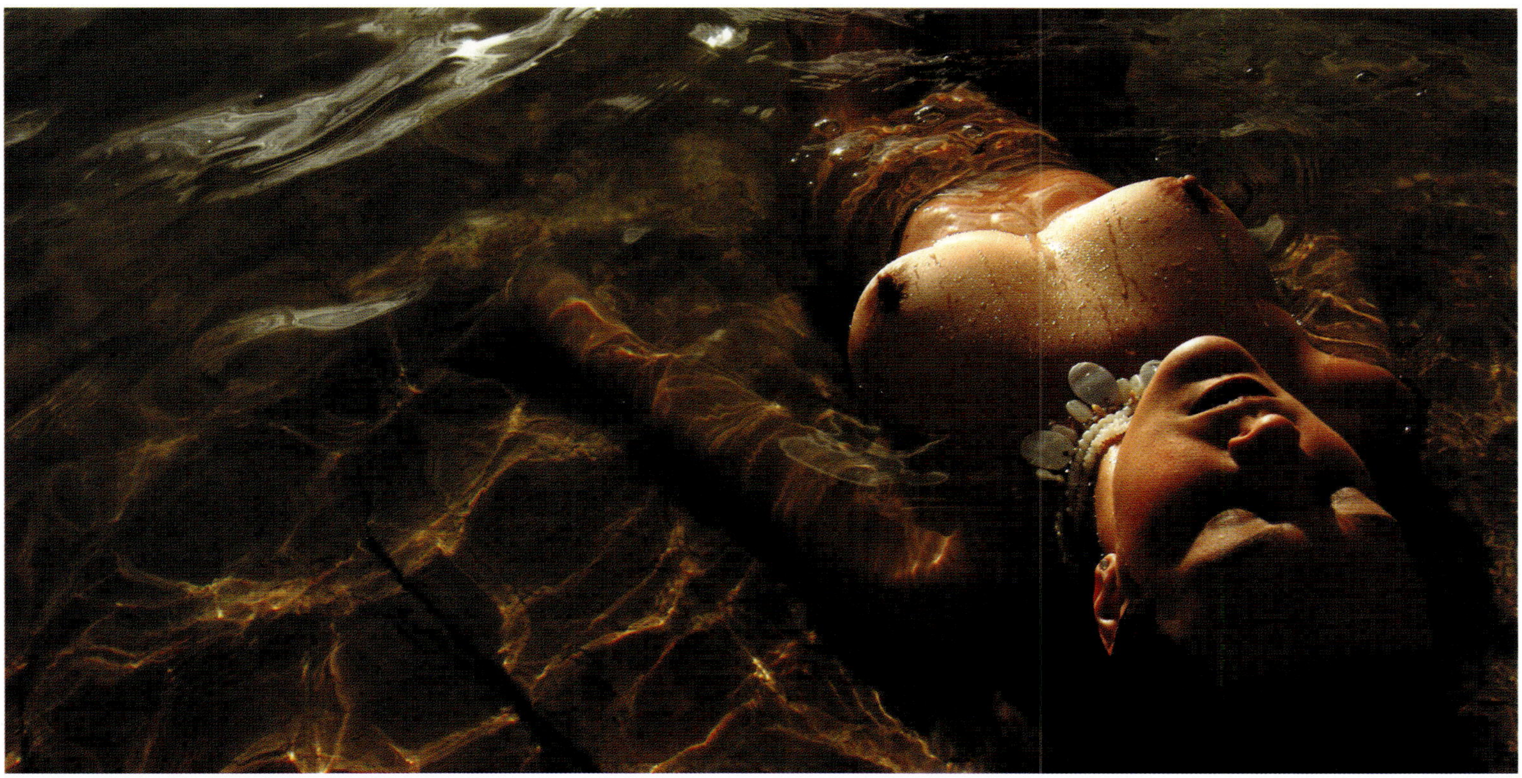

Justin Grant

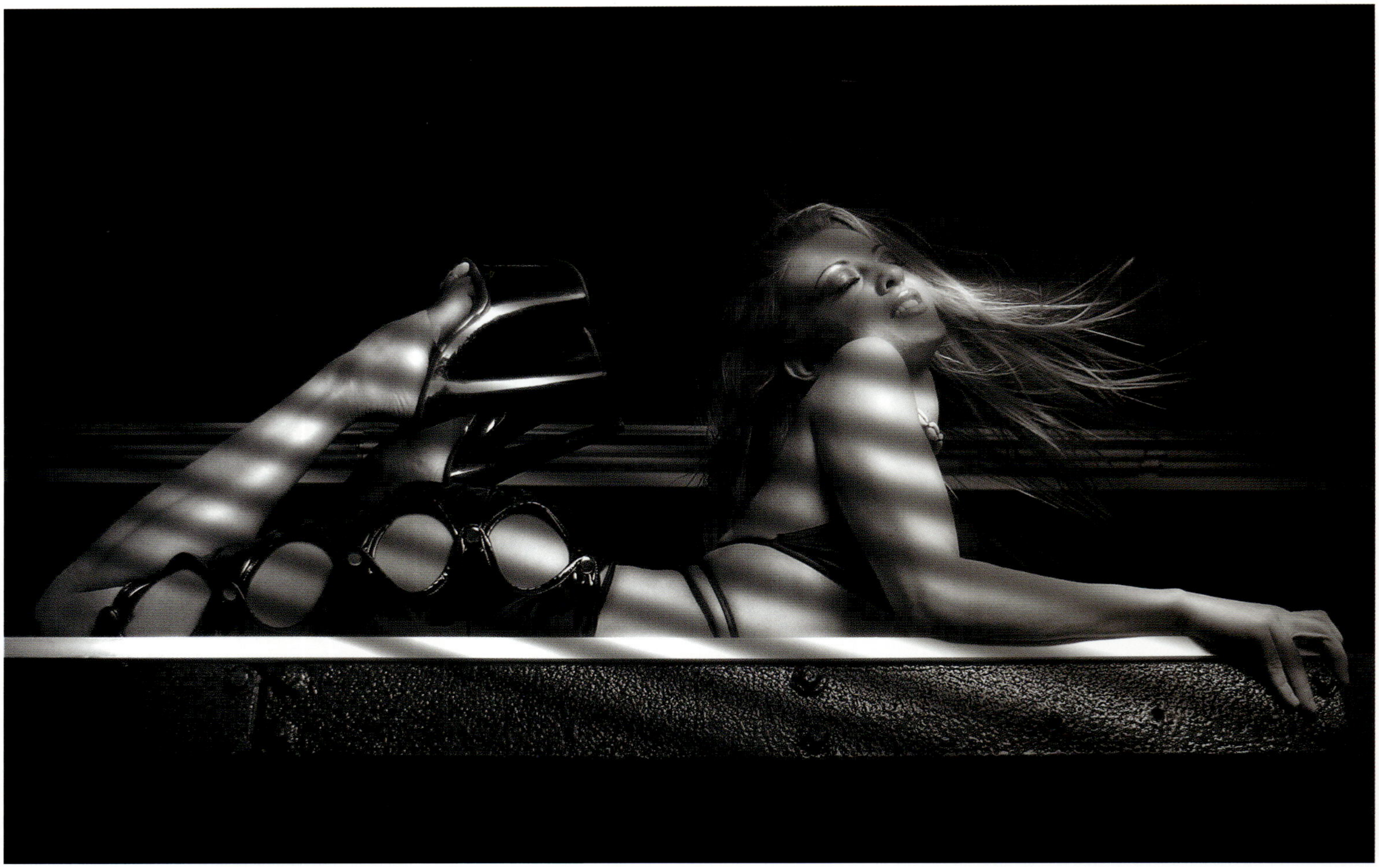

Justin Grant is a fashion and beauty photographer working in the United States. His style is easily recognizable because of his extreme posing, dramatic lighting, and erotic overtones. He believes that his digital editing skills contribute a great deal to his success, as does his ability to communicate well with his models.

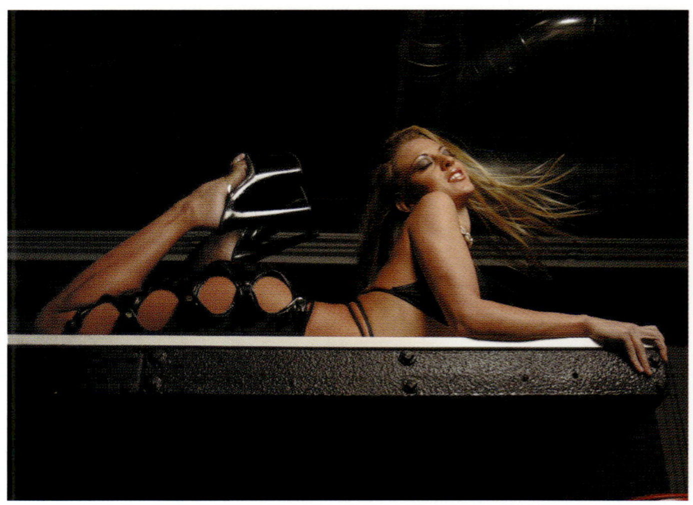

LEFT: "Shooting with Barbie is an experience like no other," says Grant. "Some models need to be guided into every pose and position, but Barbie is best when you let her do her thing! Set on a table in my studio, with loud music and a fan, she started moving and I started shooting—about 1,000 shots!" The editing was fairly straightforward for this shot. His first task is always to use the Healing tool to fix any blemishes. He then converted the image to black and white using the Desaturation tool, feeling that the picture had more dramatic impact in monochrome. The unwanted area of the ceiling of his studio was burned using Dodge and Burn tools, and then came the trickier process of creating the effect of light coming through shutters. "To do this, I made a new layer and created a long line. I then copied the layer about 20 times and distributed them evenly, then combined the layers. Then I applied the Gaussian blur effect to the lines to get rid of the sharp edge. Finally, I simply placed the layer over the photo, adjusted the opacity, and rotated it a bit."

RIGHT: There are elements of both fashion and erotica in this powerful shot. To achieve this angle, Grant had to lie on the floor beneath the model, looking up with a 19mm lens. "I turned the fan on, directed her into a dramatic pose, and asked her to exaggerate all of her movements," he recalls. "Digitally, I turned down the saturation about 50% to give just a hint of color, with a hint of black and white coming though. I then added a little bit of diffused glow to finish off the shot. I was about to remove the seamless paper backdrop in the background, but I decided it added some character to the image."

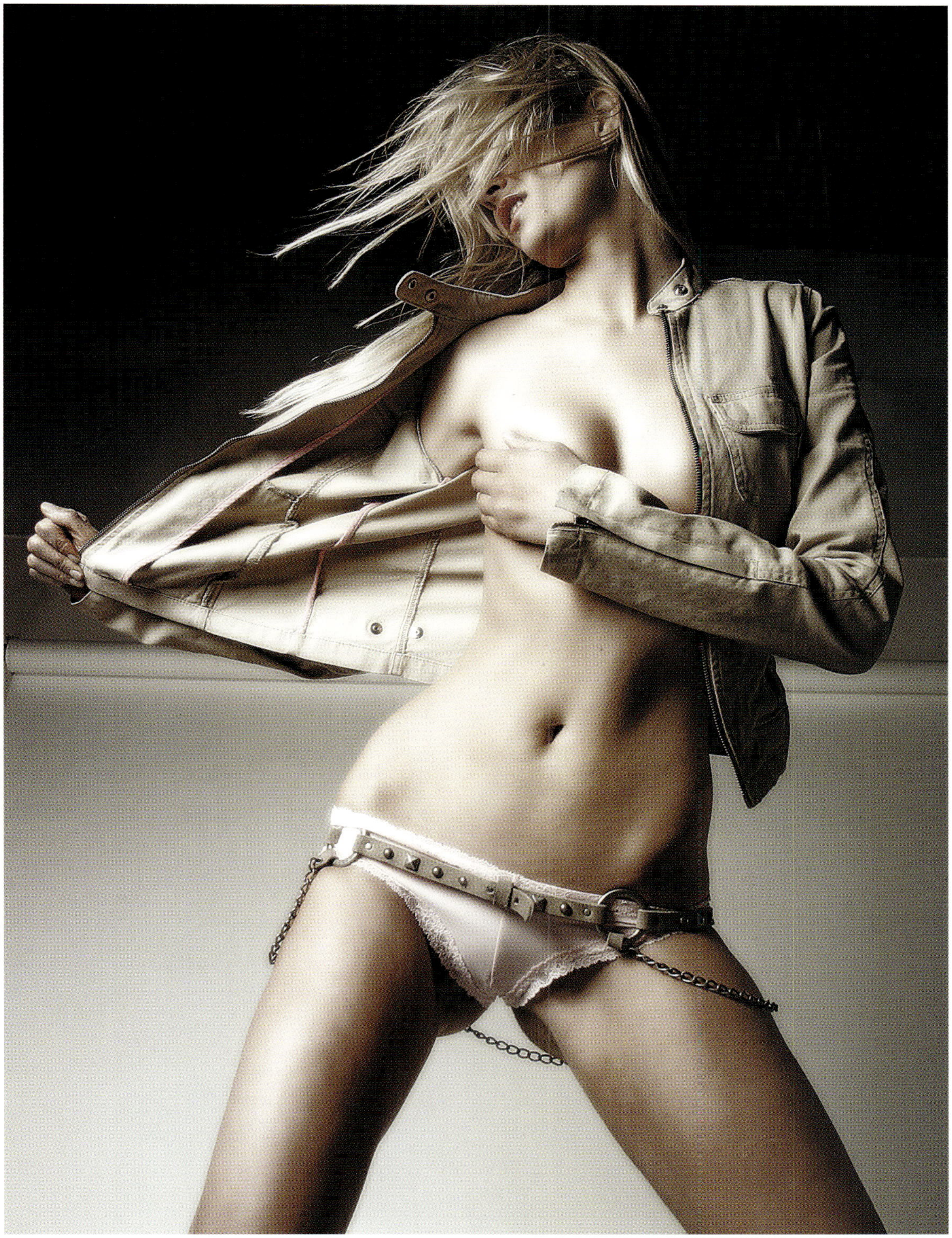

Justin Grant

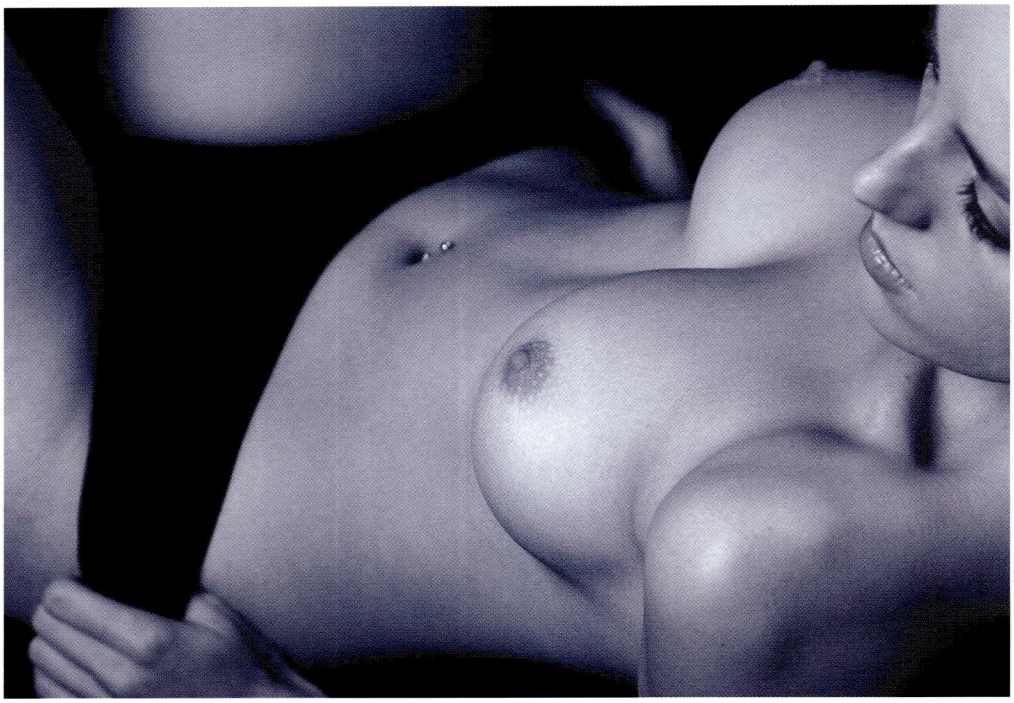

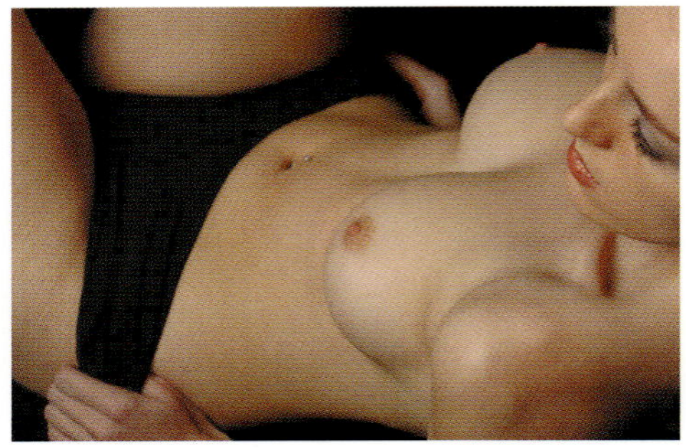

ABOVE: This model, Anna, was one of Grant's first nude subjects and he describes her as "very relaxed and confident, which made my life easy." The success of this shot lies in the sensual pose and the careful, tight framing, which was achieved in the camera, with no need for cropping afterwards. Grant used a 75-300mm lens at around 200mm, which had the effect of flattening the body, rather than a wide angle, which would have made those parts closest to the lens appear much larger than the parts further away. Photoshop was used to convert the image to black and white, and the Healing tool was used to touch it up. The blue tint just lifts it further out of the ordinary, and this was added by adjusting the mid- and high levels in the Color Adjustment tool. Lastly, he fine-tuned the contrast to achieve a perfect balance.

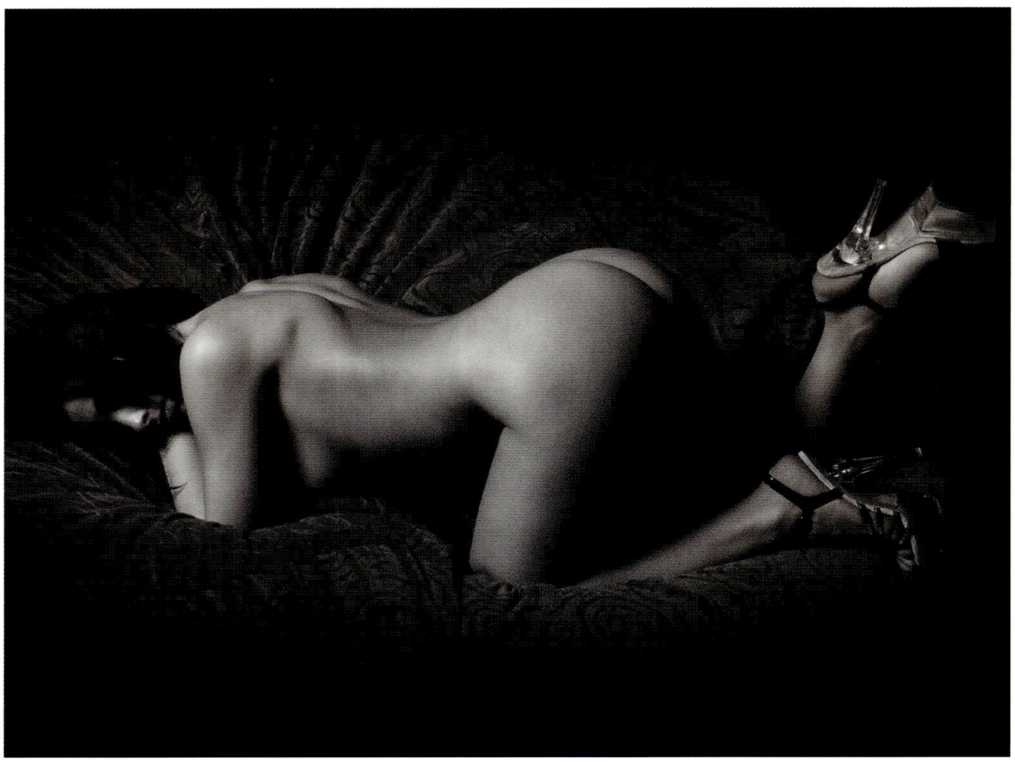

LEFT: "Wendy wanted some shots of herself that were very erotic, but that didn't reveal her identity,' explains Justin. "Using one strobe with a softbox, I was able to put her face in just enough shade so she is not recognizable but you can still see how beautiful she is. Photoshop was very simple, a little Healing tool on the blemishes, converted to black and white using the Desaturation tool, then adjusting the contrast. I also used the Dodge tool to enhance the shine of her skin in strategic places."

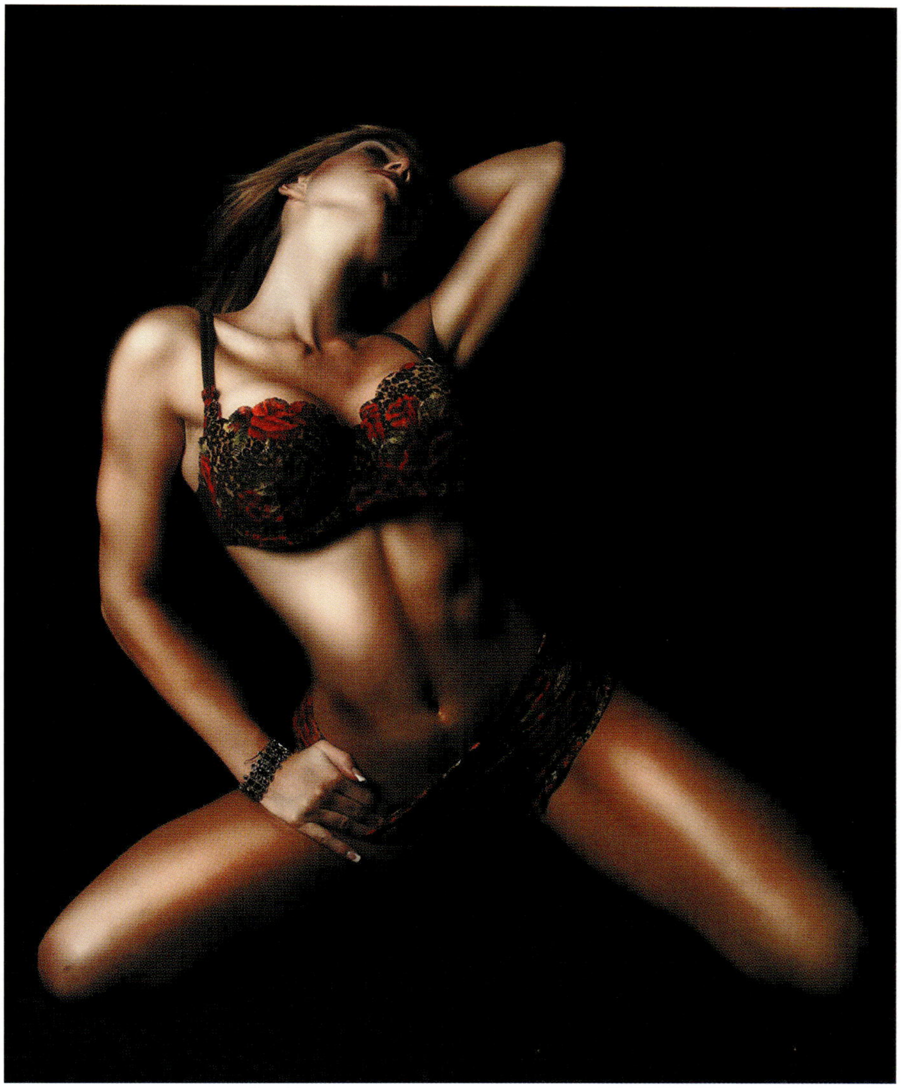

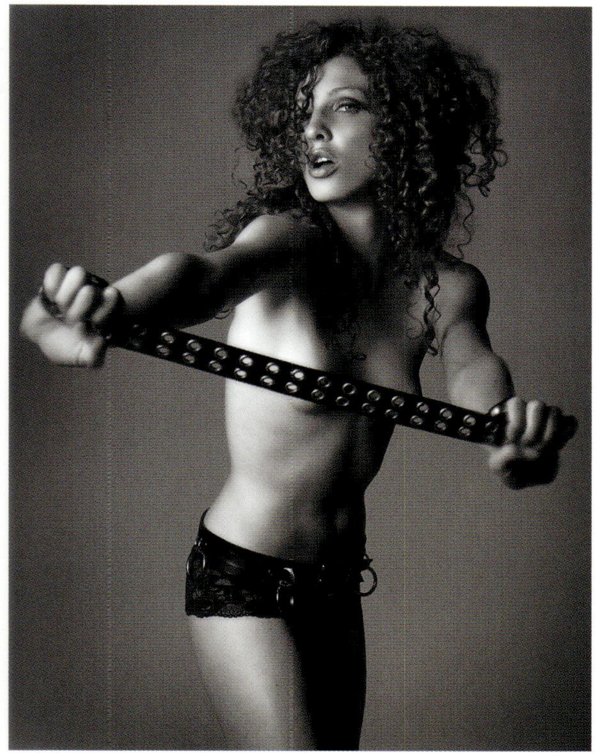

LEFT: This image of Jennifer was one of Grant's most popular early shots—a classic erotic pose with lovely rich color and tonal contrast. "Although a beautiful girl, she is quite lanky and can be difficult to pose, but the final result is very elegant," he says. "The key with her was to make her feel as comfortable and as sexy as possible, and to guide her into long, dramatic positions. I think she pulled it off. With the Dodge and Burn tools I darkened the shadows of her great physique and highlighted the sheen of her skin—then finished it off with a touch of diffused glow."

ABOVE: Grant uses movement a lot to breathe life into his pictures and digital is ideal for this, as there is no film wasted on the inevitable mistakes. "Mandilynn was having fun with this pose, moving around quite a bit between shots, which meant that I was continually moving the camera angle to keep the belt over her breasts," he says. "In my opinion, some of the most erotic images are those that hide just enough to get your imagination in gear." Editing involved first burning around the edges of the backdrop with the Dodge and Burn tools. "I then cut out the background just around her outline, made a new layer from the background, then used Gaussian blur to smooth it up a little. Also, to bring out her wonderful hair a bit more, I used the Dodge tool to highlight it a little."

D. M. Gremlin

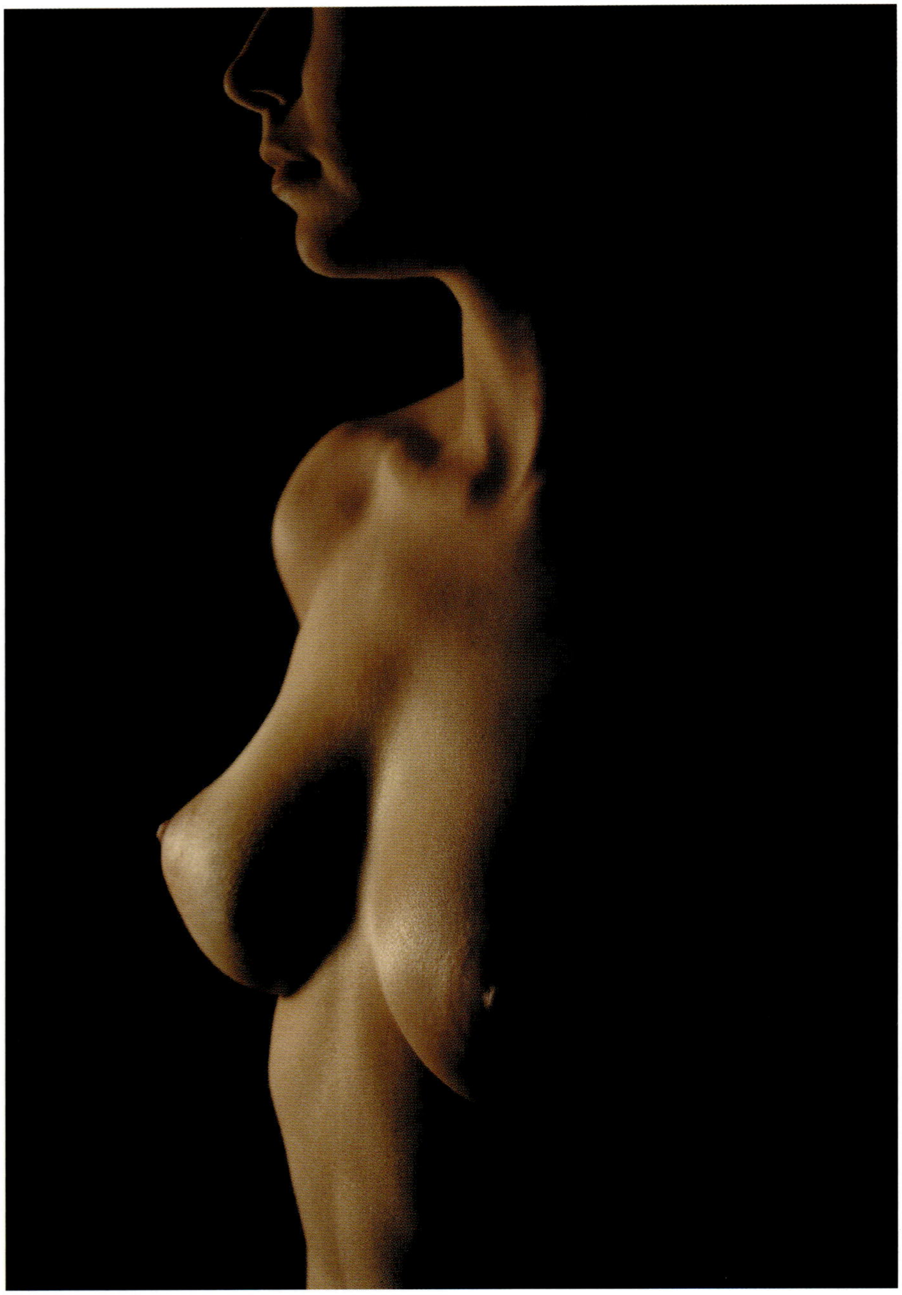

D. M. Gremlin's photographs are driven by an exacting sense of composition. Using a digital camera has enabled him to take the same shot many times with just tiny variations until he is satisfied the lines and shapes he sees are in the perfect position. He usually uses digital enhancement for subtle changes and finishing touches but also sometimes to piece together an imaginative concept.

LEFT: "This was an attempt to create a fine-art nude image in the style of those pictures I usually see done on film and hung in galleries—but with my digital camera," explains Gremlin. "This picture is a prime example of a composition based on contours and shapes that I see superimposed on the subject or object that I'm working with. A photo-black felt background was used and a single diffused spotlight shone from just a little bit behind and to the side of the model. Very little editing went into the post-processing part of this image —just a little added contrast and a few touch-ups with the brush on highlights I wanted to conceal."

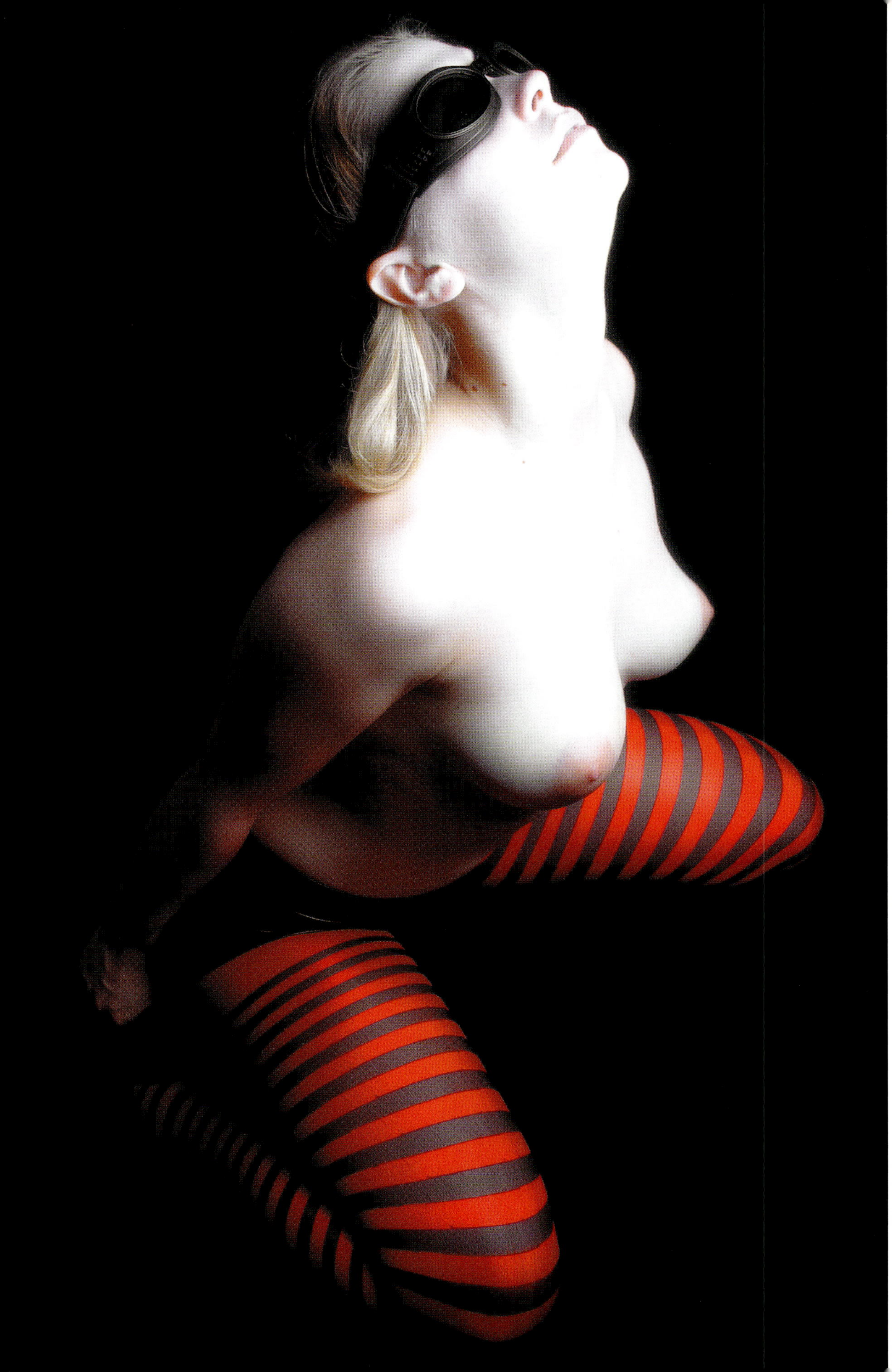

LEFT: "The concept behind this image was that the model was like a test subject embracing the radiation coming to her from the light source," explains Gremlin. "Life is full of many unseen interactions of energies, and this projection and reception of energy is a recurring theme in a lot of my compositions." The picture was taken with the model crouched on a black felt background and lit with a softbox positioned close to her face. This light produced a bleached-out effect in key areas, providing the basis for the subtle glow that was added later. "Basic effects were used to finish the shot," says Gremlin. "A selective color layer enhanced the blacks and darkened the background without blowing out the contrast—a danger due to the already partially washed-out face and chest area. I also used a Hue/Saturation layer to remove a slight blue cast caused by the flash and to saturate the reds, and finally a Screening layer with some blur added to create the subtle glow—all elements combined to give the image its 'radioactive' effect."

D. M. Gremlin

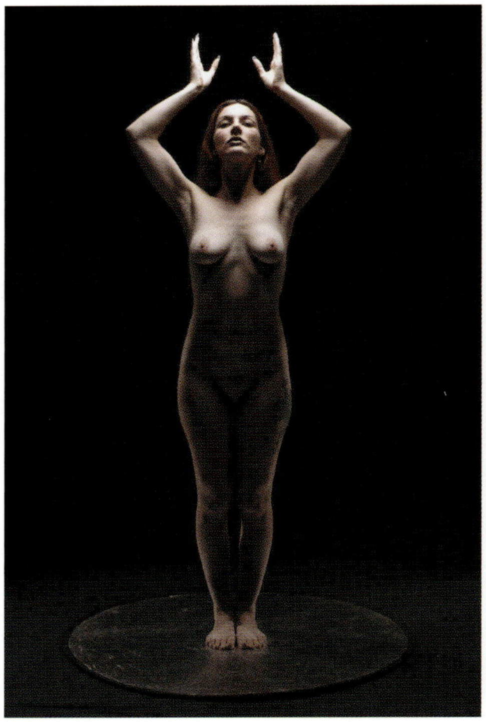

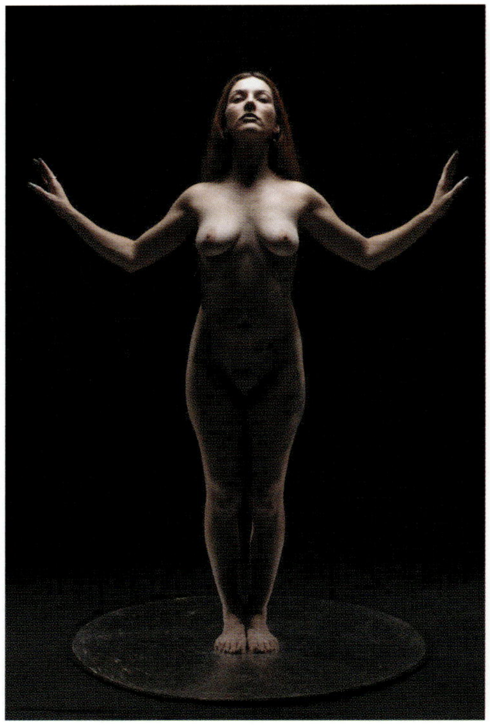

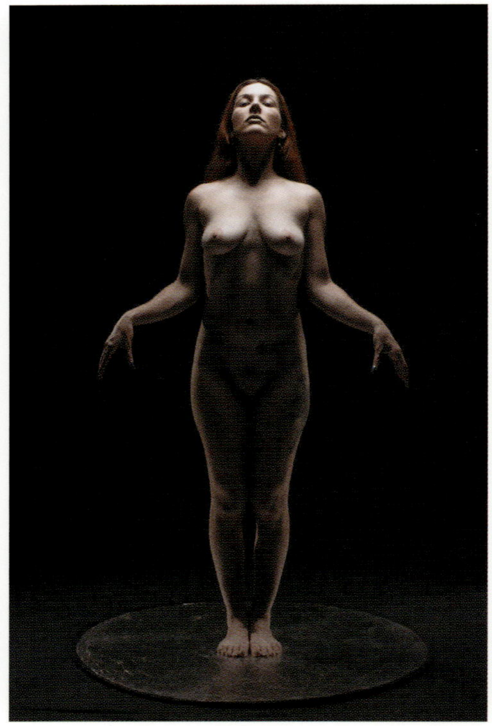

ALL IMAGES: Although this image is clearly modeled on the goddess Shiva, Gremlin didn't begin the shoot with that in mind, as he explains: "The idea came rather spontaneously. The model's name was actually 'Shiva' but the connection didn't hit me until she was moving around on this silver platform. I had improvised it as part of a completely different digital composition." Once he had decided on the new course of action, Gremlin took several pictures of the model in exactly the spot, with her arms in different positions. The lighting behind the raw images was very specific—an overhead-mounted snoot firing straight down to create an effect of reception of energy from the heavens. There were also two strobes with barn doors mostly shut and aimed at the outer sides of her body, to give it a rim-lit effect. "In blending the images together, I set out to make the result fantastical, but also realistic enough that if you took a close look at where the arms joined, you could almost believe that such a creature could exist. The arms, joints, and muscles had to look like they fitted together properly and would actually function." Finishing touches were added with a textured blue layer, masked so that it would seem to be behind and around Shiva. An unmasked duplicate of that same layer was used as an overlay to blend the skin tone with the partially masked layer.

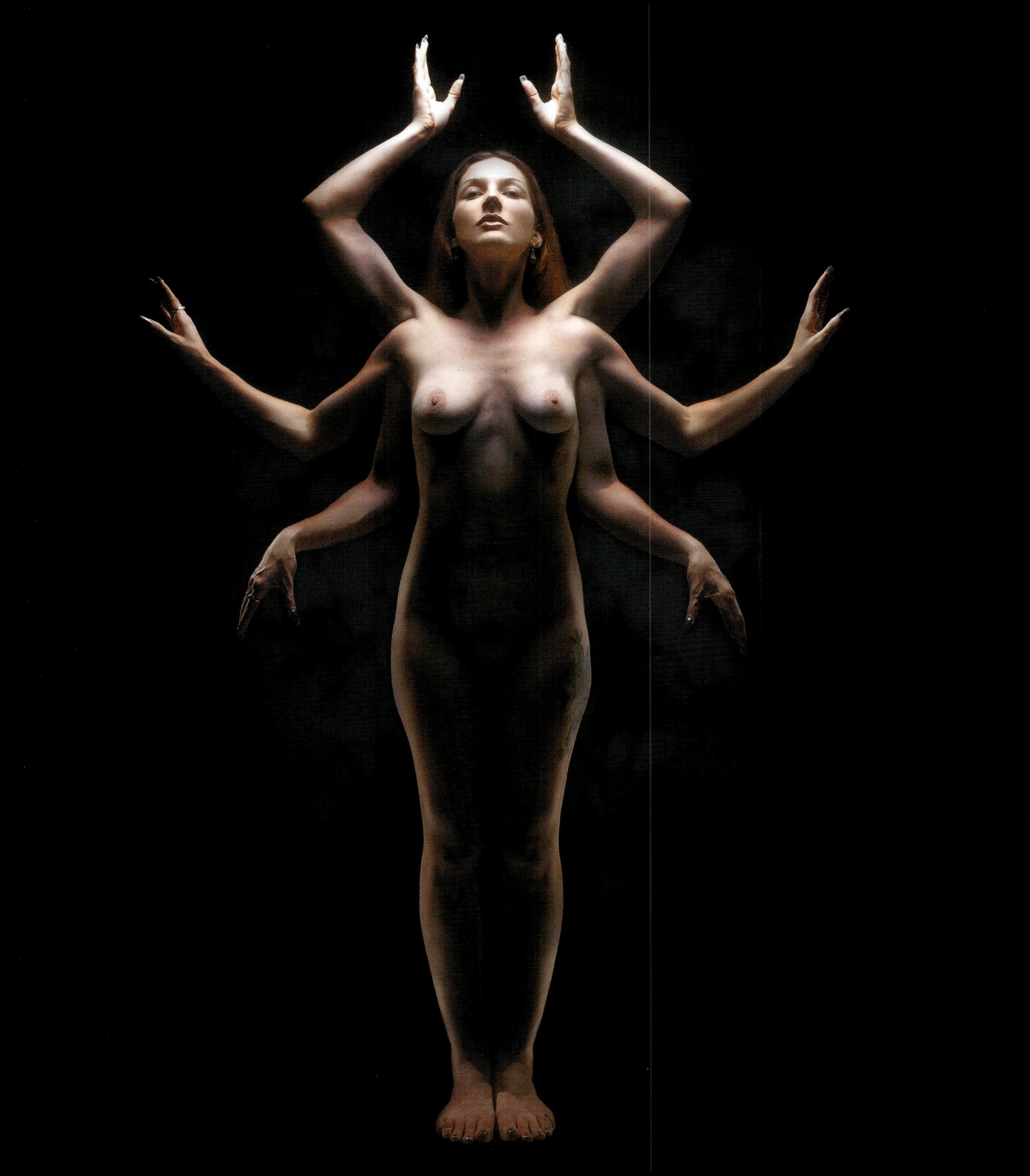

Paul Grupp

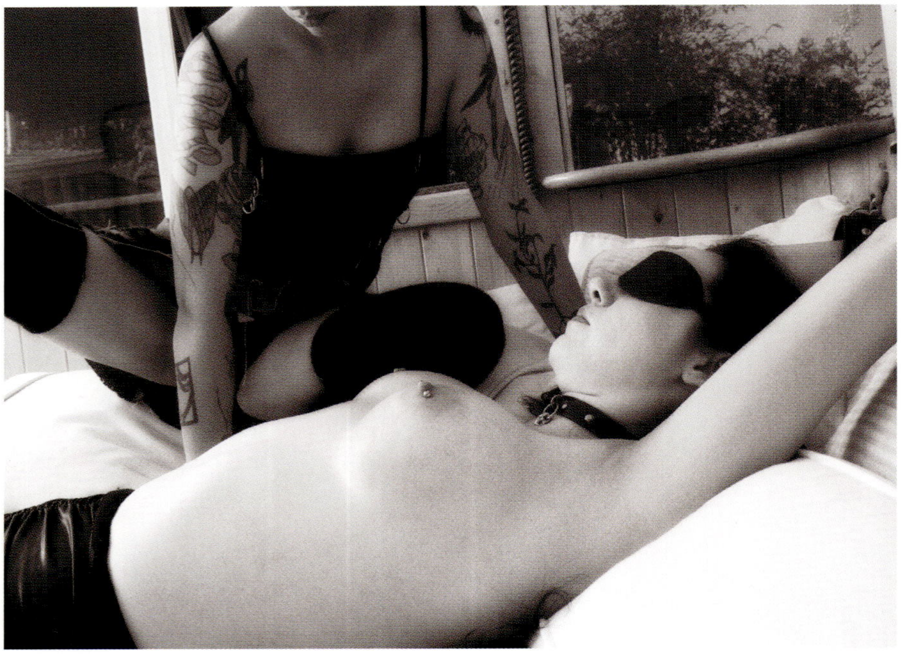

ABOVE: "Two girls, a digital camera, and two Alien Bees AB400 strobes in a vintage Airstream caravan on a hot summer afternoon... anything can happen," says Grupp. "Geitia's pierced nipples add an exotic touch to the scene, and I pushed that feeling a little further by fitting her with a simple bondage collar. For the lighting, one strobe was positioned high, at the girls' feet and another was next to the side of the bed. Both strobes had medium softboxes to keep the light gentle and even. In the tight quarters of the trailer, there was barely room to turn around, so I used PocketWizard radio slaves to trigger the strobes without having to worry about tripping over a sync cord. To capture subtle nuances like this when working with models, it helps to have a large memory card and just keep shooting until something interesting happens. The Canon 1D's high frame rate and ability to write the buffer to the memory card quickly, even in RAW mode, is perfect for this kind of work. With a slower camera, I probably would have missed the shot. Before processing, the picture had bright, accurate color that was a little too clinical for my taste. Running the picture through a nik Color Efex Pro! 'Monday Morning' filter gave an ethereal sensual look that fits the scene perfectly."

BELOW: Again from the caravan shoot, the tight crop, eliminating the eyes and mask, work to add tension and mystery to an already sensual setting. The main light was an Alien Bees AB400 with medium softbox just below the camera position. A second AB400 and softbox at the foot of the bed added some definition and drama to the lighting. The original file was shot in color and converted to black and white using the Photoshop RAW converter. A nik Color Efex Pro! "Monday Morning" filter added atmosphere, and the color balance was tweaked slightly to warm the tone.

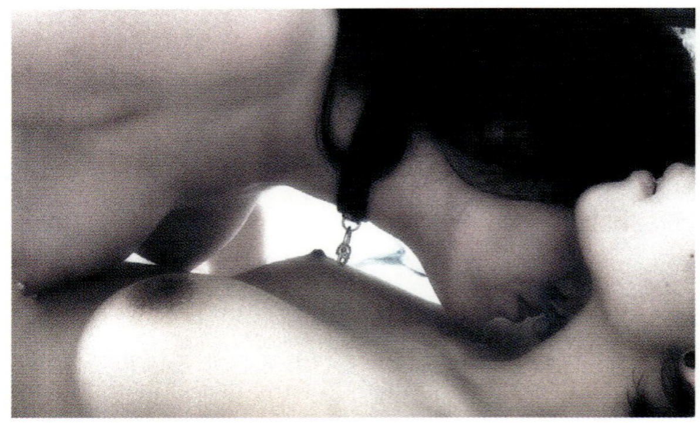

BELOW: "While preparing for the photo shoot in the Airstream caravan, I was concerned that it would be easy to make images that were merely pornographic and not truly erotic," remarks Grupp. "To combat that tendency, I drew up a list of scenarios to have the models play out during the shoot. The idea of one pouring Scotch in the other's navel and then licking it up struck me as having great possibilities for a striking image."

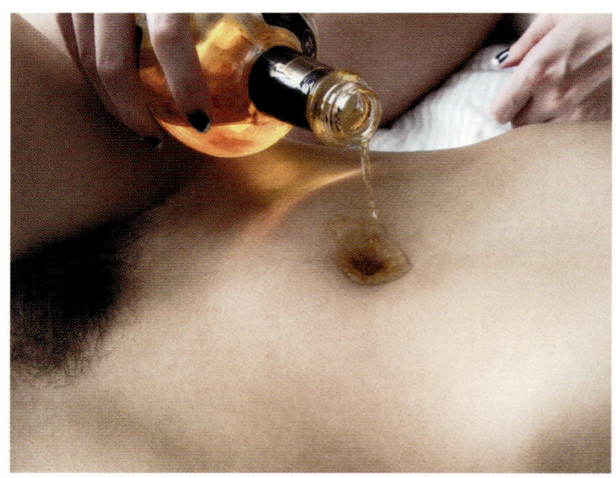

A keen photographer since childhood, Paul Grupp began shooting nudes and erotic images fairly recently, embracing digital as the ideal medium to experiment with the subject. Rather than aiming to shoot perfect bodies, he believes that an erotic photograph has to have a human element to evoke a response in the viewer and tell a story. His approach to digital editing is to "roughen" up the image —shifting the color and restricting the palette, adding noise and manipulating the tonal curve to produce organic results that he couldn't achieve in the darkroom.

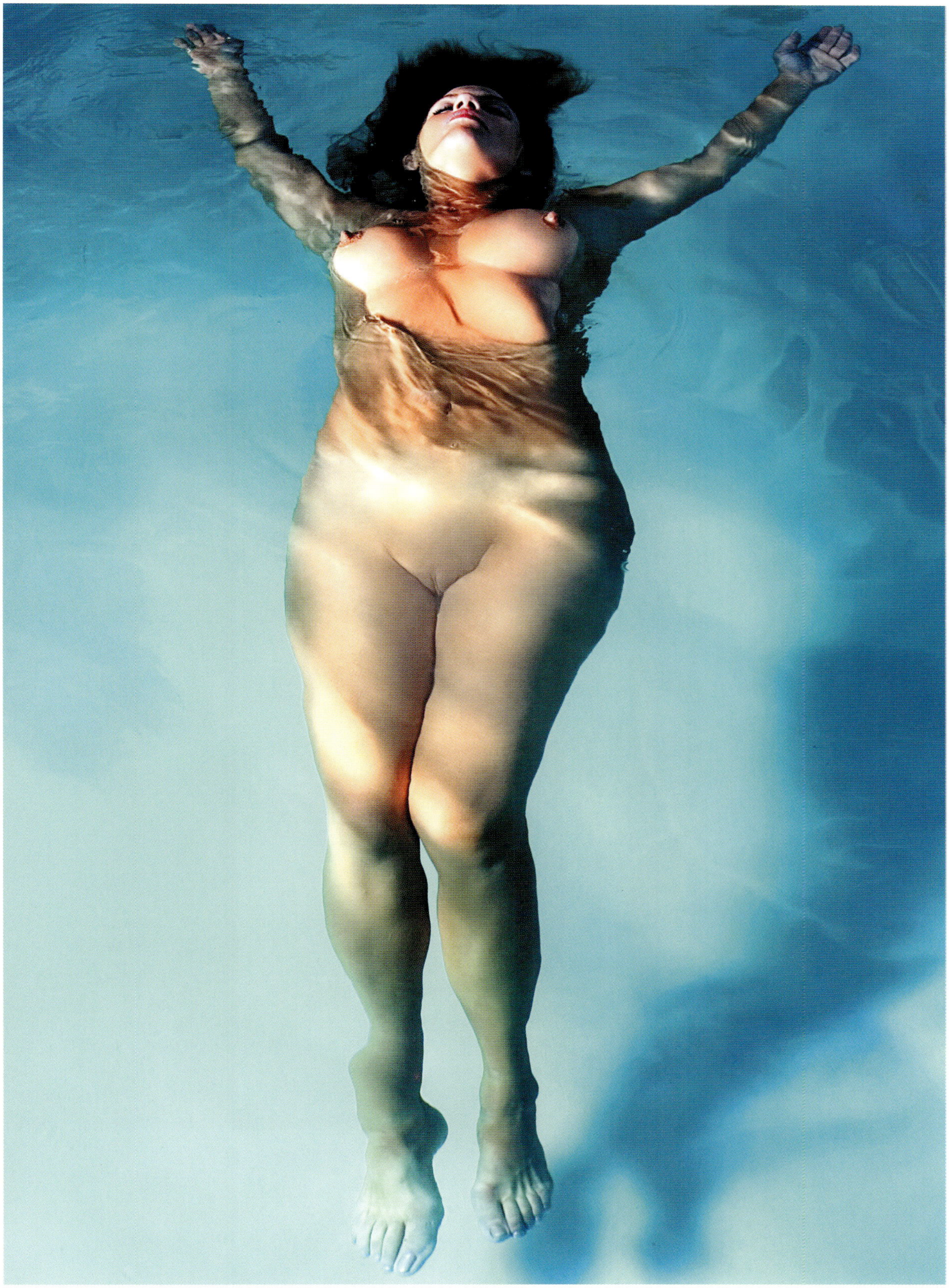

LEFT: "Rachel is floating in a swimming pool in late afternoon/early evening light. To add a little drama, I placed a 160WS strobe high and to her left, and balanced the exposure with the receding daylight. Post-processing included boosting the color saturation and using the Color/Replace function in Adobe Photoshop CS to make the pool water more blue."

Chris Gustafson

Chris Gustafson has been shooting in digital and working with Photoshop for the past eight years, and his distinctive style has won him much attention. He finds that using layers and erasing sections back to the original is the most powerful function of digital editing, allowing him to work on the contrast and saturation of just a small part of the image.

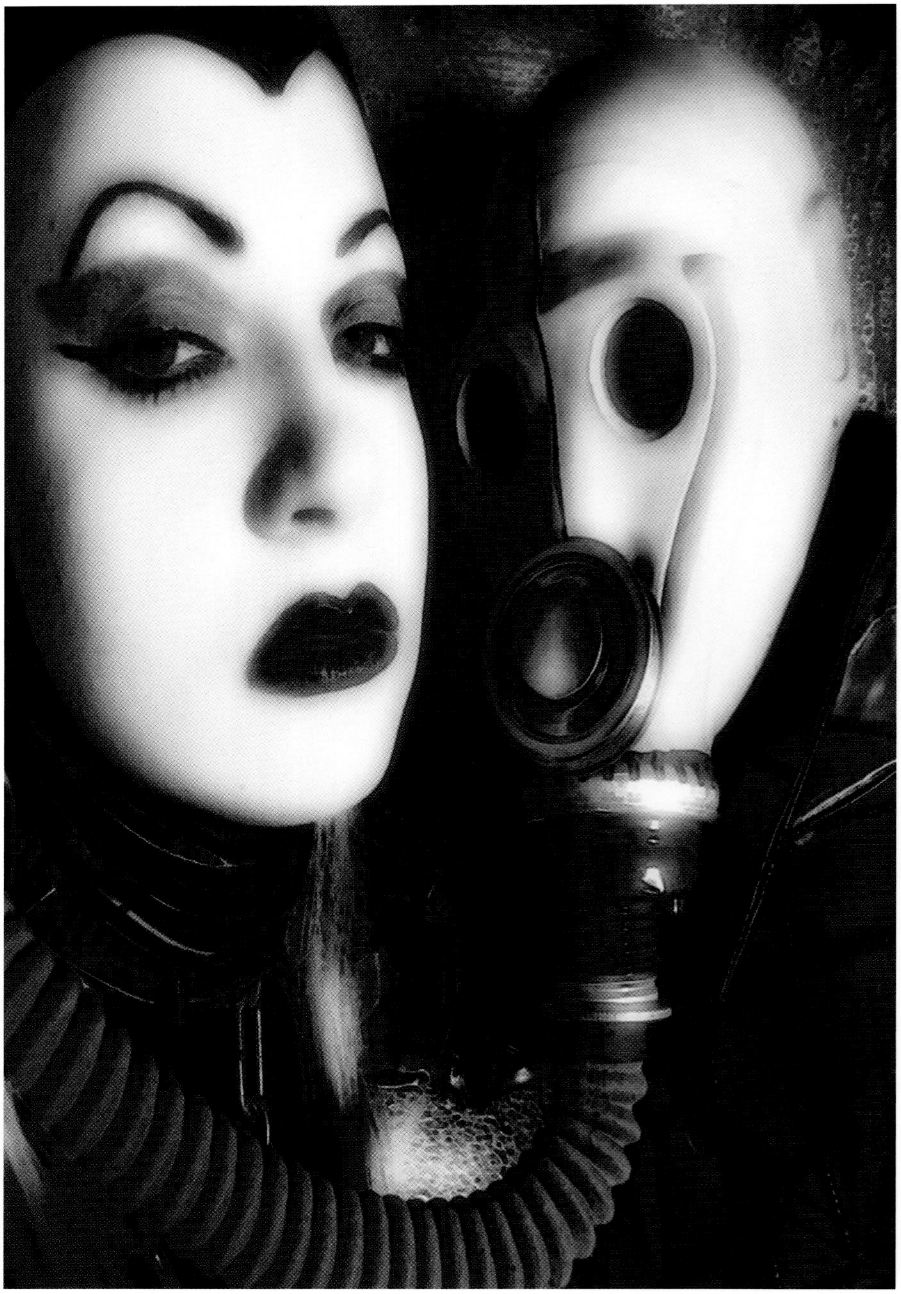

RIGHT: This eerie image started out in color and was lit with a diffused hotlight placed very close to the model, who was chosen for her extremely pale skin. "Then, in Photoshop, I used Diffuse Glow set to white and, with layers, erased the glow back to the original around key points such as her eyes and lips to bring back the sharpness," Gustafson explains. "When I got the skin tone the way I liked, I flattened the layers and adjusted the black levels until it looked believable again."

RIGHT: This image was inspired by a bar in the Detroit area, and in particular its distinctive mural. Gustafson lit the shot with several flash units bounced off walls and the ceiling, and then he worked on the contrast and brightness of specific areas, using layers to bring out a lot of subtle detail that would otherwise have been lost.

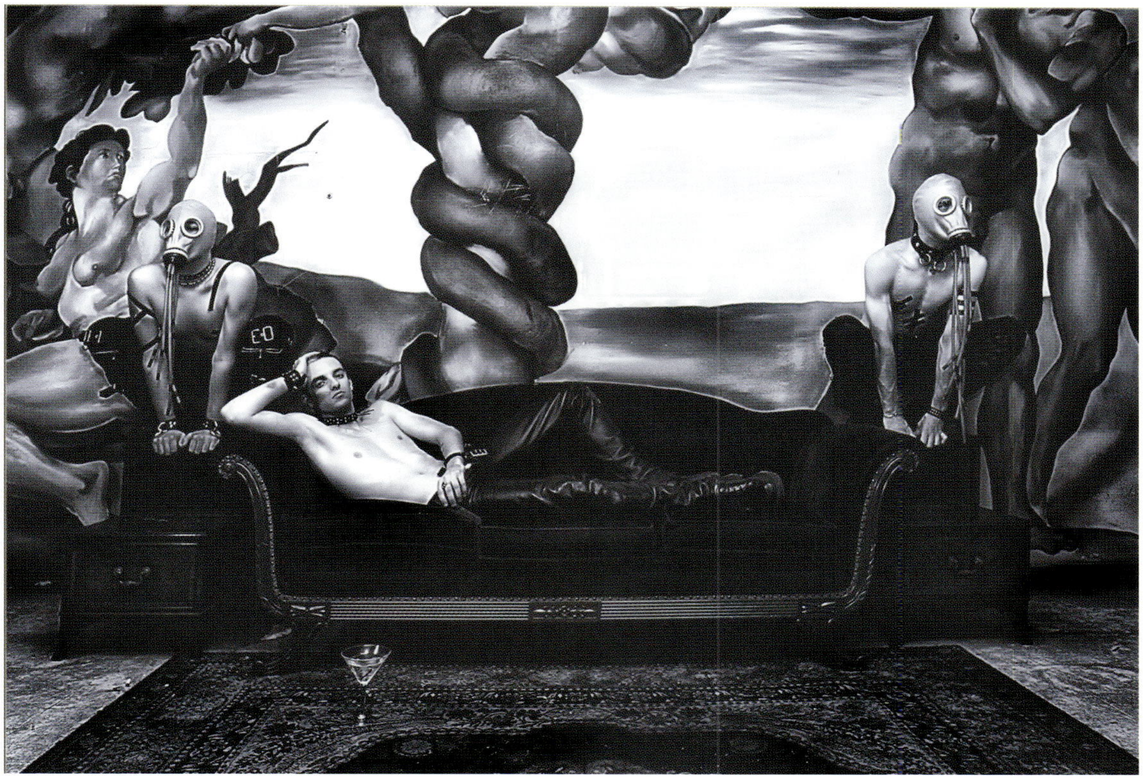

RIGHT: Photographed in the basement of his house, *Succubus* was lit with two 750-watt lights, one on either side of the models, both lights diffused heavily to help even out the skin. The models were on a black sheet on a concrete floor. The woman had very pale skin and the male model was tanned, but the color contrast between them was increased even more to give this strange, almost painterly effect.

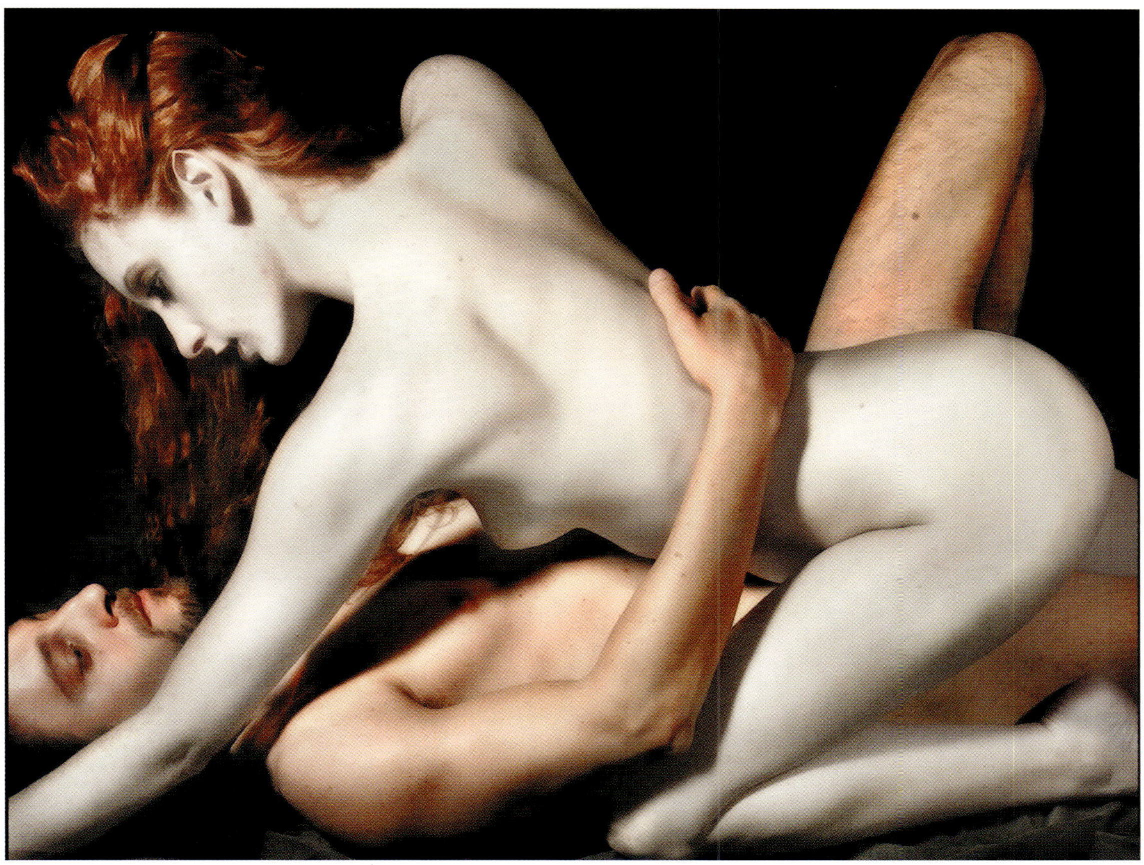

Chris Gustafson

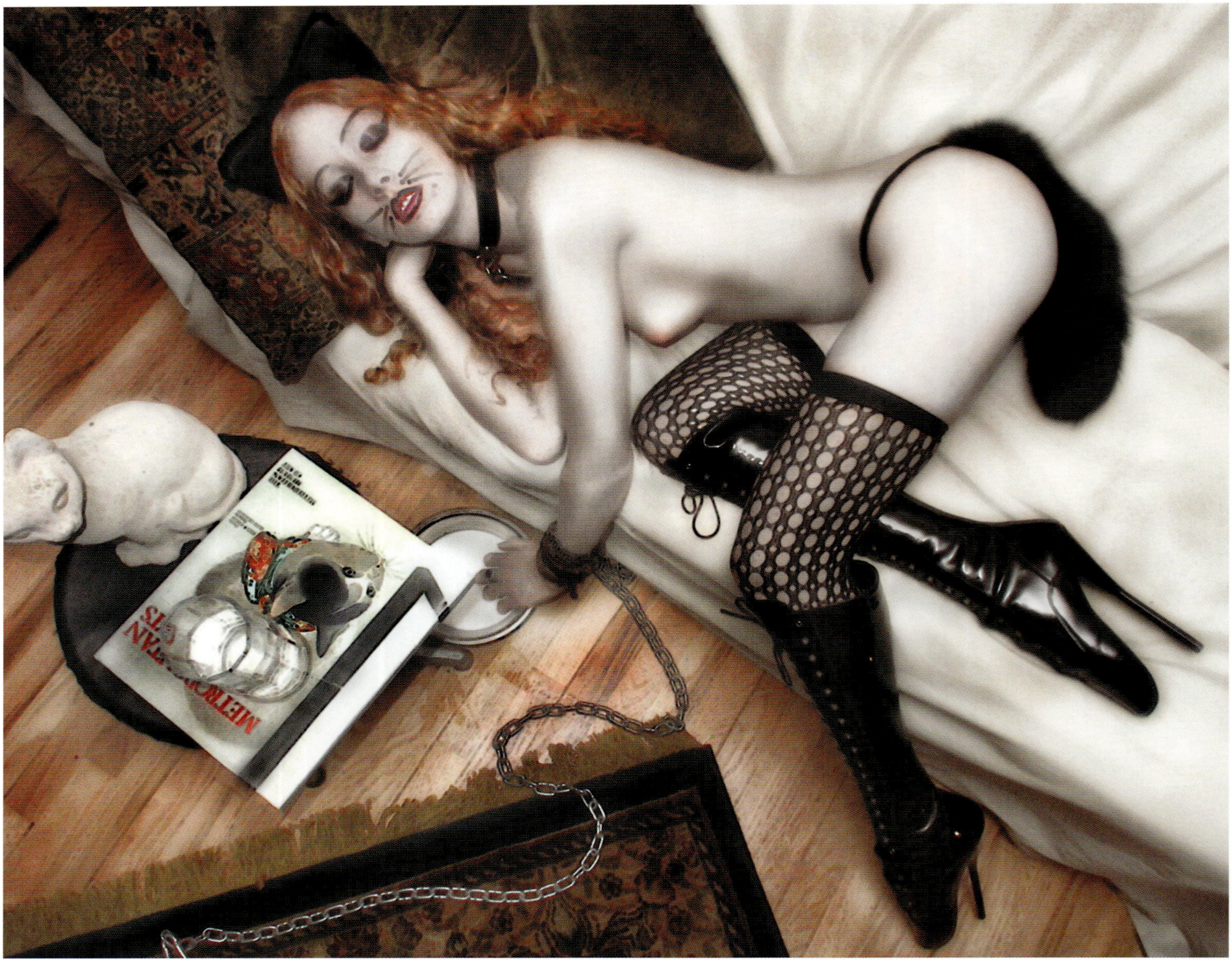

Gustafson has been working on what he calls his *Catnap* series for several years, and it is still in progress. With each model he works with, he produces a set of around five images, which all have to be worked on individually in Photoshop but have a similar final appearance. "It isn't hard to get one image to look good from a given shoot, but to try to get five to print up and look the same can be tedious—there is no single button to press to get that look," he says. Because his technique is to slightly underexpose the shot, he chooses models with very pale skin, then works on it in editing to look almost like alabaster. "If the color value of the skin is too dark to start with, it's virtually impossible to get that look," he adds.

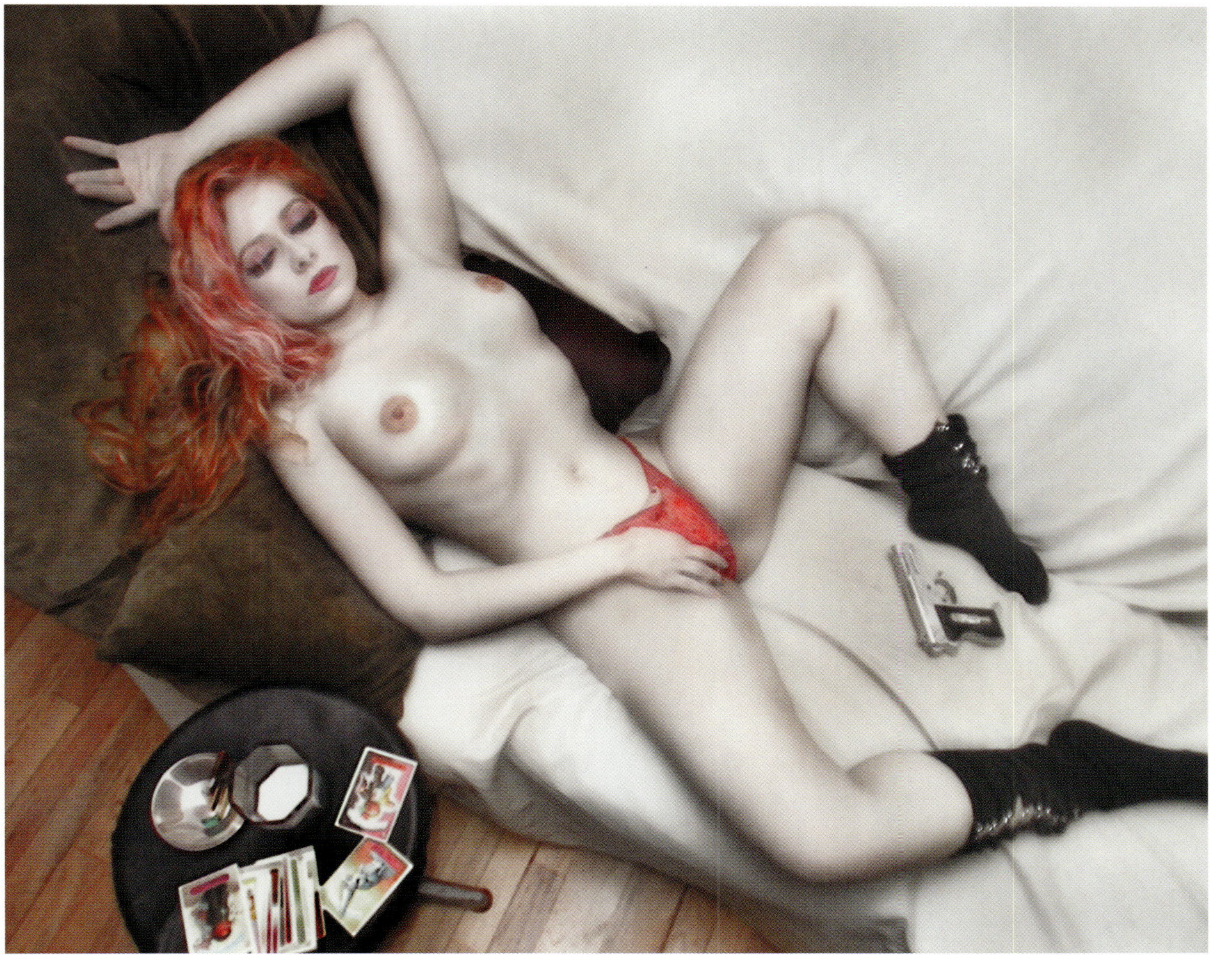

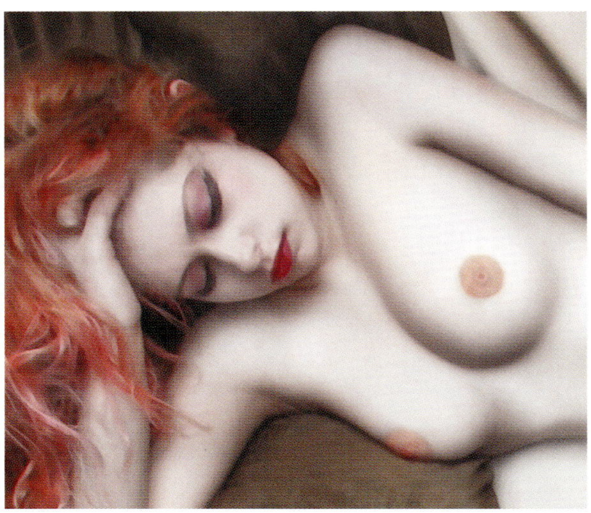

LEFT: This is the same model, but this cropped version without the props gives this a much softer feel. "I have always been a huge fan of what could be called the 'classic pin-up'—women in very sexy positions and poses but not necessarily sexual," he says. "In some of my pictures very little is showing, but nonetheless they are sexy as hell."

ABOVE: Gustafson often constructs quite detailed sets for his images, using them to tell a story—or to allow the viewer to imagine their own. The vivid pink color in the *Catnap* image is anything but subtle, but it is certainly eye-catching.

Chris Gustafson

OPPOSITE PAGE: Taken at a shared studio space in an art club in downtown Detroit, the lighting came from two strobe flash units with umbrellas and the set was made up from props borrowed from a friend. Gustafson developed his signature post-production technique by accident some years ago when he tried to rescue some underexposed images of a pale-skinned model from a lingerie shoot. "I started playing around with layering in Photoshop and using just a couple of stock filters, and after many, many painstaking layers, the resulting style came to be."

RIGHT: A less revealing pose from the same set of pictures taken in Gustafson's studio space. The colors and tones he manages to achieve digitally almost makes this look as though it is a black-and-white print that has been hand-tinted with a brush.

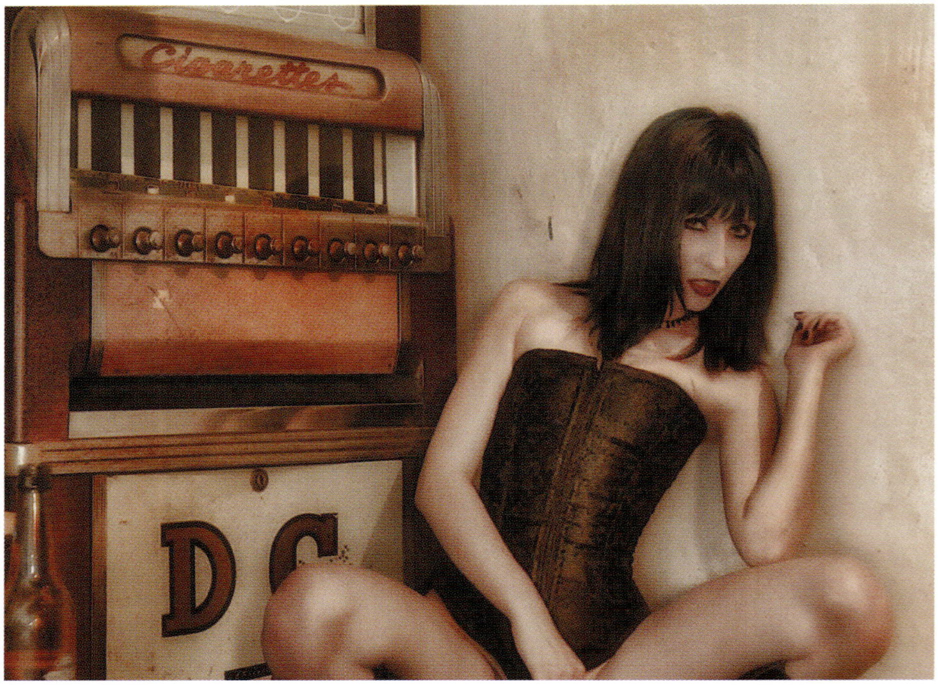

RIGHT: Once again, Gustafson's set has been carefully constructed, this time with more than a hint of fetishism—and voyeurism, by way of the figure in the background, mysteriously seen through the mirror. This was taken in an attic room using only available light from two windows and Gustafson relied on the speed of his f.2.8 lens for Canon D10 to give him sufficient exposure. Brightness and contrast were then selectively adjusted in Photoshop.

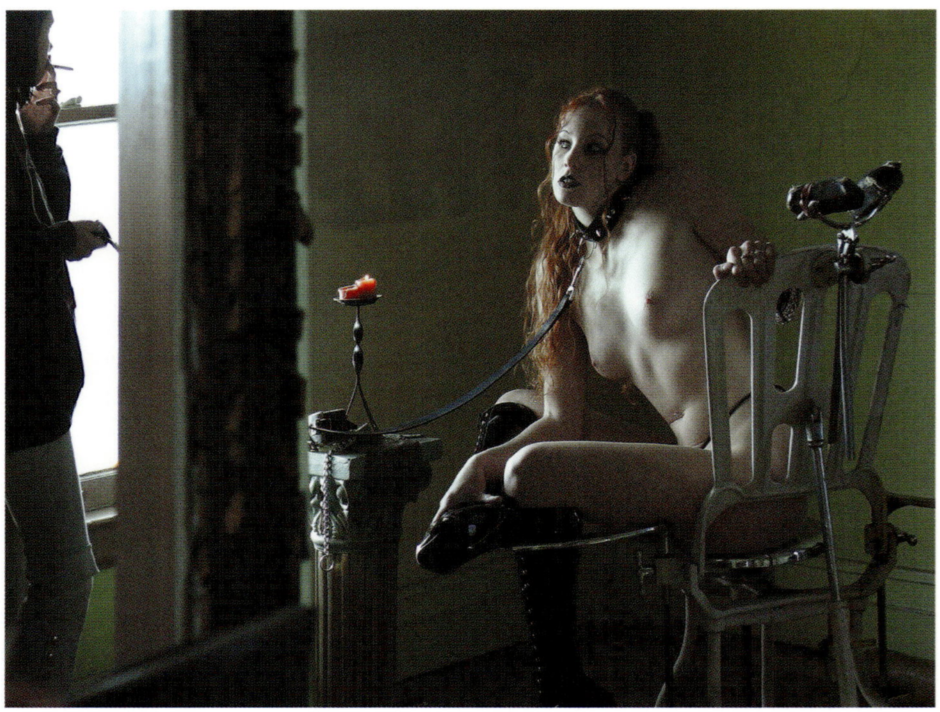

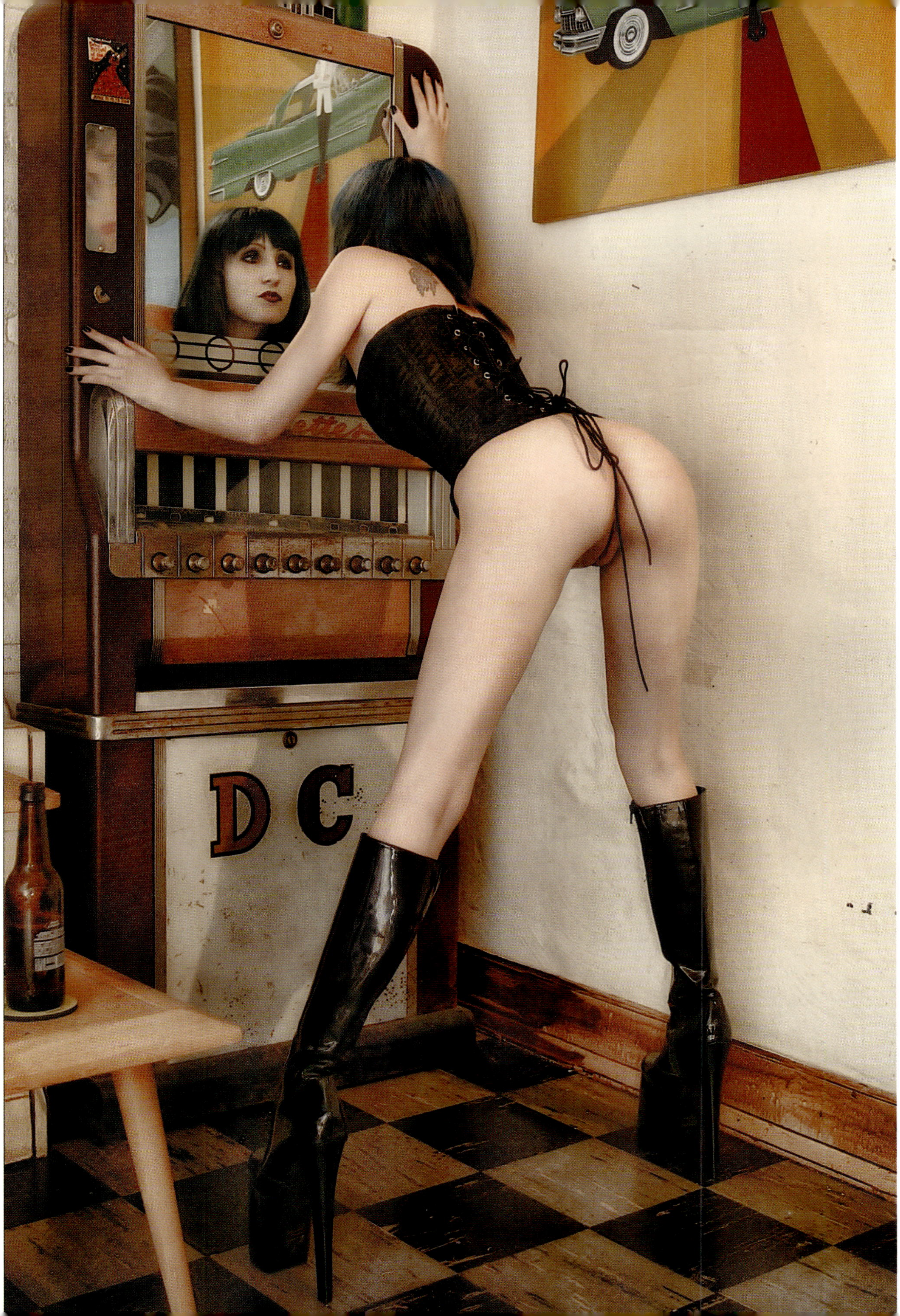
DC

H. James Hoff

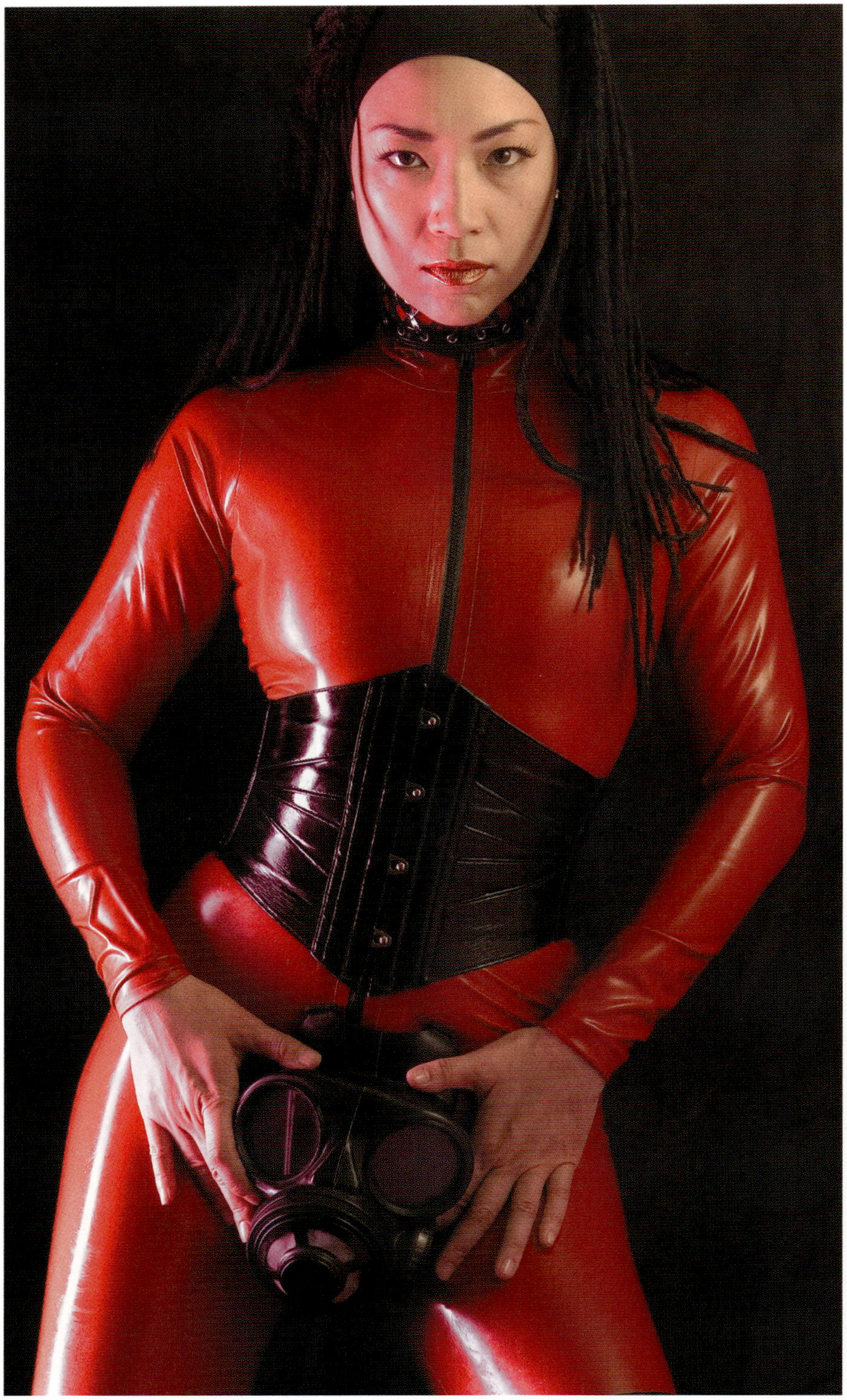

New York-based photographer H. James Hoff holds a master's degree in printmaking and has also trained as an artist, continuing to exhibit paintings and drawings. He brings his formal skills in traditional art to bear on his photographic work, regarding his final images as graphic rather than photographic.

LEFT AND BELOW: These two images prove that not all erotic images require nudity. Here only the model's face and hands are uncovered, but the erotic impact is unquestionable, deriving partly from the costume and the model's direct and challenging gaze, but also from the way the photographer exploits color and line. The idea was to create the type of character found in manga or graphic novels.

"I wanted to suggest strength and fearlessness and also draw on the notions of fetish, which are frequently found in Manga art," explains Hoff. "I asked the model, Mayan Lee, to pose because her look is perfect and she is very willing to play with ideas. I think of the two images shown here as forming a kind of diptych, or maybe adjacent frames from a Manga sequence."

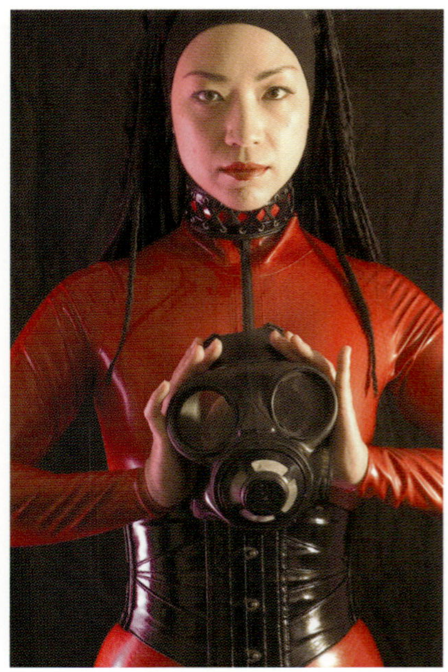

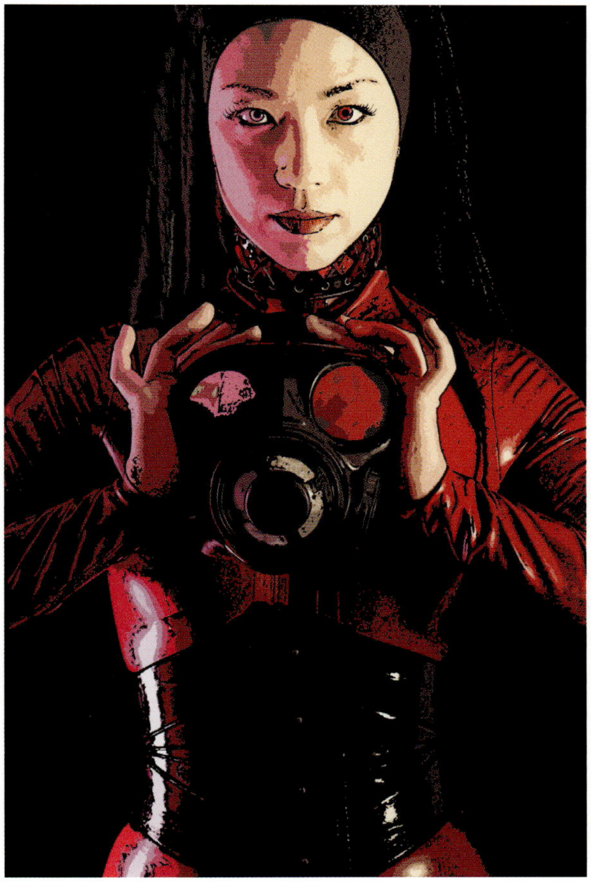

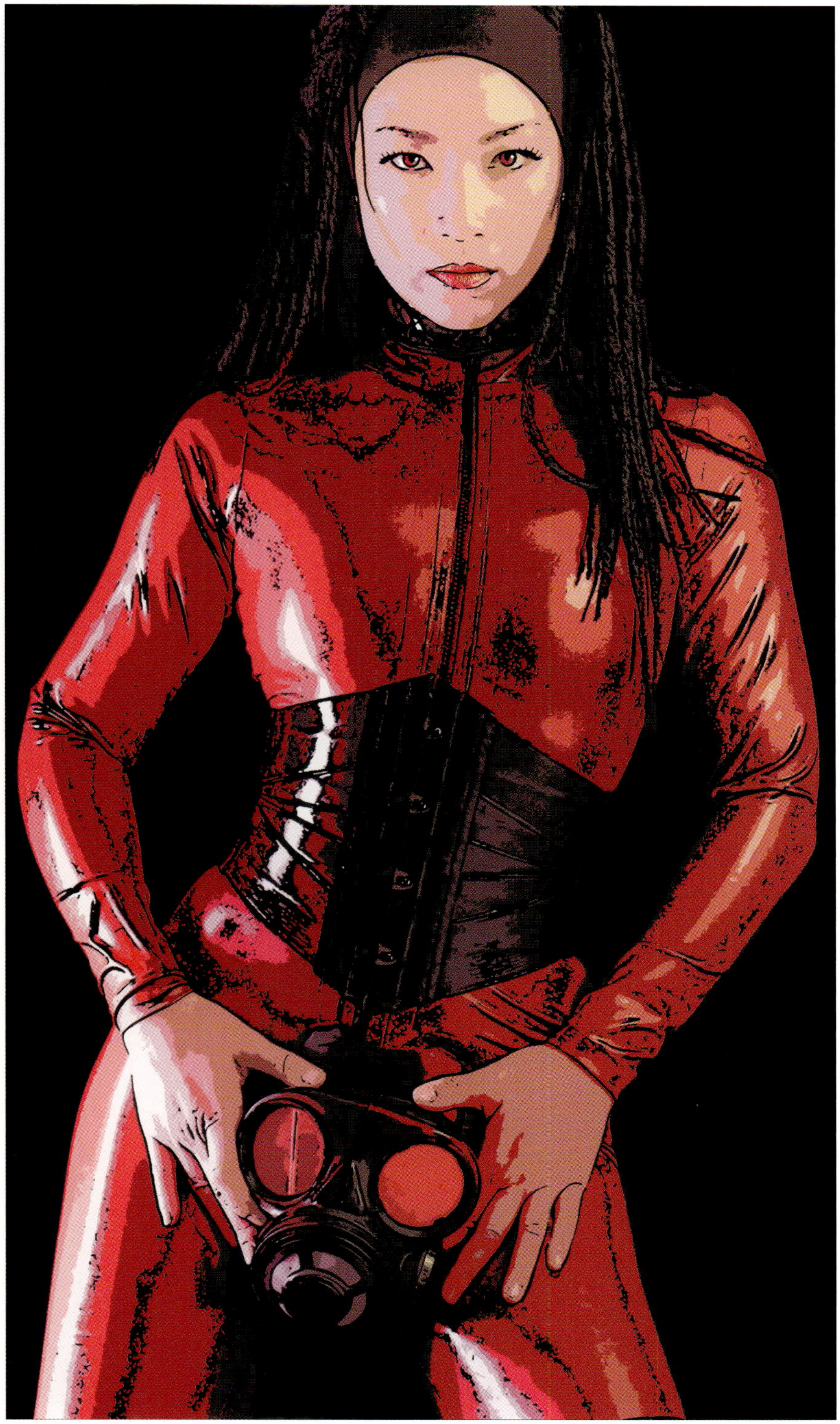

ABOVE AND RIGHT: Hoff shot the original images with a magenta gel over one flash head to provide a color accent. He then set to work on them, by hand and on a computer, to give these finished results, which have much more dramatic impact than the originals. He describes the process, which was repeated for each image: "First I used Photoshop to increase the saturation of the colors, and to break the image into separate planes, which I could then fill with color individually. This was done particularly on the face and hands and around the specular highlights on the model's right side, with the effect of bringing the image closer to the drawn and painted look of manga. I still found the image too 'normal,' particularly in the model's expression and the textures of her costume. To change this, I printed it out on a high-quality inkjet printer and set to work on the print with a pen and India ink to add a layer (so to speak) of line work. As a printmaker, I'll sometimes use the technique to correct the proof of an etching or engraving, so it was a small step to try it on a photograph. Photoshop lets you undo the last several changes you've carried out and, while I wouldn't say that makes you careless, working with 'real' materials is certainly a different experience! Finally, I wanted to show the work on the Internet, so I scanned the inked-in image again at a high resolution. I then went over it again, making a few final adjustments to the inking—using the computer this time!"

Brandon Luna

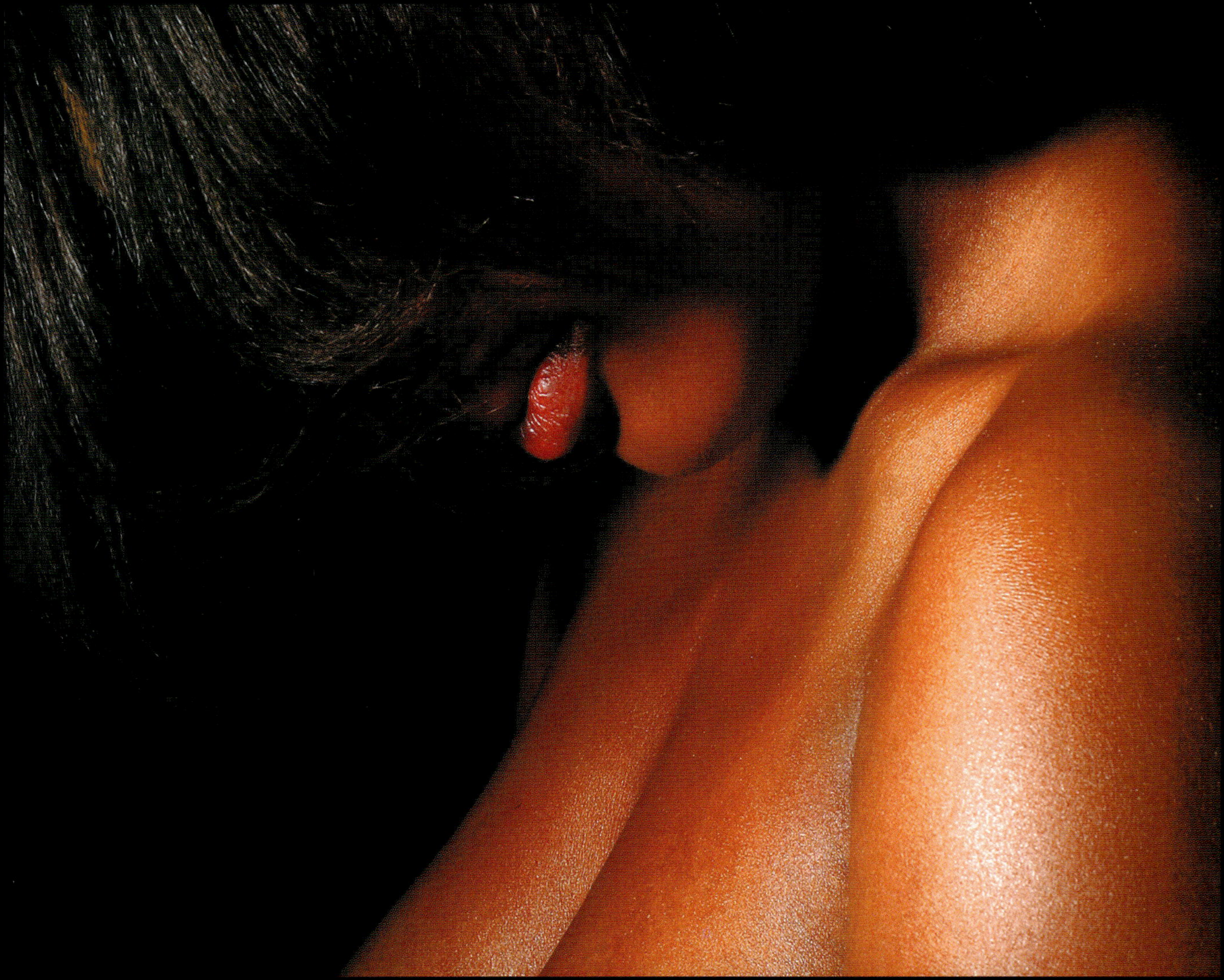

Brandon Luna was only introduced to photography a couple of years ago, and, since his first camera was a Nikon D100 SLR, his experience has been almost wholly digital. Nevertheless, he aims to capture his images as he sees them through the lens, using the computer only for minimum retouching and for showcasing his work.

ABOVE: Luna's shot *Exhaustion* shows that less can be more when it comes to erotic imagery. It was created in a studio environment with a single light set-up. The model was positioned against a black backdrop with the light source placed slightly above her head. "Since this was near the end of our shoot, I had asked Zequille to relax a bit. She naturally fell into this pose and that was the moment I captured," says Luna. "I was very pleased with the way the model's dark skin tone looked against the high-contrast lighting, so I decided to start a series of shots dealing with stark light and dark skin. Very little was done to this image post-production in Photoshop, with the exception of basic skin retouching, and a slight enhancement of the color to really give the image some 'pop.'"

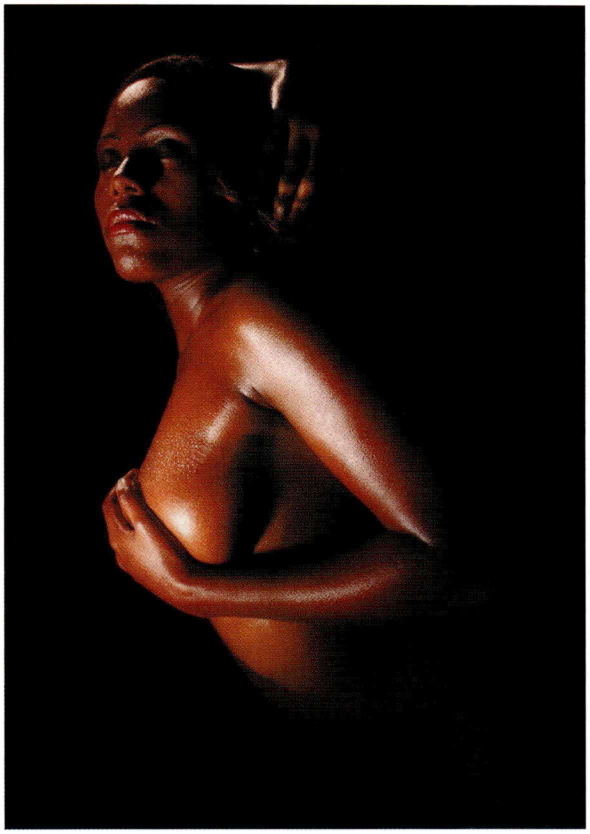

LEFT: Following the same theme of dark skin in stark light, Luna positioned his main light in front of the model with an additional hair light above. The latter was fitted with a chocolate-colored gel to match the model's complexion and reduce the harshness of the light. "As I was preparing to take this picture, I had the model move into quite a few poses until I found one that worked," he says. "When she moved into this position it seemed very statuesque to me, and I think I successfully captured that feel in this image."

RIGHT: *Droplet* was created in a studio environment, in much the same way as *Exhaustion*. Again, a single light with a grid was placed in front of the model at a slight angle. The difference, though, was that this shot was carefully planned. "I had this image clearly in mind for some time, but this was my first chance to capture it," explains Luna. "My idea was to show a part of the female form in a way that had yet to be seen, but rather than make it the central focus of the image, I wanted the focus to be a droplet of water. It wasn't easy to achieve, as I wanted to acquire the desired effect in the camera and not in post-production. After baby oil was applied, I used a small spray bottle to create the beads of water. On the twelfth try, I had captured the image I wanted. Once again, very little was done to this image post-production apart from skin retouching and boosting the color."

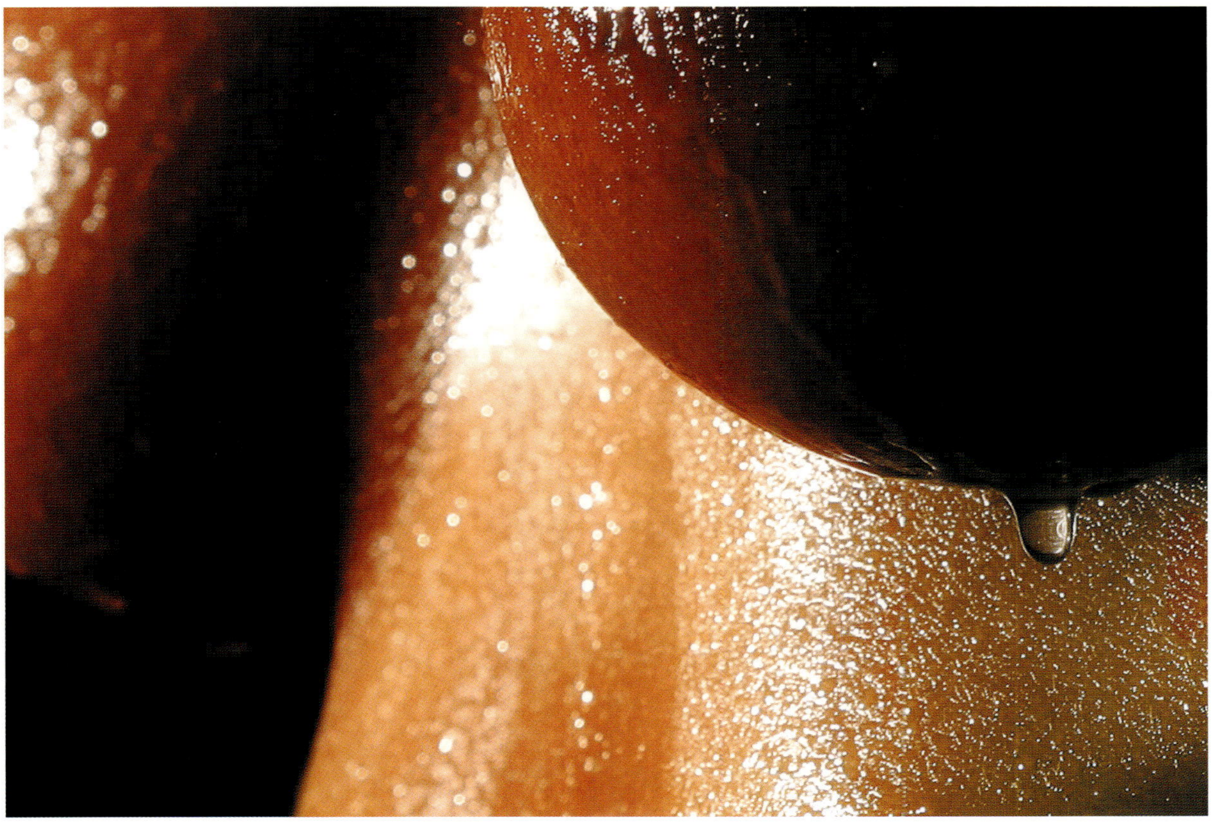

Brandon Luna

BELOW AND RIGHT: Working in a studio is ideal for exact control over lighting and, of course, privacy, but for an injection of fresh ideas and a more realistic feel to images, outdoor locations are worth exploring. Luna chose a back alley for this shot, *Night Moves*, which gave him the urban look he was after for the background. It was shot using available light from the surrounding buildings, with a reflector placed underneath the model to bounce light up onto the skin. The low camera angle maximizes the dramatic impact of the pose and also allowed Luna to include the horizontal line of the edge of the building and the bright light on the wall. A slow shutter speed allowed a little of the model's movement to register, which also gave the picture its edgy feel. "The image is strong in color but I wanted it to have more of a dreamlike quality, so I made it black and white and gave it a slight glow in Photoshop using Diffuse Glow."

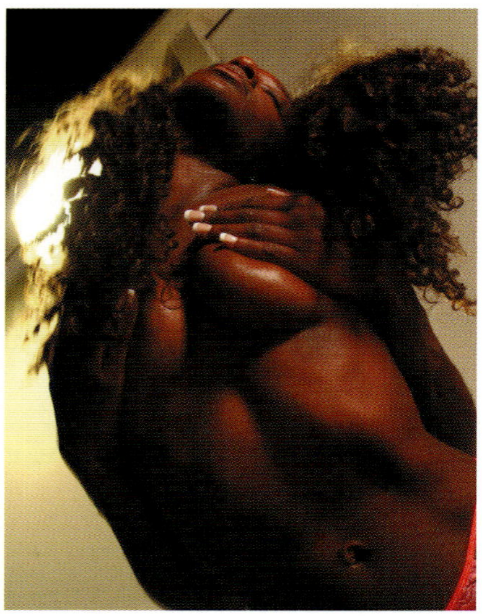

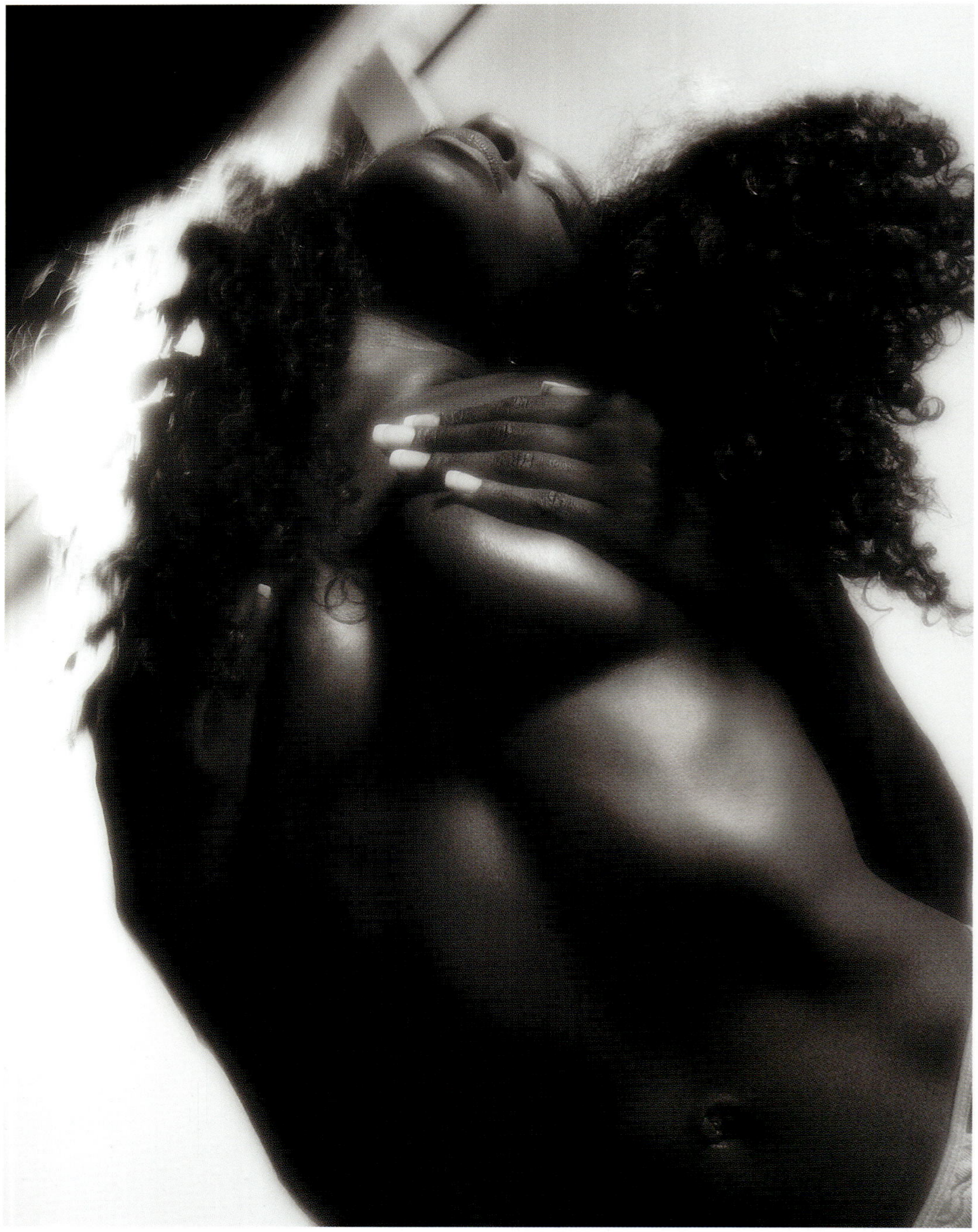

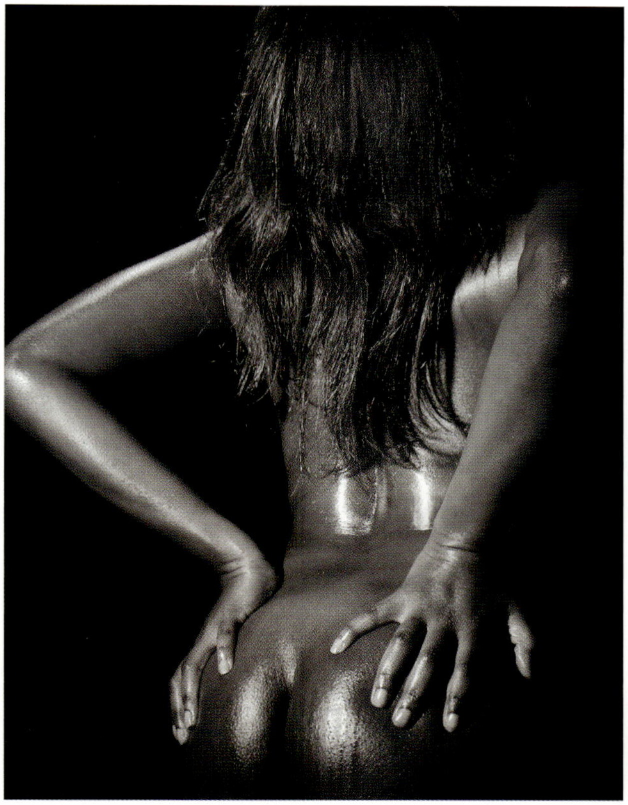

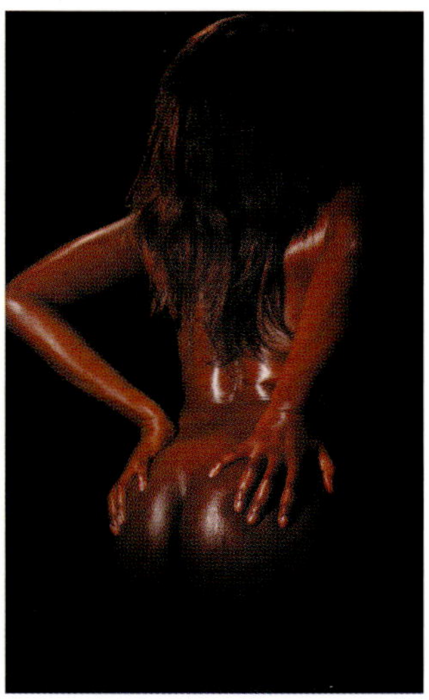

ABOVE AND LEFT: This was one of a series of figure studies that Luna produced in the studio, using light to bring out subtle tonal variations in the model's skin and hair against the deep black background. Converting the image to black and white made the highlights stand out even more strongly, better emphasizing the erotic lines and contours of the body.

RIGHT: *Night Creature* was taken on the same night as *Night Moves* and at the same location—a back alley. With both model and photographer lying on the ground, Luna tilted the camera to get this dramatic angle and lift the image out of the ordinary. "I wanted to give the image a feel of eroticism and danger at the same time," he explains. There was little available light at this level, so Luna used a single spotlight on the model. Small adjustments to boost the color were all that was required at the editing stage.

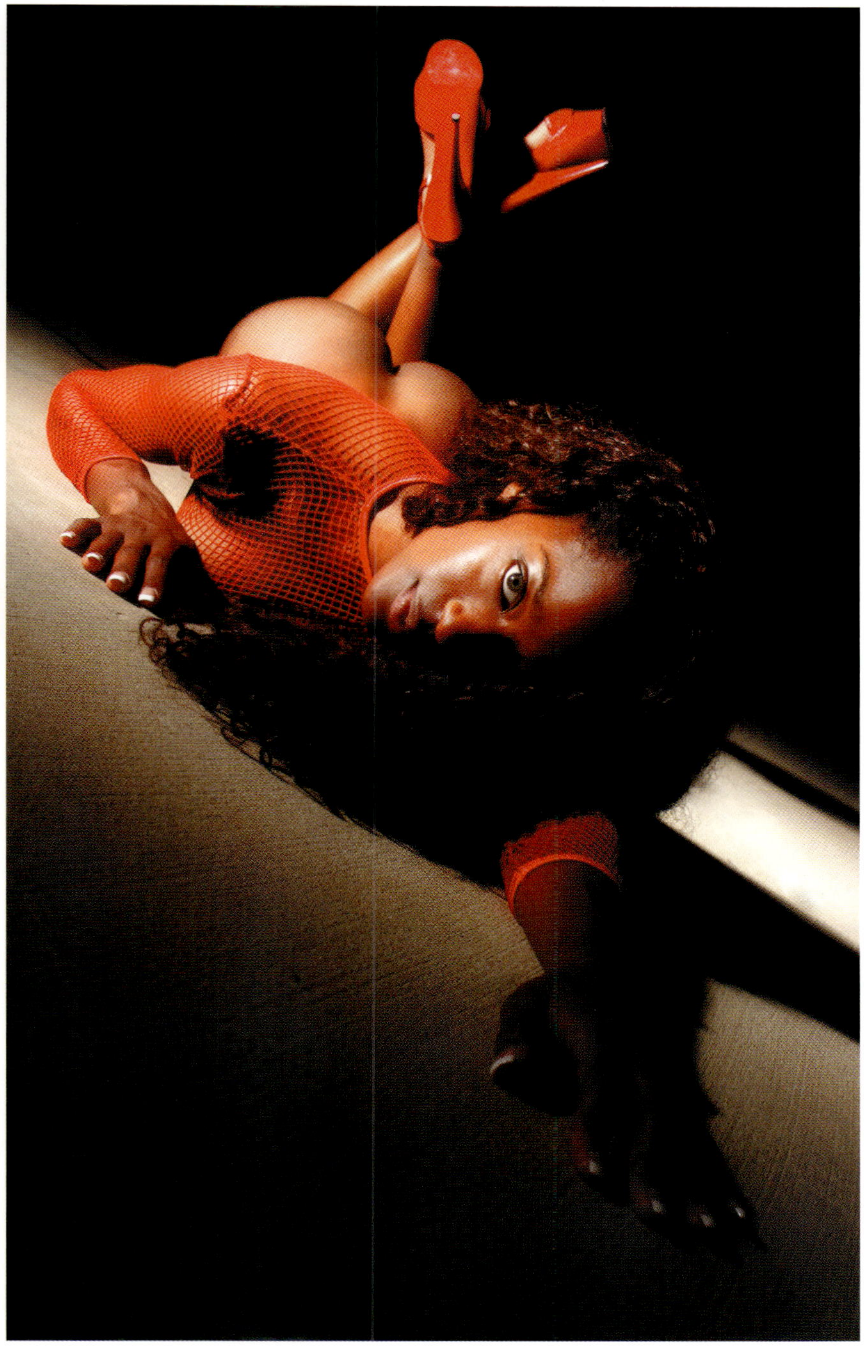

Brandon Luna

BELOW LEFT: Although this image looks as though it has been heavily retouched in Photoshop to produce the luminous color and glow of the skin, it was achieved at the time of shooting by "painting with light." The model was positioned on the floor against black muslin in the fetal position, while a flashlight was used to trace the line of her body during the three-second exposure.

BELOW RIGHT: "*Water Beads* was a continuation of my figure-study theme, but I moved away from dark-skinned models and changed from using one light to two," says Luna. "My intention was to create an artistic image that was arousing but in a non-offensive way." The tight crop was achieved in-camera with the negative space on the right used to emphasize the outline of the body. Luna had thought he would convert this to black and white but found that the contrast between skin and background was more powerful in color.

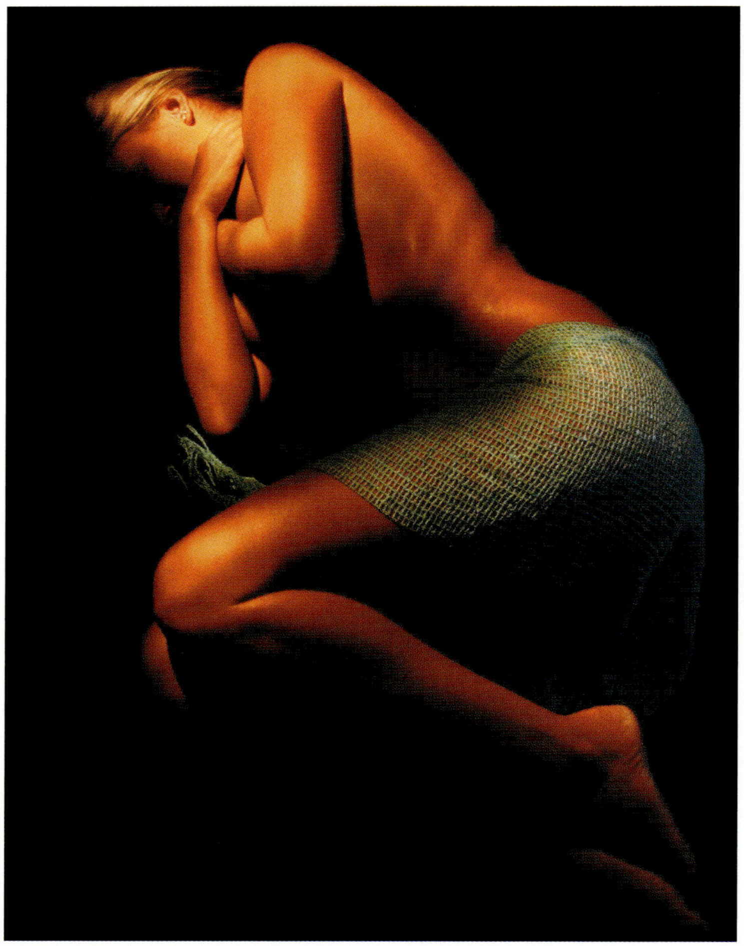

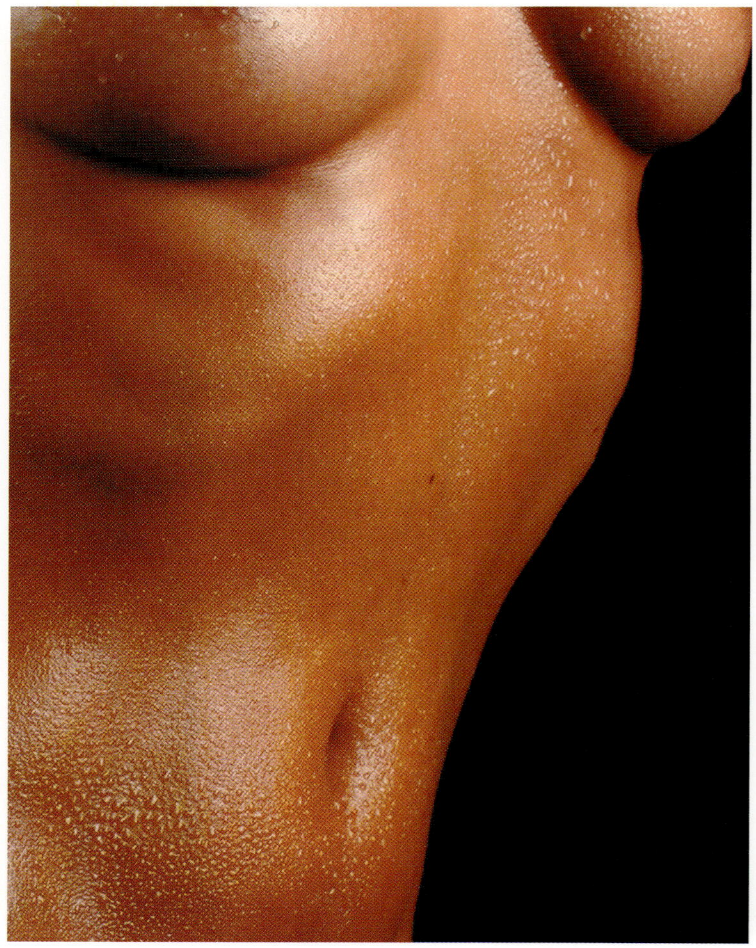

BELOW: "*Zing* was created in the studio using two studio lights and a string of Christmas lights," explains Luna. The model was frozen in time with a quick flash of the studio strobes, but the shutter remained open for two seconds so that we could swing the Christmas lights behind her a few times. As usual, I attempted to capture 100 per cent of the image I wanted in the camera so I would have to do very little in post-production. I felt the image worked better as a horizontal, so I cropped it, and did some basic skin retouching and color adjustment."

RIGHT: "This hi-key shot was created in the studio to show off the model's long legs and ability to move," Luna recalls. "It took a few tries to get the hair just right, but both the model and I were very happy with the results. This image remains one of my personal favorites because of its movement, its sense of fun, and the color contrast between the white background, the model's dark skin, and the bright pink clothing. A few stray hairs were removed in Photoshop, and the color was turned up a notch."

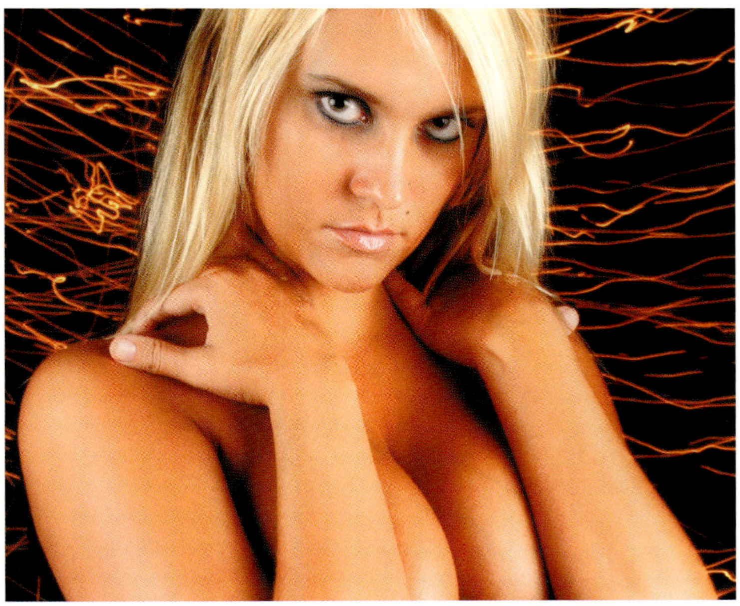

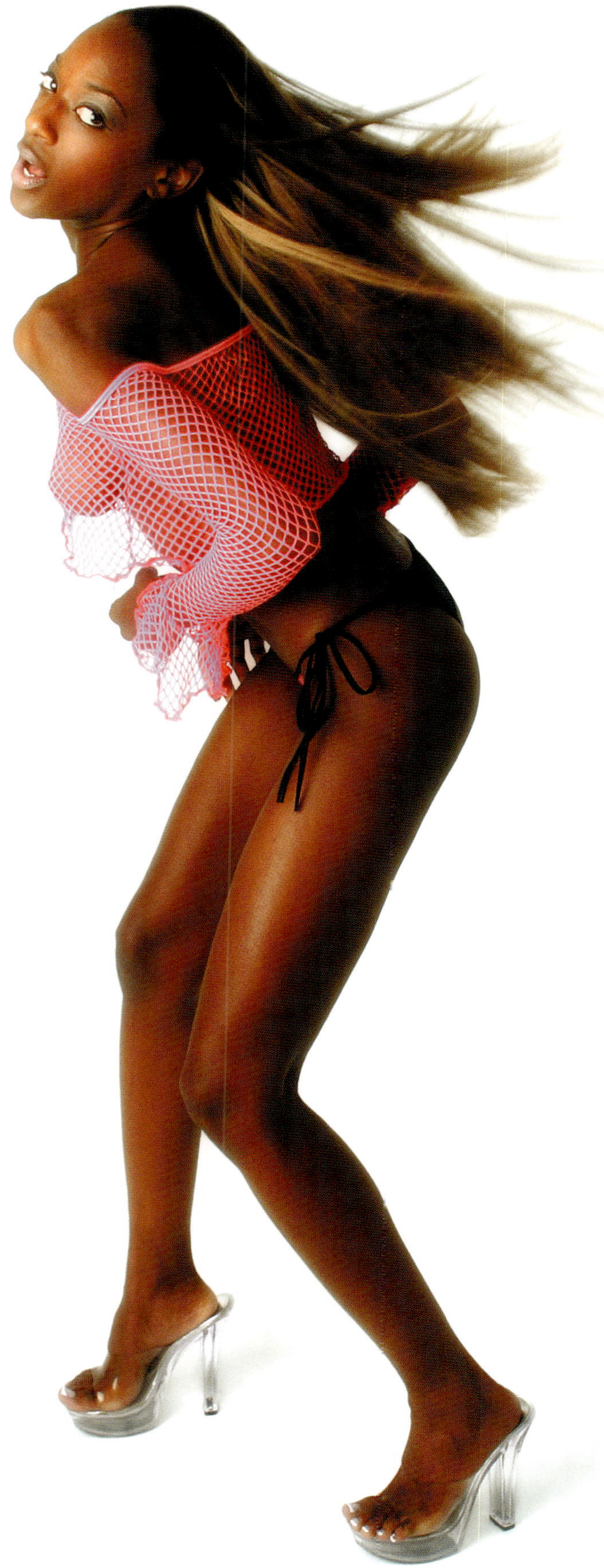

Holger Maass

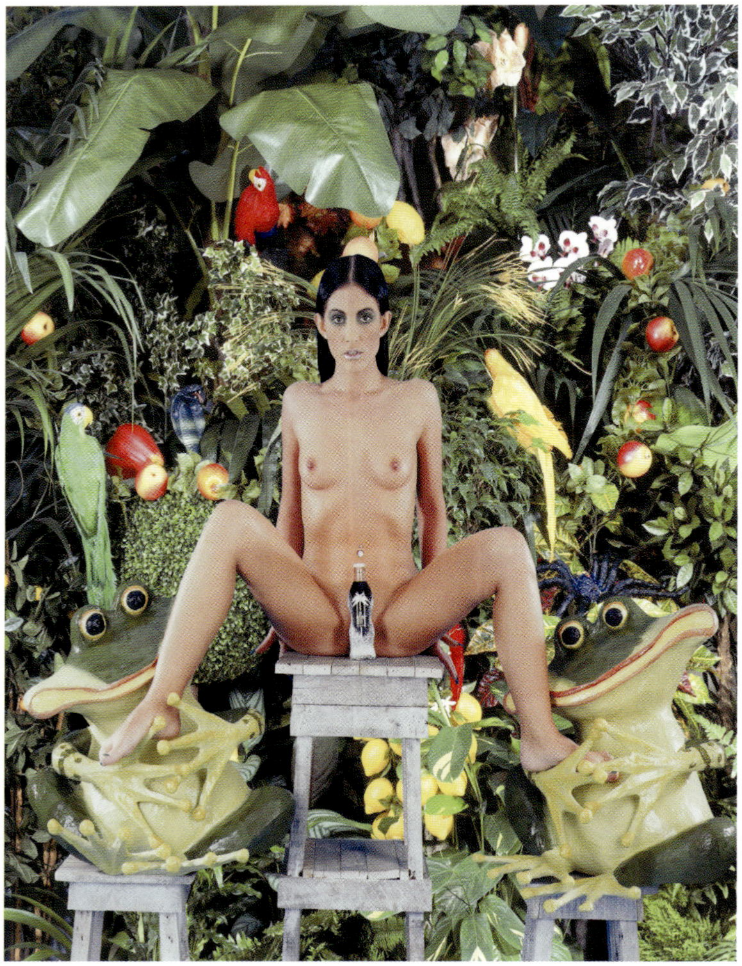

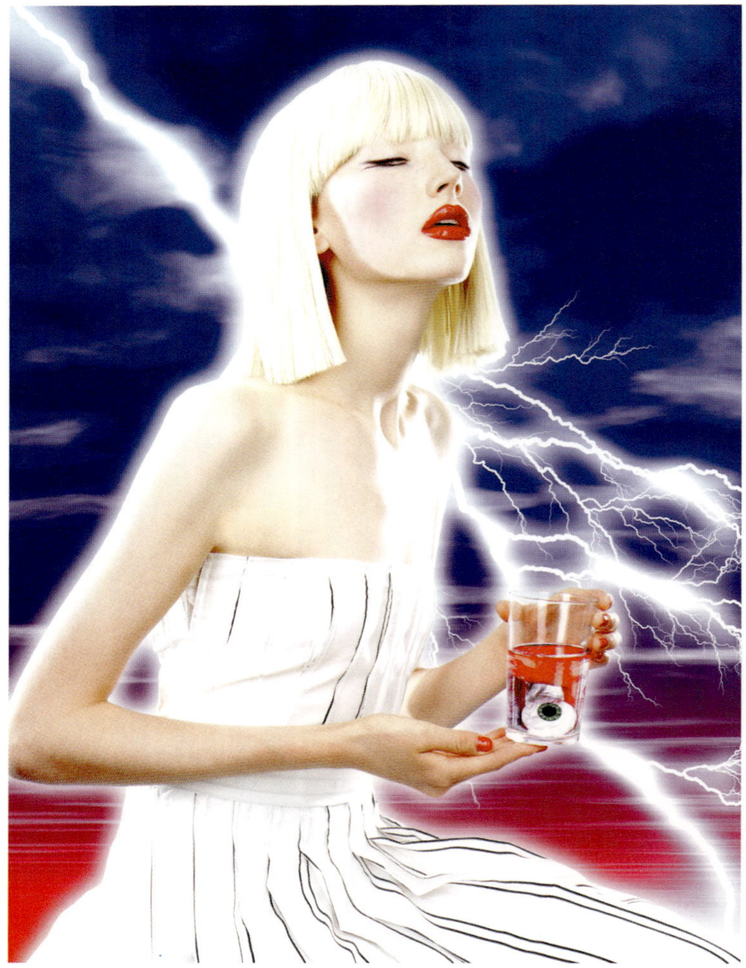

Holger Maass owns and runs Studio Maass, a photographic studio in Munich, and is represented in New York. Together with a team of assistants and outside specialists he produces striking and individual images, concentrating on celebrity portraits and fine art photography. The work is published in many magazines and displayed internationally in art galleries. In 2004, Maass won prizes in the Epson Digital Portrait contest, Canon Profashional Award, and NoLimits Digital Awards.

ALL IMAGES: The vivid, eye-catching compositions of Holger Maass are produced in his studio through a combination of traditional photography and digital techniques. All pictures are originally shot on film, with a Mamiya 6x7 Pro 11 camera. The styling, props, and backdrops play a key part in many of the images and these come from collaborating with professional set-designers and special effects artists from companies that usually work with television and film projects.

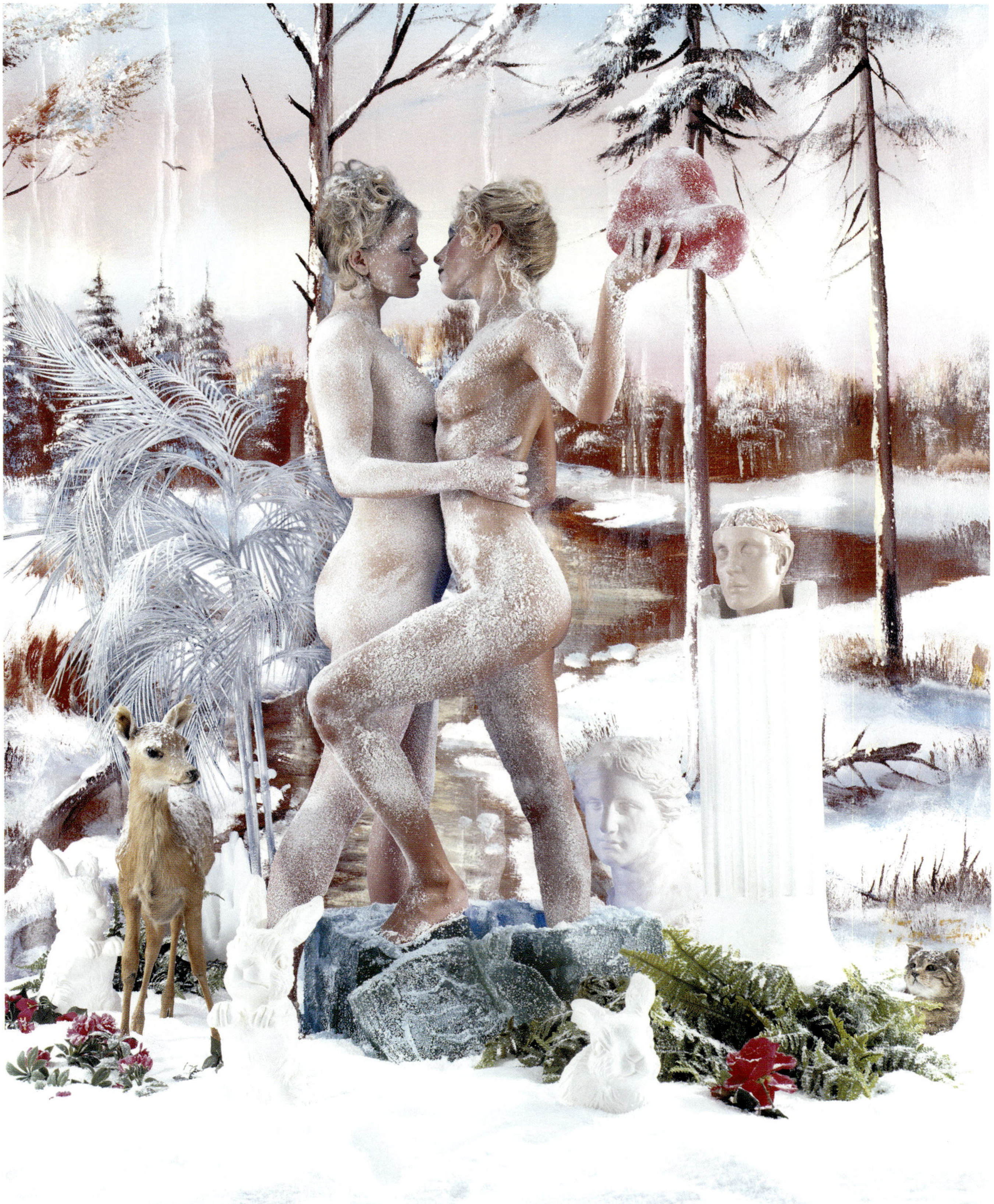

Holger Maass

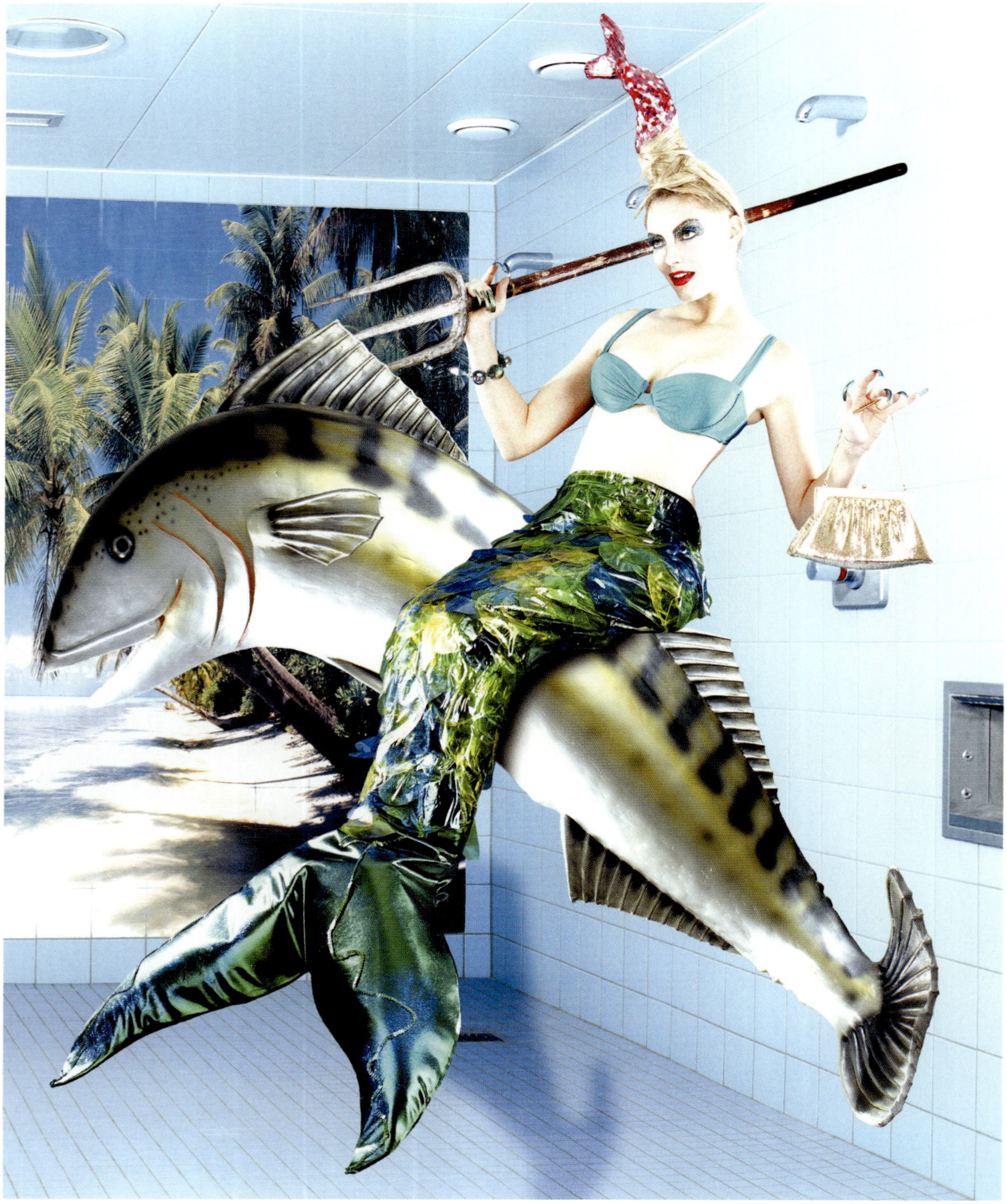

ALL IMAGES: "Working with a bigger team and within a complex environment requires accurate project planning and a detailed schedule before the shooting even takes place," Maass explains. "For the conception, realization, and post-production processes of each image, I am supported by assistants, who help keep the whole thing running." While the greater part of Maass' images are created in-camera, digital techniques are used for color and contrast enhancement, and sometimes for layering different images to introduce other elements or a new background into the image.

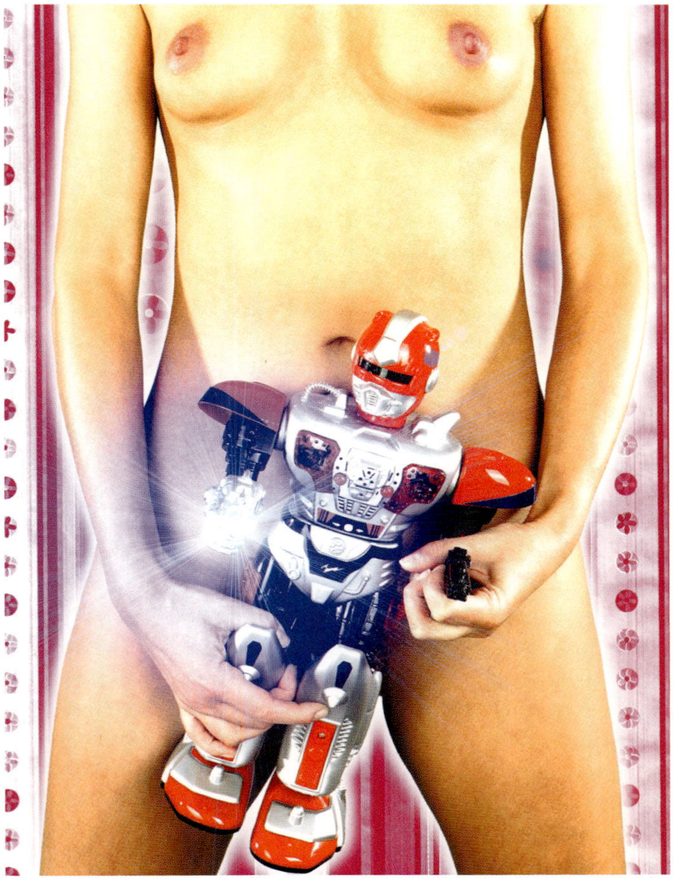

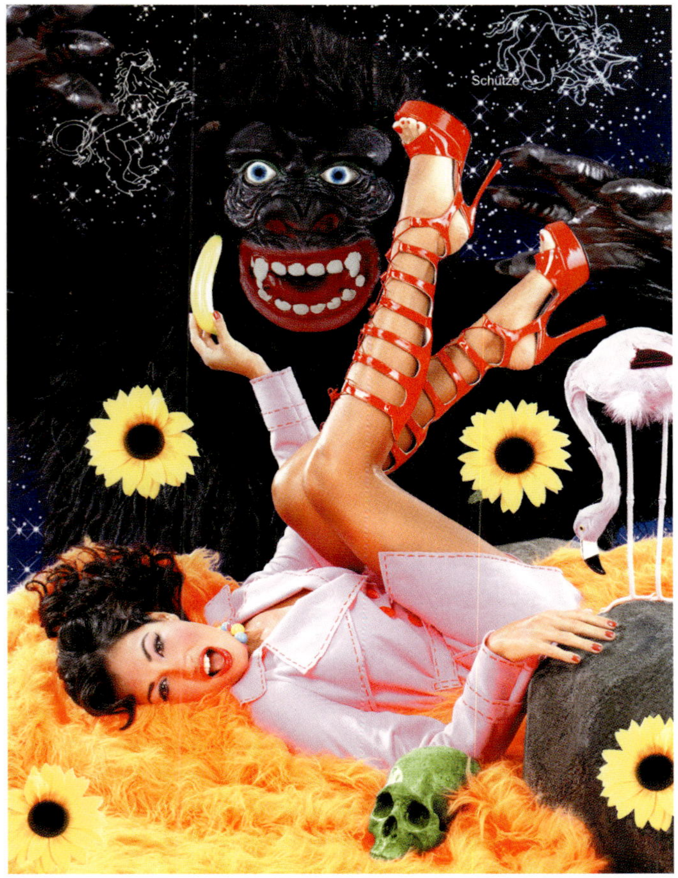
Schütze

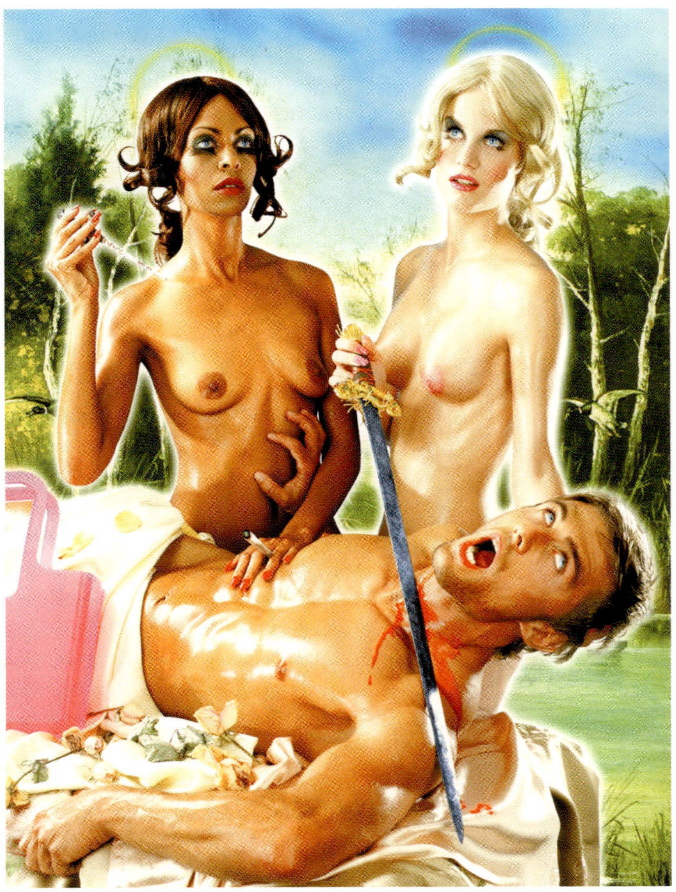

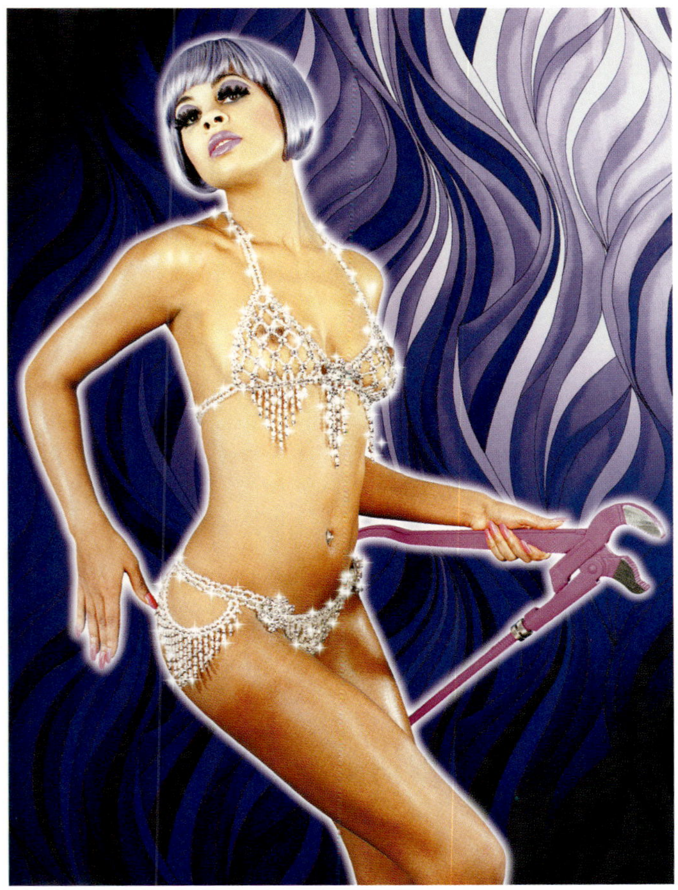

Dave McAleavy

Dave McAleavy is a Scottish photographer whose work often makes use of light painting—working in spaces ranging from a blacked-out studio to the ruins of a Scottish castle, and sweeping a light source such as a handheld flashlight or a laser across the model to produce uneven, atmospheric lighting.

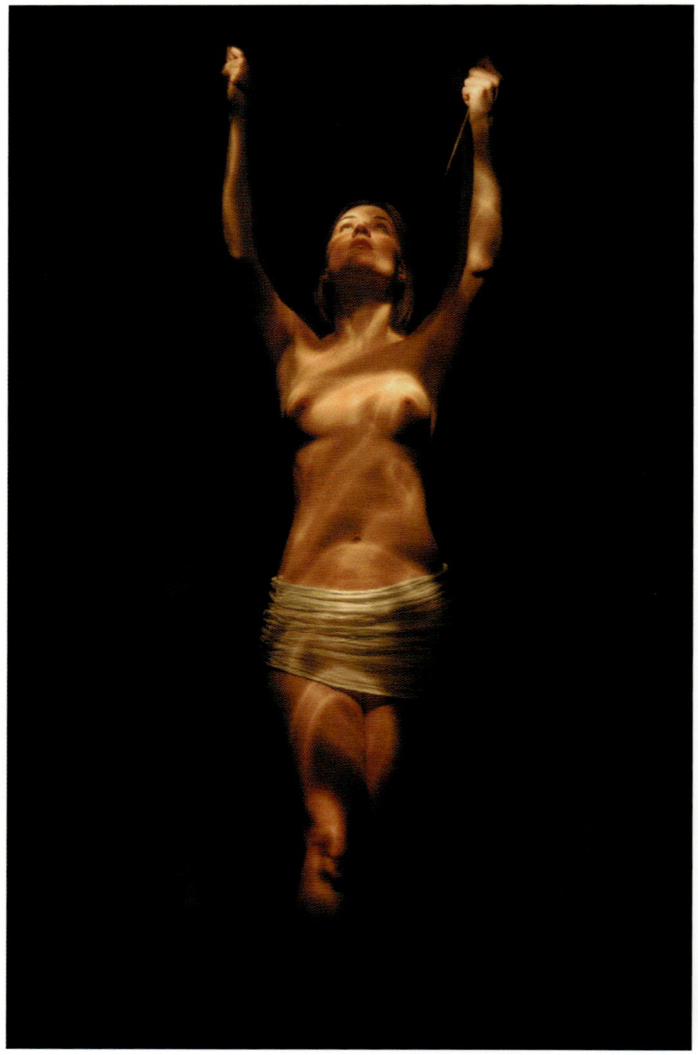

BELOW: Dave McAleavy's inspiration for this montage came from the photographic technical term "modeling light," which suddenly struck him as a possible description or concept for an image. The starting point was the bulb itself, as McAleavy explains: "I shot it switched on and switched off, against a couple of different backgrounds. I'd wired it to a dimmer, so I could vary its intensity when it was switched on, and I also bracketed the exposures widely. This gave me a good collection of elements to mask and layer together, creating the most 'real' look for the final image. It's important when you're working on montage images like this to shoot the options you need all at the same time, so you don't have to try to recreate an identical setup later. Altogether, the final image used four different shots of the bulb, masked and layered in various ways, to create a convincing image with just the right reflections."

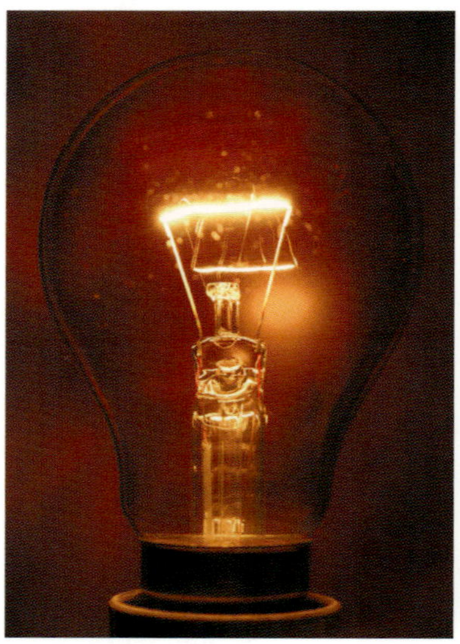

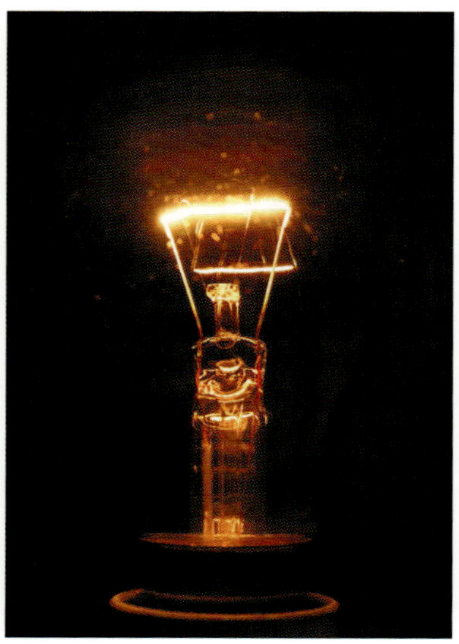

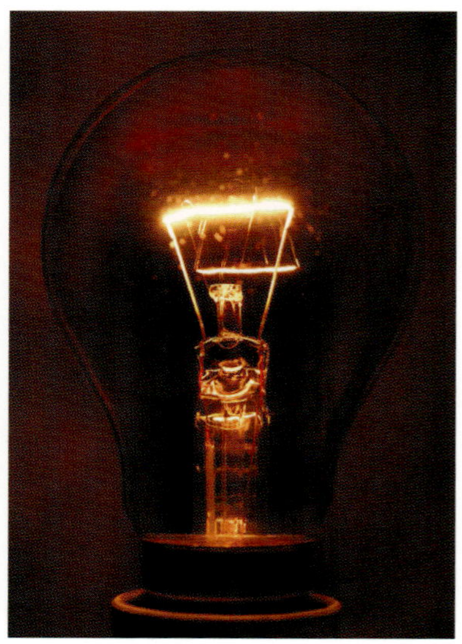

ABOVE: This model was shot using the bulb test shots as a reference to get her arms at the right angle. The initial shots were taken with a boom-mounted flash head directly above her to simulate the filament. "This proved to be far harsher than I expected, so I swapped to a lightpainting approach," says McAleavy. "The final shot was lit with a flashlight, swept from head to foot while the shutter was open. This relies on the model's ability to hold a pose, in the dark, with minimal movement, for about 30 seconds. Fortunately, Charlotte is extremely good at this, and the image was acceptably sharp. The result is also nice and uneven, removing the need to distort the image later to give it a wavy 'through glass' look."

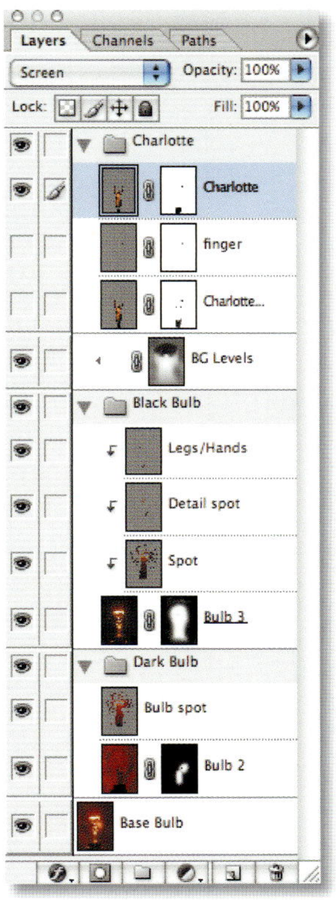

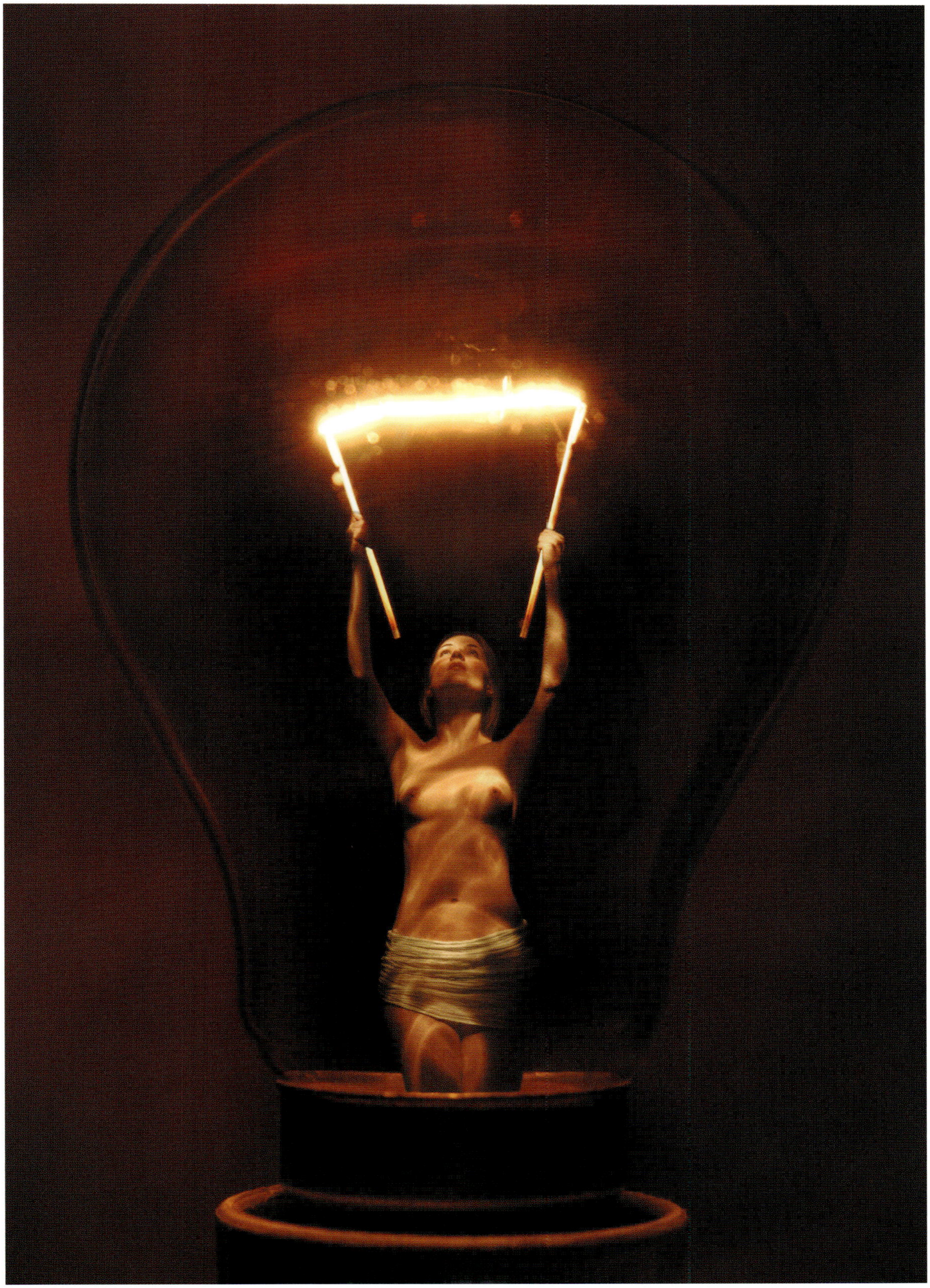

RIGHT: In this final image, the model herself becomes part of the source of illumination as she supports the glowing element of a lightbulb. "Fitting Charlotte into the bulb was less complicated, once I'd scaled the image of her to fit correctly into it. The only problem was that after cutting her out of her original background, I discovered that her left hand didn't quite fit around the filament support wires, so I had to partly 'rebuild' the hand, replacing a finger that wasn't visible enough in the original. I also used Photoshop's Liquify tool to reshape the hand so that it wrapped around the filament wires more satisfactorily."

Michael McGrath

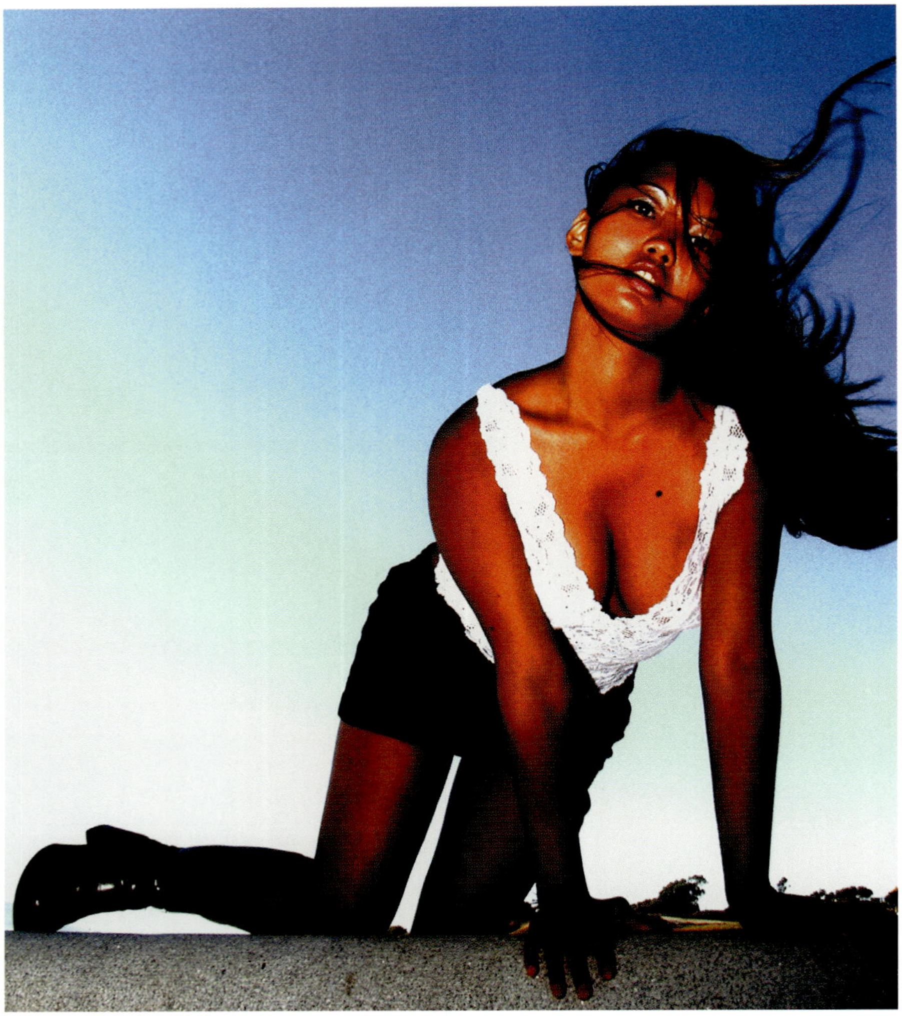

Michael McGrath's career as a photographer began at the age of 18, when he got a Canon AE-1. He trained under two photographers, Tim Crowson and Rancisco Ballesteros. He has been shooting for over 30 years and running his own business, Images of Elegance, for over three years. His passion is photographing women, either in the studio or outdoors. What interests him is creating sensual portraits, revealing something of the subject's soul, which often means concentrating on lips and eyes in tight head shots.

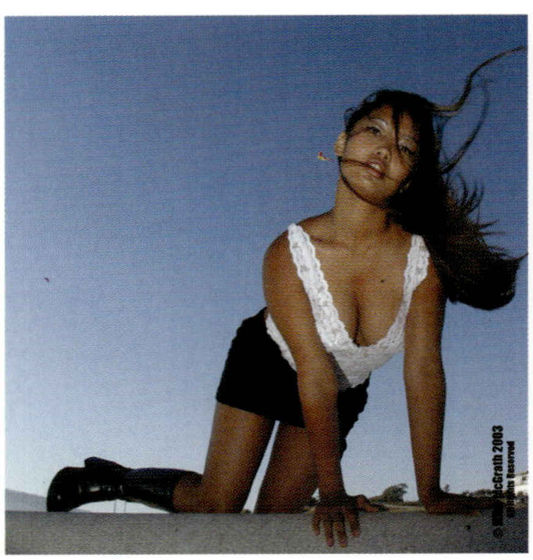

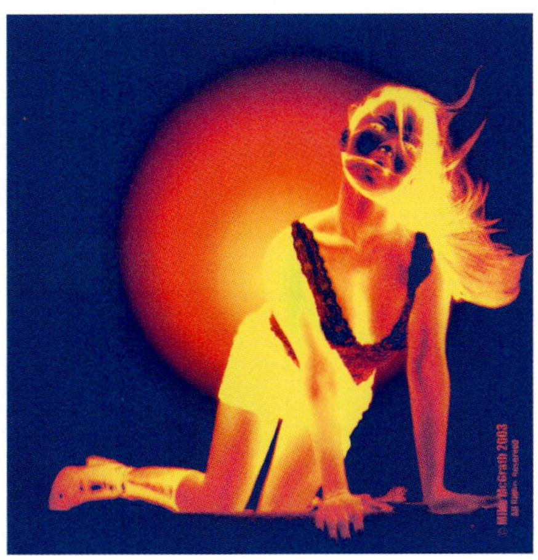

THIS PAGE: For this sequence, McGrath used an Olympus E-20N on ASA 80 set at 1/160 f 7.1 with flash. He shot outdoors at a pagoda overlooking the Pacific Ocean. He positioned the model, Azaylia, on a stone railing. "It was late in the day, around 4pm, and it was very windy, with gusts up to 30 knots. I had intended to use an umbrella flash but it was much too windy. The sky was overcast and there was very heavy fog, but at times it lifted a bit. The wind was blowing so hard we were unable to keep Azaylia's hair in place. I wanted the shot to feel very free and for Azaylia to be part of the sky and to flow with her hair in the wind. My aim was to capture and reveal both an innocence and a definite sensuality without tipping over into aggressive sexuality."

For the image (above left), McGrath manipulated the contrast to bring out a gradient sky, and warmed up the face and made Azaylia's cleavage appear more prominent, as well as darkening the stockings.

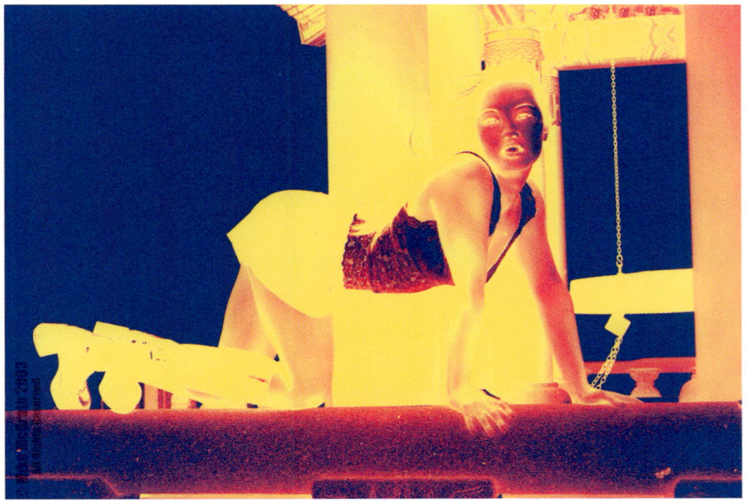

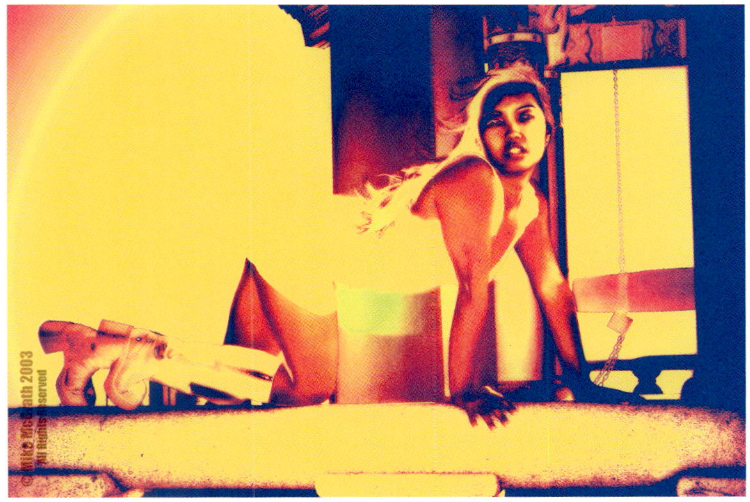

THIS PAGE: For this sequence, McGrath shot with an Olympus E-20N on ASA 80 set at 1/125 f8 with flash. Azaylia was on all fours directly in front of the bell of the pagoda. "As you can see we were still blanketed in with fog. For this shot I wanted a very sensuous look on her face with an 'almost nude, but not nude' sort of tease going on as far as clothing is concerned."

ABOVE LEFT: McGrath says, "We were getting some hot blues and yellows, but the picture still feels flat-to-calm." He used an infrared filter on an Olympus E-20N set at 1/125 f8 with flash on ASA 80.

ABOVE RIGHT: "I made two attempts at the image, and this is the second attempt. I wanted it to feel hot—molten—I wanted to feel the heat from her body. At first I solarized the image, carefully adjusting exposure time, and digitally fogging the image with white light. The last step was to apply the infrared filter. The final effect was of a sun goddess with a sexuality so intense that being any where near her would envelop you in flames of passion."

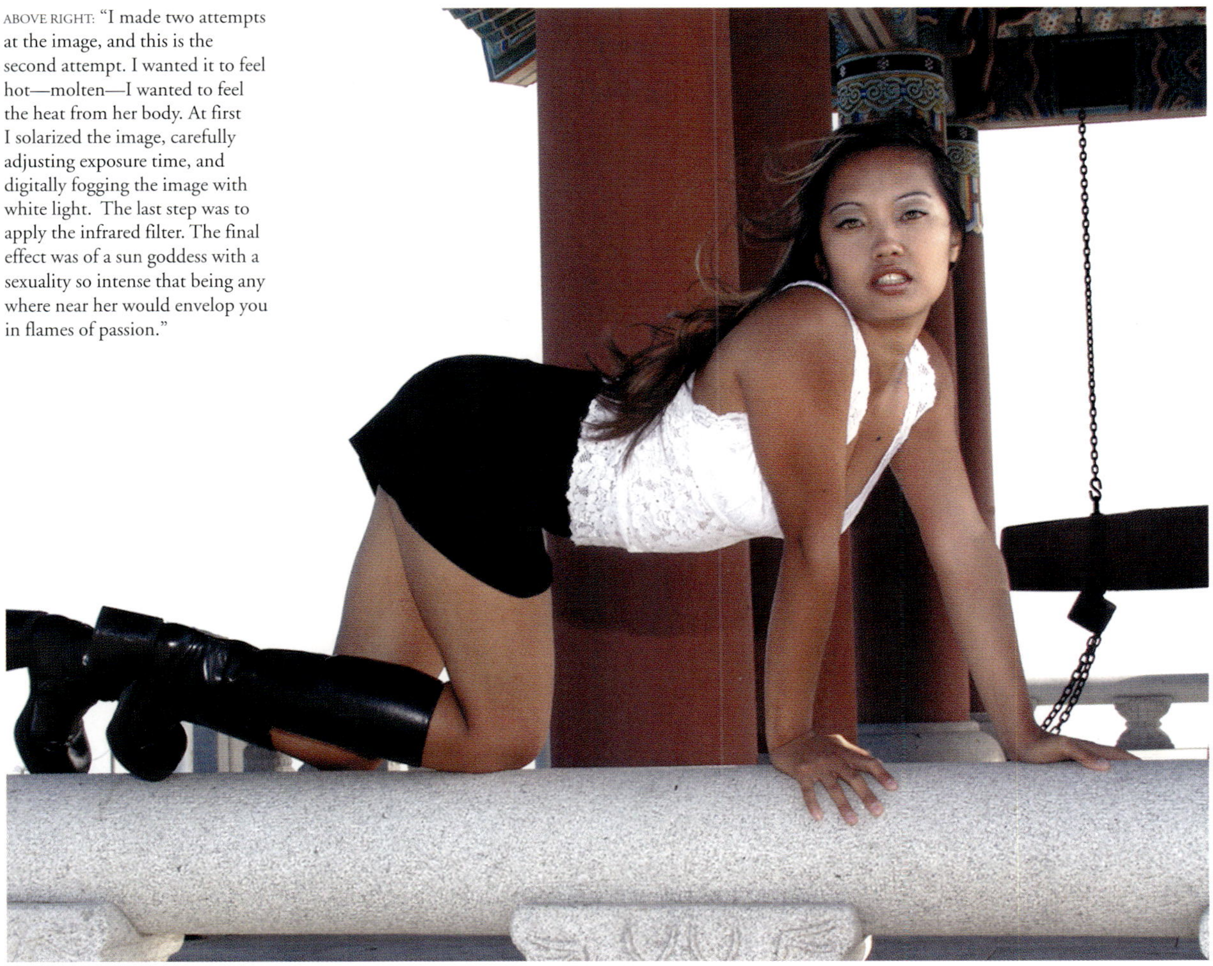

Michael McGrath

THIS PAGE: "On the original pictures my flash didn't fire, but... I liked the composition of the shot, so I saved it and worked on it. I chose this spot and this pose for their not-so-subtle sexuality. If you look closely at this picture you will see a few elements suggestive of phallic symbols—for example, Azaylia is crawling up the cylindrical rail, and directly in front and to her right is another cap that is phallic in shape."

On the second shot, McGrath used a high-pass filter to darken the overexposed background and he added a soft, white halo around the subject, followed by a Neon Glow filter, which darkened the image further and gave it an "X-ray" effect. It was shot on an Olympus E-20N set at 1/160 f 7.1 in available light.

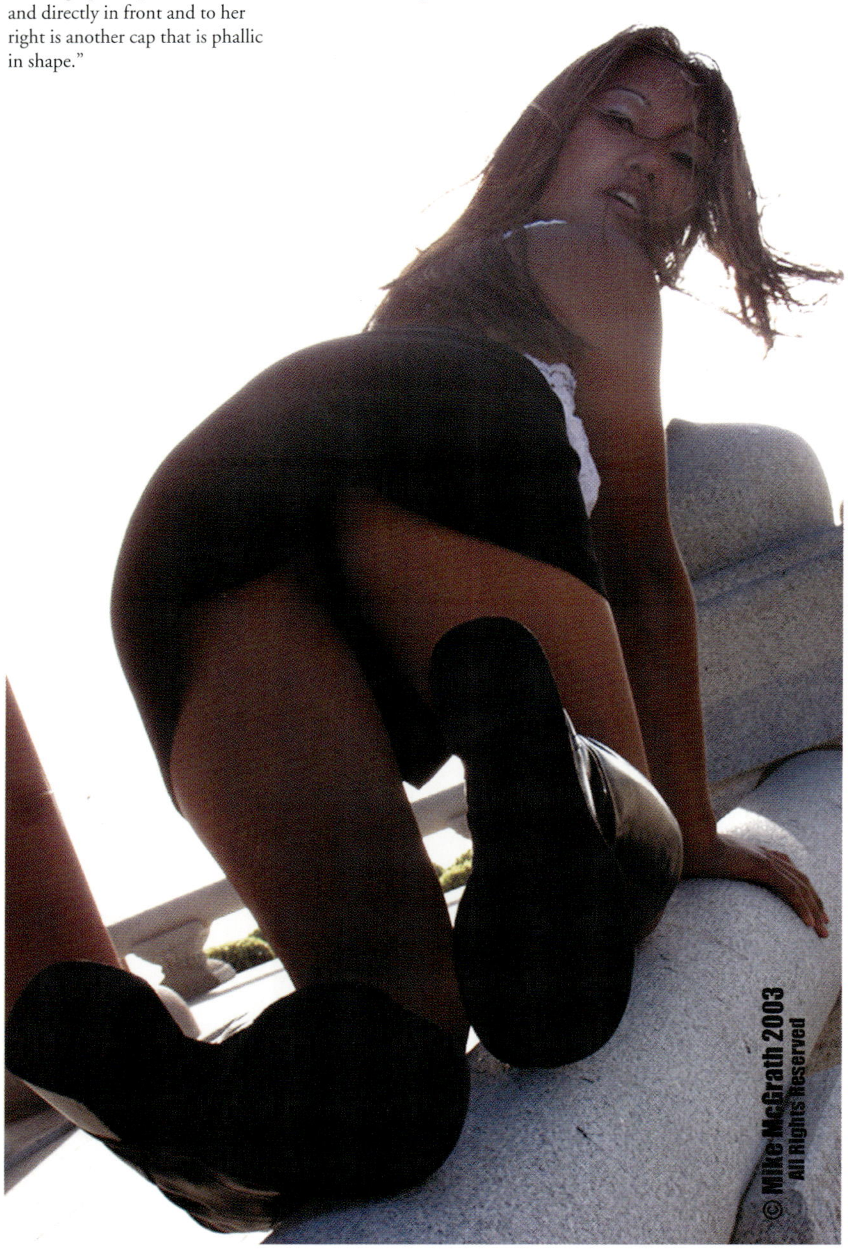

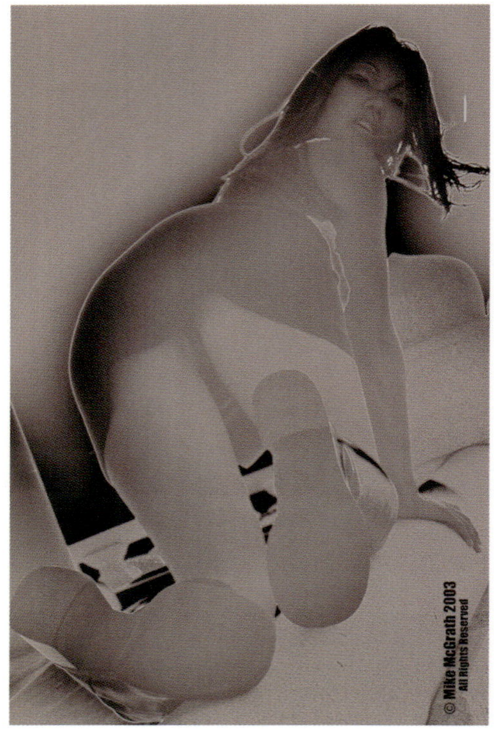

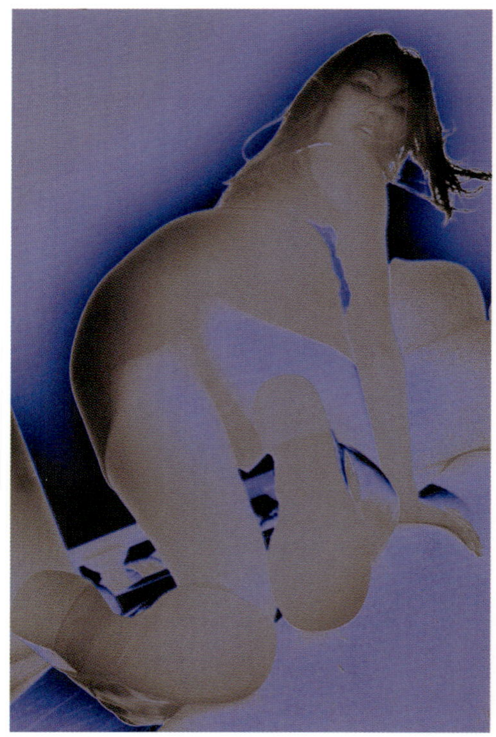

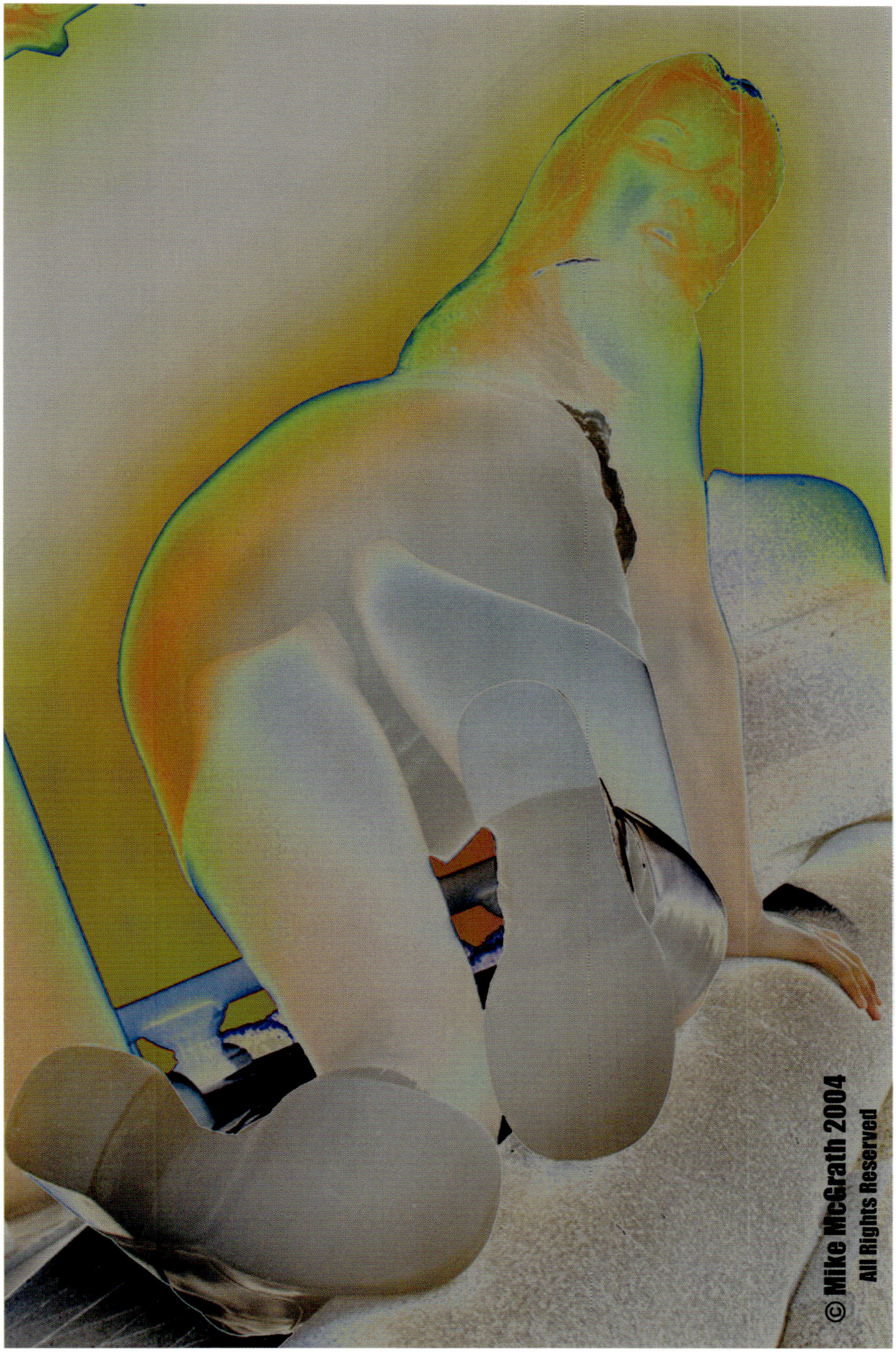

LEFT: On the final image in the sequence, McGrath used a high-pass filter followed by Neon, then Desaturation, winding up with well-defined rim light and reduced glow, which gave better definition to the subject's thighs.

Michael McGrath

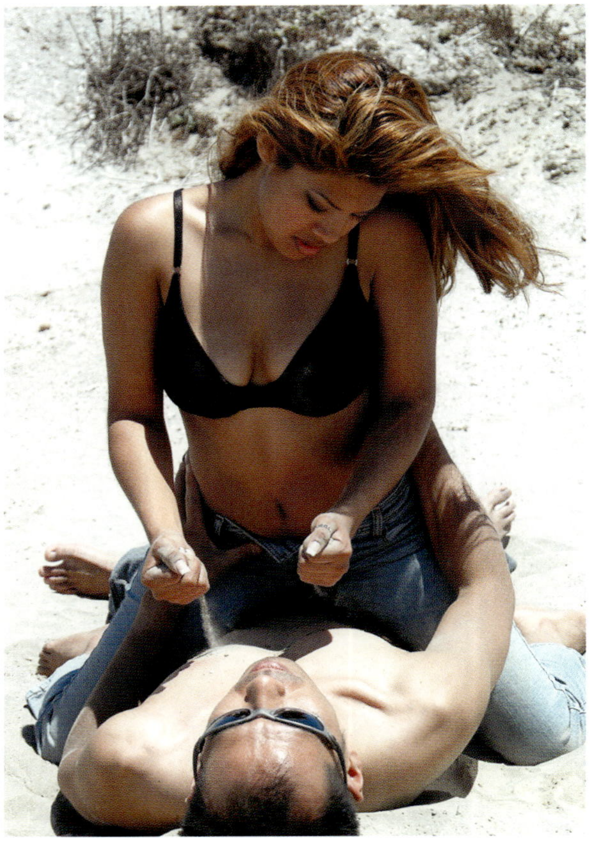

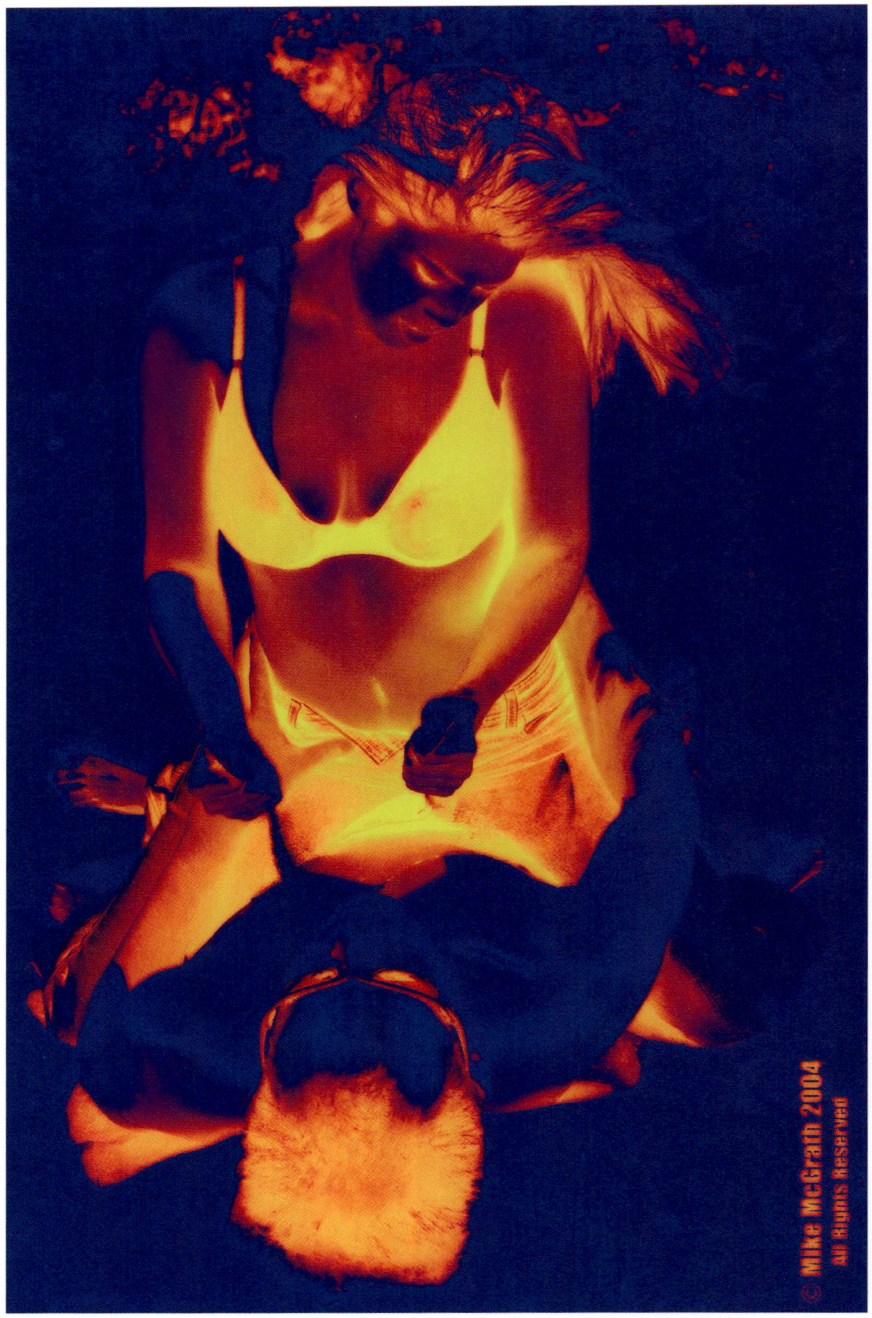

THIS PAGE: McGrath's shoot for this series took place on a deserted beach in southern California on a very clear, bright afternoon. He wanted to work on a theme of dominance and disempowerment.

"The first image in the *Burning Sand* sequence was fine, but I still wanted to create a searing heat combined with passion. To do this, I needed to use an infrared effect, which mimics the effects of an infrared filter on conventional cameras. Infrared gives your image a thermal look wherein different temperatures are indicated by different colors. You can achieve these effects digitally using nik Color Effex Pro 1.0. It has three adjustments: center size, blur, and color.

"In this shot I wanted to have the model pour the sand into his body. In the untouched first shot the sand was poured upon him, and after adding the infrared filter for the second shot it becomes evident that the sand is not just sand but a potion, an incredible life force, an element that is entering and becoming one with him. Rancisco's glasses reflect the intense temperature radiating off Uniquea's body. I used a Nikon D-70 on ASA 80 film and set the shot at 1/500 sec, f8, using available light."

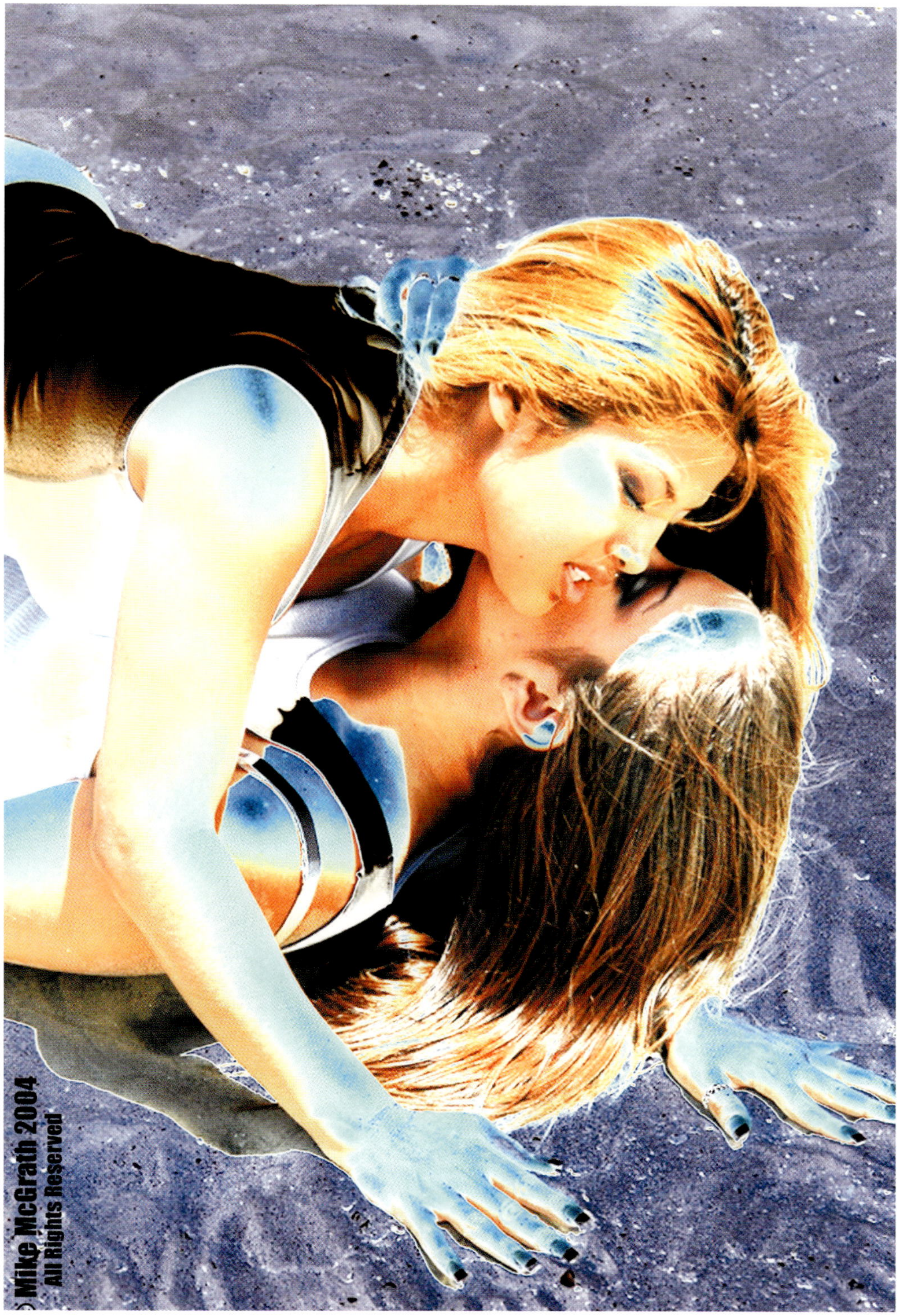

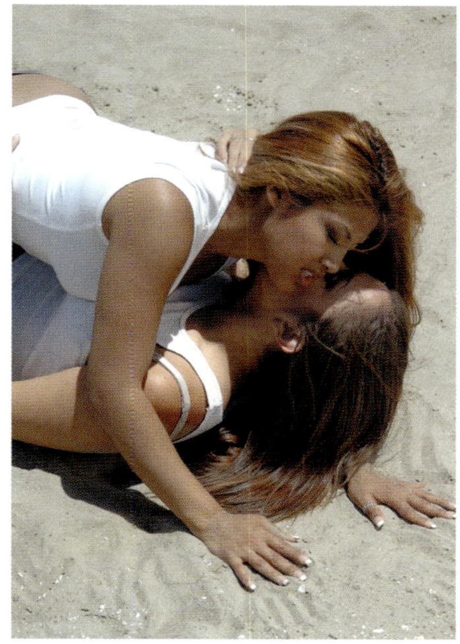

THIS PAGE: "Two young Latina beauties. Jessyka, a very experienced professional model/ make-up artist, and Uniquea, a model on her first shoot. They knew each other prior to the shoot and felt comfortable together. My theme was to present a powerless young woman, overwhelmed by the heat of the moment and unable to resist her aggressive partner." McGrath used a Nikon D-70 set to 1/1000sec, f5.6, shooting on ASA 200 with a solarization filter in available light.

"Solarization, also known as Sabattier, can be achieved in standard developing using either print or negative. The image is fogged by overexposure to white light during its development. You can achieve a similar effect in the digital darkroom. I created my solarization effect with nik solarization. It blends negative and positive images, working on image density and luminance. You can adjust exposure time, mimicking the traditional white-light fogging technique."

Sylvio Pennucci

Sylvio Pennucci is a photographer of many talents. In addition to shooting for almost 20 years he has been an actor, executive producer, pageant judge and sponsor, and CEO of a software company providing programs for the talent, modeling, and casting agent industry. Based in California, he is married with two young children.

BELOW: This was from a shoot that Pennucci did with New York model, Lady J, in a large private home in Encino, California. He used a Canon 10D digital SLR camera with a Canon 24-70mm lens. The lighting came from two Canon 550 EX flash units with large, silver reflectors, fired using a wireless infrared transmitter. The image required very little work to complete, just some cropping, adjustment of brightness and contrast, and a small amount of smoothing of the skin to give the flawless appearance.

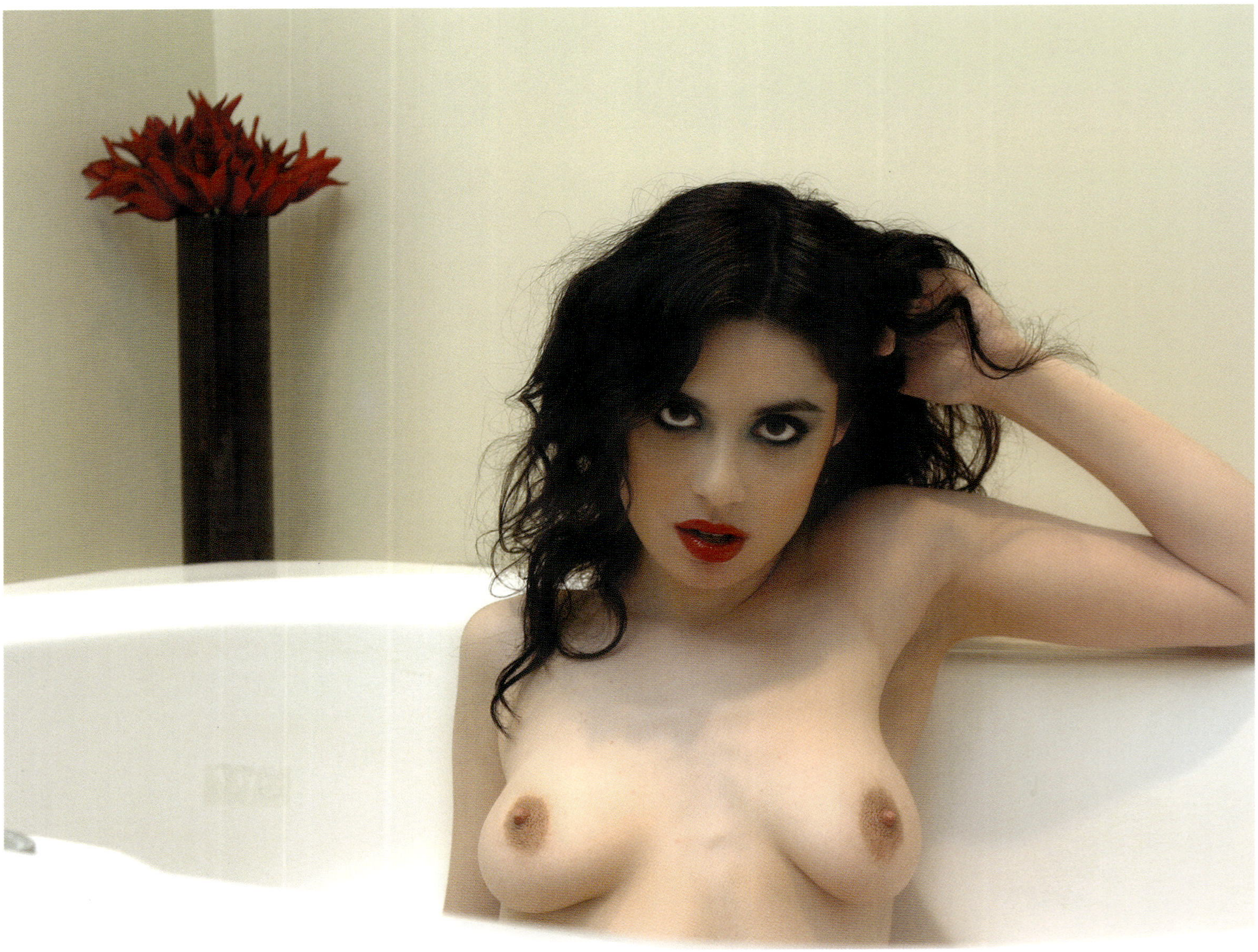

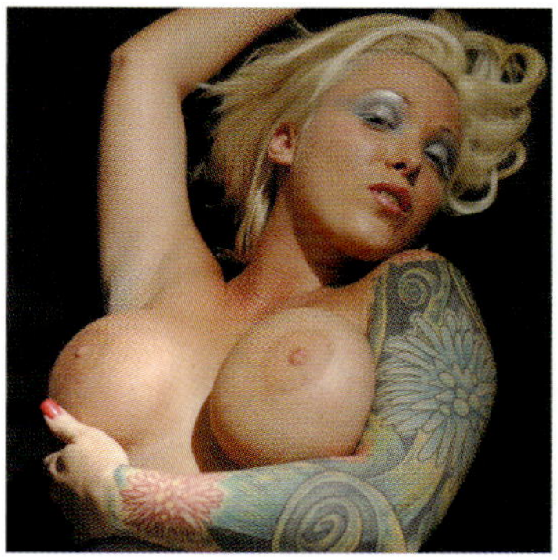

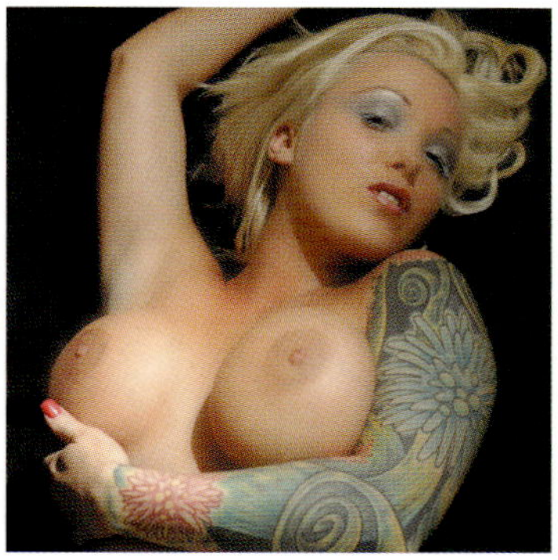

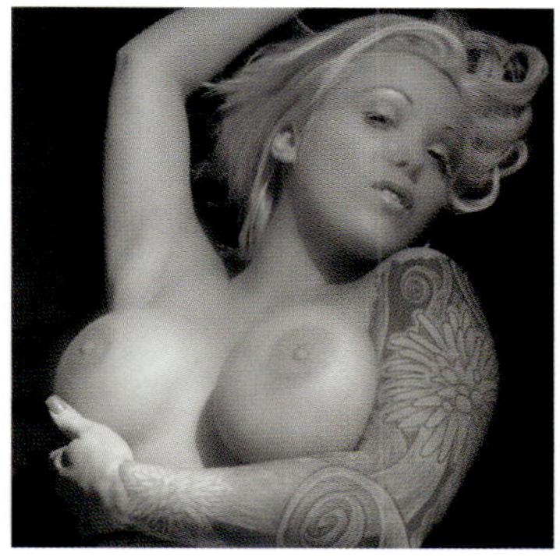

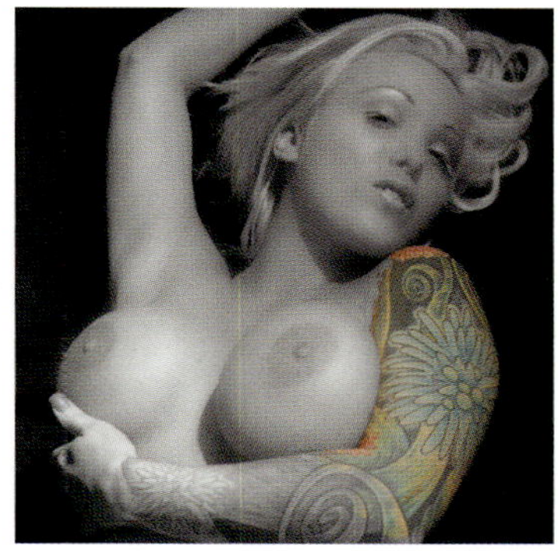

THIS PAGE: Before the arrival of digital-imaging programs like Photoshop, choices about the color of a photograph were limited—you used either color or black and white film and that was pretty much that. Of course hand-toning and tinting a monochrome print was always an option—and still is—but applying color selectively with a brush requires a lot of patience and skill to produce an impressive result. That is still true with digital techniques but to a lesser degree, and if you make a mistake, you can always undo it. In this sequence, Pennucci started with a full-color shot and decided this was too harsh for the composition. His first step was to soften the skin tones to remove blemishes and unwanted highlights. After creating a layer, he removed the color from it altogether and then, with a second layer, he partly erased the black and white, allowing some of the color of the tattoo to show through. In the final image, these layers have been merged and the color balanced, saturated, and sharpened.

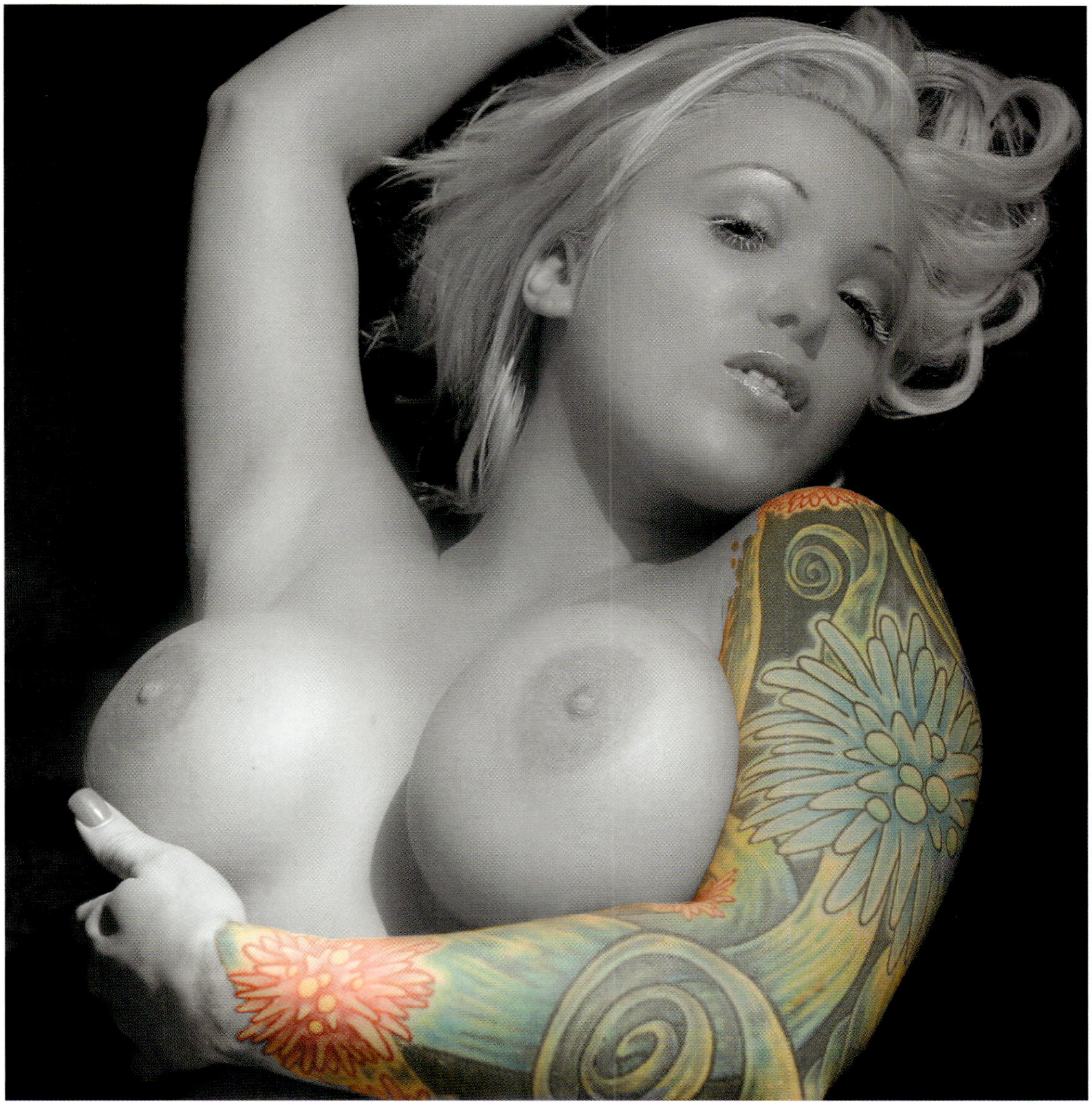

Photochimera

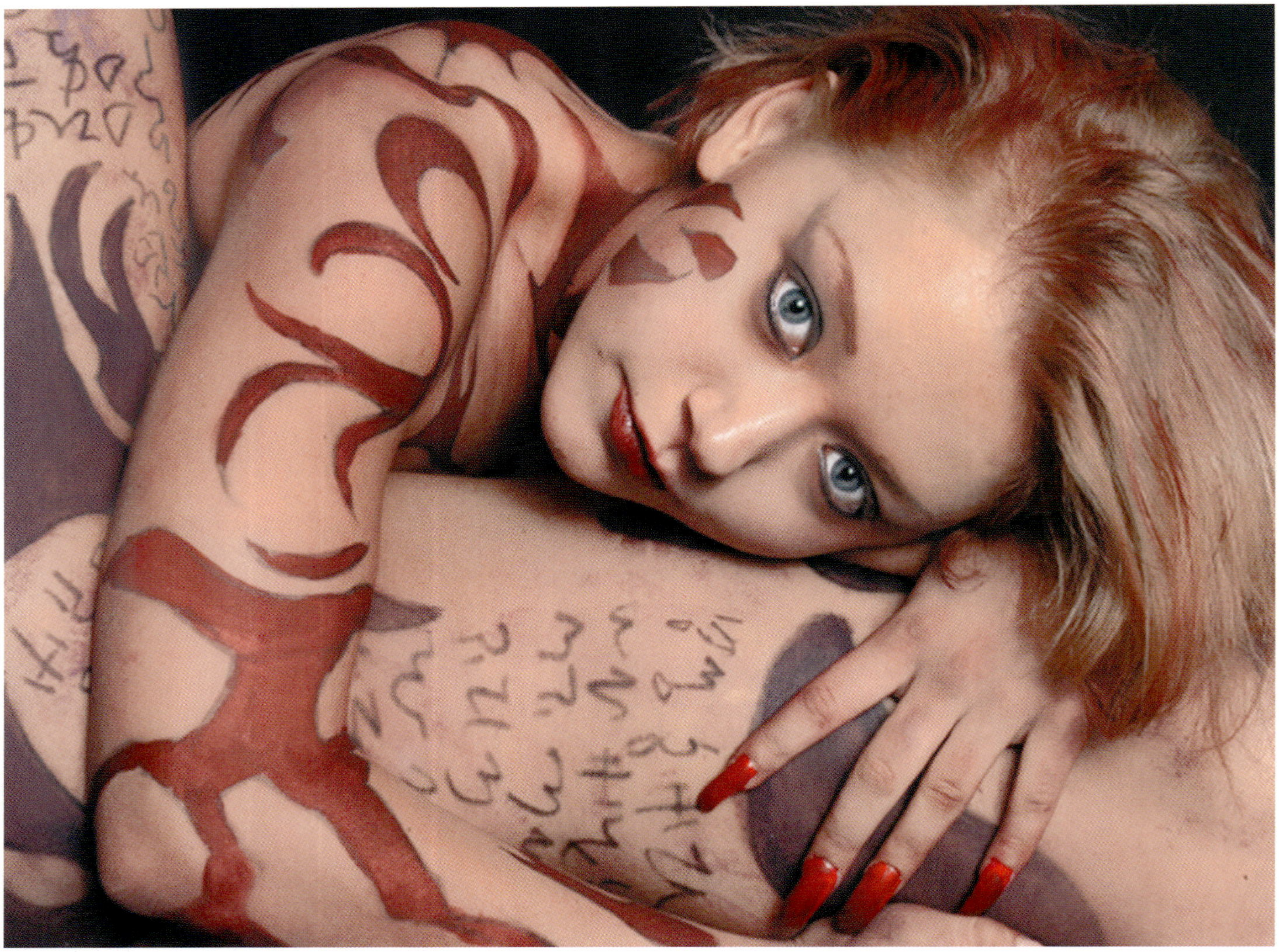

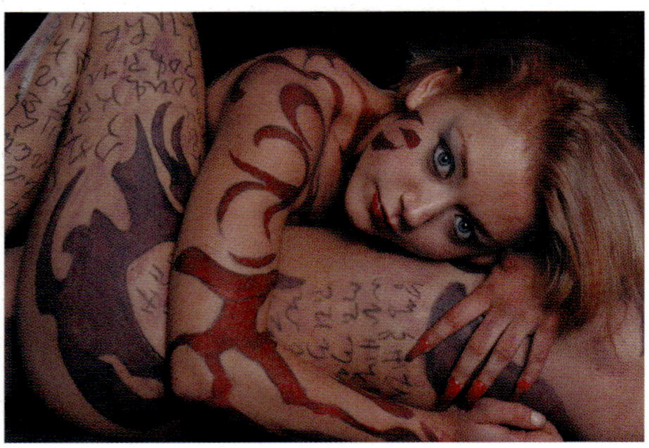

Victor and Lynne Ciccarelli, aka Photochimera, are a husband-and-wife creative team who rely heavily on costume, body paint, and make-up special effects to achieve their own brand of fantasy. Their methodology is based on creating a character for their subjects, often inspired by wildlife. This approach has taken them all around the world.

ALL IMAGES: "These images, shot in our San Diego studio one Sunday afternoon in 2003, were the creation of a four-person makeup team. The concept was to create an Elvin inscription using flesh as a canvas. The script that features in this series is New Area Druidian, which is a subset of Ancient Oogam, a language originally spoken on the outlying islands of Scotland. The models were painted with standard body paints.

"When I am shooting for a high-contrast image I find the best effect for me is to slightly underexpose the image then increase the contrast and saturation in post-production, a process that I find very similar to push-processing in film. Clearly some detail is lost but I find the overall effect pleasing."

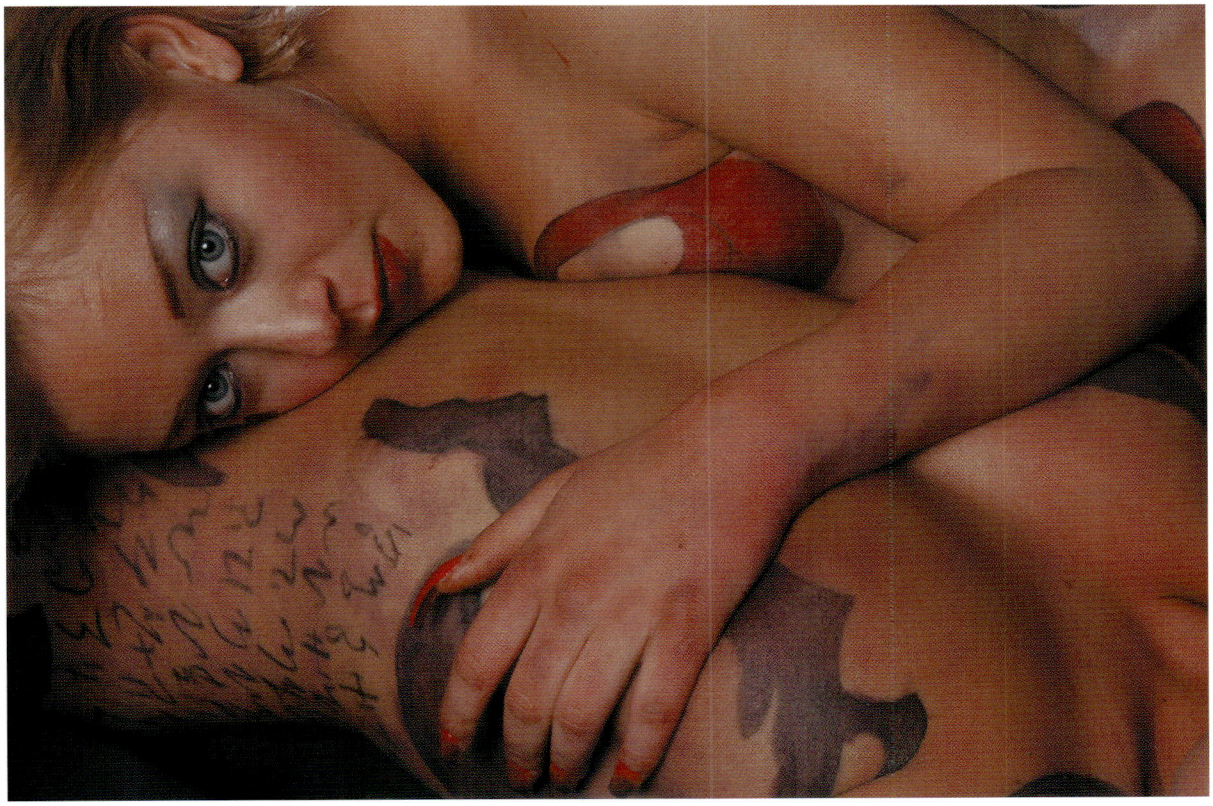

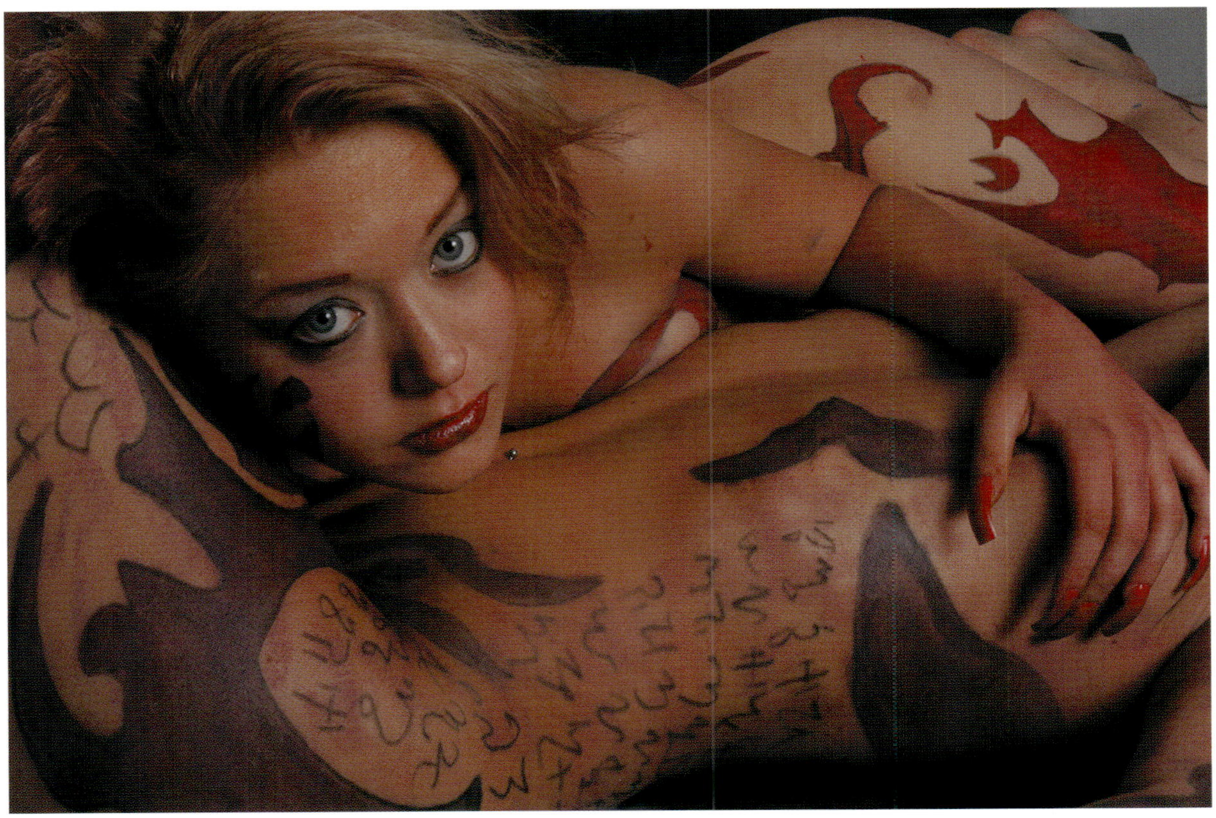

Photochimera

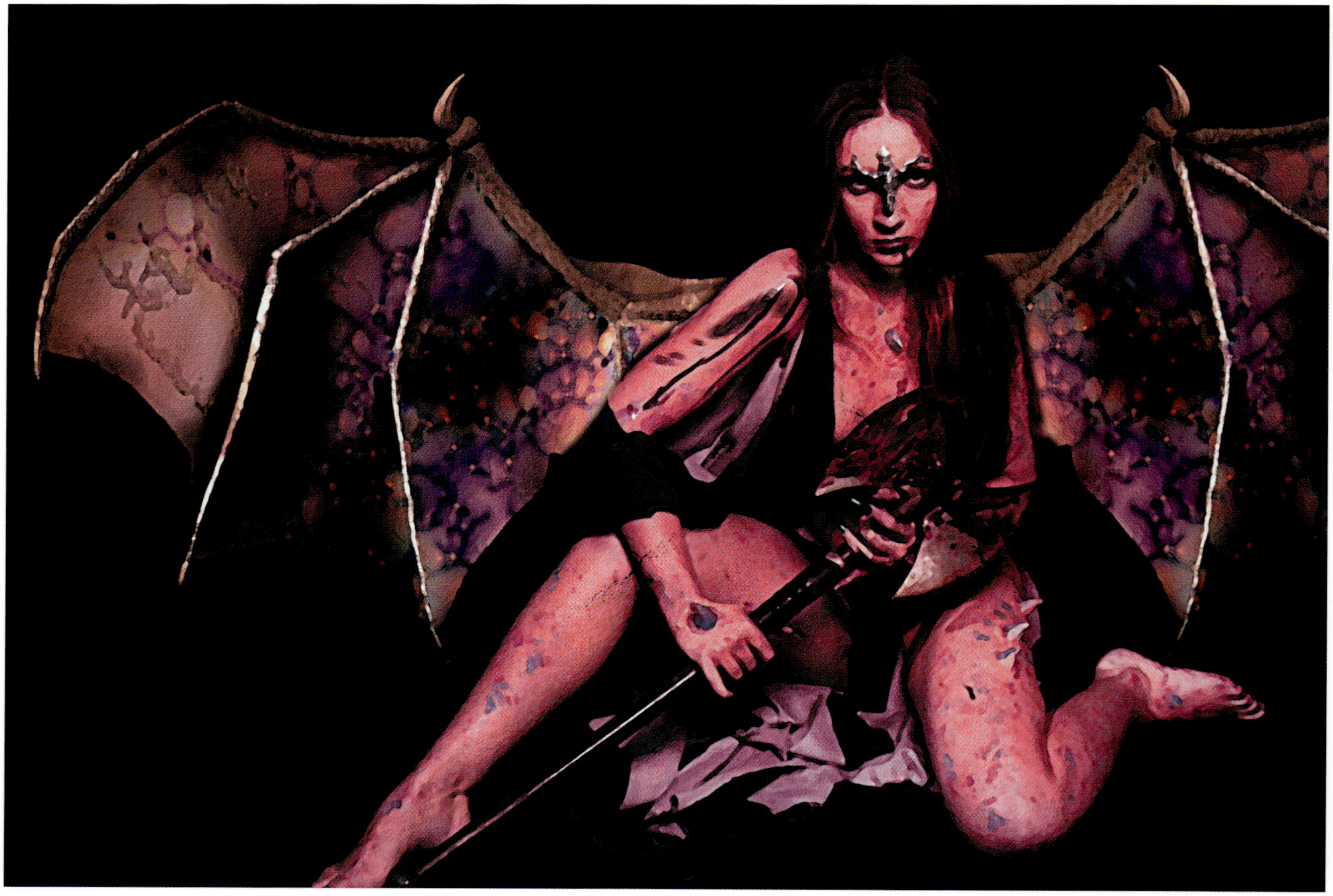

THIS PAGE: "*Crystal Dragon.* This image features a sexy dragon chained to a dungeon floor. Our model Crystal was the makeup victim for the day. For the makeup we started with clay and latex prosthetics and applied a complete coat of body paint. The costume consisted of some torn and shredded cloth draped from the body. The wings are imported from the DAZ Poser collection (right), utilizing their standard textures and overlays."

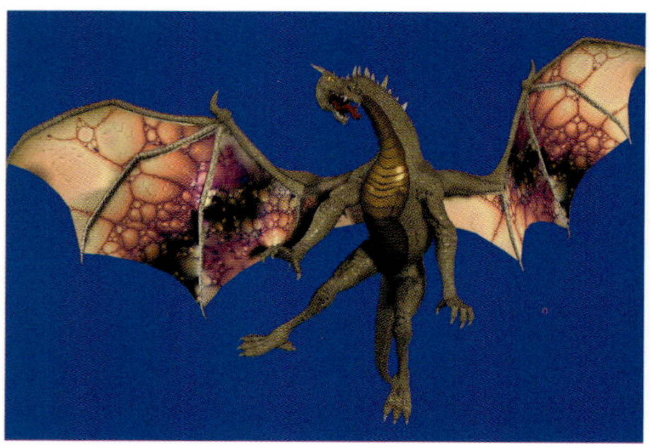

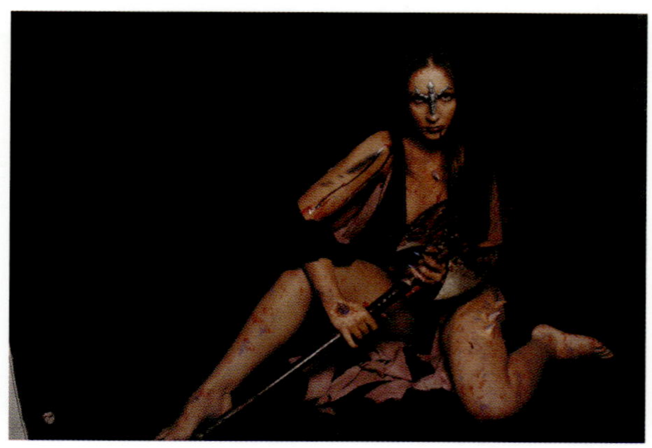

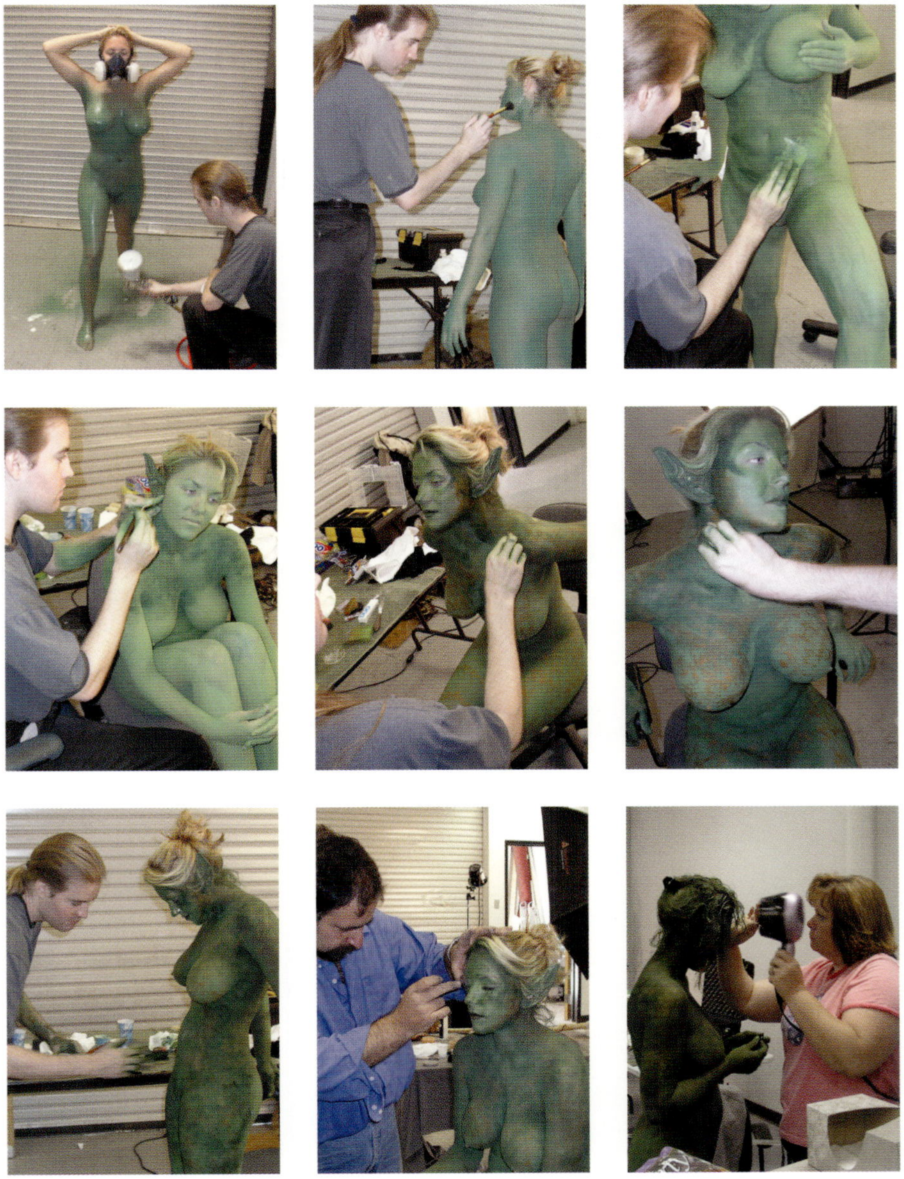

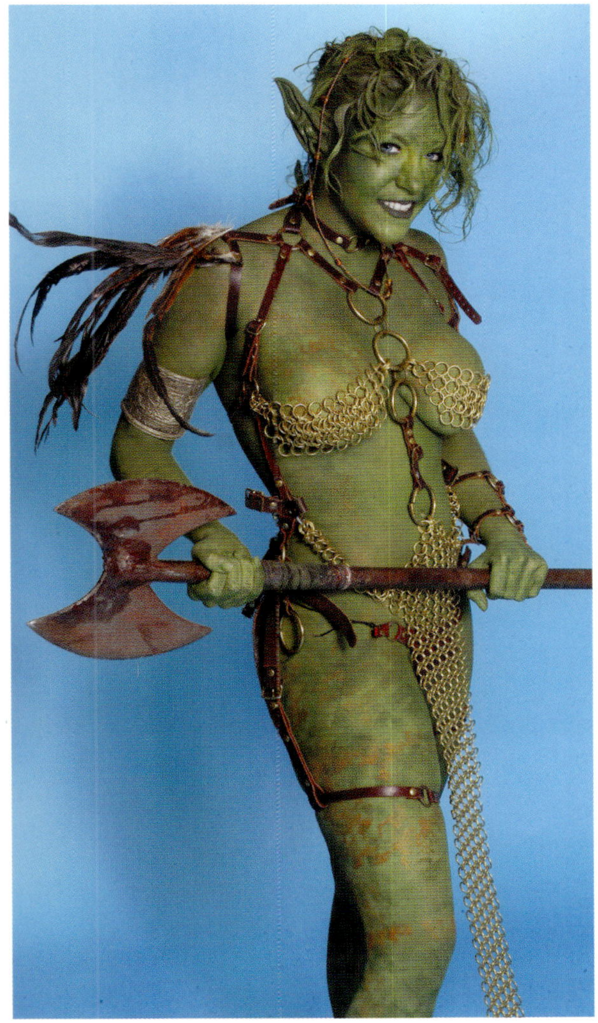

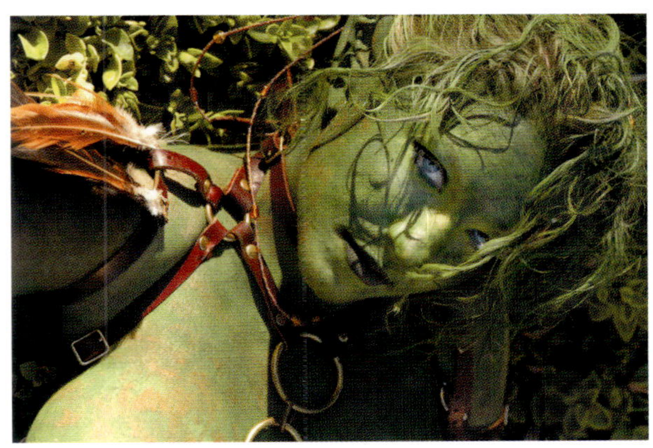

THIS PAGE: *"Green Goblin.* One of our most popular techniques is the application of painted skin. This seemingly simple technique takes lots of practice to get right. Shawn Strider, pictured above, applies one of 17 coats that make up the layers of color. Our first layer, a solid base color, is sprayed on with conventional spray equipment. Subsequent layers are sponged on and built up over time. While spray gives a perfect, smooth coat, skin is not perfect or smooth and requires the depth and texture that can only be achieved with sponge application. The custom costume is applied over the paint, and the character is ready to shoot. For us, the goal is not to make our subjects beautiful, but to make them characters. We talk to our models about emotion and acting rather then posing. Most models are very excited about this, as it is a total departure from daily fashion or glamor modeling. Others are very upset that a photo will not show them in the best light. Make sure you talk to your model before you spend hours in makeup. Frequently with a shoot we easily spend 10 to 20 hours on costume creation, special effects creation, and prosthetic casting and post-production. Anything worth doing takes time."

Dan Santoni

BELOW LEFT: Much of the success of Santoni's work is due to his studio-lighting effects, often using multicolored gels, which he has developed over 15 years. Before embarking on photography he was involved in the 1980s in the underground music scene, organizing club events with still and movie projections, multimedia sculptures, and artwork. This background has had an influence on the photographic images he now creates. This shot, *Cyber Military Shoot,* was created entirely in the studio and shot with a digital SLR camera. Again, Photoshop was only used for color saturation and to add a slight blur.

BELOW: *Mummy* was created in Santoni's studio and, like many of his shots, required careful planning to execute. Eight bags of sand were brought into the studio and emptied on the floor, and the

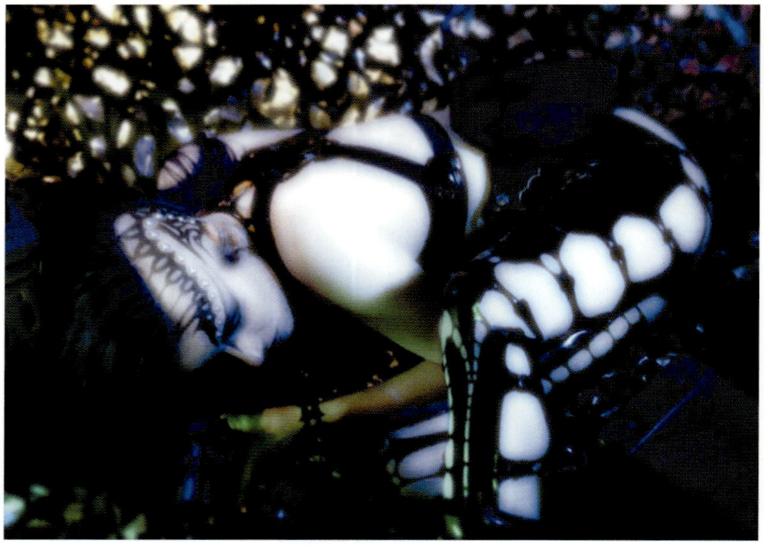

A photographer, effects animator, and art director, Dan Santoni's images range from the macabre to the ethereal. He aims to show beauty, but with an unsettling edge, and cult and zombie movies are among his influences. The images here were constructed in the studio and shot with a digital camera, with post-production kept to a minimum.

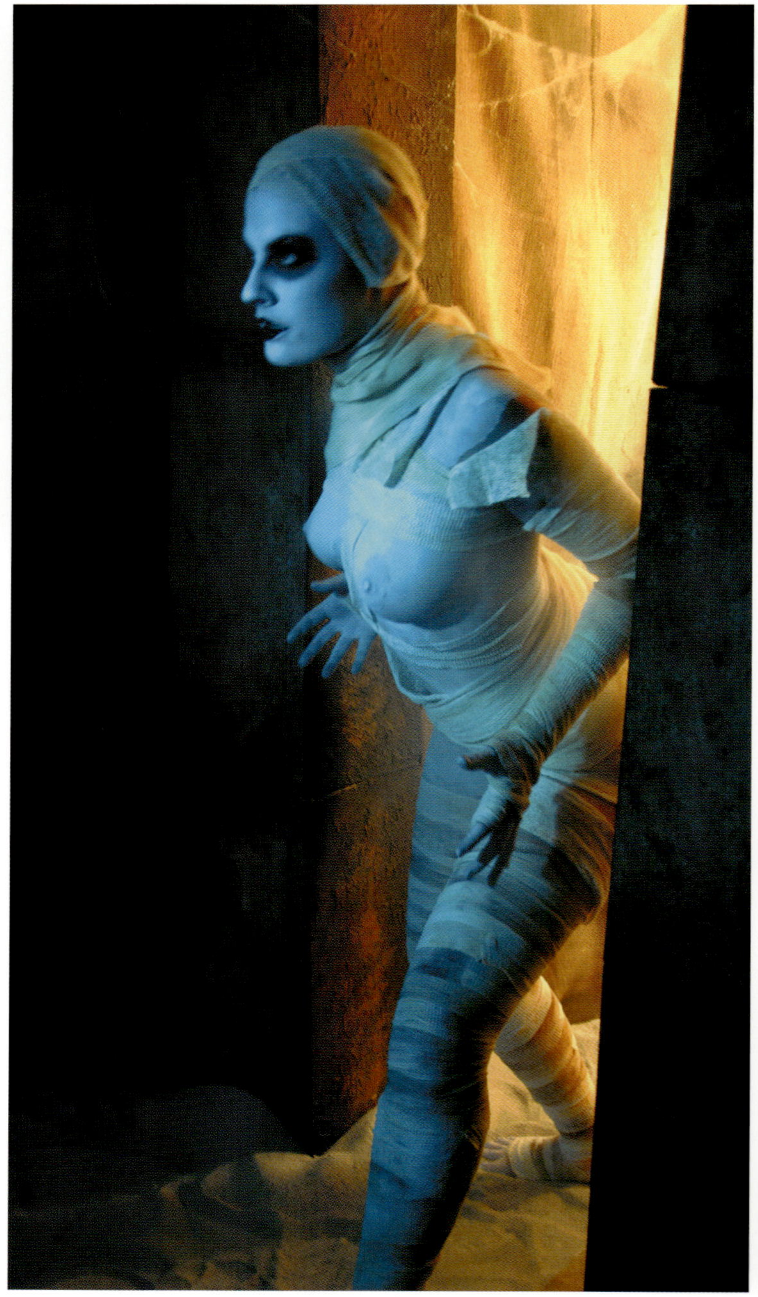

"Egyptian" walls were painted on collapsible cardboard boxes stacked against the studio walls. Burlap sacks were hung up in the background hallway and lit with very strong lights. Jenn Rose was responsible for the makeup and bandaging of model Audra. No post-production was necessary as the composition and lighting were achieved in-camera, a Nikon D100.

BELOW: "This was a tribute to the *Hellraiser* movie series, based on the demonic Cenobite characters," explains Santoni. "It was shot in an old, run-down garage with chains hung from the ceiling. Jenn Rose did an amazing job with some prosthetic effects on Mistress Persephone. This was entirely shot in-camera with no post-production used."

BELOW RIGHT: "*Ice Queen* was loosely based on the European movie *The Snow Queen*," says Santoni. "Art direction was by Adrian Grey and myself, with Amazing Airbrush makeup provided by Alquin. All of the lighting effects and the composition were done in the studio, which was hung with tree branches. The model was behind clear plastic sheeting that had been painted, and I added some blur effects and color saturation in Photoshop."

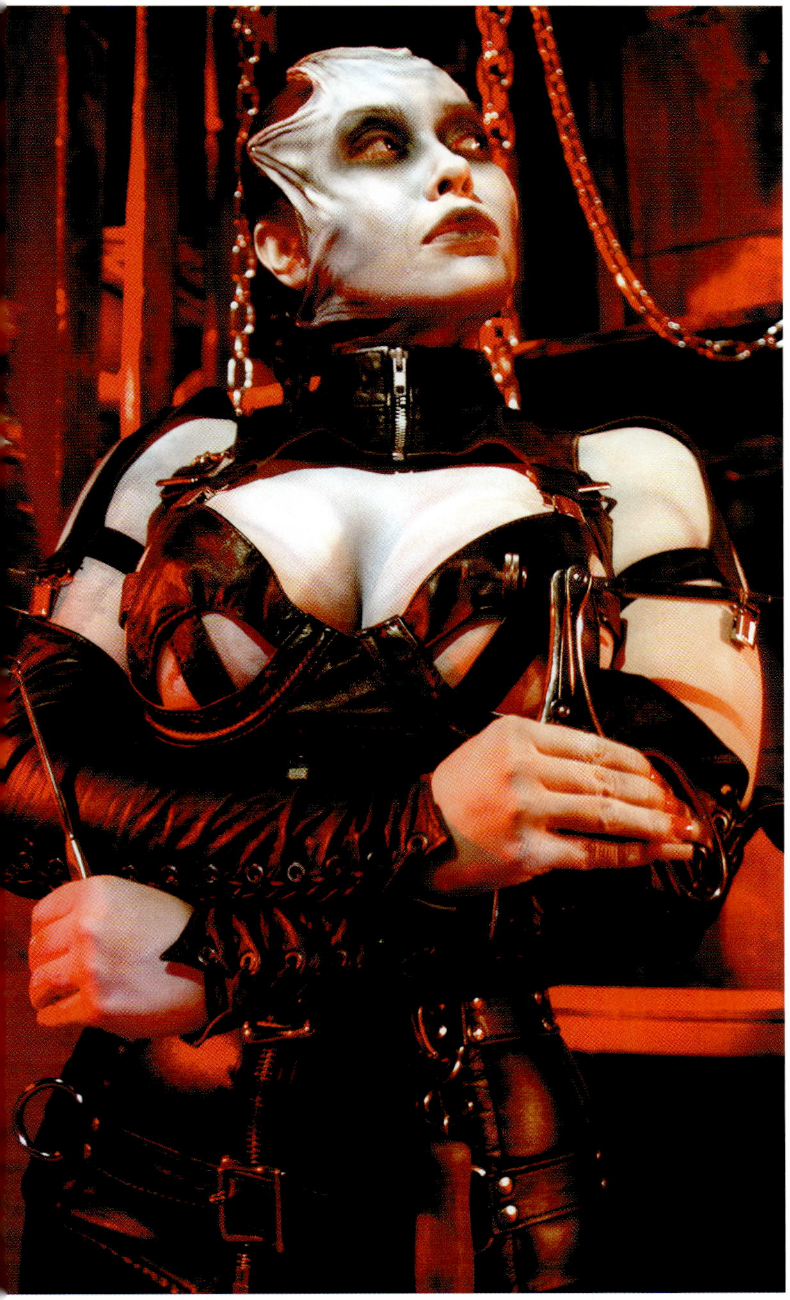

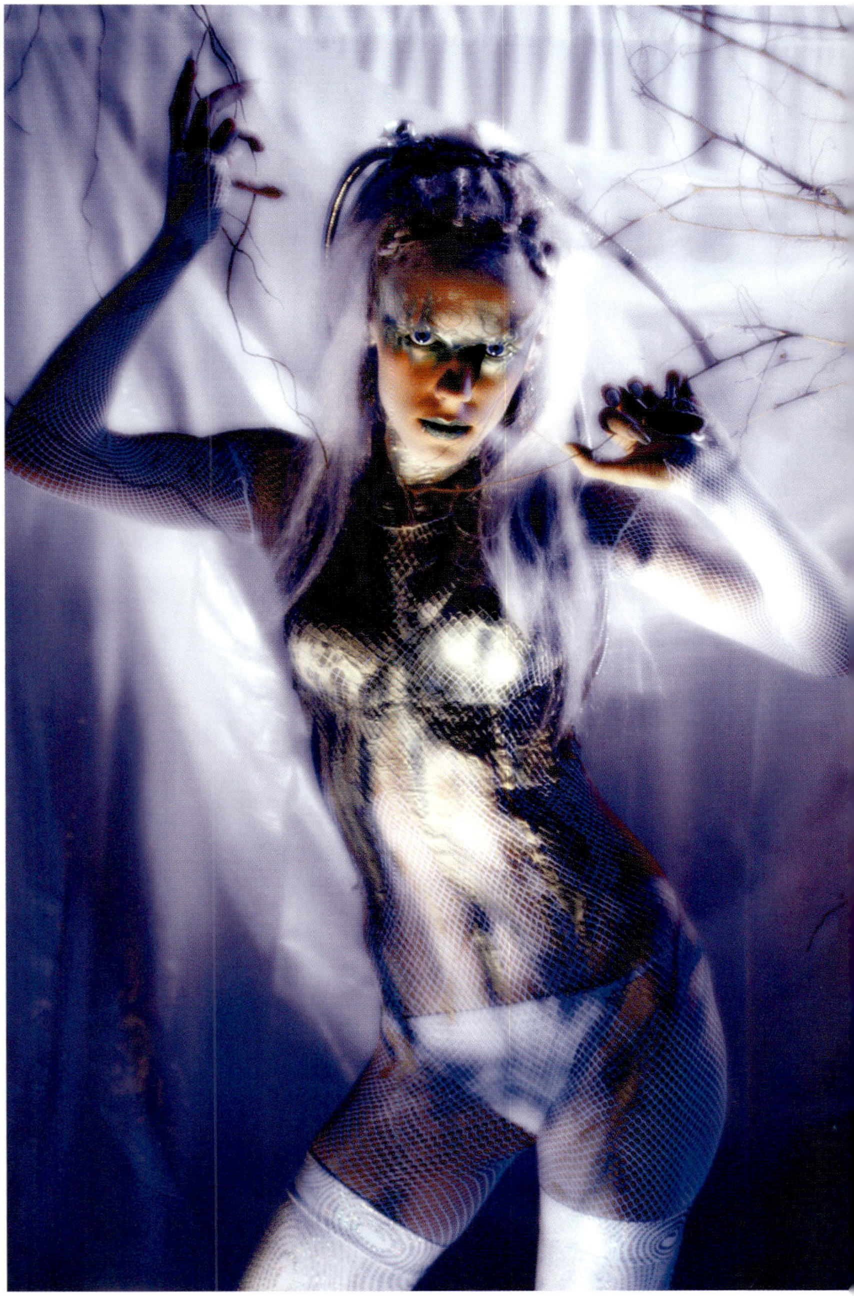

Jeffery Scott

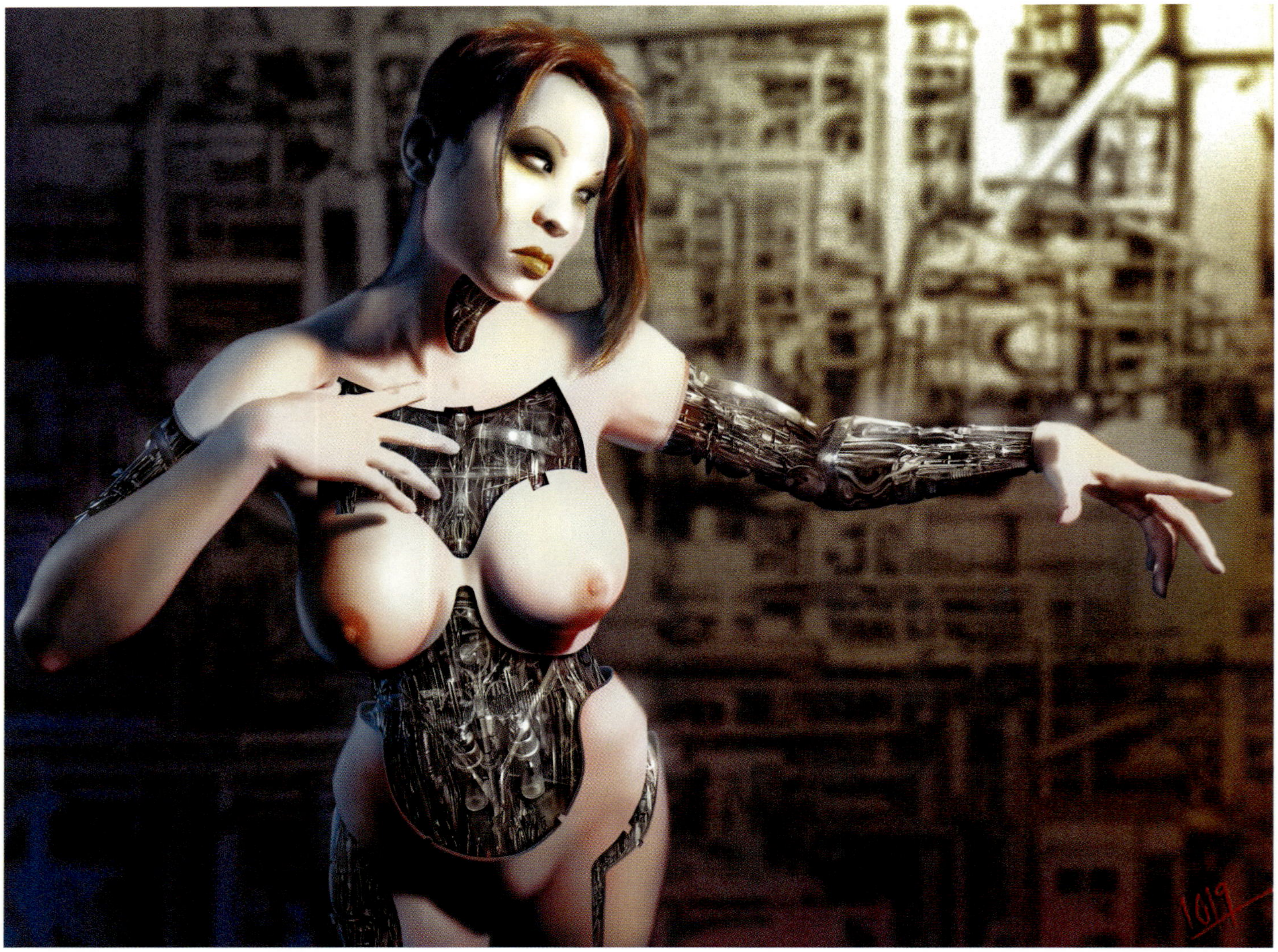

ABOVE: *Cold Hands, Warm Heart* showcases a number of digital montaging techniques. Jeffery Scott says: "Every element in this image is photographic. The biomechanics are made up of carefully placed and photographed assemblages of vintage surgical instruments, which are then repeated, digitally adjusted to enhance their metallic sheen, and precisely realigned with each other to create the visual symmetries on which the image depends. The background is a digitally manipulated shot of an industrial plant in Huntington Beach, California. And the computer has been used to create that almost synthetic texture and look of the model's skin."

OPPOSITE PAGE: *From the Ministry of Decay* illustrates how the visual quality and mood of an image can be transformed through digital manipulation. The sequence begins with the original photograph and traces its development through to the final image.

The original picture's erotic strength lies in the sensuality and challenge of the model's gaze, combined with the lighting, which comes almost from floor level, producing very unnatural shadows. At the same time, the surroundings are familiar and, in this form, not particularly striking—a room, a filing cabinet, a doorway….

Scott has added an element of decay to the room by superimposing photographed patterns of cracks and fissures. Several different photographs may be required, or the same photograph may be superimposed more than once.

OPPOSITE PAGE, TOP: The Photoshop layers containing the signs of decay, and the edges of the paving

Jeffery Scott is an American photographer whose work is an eclectic mix of photography, painting, and sculpture. Digital manipulation allows him to create images in which every element either retains its separate identity or combines with others to produce new textures and surfaces.

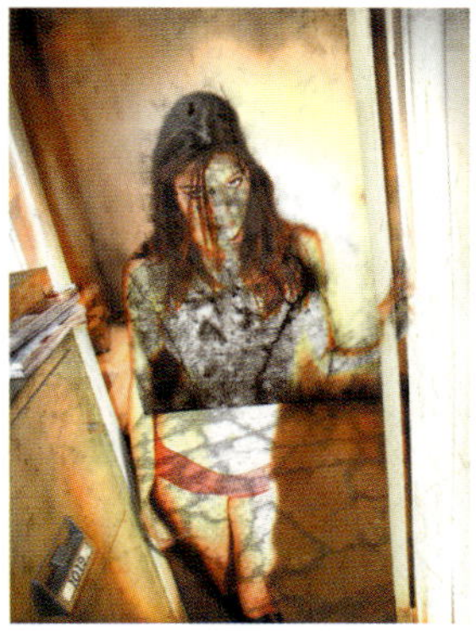

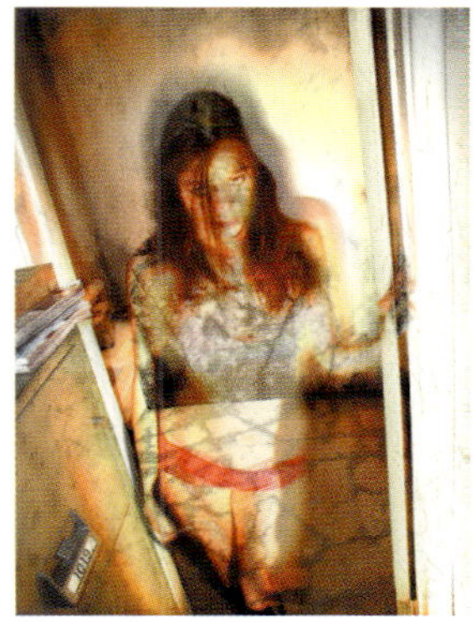

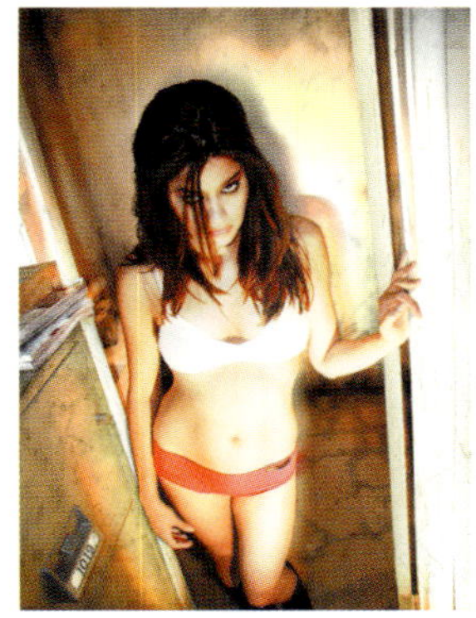

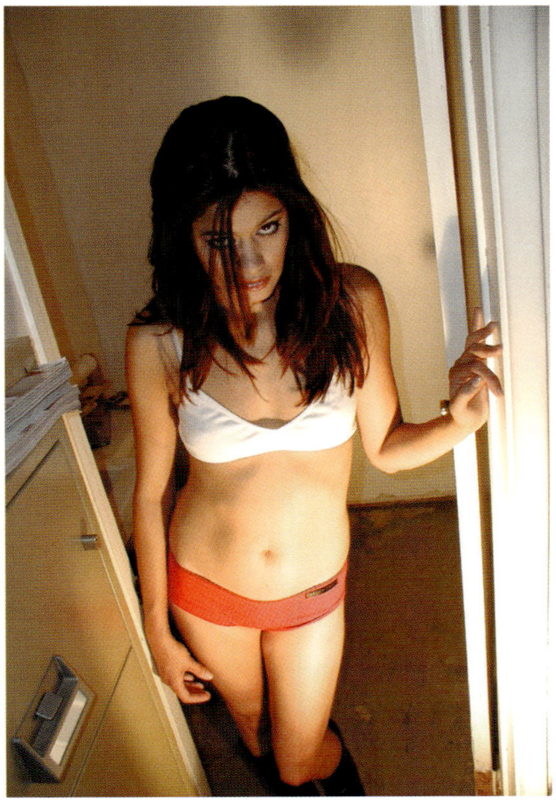

stones added to the floor, are all superimposed above the base layer of the model. The edges of the images in some layers are clearly visible. Now a ghostly double-image of the model has been created, as if she, too, is subject to the same principle of decay as her surroundings. This layer is also above that of the model. With the order of the layers changed, we can now see how the image is going to work. The signs of decay are no longer visible on the model, and her double image has almost taken on the aspect of a halo completely surrounding her. However, the lighting is fairly even across the whole image.

RIGHT: Scott has darkened the area around the model, thus re-emphasizing her place in the composition.

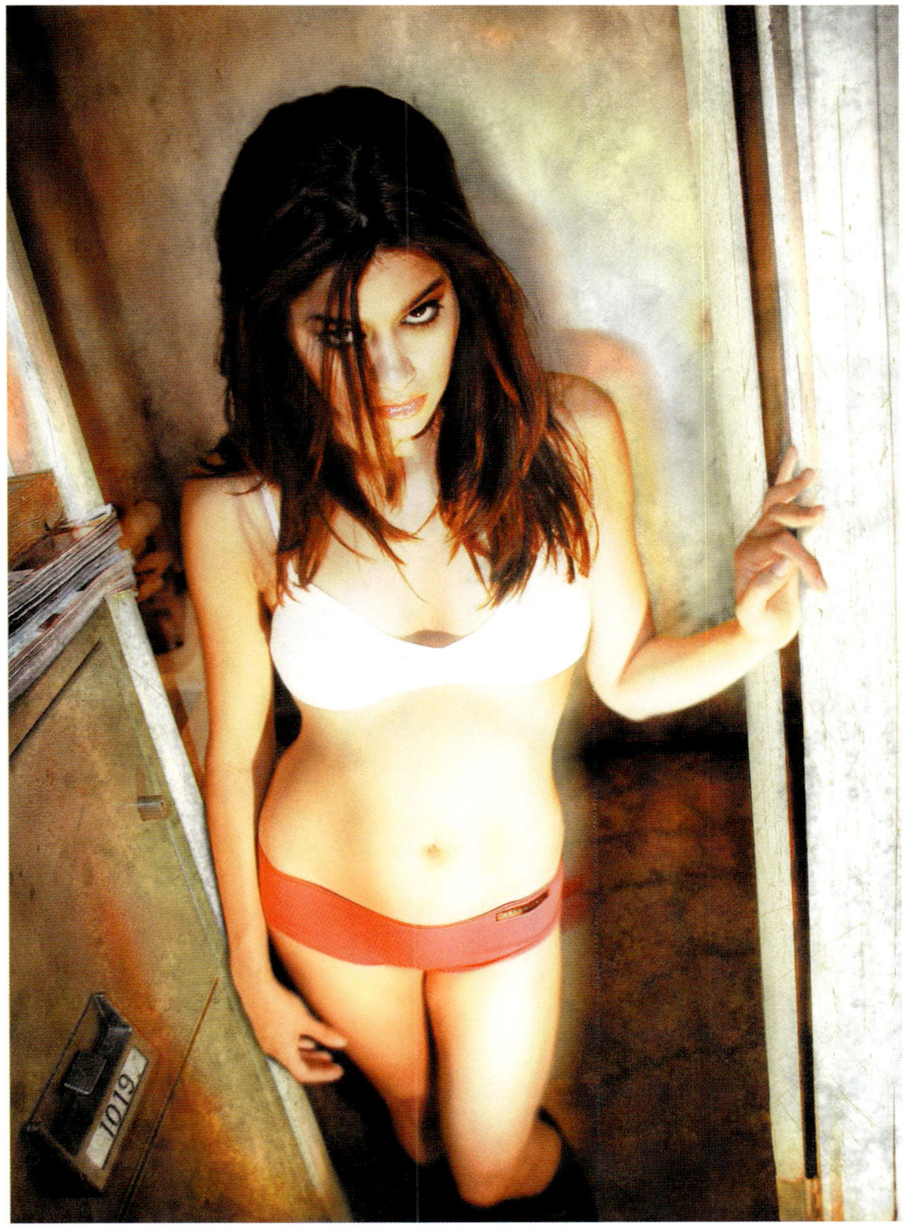

Roberto Segate

Design is very important in Roberto Segate's work. He began introducing textual elements to images in the darkroom but found that digital methods opened up exciting new challenges. His inspiration comes from old buildings, churches, and warehouses, and he is always on the lookout for textures for his images. His recent work focuses on issues surrounding female dominance, woman's role in society, and her relationships with men.

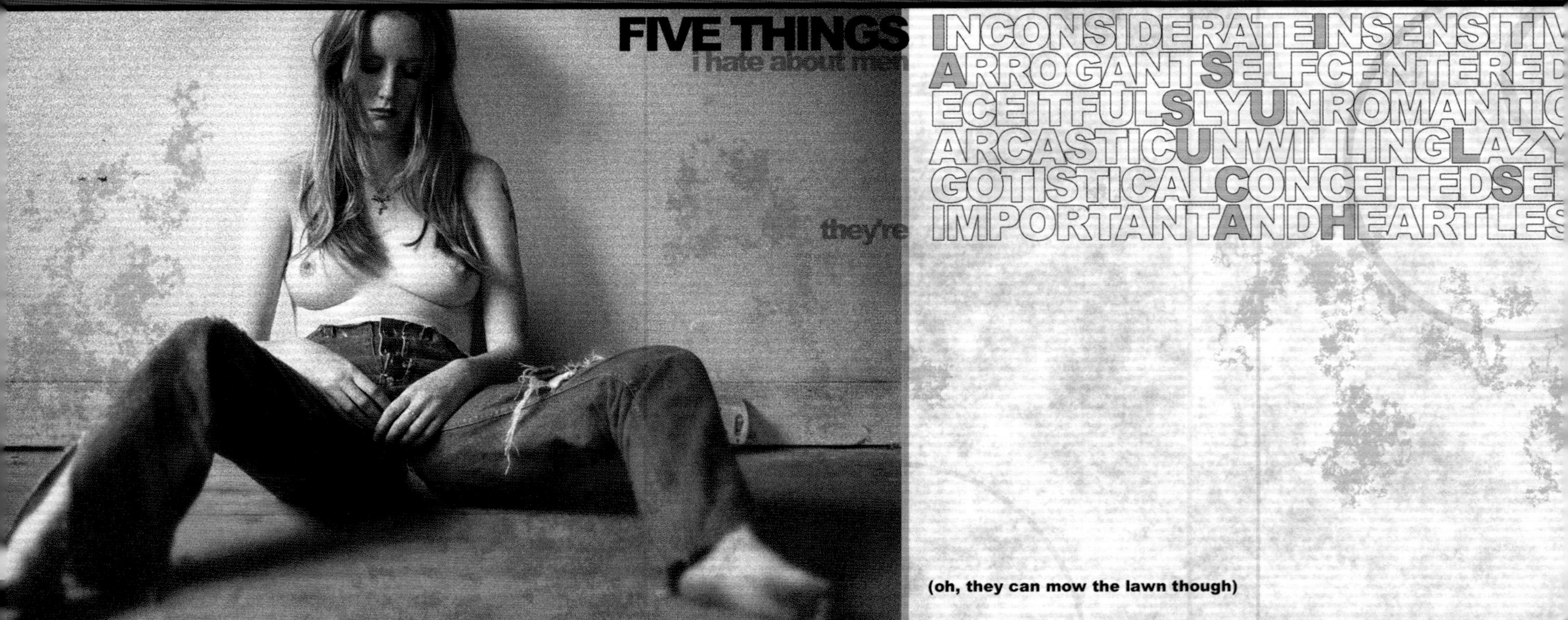

ALL IMAGES: Segate's concept behind this series of images was to reflect the changing roles of men and women, particularly in terms of growing female confidence and self-assurance, while introducing an element of humor. "I wanted the images to be photographic with a strong use of text, which was to communicate the subject's strength and confidence," he says. "The models were deliberately photographed on a flat day—gray but quite bright. This allowed me to capture a full range of skin tones without worrying about bright highlights and deep shadows. Scanners are not particularly good at wading through dense highlights and, once images are scanned, I can retouch and tonally adjust, dodge and burn the image as I want, while maintaining detail in all areas."

Segate photographed the models in a clutch of run-down buildings to create a striking visual contrast. "I wanted a 'grunge' feel, and this was made by scanning textures, found objects, decay, and so on. I created a custom Photoshop brush that could 'paint' the mess anywhere in the image, tying together the design and the photographs."

The copy for each image was researched by talking to friends and family. "Particularly funny, and at the same time quite tasteless, are the put-down lines commonly used to shake off unwanted male attention." Segate added the text using Arial, placing words and sentences to allow them to flow as if spoken. "By using a combination of size, tone, and placement, I was able to position the text to reflect the way that particular put-down could have been spoken," he explains.

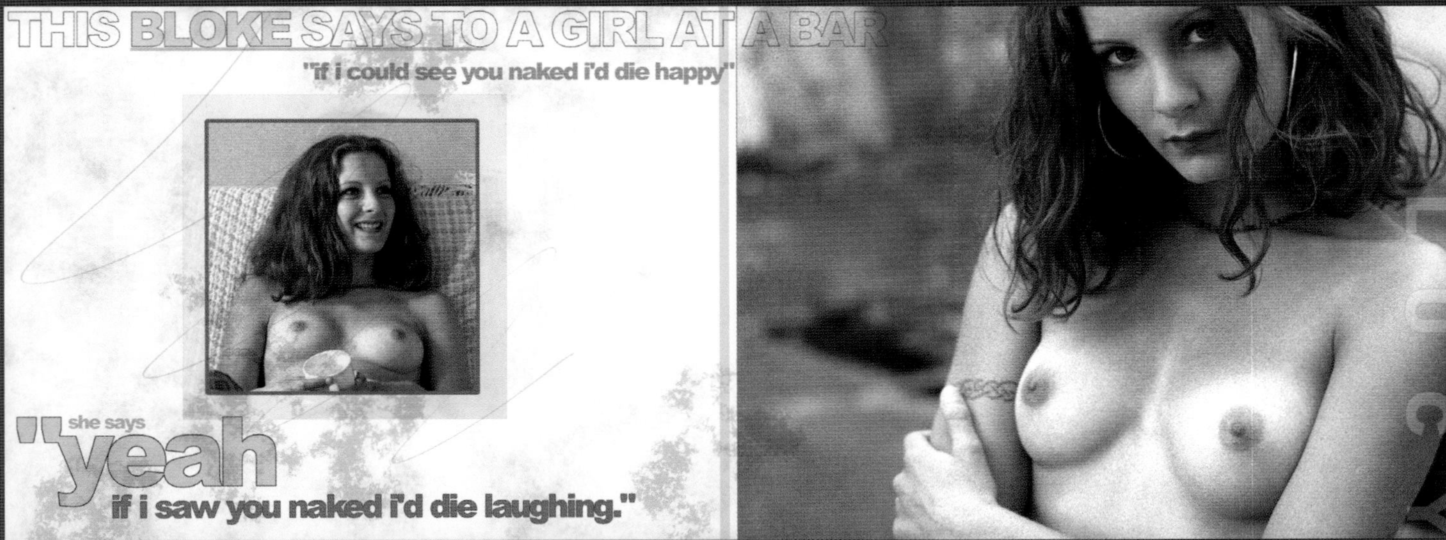
THIS BLOKE SAYS TO A GIRL AT A BAR
"if i could see you naked i'd die happy"
she says
"yeah
if i saw you naked i'd die laughing."

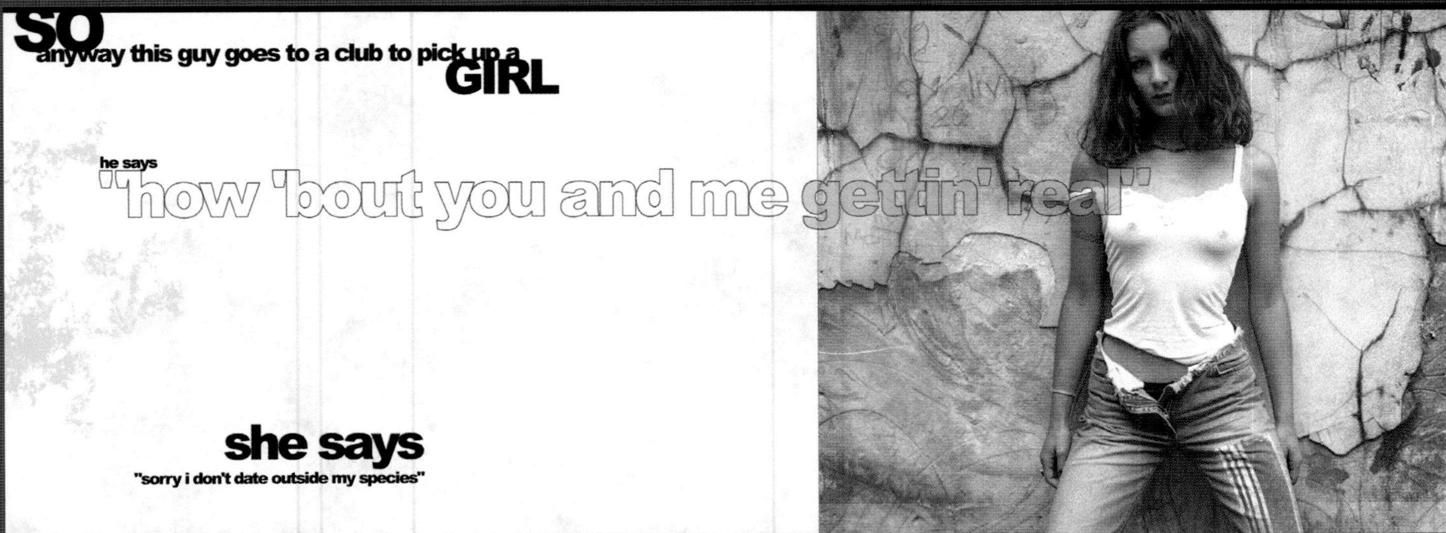
SO
anyway this guy goes to a club to pick up a
GIRL
he says
"how 'bout you and me gettin' real"
she says
"sorry i don't date outside my species"

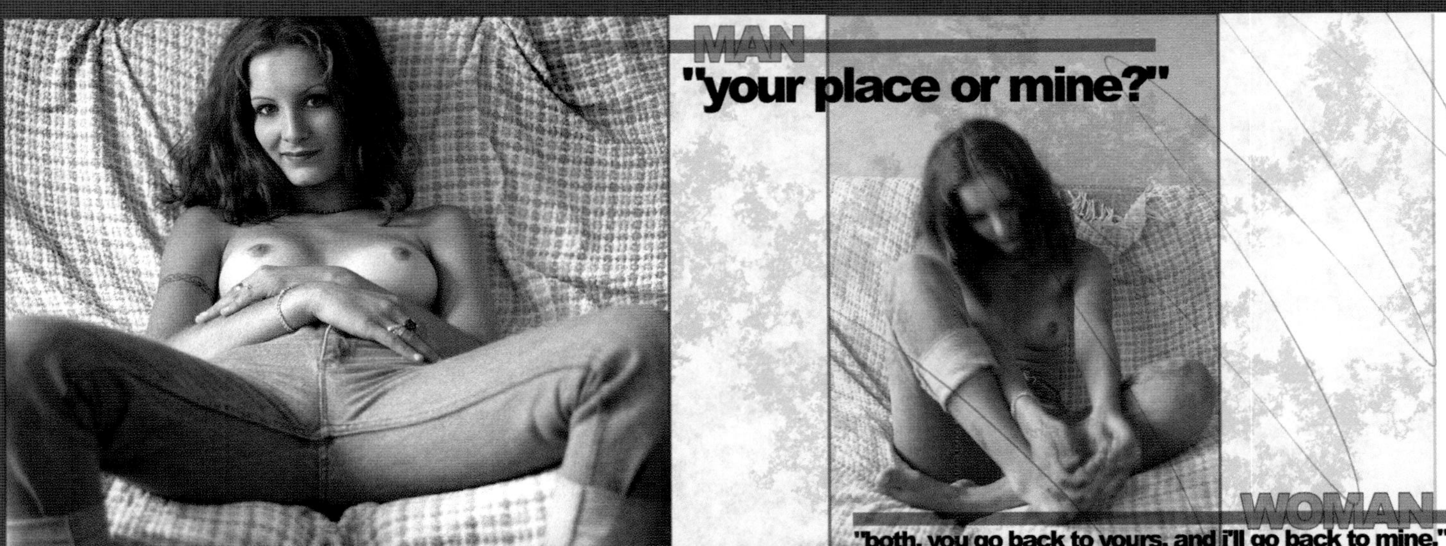
MAN
"your place or mine?"
WOMAN
"both, you go back to yours, and i'll go back to mine."

Roberto Segate

ALL IMAGES: "My photography is important to me. The ability to make my images convey feeling is something I constantly seek. To provoke some sort of reaction is better than no reaction. My work is a mess, full of imperfections. I purposely include scratches and dirt and other grunge elements to enhance a feeling."

"Working digitally, it is important that I try to produce organic work, to try and remove any trace of the computer's clinical hand. These days I solely work digitally; while I work from negative stock I almost never use chemical processing anymore. I was a die-hard darkroom worker, but I began to fail to achieve exactly what I wanted. I became frustrated with the waste and increasingly dissatisfied with my work. Digitally I can layer images, move and delete sections, and—while I haven't done so here—add type to the image if I wish. This is very important to me."

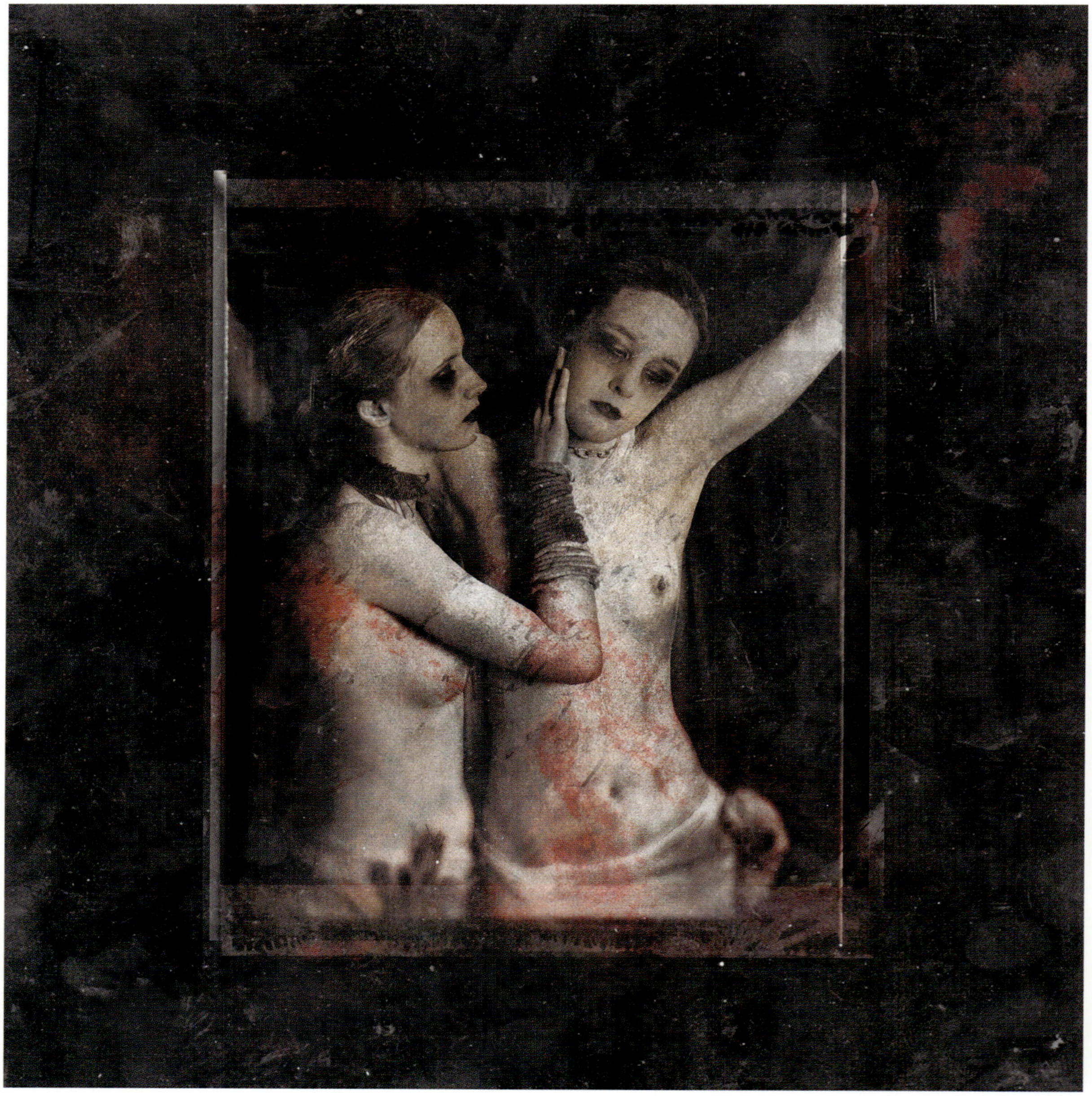

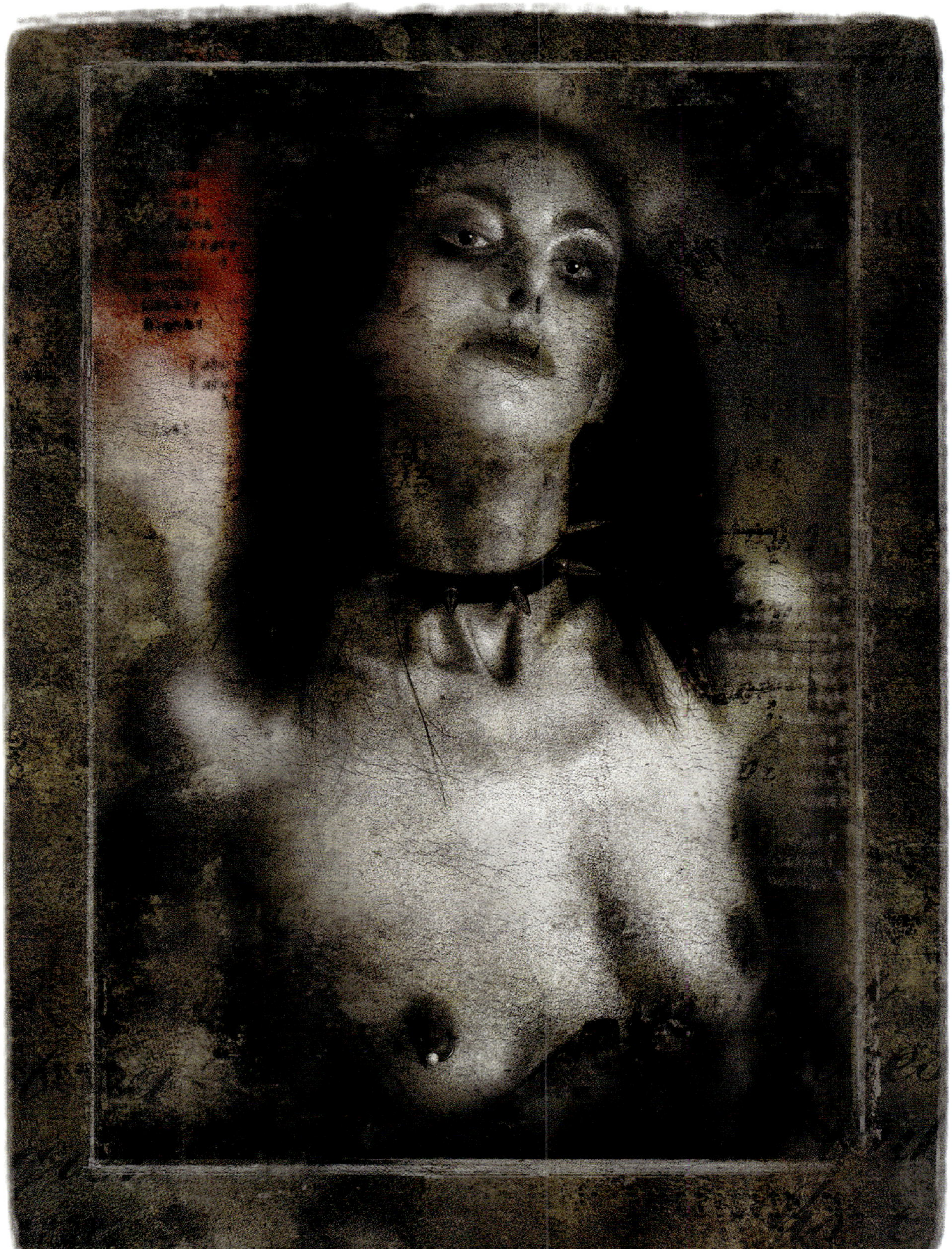

Greg Slaughter

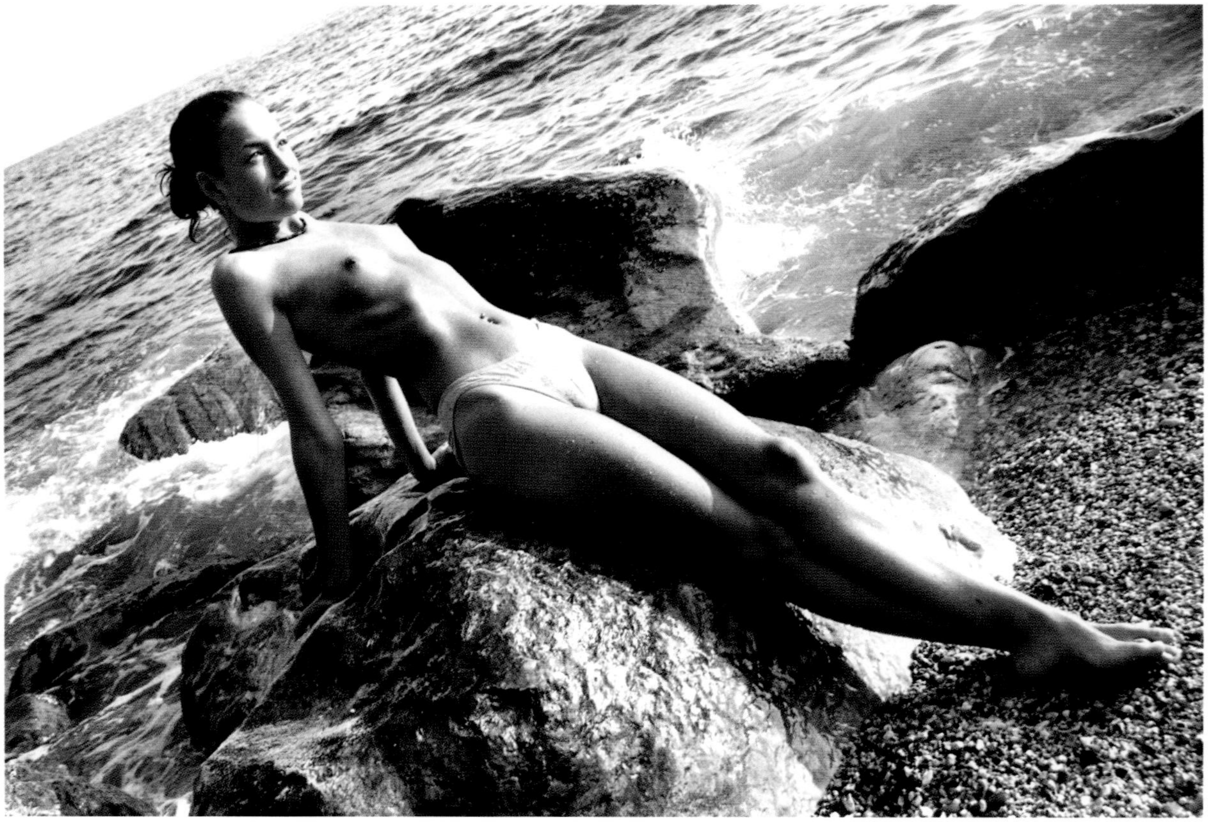

Greg Slaughter has traveled the world photographing the nude for almost 10 years. His photos have won awards and been exhibited in the US and Japan. Lately he has developed techniques for using digital processes to create quality prints that look like fiber-based, selenium-toned prints produced in the darkroom.

ABOVE: Slaughter used a Leica with 35mm lens and 100 ISO negative film for this shot, and tilted the camera to get this dynamic angle, with the model's body forming a horizontal right across the frame. Again, Slaughter used his digital "printing" technique, which he developed as a result of experimentation. "I felt that many of the recipes for creating black-and-white digital prints are too complicated," he says. "My goal was not to do any manipulations that would not normally be done in a darkroom."

RIGHT: The combination of sea, sun, and a great model is an alluring one for nude photographs. This is a classic pose, taken in strong sunlight from behind the model, on the Hawaiian island of Oahu. Once again, Slaughter used a conventional, medium-format Hasselblad camera and then produced a digital print. "After mounting under clear, archival plastic, I really couldn't tell whether it was fiber-based or a digital print," he comments.

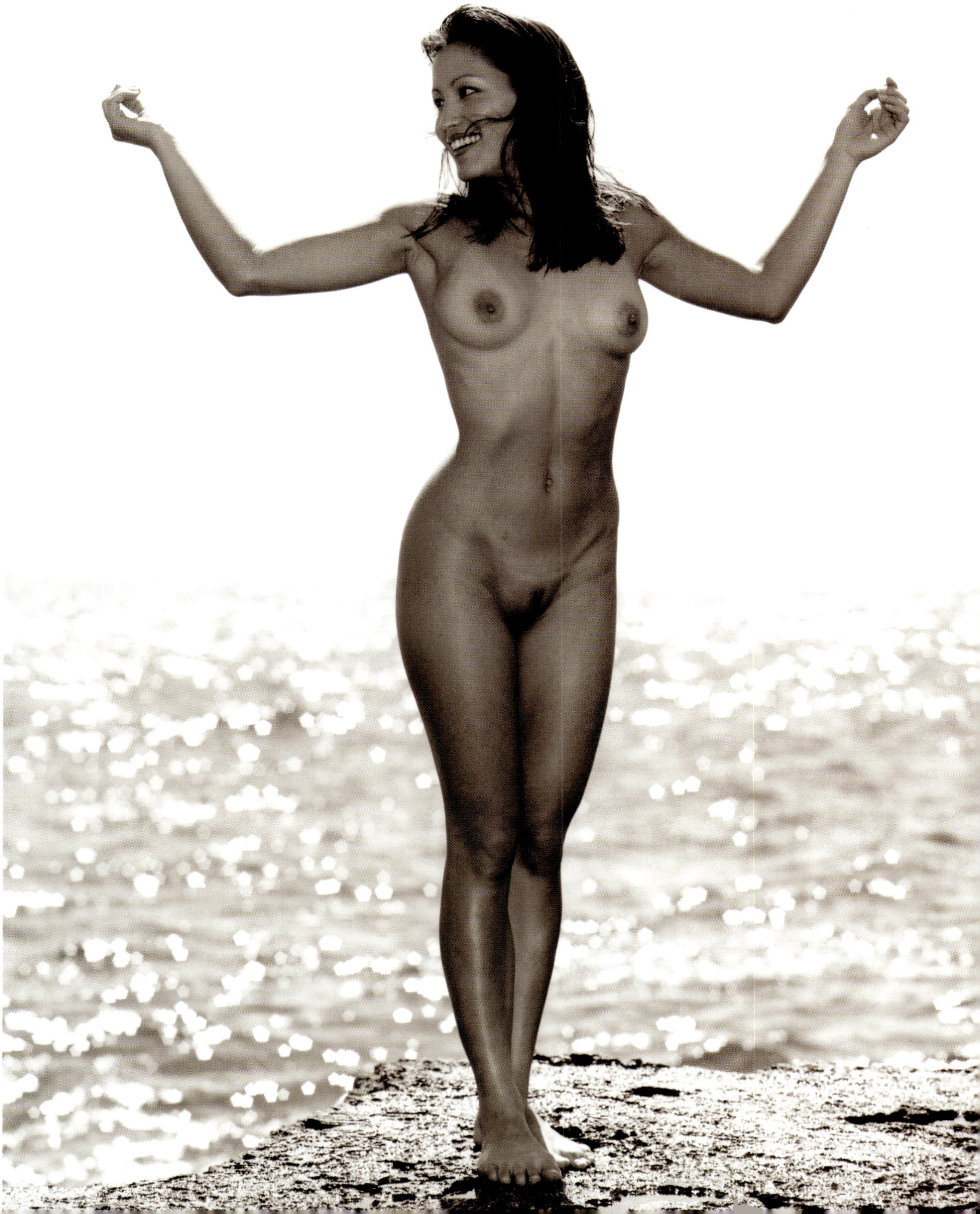

Greg Slaughter

BELOW: The vast empty space of Death Valley, California, was the setting here, with the low sun of late afternoon producing the long, deep shadow that helps give the image a graphic quality. Slaughter took the picture with a Hasselblad 503CW camera with 50mm lens and Kodak T-Max 400 negative film. His initial prints were made using conventional darkroom techniques on warm-tone fiber-based paper. This version, along with the other images on these pages, was produced digitally, with the aim of matching or improving the quality. His method is to first scan the film in RGB to 4,800 dpi. In Photoshop he uses *Image>Adjust >Brightness/Contrast* to change the brightness and contrast until the photo looks right on the monitor. Next, he creates a 5x5 grid of small versions of the image, where the contrast is varied on one dimension and the brightness is varied on the other dimension. In terms of the Photoshop Brightness/Contrast control, the five variations are -10, -5, 0, +5, +10. This results in 25 small versions of the image, which are then printed on one sheet to save paper and time. He picks the correct adjustment of brightness and contrast from the 25 small images. Often, for ultimate perfection, an in-between variation, such as –7, is chosen. After making the adjustment in brightness and contrast, he desaturates the image using *Image>Adjust>Desaturate* in Photoshop. To create the warm, selenium-toned appearance, the *Image>Adjust>Color balance* control is used. The photographer chose 30 units of red and 15 units of yellow, but it is up to personal taste to pick the right combination of colors.

For Slaughter, the critical step in achieving the look of a fiber-based selenium-toned image is printing the photo using an Epson 2200 printer on Epson Premium Semigloss paper.

RIGHT: Sea cliffs on the island of Oahu in Hawaii provided the location for this shot, taken in bright sunlight to provide the strong shadows. "I was employing a Cubist technique, with the model's shadow showing how her figure looks from the side at the same time as her direct image shows her from the front," Slaughter explains.

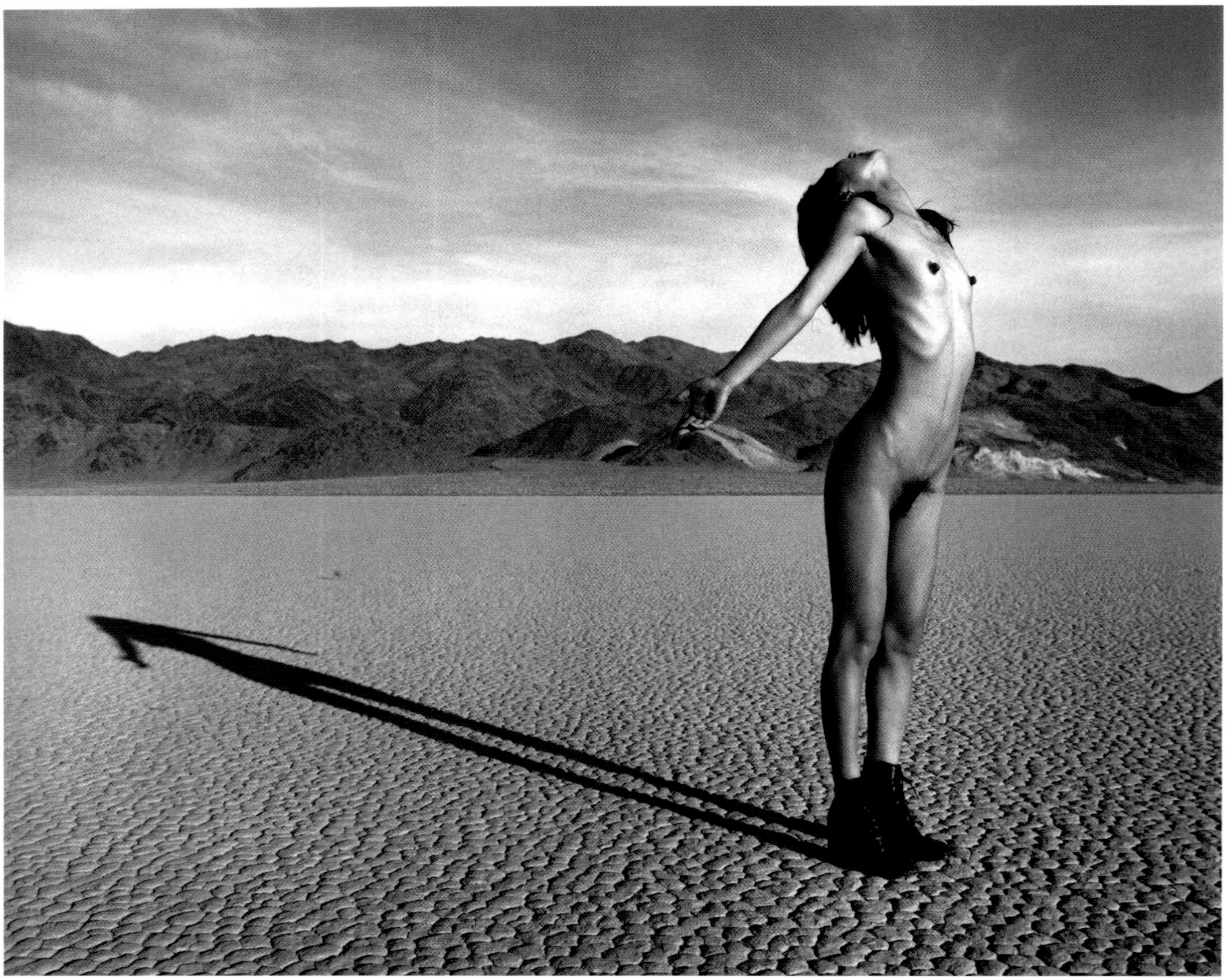

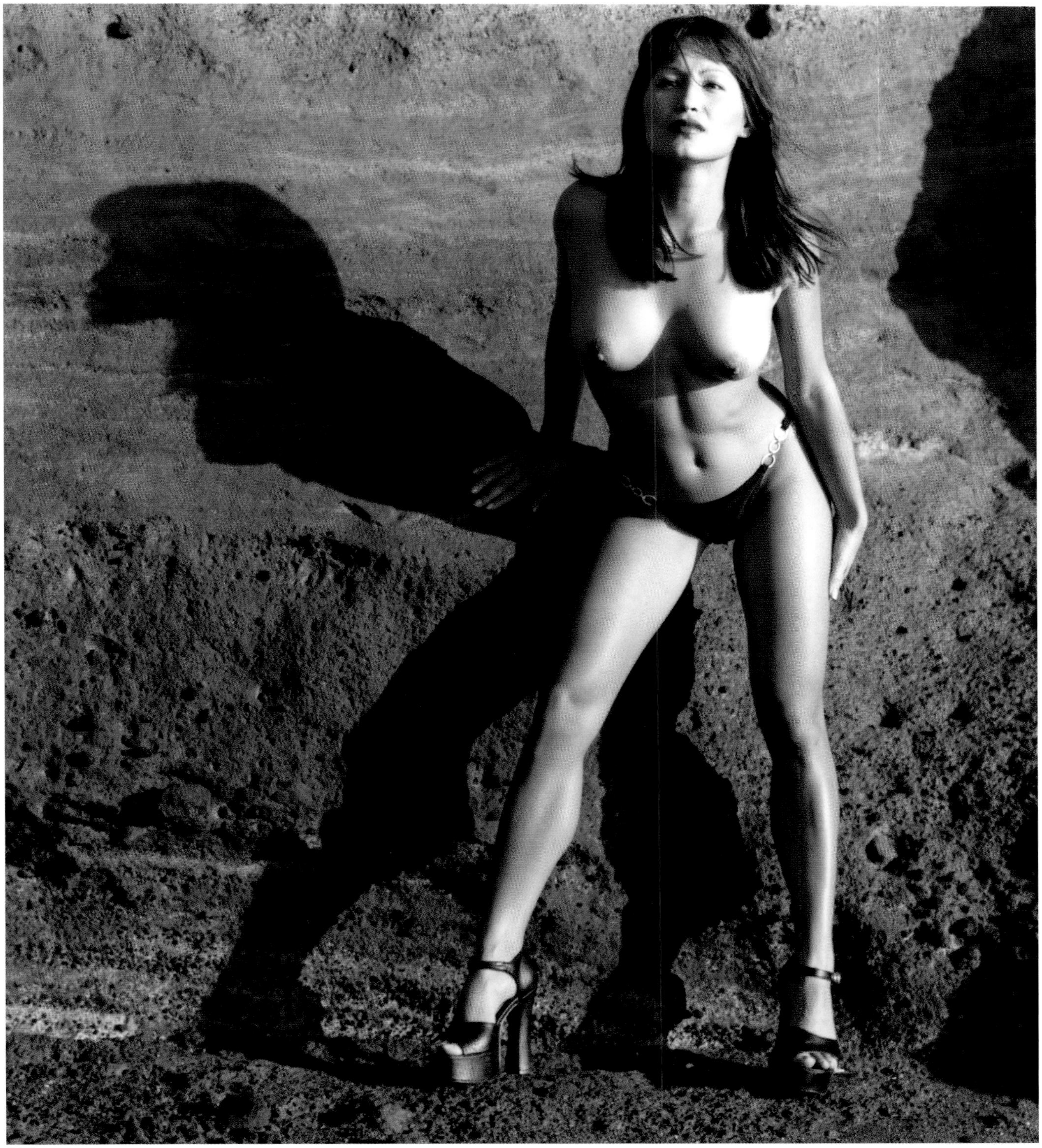

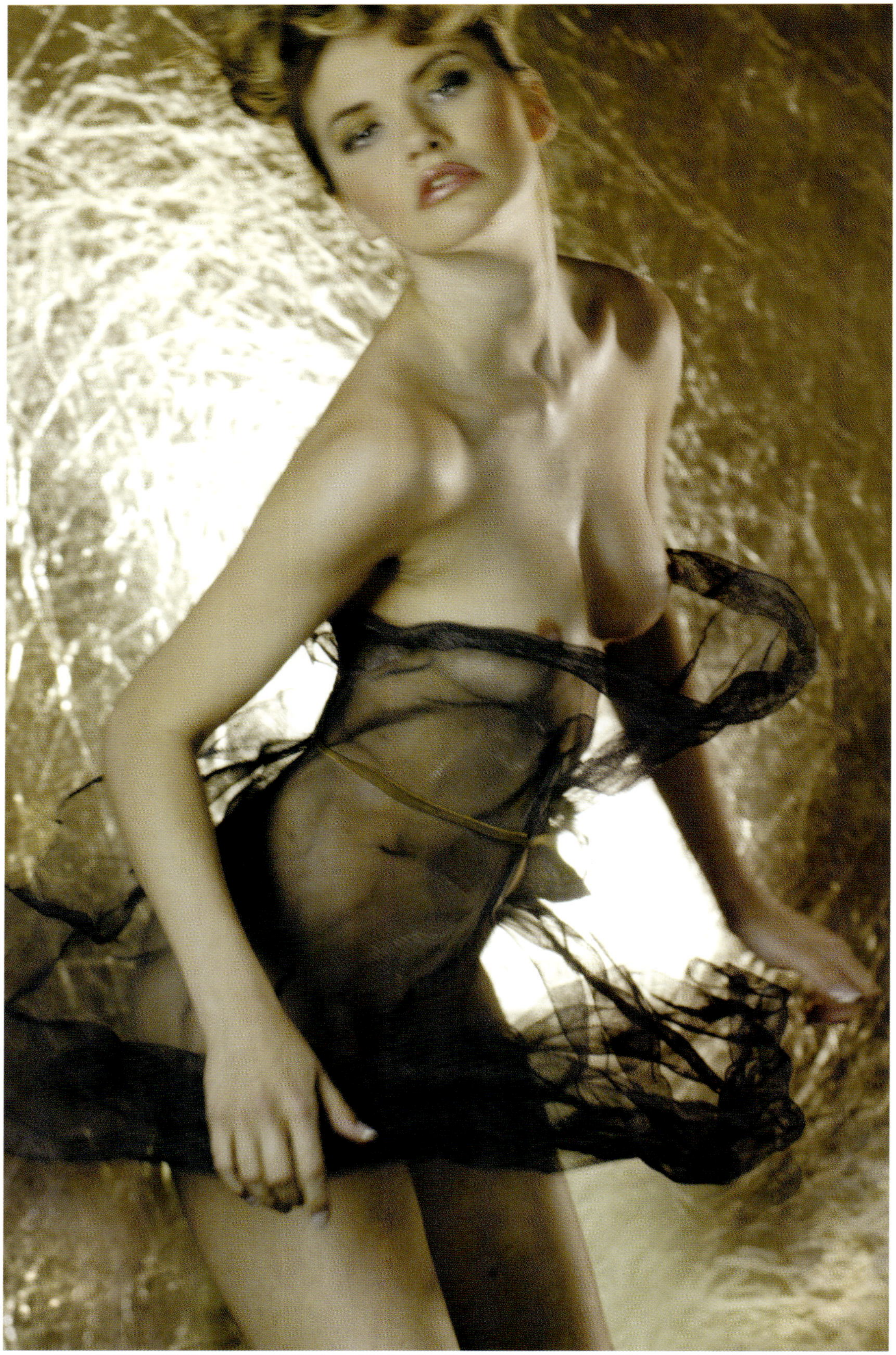

Directory of photographers

Bang Bang Photo
(Paul Grupp)
14611 Appleby Lane
Poway, CA 92064, USA
00 1 (858) 395-5298
www.bangbangphoto.com
pgrupp@bangbangphoto.com

Charly B
(Charles Bealmer)
15025 Gard Ave.
Norwalk, CA 90650, USA
00 1 (562) 746-2896
Charly@charly-b.com
chasbealmer@earthlink.net

G. W. Burns
Gwburns@gwburns.com

Derek Caballero
Theinvisiblelife@hotmail.com

Matt Conrads
00 1 (480) 283-5256
Onlineportfolios@cox.net
www.onlineportfolios.net

Heather Dellinger
Hmdphotos@hotmail.com

Christopher Donovan
Chris@chrisdonovan.com

Explorelight
(Ed Gordon)
00 1 (777) 498-0999
edwgordon@hotmail.com

Steve Gatlin
steve@gatlinphotography.com
www.gatlinphotography.com

Justin Grant Photography
Salt Lake City, Utah, USA
00 1 (801) 424-3700
justin@justingrantphotography.com
www.justingrantphotography.com

D. M. Gremlin
6053 Atlantic Avenue
Long Beach, CA 90805, USA
00 1 (866) 334-4364
www.dm-gremlin.com
dmg@dm-gremlin.com

Chris Gustafson
Ckreationz@aol.com

H. James Hoff
Jhoff1@optonline.net

Luna Digital
(Brandon Luna)
00 1 (469) 450-7415
lunadigital01@yahoo.com

Holger Maass
Info@studio-maass.de

Dave McAleavy
Dave@illudium.demon.co.uk

Michael McGrath
mikemcgrathnyc@yahoo.com
www.mybeautifulfilipina.com

Sylvio Pennucci
00 1 (818) 769-6800
sylvio@scnetwork.com

Photochimera
(Victor and Lynn Ciccarelli)
8011 Mission George Road
Santee, CA 92071, USA
00 1 (619) 448-0253
victor@photochimera.com

PhotoGecko
(John Campbell)
1413 S. 1st Street
Austin, Texas, USA
Gecko@photogecko.com
www.photogecko.com

Dan Santoni
Dansantoni@earthlink.net

Jeffery Scott
Numatrix.artist@verizon.net

Roberto Segate
Robhowells@madasafish.com

Greg Slaughter
Gls@onemodelplace.com
Zzyx_gs@yahoo.com

Glossary

Ambient light
The natural light in a scene.

Application
A computer program, such as an image editor or image browser.

Archival
The ability of a material, including some printing papers and compact discs, to last for many years.

Brightness/contrast
A common adjustment to improve the appearance of an image. Different amounts can be applied to specific areas.

Buffer
Memory in the camera that stores digital photos before they are written to the memory card.

Burning
Selectively darkening part of a photo with an image-editing program.

CCD
Charge Coupled Device. The image sensor found in many digital cameras and scanners.

CD-R
CD-Recordable is a compact disc that holds either 650 or 700 MB of digital information, including digital photos. Creating one is commonly referred to as burning a CD. A CD-R disc can only be written to once, and is an ideal storage medium for original digital photos.

CD-RW
CD-Rewritable discs can be written and erased many times.

CompactFlash
A common type of digital camera memory card.

Compression
The process of reducing the size of a file. Lossless compression makes a file smaller without losing data and degrading the image. Lossy compression reduces the size of a file but as it loses some data in the process it can't be restored to its original quality.

Color balance
The overall accuracy with which the colors in a photograph match or are capable of matching those in the original scene.

Contrast
The difference between the darkest and lightest areas in an image. The greater the difference, the higher the contrast.

Curves
A method of adjusting parts of a tonal range by dragging points on a line representing that range.

Dodging
Selectively lightening part of a photo with an image-editing program.

Download, downloading
The process of moving computer data from one location to another. Also used to describe the transfer of photos from a camera memory card to the computer.

DPI
Dots per inch. A measurement of the resolution of a digital photograph or digital device, including digital cameras and printers. The higher the number, the greater the resolution.

File
A computer document.

FireWire
A type of cabling technology for transferring data to and from digital devices at high speed. Some professional digital cameras and memory card readers connect to the computer over FireWire. Also known as IEEE 1394, FireWire was invented by Apple Macintosh but is now commonly used with Windows-based PCs as well.

Grayscale
An image made up of 256 tones varying between black and white.

Highlights
The brightest parts of a photograph.

Histogram
A graphic representation of the range of tones from dark to light. Some digital cameras include a histogram feature that enables a precise check on the exposure of the photo.

Hue/Saturation
A useful control for choosing and adjusting color and its intensity.

Image browser
An application that enables the viewing of digital photos.

Image-editing program
A computer program, such as Adobe Photoshop, which allows you to adjust a photograph in many different ways to improve its appearance.

Image resolution
The number of pixels in a digital photo is commonly referred to as its image resolution.

Inkjet
A printer capable of photo-quality output.

ISO speed
A number rating indicating the relative sensitivity to light of an image sensor or photographic film. Faster film (higher ISO) is more sensitive to light and requires less exposure than slower film.

JPEG
A popular digital camera file format that uses lossy compression to reduce file sizes. Developed by the Joint Photographic Experts Group.

Layers
A facility in Photoshop that enables work to be carried out on parts of the image without changing the original until the end of the process.

LCD
Liquid Crystal Display. A low-power monitor often used on the top and/or rear of a digital camera to display settings or the photo itself.

Levels
A control found in image-editing programs for adjusting the tonal range of an image.

Media
Material that information is written to and stored on. Digital photography storage media include CompactFlash cards and CDs.

Megabyte (MB)
A measurement of data storage equal to 1024 kilobytes (KB).

Megapixel
Equal to one million pixels.

Memory stick
A memory storage device developed by Sony.

Noise
Pixels on the image sensor that misread the light. The effect is similar to grain on an image taken with fast film.

Operating system
The program that controls the camera or the computer's hardware.

Pixel
Picture element. Digital photographs are comprised of millions of them, arranged in groups. Individual pixels are tiny and indiscernible, so that the image resembles a continuous tone picture.

Pixelation
An effect seen when a digital image is enlarged too much and the pixels become obvious.

RAW
A type of digital image file containing the raw data from the CCD plus information about the settings used to take the photo. Acts as a digital "negative."

Recycle time
The time it takes to process and store a captured image.

Removable media
Storage media that can be removed from a camera or computer.

Resolution
An indication of the sharpness of images on a printout or the display screen. It is based on the number and density of the pixels used. The more pixels, the more detail can be seen and the higher the image's resolution.

RGB
The color system used in digital cameras where red, green, and blue light is captured separately and then combined to create a full color image.

Saturation
The strength and richness of the colors in an image.

SD memory card
A rival memory card format to CompactFlash.

Scanner
An input device that uses light to read printed information and flat objects, and transfers it into the computer in a digital format.

Sharpness
The clarity of detail in an image.

Shutter speed
A measurement of how long a camera's shutter remains open as the picture is taken. The slower the shutter speed, the longer the exposure time.

Thumbnail
A small, low-resolution version of an image for viewing several or even dozens of pictures at a time.

TIFF
Tagged Image File Format. A lossless image format that creates a bigger size than a JPEG or RAW file.

Underexposure
Exposing the film to less light than is needed to render the scene as the eye sees it, resulting in an overly dark photograph.

USB
Universal Serial Bus. A protocol for transferring data to and from digital devices. Many digital cameras and memory card readers connect to the USB port on a computer.

USM
Unsharp Mask increases contrast between defined pixels, improving the apparent sharpness.

White balance
An automatic or manual control on a digital camera to compensate for different colors of light being emitted by different light sources.

Index

Index

Acknowledgments

My deepest thanks go to all the models—Naomi, Alex, Clare, Emmy, Honesty, Jackie, Keri, Lexi, Martha, Medea, RedLilly, Rosewood, Wicilha, Zenith, and Zoey—and the many talented photographers who've contributed so willingly and generously of their expertise.

Many friends have provided support and advice. Rick Martin has had first view of much of my work over the past year, and I have benefited from his sharp eye and forthright opinions. Janet Croft has once more helped me keep it all together, I hope more easily than last time. Susan Meredith, Mike Nott, and Peter Chapman have remained staunch and helpfully skeptical friends.

The members of the Norwich, Cambridge, and Bedford Munches, with their very diverse definitions and embodiments of the erotic, have contributed much to my attempts to pin-down what this elusive word means today. My thanks go to Ali, Alison, Bob, Derek, Geo, Glenn, Peter, Teresa, and Wil, but most of all to Nichola McLeod. My contribution to the book is dedicated to her.

Roderick Macdonald